The New Woodworker Handbook

The New Woodworker Handbook

By Tom Hintz

Fox Chapel Publishing
1970 Broad Street • East Petersburg, PA 17520
www.FoxChapelPublishing.com

Alan Giagnocavo
Publisher

Peg Couch
Acquisition Editor

Gretchen Bacon
Editor

Troy Thorne
Book Design & Layout

Lindsay Hess
Layout

Photography Credits

Many of the interior photographs in this book were provided by Tom Hintz. Other contributors include:

John R. Dingman, Sr.: p. 3, p. 5, p. 7

Tom Ferone: p. 9 (all)

Delta Machinery: p. 34–35, p. 47, p. 48 (left), p. 56 (top), p. 59 (top), p. 61–67 (all)

Woodcraft Supply LLC: p. 36–37

Rockler: p. 38, p. 40 (bottom), p. 78–79

IRWIN Industrial Tools® – A Newell-Rubbermaid® Company: p. 42–43 (all)

Bosch: p. 49 (all), p. 55 (bottom), p. 75 (top)

Porter-Cable: p. 50 (top), p. 54

DeWALT: p. 58, p. 60 (top), p. 69, p. 70 (top), p. 74 (left), p. 76 (bottom), p. 77 (top)

Dedication

This book is dedicated to:

My father, who passed away too early but who continues to inspire me every day. He taught me that accuracy is a good thing and that I can be accurate when I want to be. He always knew when I wanted to be.

My mother, who, when I was seven or eight years old, told me, "One day you will be a writer." What I have gone through between then and now makes this a truly remarkable prediction.

My wife, Beth, and daughter, Jenny, who have read and edited far more than they could have anticipated. Despite the never-ending stream of pages to be read and the sawdust trail between the shop and office, they continue to be supportive and allow me to live indoors.

Peg Couch, acquisition editor for Fox Chapel Publishing, for finding me and believing. Peg's encouragement and guidance, along with that of publisher Alan Giagnocavo and the entire Fox Chapel staff, have made this effort not only possible, but also enjoyable.

ISBN 978-1-56523-297-6

Publisher's Cataloging-in-Publication Data

Hintz, Tom.

The new woodworker handbook / by Tom Hintz. -- East Petersburg, PA : Fox Chapel Publishing, c2007.

p. ; cm.
ISBN 978-1-56523-297-6
Includes index.

1. Woodwork--Handbooks, manuals, etc. 2. Woodwork--Technique. 3. Workshops--Equipment and supplies. I. Title.

TT180 .H56 2007
684/.08--dc22 0703

To learn more about other great books from Fox Chapel Publishing, or to find a retailer near you, call toll-free 1-800-457-9112 or visit us at *www.FoxChapelPublishing.com*.

Printed in China
10 9 8 7 6 5 4 3 2 1

Note to Authors: We are always looking for talented authors to write new books in our area of woodworking, design, and related crafts. Please send a brief letter describing your idea to Peg Couch, Acquisition Editor, 1970 Broad Street, East Petersburg, PA 17520.

About the Author

Shortly after Tom Hintz and his wife, Beth, moved into their first home in the mid-1970s, he built a workbench for the new house. That project ignited a passion for woodworking, a passion fueled by a sign-making business he owned. "It gave me an excuse to buy a table saw and other basic woodworking tools," he says.

Influenced by his father, a master machinist whose capabilities in metal inspired him, and Norm Abram, host of the PBS television program *The New Yankee Workshop* and master carpenter of *This Old House*, Tom avidly pursued his woodworking hobby while he pursued his other passion, car racing. The Vietnam veteran spent 30 years in stock car racing before becoming a writer/editor/webmaster for such car magazines as *Circle Track, Stock Car Racing,* and *Open Wheel.* In 2001, he left his day job and turned his longtime woodworking hobby into a full-time career when he launched the Internet site *www.NewWoodworker.com.* The website serves as an online reference and forum for new and experienced woodworkers.

Largely self-taught, Tom says that he took the opportunity to learn from others along the way, but he's learned the most from the new woodworkers who visit his website. "Helping them find answers to procedural and technique questions has been an intensive learning process that has brought me a long way," he says.

But don't call him a woodworking expert. "There are lots of real experts out there, and I'm not one of them," he says. What he is an expert at is taking complex ideas and procedures and translating them into something comprehensible. "I am good at explaining things in a way that others understand. I think that is my strongest trait and the reason *NewWoodworker.com* is doing so well," he says.

His commitment to continuing education is embodied in the motto on the home page of *www.NewWoodworker.com*: "Because there is always more to learn."

Contents

Introduction

I began woodworking thirty-some years ago when I needed a basement workbench. Not liking those that were available commercially, I designed and built one myself. That bench turned out a little crooked and wobbly, but the experience of making it was very rewarding. It also sparked a lifelong interest in woodworking.

When I began searching for information to help me learn more about woodworking, I got frustrated. The few books and magazine articles I came across either were overly simplistic or assumed I knew far more than I did. That frustration simmered within me for a couple of decades, eventually re-emerging as the inspiration for *www.NewWoodworker.com*. No longer do new woodworkers need to feel frustrated for lack of suitable information. During its first five years in existence, *www.NewWoodworker.com* was flooded with thousands of questions, comments, and suggestions from new woodworkers who visited the website. Those questions, comments, and suggestions serve as the basis for this book and provide a foundation for the new woodworker seeking clear, concise, understandable, and accessible information.

How to use this book

The goal of this book is not to make you a master woodworker. Instead, I want to get you going in the hobby with a core set of skills that will let you find out if you are a master, a happy weekender, or maybe even a contractor in the wrong job. You will find your place in woodworking as you go, and I want to help make it easier, safer, and more enjoyable to get started.

I'll start with the basics of laying out a shop, buying tools, and setting up and aligning them, and then I'll address safety and move on to what you need to know about wood, adhesives, fasteners, joinery, and finishing. The material is organized so that each chapter builds on the one before it. The projects in the final chapter depend on your learning the information in the chapters before them. Building the projects in the order in which they are presented will familiarize you with a core set of techniques that you will use in virtually every project you build in the future.

Remember to go at your own pace. The people attracted to woodworking are as diverse as the hobby itself. Since everyone learns at a different pace and has varying amounts of time in which to do it, there are no time-specific goals in this book. The material is presented in a step-by-step format that allows you to follow along at a pace that is comfortable for you, in the hours your schedule permits. The class ends when you say it does, and there are no other students to hold you back or force you to move on before you are ready. This book also provides information to help new woodworkers decide what tools and machines are best for their situation and budget, not someone else's.

One of the best things you can do in using this book and in woodworking is keep a positive attitude. There will be bumps along the road to learning the skills presented here, but you can succeed, so be sure to keep the following principles in mind:

Keep your expectations realistic. In many endeavors, having realistic goals may mean lowering expectations. In woodworking, the opposite is more apt to be true. Of the literally thousands of woodworkers I have had contact with, only a handful were disappointed in their early progress. Most were surprised by how quickly they learned the basic skills and by the rapid expansion of the types of projects they felt capable of building.

Part of the reason that people tend to advance in woodworking faster than they anticipate is that so much of it is based on a relatively small number of basic skills. With each basic technique or skill learned, the number of projects you can realistically take on expands. Nothing inspires a new woodworker more than completing a project he or she felt incapable of building only a short time before.

Give yourself plenty of time. Occasionally, a new technique will seem foreign or hard to grasp. Get used to this feeling because it will probably recur as long as you do woodworking. The key is to work through it, step-by-step, and repeat a technique or procedure as many times as it takes for you to become comfortable with it. Knowing how something is to be done can be vastly different from being comfortable with it. Whether it is a new tool, machine, or procedure, nothing beats experience, so keep working until you get it. How fast you learn something is of no consequence. How well you learn it, is. The only indicator of progress you will need here is a bookmark.

Be patient and read through all of the material. The success-induced bit of euphoria that can be found in woodworking has a downside. It can tempt you to skip ahead in the learning process—and in the book. While there may be a skill or procedure in later chapters that seems more interesting, there is a very good chance it is based on at least one of those skills or procedures you passed over. Do yourself and your budget a favor: Complete each step in the order in which it is presented. You will learn faster, and the pile of wasted wood will be smaller.

There may be parts of this book that deal with a machine or tool you do not (yet) have or may not even be considering at this point. Read those parts as well. Understanding how various machines relate to procedures or techniques may clarify your need for it in your shop. These descriptions can also provide insight on how to accomplish the same thing on another type of machine you may already have.

For those who have yet to equip their shops, understanding how a machine is used will be valuable when it comes time to choose from those on the market. Since most of us cannot buy all of the tools we want, it's important to get the most from what we can afford. This kind of information can be very helpful when convincing the other checkbook-authorized person in the house that buying a specific machine is a reasonable expenditure. Facts and real-world uses are much more persuasive than whining about how cool that tool is.

Give yourself a break. While repetition is a good teacher, it can become frustrating at times. When those feelings set in—and they will occasionally—it's time to stop for the day, or at least to take a break. A frustrated mind learns little. When power tools are involved, that loss of focus can be dangerous. Drop the bookmark in and close the book. That lesson will be better learned tomorrow.

Most of all, relax. Woodworking is fun and should be relaxing—even during the learning process. If you take your time and keep your mind on what you are doing, you can get through any bumps along the way without any extra bumps on you.

Remember, you control the class time. I won't be calling to check on you. There will be no tests other than the ones by which you grade yourself. If you can avoid rushing and skipping ahead, I promise you will be at least as impressed as I was with my first projects. It's a great feeling.

Ready to go buy tools? Not so fast there. We need to talk about where you are going to put them. Read on.

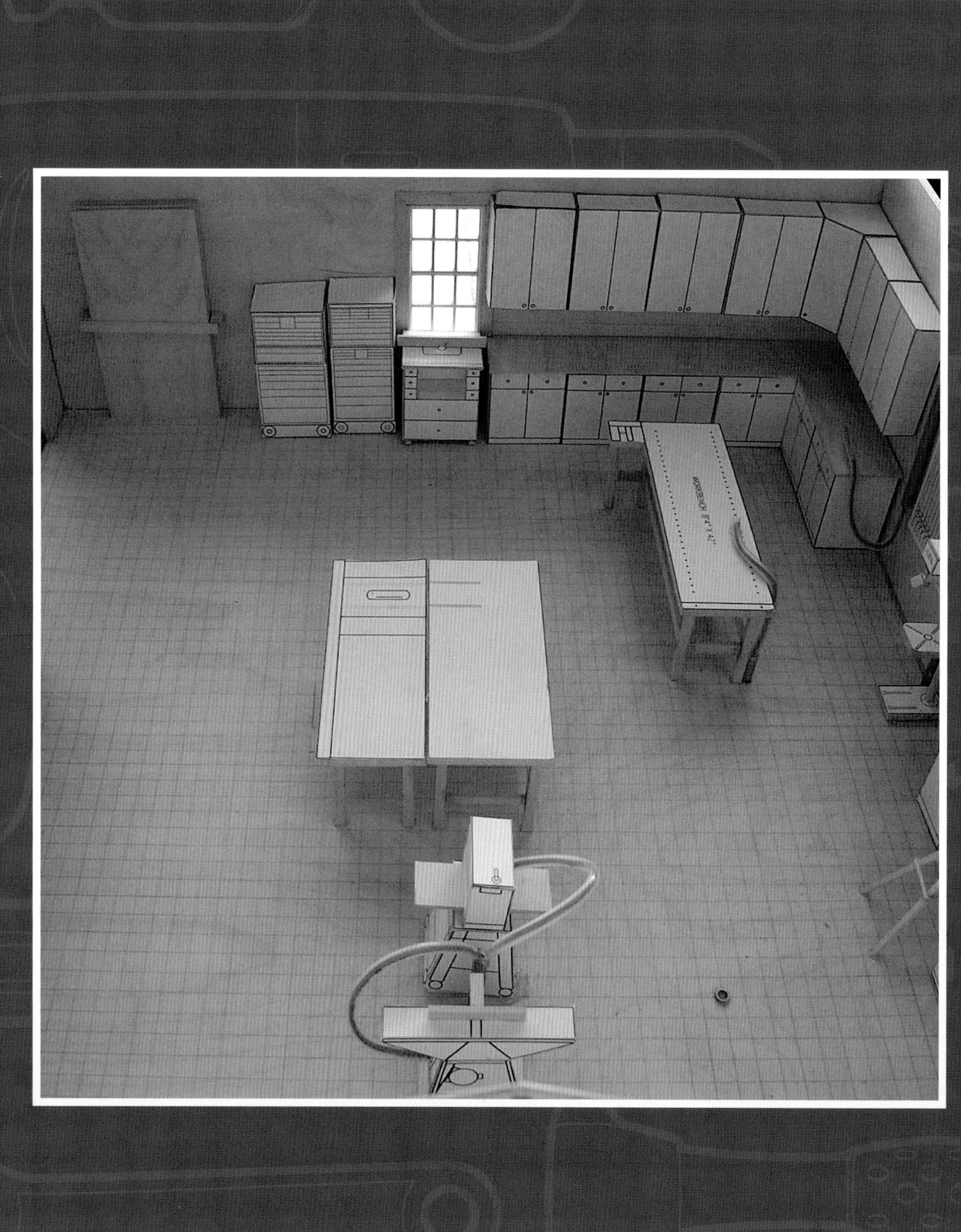

Chapter 1

Setting Up Shop

Setting up a place to work would seem to be the logical first step to beginning in woodworking. However, for most of us, the first shop space was developed in stages as needs for early projects were realized. Taking the time to plan a basic shop area early on can make getting into woodworking easier and safer.

You can begin very simply in a portion of the garage, in a corner in the basement, or out on the deck, but the need for a real workshop of your own will soon become apparent. Regardless of whether you can build the ultimate freestanding shop or whether you will share the garage or basement with household equipment and belongings, you'll want to put some thought into the space that you plan to use so that it is safe and reaches its full potential.

While budget and available space will be most influential in how you set up your shop, the information and planning that we'll cover in this chapter will show you how to make the most of your budget, allow for future growth, and set up for safety and efficiency. We'll take a close look at the three most popular types of shops—basement, garage, and freestanding building—discuss the pros and cons of each, and address special concerns for woodworkers, like lighting, electricity, safety, and adequate space for woodworking machines. Finally, we'll walk through the steps of actually planning out your space—including using graph paper and templates—so that you can set up a shop that best suits your needs.

What's a shop for?

As you think about workspace, remember that it is not just a place to work. There is more to it, and you'll want to consider all aspects of it. I'll give you a list since there may be elements that haven't yet occurred to you:

- You need a place to do the work itself, that is, a place for your own self, for the pieces of your current project, and for the tools and materials you're currently using.
- You need space to park and use your machinery, and to store your portable power tools and hand tools.
- You need storage space for incoming project wood and for glue, screws, varnish, and other materials.
- You need space for leftover wood, short ends, and cut-offs, everything that is too valuable to throw away but not quite what you need at the moment.
- You need space for projects that aren't yet completed. Nobody plans it this way, but you will probably be surprised by how many projects you'll start and then put aside for some reason or other. Maybe you don't quite know what to do next, or it's not coming out the way you wanted, or something more urgent has come up.
- You might need space for your tool catalogs, woodworking handbooks, magazines, and project drawings.

Types of Shops at a Glance

	Basement	Garage	Freestanding Building
Space	- Often spacious, but you may need to work around furnace, laundry, and water heater - Headroom can be inadequate, making it difficult to stand pieces vertically - Cement floors provide a smooth surface to roll machinery but can be hard on the back - If present, carpet will need to be pulled up	- Can be spacious, but you may need to share with an automobile and/or lawn equipment - Overhead rafters can provide great storage for unused wood - Cement floors provide a smooth surface to roll machinery but can be hard on the back	- Space is optimized because you will not have to share with household facilities or automobile - Large machines and workspaces can be permanently installed, improving safety and efficiency
Electrical Systems and Lighting	- Solid groundwork for electricity - Might be dark and gloomy - Electrical upgrades can be easy in a new home but expensive in an older one	- Electricity may need to be installed or, if present, upgraded - Natural light can be an advantage	- Electricity and lighting will need to be installed - Running service may be costly but can add value to the home
Environmental Control	- Built-in climate control - High humidity can cause rust - Ventilation is often lacking	- Heating and/or air conditioning will most likely need to be addressed - May be susceptible to humidity or other weather conditions causing rust or wood movement - Open doors and windows provide good ventilation	- Heating and/or air conditioning will most likely need to be addressed - May be susceptible to humidity - Open doors and windows provide good ventilation
Access	- Convenient if doors provide direct outside access - Cumbersome if stairs need to be navigated - Shop may be accessible to children	- Large doors provide easy access for machinery, wood, and projects - Shop may be accessible to children	- Ground-level entry can provide good access, but it can be compromised if far from the driveway - Easy to lock so that children cannot access
Effects on the Home	- Dust can spread into the home - Noise travels throughout living spaces	- Dust is contained primarily to shop area - Noise is isolated from living spaces, but not from neighbors	- Dust is contained to shop area - Noise is not an issue unless shop is close to a neighbor

Also, consider whether you really want or need to have your workshop confined to a single space. Woodworkers very commonly find there just isn't enough room in the workshop itself for storing materials and half-finished projects. So you might have a workshop in the basement, with materials stored out in a garage or shed.

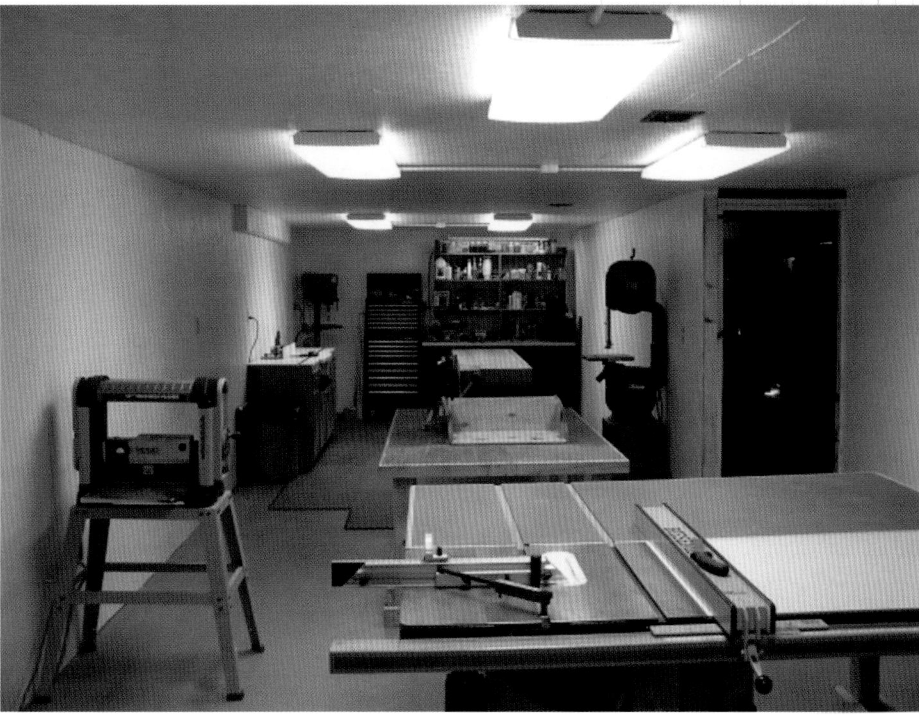

Figure 1.1. A basement shop is convenient and already contains the groundwork for heat, electricity, and air conditioning. Take care to maximize the available space and to minimize dust migration to the rest of the house.

Types of shops

For most woodworkers, the choice of where to set up shop is dictated by the space that is available. Most shops land in one of three different kinds of space: basement, garage, or freestanding. Each, of course, has its advantages and disadvantages. Some people also manage to shoehorn shops into large closets and spare bedrooms, which can be great if what you make is small and you don't have any large machines. Before you choose your space, let's take a look at some of the different features of each type.

Basement

Basement shops can be great for new woodworkers. Because they are attached to a house, basement shops offer convenience and solid groundwork for temperature control and electrical systems (see **Figure 1.1**). They're often as spacious as the house above (see **Figure 1.2**), so they can be used for very large home repair and remodeling projects, kinds of woodworking that can go a long way toward convincing your significant other that buying more tools will benefit the entire household, not just your woodworking habit.

Space

Although basements usually are spacious, many do have a low ceiling, which can be an ongoing problem. Occasionally, you will want to stand pieces up vertically to make a cut or form joints, or to assemble a large project. A low ceiling, often reduced further by suspended lights, can make these tasks difficult, and even dangerous if the workpiece whacks into something overhead—a fluorescent tube, for example—while it is being cut or maneuvered around.

If the basement houses the furnace and hot water heater, and perhaps the laundry, they'll be fixed in place, and you will have to work around them. You'll soon also want to box them into their own room or rooms, for safety as well as for dust control. These moves may leave you with some rather awkward spaces to use as your workshop, which you will have to plan around.

Basements almost always have a cement floor, with or without carpet or vinyl tile, and it is often not level. There may be a drain that everything slopes toward. While it is easy to roll machines around on cement and is usually easy to sweep up, hard concrete is not the kindest material underfoot, nor is it any good for dropped tools. You can put down work mats for that, but if there is carpet or industrial carpet in the proposed shop area, you'll probably want to pull it up before it becomes a huge magnet for sawdust.

Electrical systems and lighting

The basement in a newer house probably has some lighting installed, and it's probably not too far to the main electrical panel, so upgrading the electrical system can be easy. If you are lucky, there may even be more than one electrical outlet in the proposed shop area. But you are almost certainly going to need to add electrical outlets for tools and machines and more overhead lighting.

In an older house, both lighting and electrical outlets can be a real problem. You may have to install both, along with the electrical capacity they require, and that may cause you to upgrade an older electrical panel, which can run into real money. On the other hand, upgraded electrical service is a selling point when it comes time to market that older house, so the news is not all bad.

Environmental control

By being in the house itself, the basement is probably connected to the heating and air conditioning systems. Even when they are shielded from outdoor humidity, basements can have relatively high and consistent humidity levels that may keep your wood in a relatively damp condition and may also induce rust on your tools and machines. Dehumidifiers and air conditioning can help, but an ongoing tool maintenance program remains a good idea, as does storing your hand tools in closed cabinets and covering your machinery with breathable covers when it's not in use. And if the rest of the house is always drier than the basement, you'll have to learn through experience how that affects the dimensions of your wood, and how you can compensate for dimensional changes caused by changes in humidity.

Ventilation—or more specifically, the lack of it—can be a significant problem for basement shops. Finishing, even with many water-based materials, requires significant ventilation. Just blowing basement air out of a basement window is not enough. Finishing materials with solvents or other volatile components can present serious fire/explosion hazards because of the lack of ventilation, a confined area, and the presence of ignition sources including, but not limited to, water heaters and furnaces.

Access

Unless you have a direct outside access, getting machines and wood into a basement shop can be difficult on a good day and outright dangerous the rest of the time. Even with direct outside access, stairs are generally part of that entry and pose significant safety issues when trying to bring machines that weigh 200, 300, or more pounds into the shop. A good hand truck, the kind appliance movers use, and a friend to help can take the sting out of that.

In newer houses, the basement might have sliding glass doors leading directly to the outside, and if that's the case, you're in heaven. You can get anything in and out, and they'll also give you great natural light.

Another pitfall related to basement access is moving large projects out of the basement, particularly when the stairs make a turn or face a wall at the top. I know a fellow who built a beautiful entertainment center only to discover there was no way to get it out of the basement. That led to strained negotiations with his wife, resulting in a basement family room with a very nice entertainment center, which reduced his shop space. That's why professional cabinetmakers always measure access in the first place, and also why they tend to build large units as assemblies of a number of smaller units. This is also the reason that traditional highboy chests come apart at the waist. This strategy is no help for boatbuilding, though.

Effects on the home

Dust migrates farther than you could ever imagine. If you have forced-air heating in the house, it will propel the fine dust throughout the building, usually before you complete sanding the project. Enclosing the shop space helps but will not prevent dust from finding its way into the

Figure 1.2. Storage is a problem in any shop. For this shop, a blank basement partition wall provides a great space for a large set of clamps. Unfortunately, most of us only dream of a free wall in the shop!

living spaces in easily noticeable quantities. While sanding is unlikely to generate enough airborne dust to support a dust explosion, wood dust can build up in dangerous, often unseen places within furnaces and water heaters. Eventually, this dust buildup can ignite and start a fire, so along with enclosing the shop, you may also need to create a partition to further separate the furnace and hot water heater from your work area.

Using a good dust collector helps, though none of them are 100% effective, especially when it comes to the ultra-fine particles that are so adept at escaping the shop area, and some collectors are too tall for most basements. Along with a dust collector, an air filter unit purposefully designed for the woodworking environment can be a big help since these machines are designed to catch the dangerous sub-micron particles that escape regular collectors.

Power tools produce significant levels of noise that a basement shop helps protect neighbors from. Unfortunately, running most machines directly below the other occupants of the home does nothing to endear you to them. If you can't schedule the noisiest operations for times when nobody else is at home, consider adding insulation to the ceiling of the basement shop.

Unless the basement shop is partitioned off from the rest of the house and can be locked up, your tools and equipment can be dangerously interesting to children and unsuspecting adults. While most machines have a safety interlock, it's probably safest to lock the shop door and throw the electrical breaker when you're not in there working.

Pro and Con: Basement Shop

Pro

- Convenient
- Often spacious
- Solid groundwork for temperature control and for electricity; upgrades will be easy and relatively inexpensive in newer homes
- May have great access through double patio doors

Con

- Might be dark and gloomy
- Headroom can be inadequate
- High humidity can cause rust
- Ventilation is often poor or lacking
- Access may be a problem
- Often creates dust in the home
- Noise travels throughout living spaces
- Shop is not easy to lock and therefore can be accessible to children

Garage

Many woodworkers would consider a two-car garage, attached or detached, the ideal workshop: It is spacious, is separate from the main house, has super access, and has great natural light through those big doors (see **Figure 1.3**). Many woodworkers would find a single-car garage plenty big enough for their hobby, at least initially. The problems of a detached garage—electrical hookup, heat, sharing with a car and yard equipment—are small compared to the potential advantages, and all can be worked around one way or another. In a condo, a garage on the lower level probably is your only option, since few condos have genuine basements or yards where you could put up a shed.

Space

Garage-based shops may have to share the space with vehicles, lawn mowers, bicycles, and all the other things families keep there. Sharing the floor space can limit the size or number of machines, or at least require adding mobile bases under the heavier ones so they can be brought out for use and stowed when the car needs to come inside.

If the shop is arranged right, you have the benefit of a disappearing wall in the form of an opening overhead garage door. Aside from the obvious benefit of allowing a nice day into the shop, working with large pieces of wood can be much easier and safer when you can make use of this large opening. You won't have any trouble getting a big project out of there either, even if it is a 17-foot canoe.

In many garages, you will also have the advantage of overhead storage in the rafters. This is not the kind of accessible storage you need for materials you're using, but it can be great for long-term wood storage and half-finished projects you're intending to get back to someday.

Ceiling height is not a problem in most garages, though the floor is almost certainly going to be hard concrete, with or without a sloping drain. You'll probably want rubber mats at the table saw and workbench, or wherever you work for extended periods, to reduce the strain on your legs and back.

Electrical systems and lighting

While many garages have some electrical service available, it is seldom of sufficient capacity to support woodworking tools and machinery. Adding a sub-panel and a couple of circuits for lighting and general tool use can be expensive, but it might not be prohibitive—consult an electrical contractor.

Being able to let natural daylight in through doors and windows can help on nice days, but usually it is not enough, and it is not much help on a dark winter evening. However, once you have upgraded the electrical service for your machinery, it will not cost much more to install overhead lighting.

Environmental control

In virtually every part of the world, some amount of heating and/or air conditioning will be needed to make working in a garage bearable at various times of the year. Insulating the space is relatively cheap but does not eliminate the need for a mechanism to control air temperature within the shop. That can cost a lot if you go the deluxe route, but for evening and weekend woodworking, it does not have to be overly elaborate. A kerosene space heater or a couple of electrical space heaters will get a shop warm enough to begin to work, and moving sheets of plywood around will get you plenty warm from the inside, too. Whatever heat source is used, remember to place and use it safely. A window air conditioner will make a big difference in a garage-size space.

The ability to open doors and windows will give you plenty of fresh air when sanding or finishing. Assisting the exchange of air with a window-mounted or properly aimed fan may still be necessary. Keep in mind that while blowing dust or fumes out of a window may clear the shop, it might contaminate relations with nearby neighbors.

Garage-based shops are susceptible to virtually the same humidity as the outside air. This humidity can be especially harmful to metal surfaces near oceans that add salt to the air. Add condensation caused by rapid temperature changes, and rust can become a serious issue. The tendency for rust can be mitigated with good maintenance practices, such as cleaning and waxing the tables on saws and other machines, and using a breathable cover for protection when they are not in use. Store hand tools inside closed drawers and cabinets.

Access

Bringing heavy or bulky equipment and supplies into a garage-based shop is far easier and safer than having to hustle them through the house and down a flight of stairs. A doorway designed to accept an automobile can be a wonderful asset when dealing with odd-size machines or projects. Being able to get projects out of the shop, however, doesn't make it any easier getting them into the house.

Effects on the home

Dust is easier to deal with in a garage shop, in part because of the ventilation. If the garage is attached to the house, dust migration can still be a factor, though is somewhat easier to manage than with a basement shop. Add a storm door to the house access door, and you will have solved most of the problem. You still have the potential to track dust into the house on your shoes and work clothes, but you can minimize this kind of irritating behavior if you remember to brush yourself off and wipe your feet on a bristly mat before leaving the shop.

Your family will be less affected by the shop sounds, but now your neighbors may get an earful. Insulating garage-based shops to aid heating also substantially reduces the amount of noise that escapes. Remembering to close the doors during particularly noisy operations usually keeps the neighbors much happier.

All that wood dust and those volatile chemicals in your garage, especially if it is attached to your house, still can put your home in peril unless you take adequate safety precautions. Add the normal flammables associated with a home, such as fuel for lawn mowers, and fire remains a serious risk. You will want to invest in a fireproof metal cabinet for all flammables, including the mower gas.

Figure 1.3. Though it may share a space with lawn mowers, cars, and other equipment, a garage shop can have many benefits—it can be spacious, separate from the main house, accessible, and well lighted.

Like a basement shop, a shop located in a family garage can be accessible to children and others not familiar with the dangers of woodworking tools and machines. This makes it important to unplug or otherwise disable tools and machines when not in use, which is quite easy when there is a dedicated electrical sub-panel in the garage shop.

Pro and Con: Garage Shop

Pro

- Can be spacious
- Big overhead doors for easy access
- Isolates the noise and dust

Con

- Might be hard to heat or air condition
- Electrical upgrade can be expensive
- Outdoor humidity can cause rust and wood movement problems
- Might have to share space with cars and lawn mowers
- Shop is not easy to lock and therefore can be accessible to children

Freestanding Building

If you have the yard space and the cash, building a separate, dedicated workshop can be a dream come true (see **Figure 1.4**). You can modify two-car garage plans, or you can design your own space to precisely suit yourself. Designing a dedicated shop might not be the best choice for a new woodworker since you may not know exactly what you want. However, given a year or two of experience as a woodworker, it gets much easier to form clear ideas of your own.

While woodworkers sometimes use existing sheds and other small outbuildings for shops, this section deals primarily with purpose-designed shop buildings. The same pros and cons of a garage-based shop can be applied to those housed in sheds and similar structures.

Space

Space and designing that space specifically for woodworking are the obvious benefits of a dedicated building. Local codes and budget can limit the overall size, but having a dedicated space for woodworking is nirvana for most in the hobby. Being able to permanently install larger machines and work surfaces can make using them safer as well as more efficient.

Unless you are blessed with an existing, suitable building with the necessary features, constructing a dedicated shop building is by far the most expensive alternative. Those costs can be contained somewhat by regulating the size, but it remains an expensive proposition. However, nobody blinks if a suburban gentleman owns an expensive boat; why should anyone object if he puts the same money and trouble into a workshop building? You can even get the money back when you sell the house, if you take the trouble to insulate the building and add plumbing, since the new owners can use it for other hobbies or even as a guest cottage.

Electrical systems and lighting

The building plan has to include an electrical plan, which will include running a new service entry to the building. In that case, it's going to be best to bury the wiring underground if at all possible (and it may be required by local codes) and to install at least 100-amp service. Along with plenty of ceiling outlets for lighting, being generous with wall and even floor outlets can be a huge benefit in coming years as your equipment collection and project list grow.

Put your machinery on its own electrical circuit, not on a shared circuit with lighting. That way, if the machine overloads and blows the breaker, you won't also be stumbling around in the dark. You'll probably want a 220-volt circuit so you have the choice of converting machines with dual voltage capability to 220-volt operation, which is more efficient than 110 volts. This also makes it possible for you to install larger machines if you want.

Many people would prefer not to be under fluorescent lighting if they can help it, and it's true that incandescent light is warmer and friendlier. It also casts shadows, a good thing in some woodworking situations, such as when evaluating a finish, but not so good when you are trying to see the layout line on a dark piece of wood. Whether you choose incandescent or fluorescent lighting, it's hard to have too much of it in a workshop, and you'll find ceiling-recessed fixtures much better than drops suspended from the ceiling. The downside is you have to have planned the space rather thoroughly before you know where the lighting needs to be. The answer is install it everywhere. The same goes for the outlets.

Environmental control

Containing dust or fumes is much easier in a dedicated building. Even installing a dust control system is easier when you do not have to worry about it contaminating other living spaces. Finishes can be applied and the shop locked up until the project dries, something that can be impossible in shared basement or garage-based spaces.

On the other hand, heating and air conditioning a separate building that does not share any walls with the main house can be expensive. What you do about that, and how much you do, depends of course on your climate. Some woodworkers like to heat the shop in winter with a small wood stove that, in addition to regular firewood, may burn shop scrap. Air conditioning may be optional in some climates but can be very helpful for controlling humidity. Like heat sources that move the air, filters in air conditioning units must be maintained frequently to prevent their clogging with dust.

Since the building won't be heated when you are not in it, humidity remains the same issue it is in a garage shop, though not so serious a problem as it would be if the doors were open all the time. You may need to store hand tools and small machines in closed cabinets, put breathable covers on machinery at times of the year when rapid temperature changes are inevitable, and learn how to manage the effects of humidity on your wood. Keeping up with an ongoing maintenance program, which might include keeping bare metal surfaces clean and coated with a nonsilicone wax, goes a long way to prevent rust and corrosion.

Access

When you are building the workshop of your dreams, you can install any kind of doors you like, so naturally you will have a pair of doors that open wide for moving machines and materials in and projects out. Depending on your property, however, the workshop building might be rather far from the driveway, and it might not have vehicle access. An appliance-moving hand truck, or a robust garden cart, can solve that.

Effects on the home

Because the workshop is a freestanding building, you don't have to worry about tracking sawdust into the house, nor will noise be a huge problem unless it is close to a neighboring house.

Working in a dedicated space allows you to leave partially built projects on a bench without worry of their being in the way or "adjusted" by well-meaning family members. Having a dedicated space usually allows much better control over who enters it, particularly when you are not around. Just being able to close and lock the entrance goes a long way toward keeping inquisitive fingers out of harm's way.

Figure 1.4. If your budget allows for it, designing a large, freestanding shop is the ultimate way to go. However, careful planning and layout remain necessary to get the most from the investment. Having a large door, sliding or overhead, is a great feature. Besides the obvious access benefits, being able to let natural light inside makes the shop more enjoyable.

You might imagine that working in a dedicated shop will allow you to have as many tools and as much materials as you need. However, you probably will need to exercise the same discipline as in any other workshop, including forcing yourself to toss out or burn all those pieces of valuable wood that really are too small to be useful. No matter how much space you have, if you are of the pack rat persuasion, you will soon fill it up.

Pro and Con: Freestanding Shop

Pro

- No compromises, until your money runs out
- All the space you need
- Controls dust and noise
- You can leave projects undisturbed

Con

- Expensive
- Needs its own heat and air conditioning
- Might not have easy vehicular access
- Can encourage pack rat personalities
- Not the best thing for a new woodworker—wait until you know more about what you really need

Taking stock of your space

Once you have chosen your location or if you have a few spaces in mind, take a really good look around. Make sketches, take measurements, and write notes to yourself. Note the details of each location: Where are the windows? Doors? Electrical outlets? Lights? You'll also want to be aware of any space that is taken up by other items either permanently, such as household mechanical systems in the basement, or temporarily, such as cars.

After you've looked around your potential shop(s), draw your basic space to scale, including the doors, windows, and any other features you noted (see **Figure 1.5** for an example of a basic floor plan). A useful scale is an inch on paper to a foot on the floor; you can buy large pads of paper ruled every quarter-inch. Mapping out your shop on paper will help you avoid moving machines around multiple times and having conflicts between different machines. Plus, while you may not be able to do much about where some of the physical features of the shop are, a little planning can maximize the useable space while minimizing any negative impact of those features on the shop. Taking stock of the features of available spaces can also help you choose the best one to suit your shop needs.

Best of Both

Whatever you do for a home workshop, you will have to make compromises and tradeoffs. But if you have the right kind of space, you can solve a lot of dust and noise problems by dividing the workshop: materials and noisy, dusty machines in an unheated garage, shed, or outbuilding; workbench, hand tools, small machines, assembly, and finishing in a cozy basement workshop. Bonus: You'll teach yourself how to organize the work, and you'll work off some extra poundage trotting back and forth.

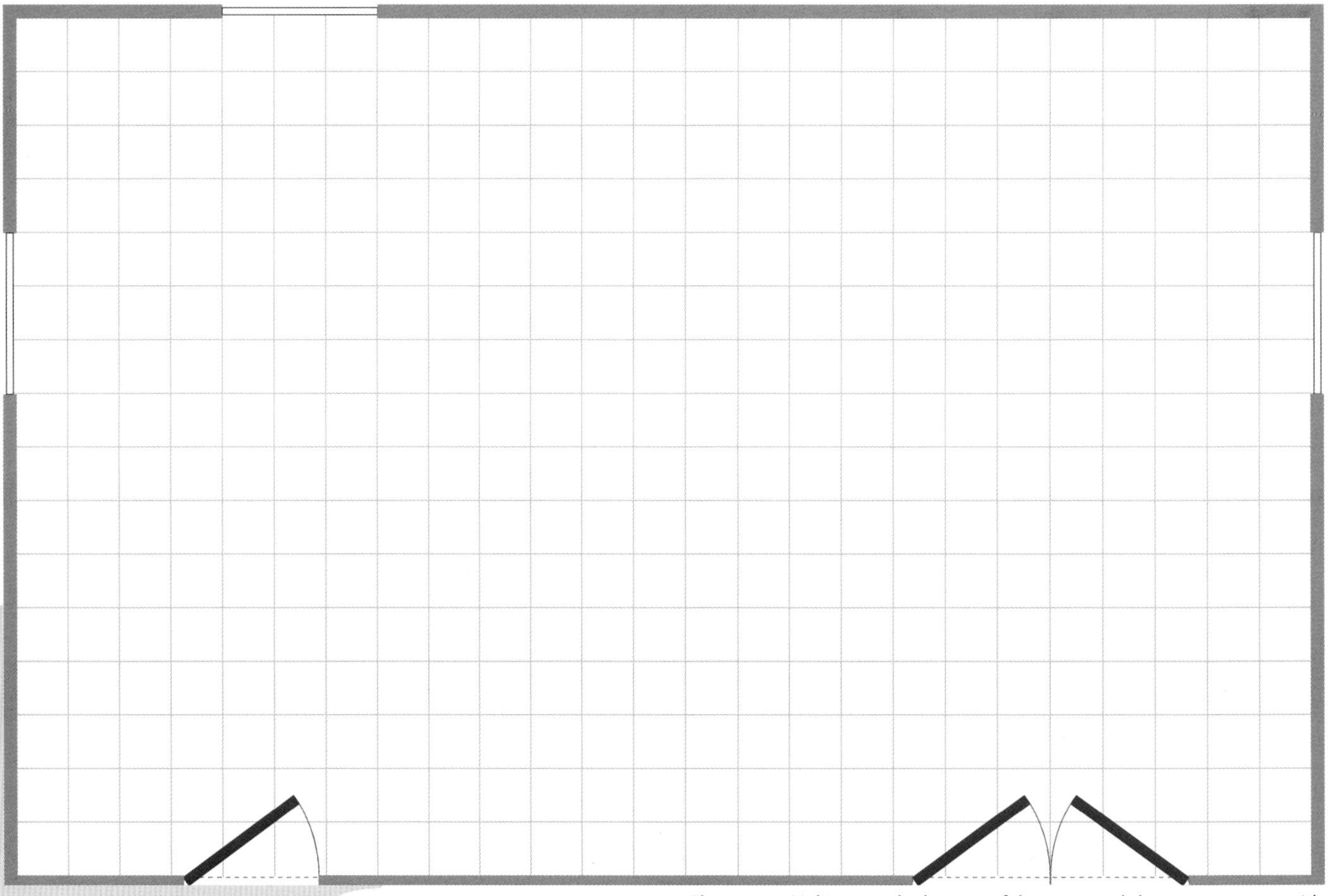

Figure 1.5. Making a scale drawing of the proposed shop space can provide a clear picture of the useable space you have. Be sure to note any permanent fixtures, including doors and windows. This basic blank floor plan was created on gridded paper to ensure accurate measurements. Here, ¼ inch equals 1 foot.

Shaping the space

Now that you have a basic layout to work with, it's time to start considering the type of shop that will best work for your space, the type of work you want to do, and the machinery that you'll need to create your projects. In the following sections, we will look at the different aspects of creating your shop.

Moving Materials

Bringing materials into the shop is an important consideration. I'll discuss materials in relationship to shop machines in a moment; right now let's think about just getting them in the door and storing them. It might be that you have an ideal slot for sheets of plywood at the far end of the workshop, but if you have to snake the plywood there, around and over all kinds of obstructions, you're probably not actually going to use it. Same for planks of wood—you need to be able to bring them in the door, store them until you need them, and then extricate them from storage to work with them.

The important consideration for materials storage is access. It's simplest if you can bring materials straight in from the driveway, through the shop door, and directly into their storage rack. Being able to access the materials safely from within the shop can also be an issue, especially in colder climates where opening a door for even short periods of time can vent expensive heat out into sub-zero temperatures.

Selecting Tools

Buying the biggest, baddest machine on the planet can be fun, but, if it is not useable in the space available, that little burst of bravado can negate a portion of the machine's capacity, and make your shop a dangerous place to work. That kind of purchasing mistake can needlessly take a major chunk out of your tool-buying budget, a type of fiscal insanity that is to be avoided at all costs. If you do fall down this rabbit hole and find yourself the bemused owner of a 24-inch 5-hp cast-iron thickness planer, the sooner you sell the behemoth, the better.

Important considerations when setting up a shop include deciding what equipment will fit in the space you have available, where you will put it, and how much space you need to operate it beyond the territory it stands on. You'll find a more thorough discussion of machines and tools in Chapter 2, "Buying Tools," on page 33, so if you don't already know what you want to purchase, you might want to skip ahead and then return to this chapter to finish your shop layout.

Building Your Own Workbench?

When building your own benches and worktables, why not make them a comfortable height? If you stand up straight, bend your elbows 90 degrees, put your hands straight out, and measure from your palms to the floor and subtract two inches, you will find a height that is very close to what is most comfortable for you (and your back) to work with. You can thank me later.

Another benefit of higher bench tops is the amount of space gained below them. Often, there will be room for another row of drawers. Storage space is always a good thing to find.

Another point of view on this is making sure that workbenches and assembly tables are either the same height as machine tables, or a smidgen lower. That way, large workpieces like sheets of plywood can glide over them, or be supported by them. Which way you go depends on how much space you have, and also on how tall you are.

> "The most important consideration for materials storage is access. If you have to snake the material there, you're probably not actually going to use it."

Making Templates

To get dimensions of a machine you are considering purchasing, measure it at a local retailer or perhaps obtain the dimensions either online or from a current owner. Then, make a paper or cardboard template using the same scale as the basic floor plan you created earlier (see Figure 1.5 on page 10). Include parts that stick out from the main body of the machine and where the blade or cutter is located. This is particularly important with table saw fences, where the longer rails take up considerably more room and greatly expand the useprint of the machine, or the amount of space required to use that machine. I've provided some common machine templates for you (see **Figure 1.6**), but be sure to modify them based on the actual machine that you wish to purchase. Making full-scale templates can be especially handy for investigating a potential shop area (see Determining Useprint on page 14).

Write the height of the work surface and that of the highest portion of the machine on the cardboard template. Be sure to note where the operator needs to stand and where access will be needed for maintenance and adjusting. Some machines, like a chop saw, can go against a wall—a chop saw needs access on both sides and in front but not from the back. Other machines, like a table saw, really need access from all sides. With this information, templates can help decide where wall cabinets, racks, and electrical outlets must be placed for easy access, and you can more easily determine where a machine will work best in your shop (see **Figure 1.7**).

Footprint versus Useprint

The footprint of a machine represents its total physical size, measured straight down to the floor at its largest dimensions—not just the area taken up by the leg set or base. These dimensions include fence rails, permanent table extensions, or anything else that projects out from the primary mass. The footprint of a machine is most important when it is not in use.

More important is what I call the useprint. The useprint is the amount of space required to actually use the machine to cut or process wood, not the physical size of the machine itself, as shown at right. The useprint includes where you stand. If the useprint is not considered, the capacity and capabilities of the machine can be reduced by obstructions.

Even more important is the effect inadequate free space around a machine can have on safety. If the wood contacts an obstruction while being cut, it can initiate a dangerous kickback, which occurs when the blade or cutter grabs the wood and throws it off the machine. At the very least, contact may cause the cutter to take a hunk out of an otherwise clean edge and ruin it.

Being able to see the actual footprints and useprints will help avoid conflicts between machines, benches, and other shop cabinetry.

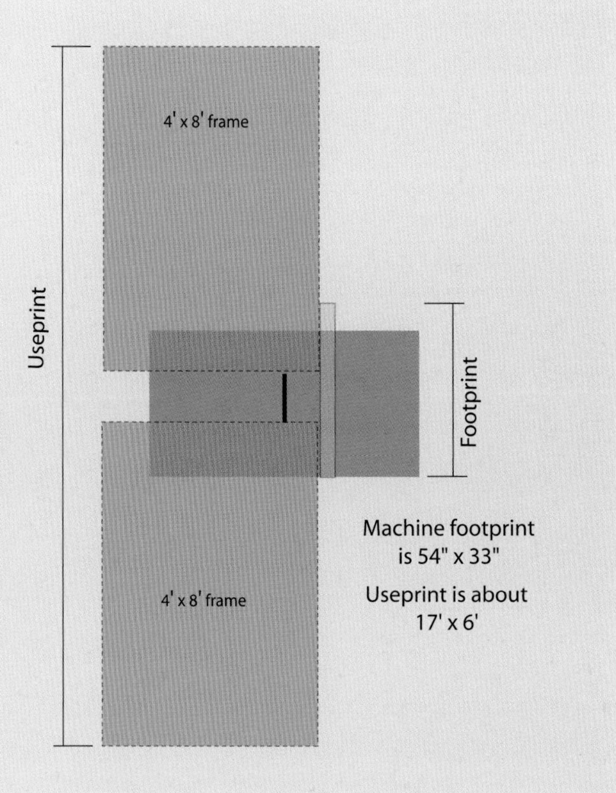

Machine footprint is 54" x 33"

Useprint is about 17' x 6'

Figure 1.6. These templates match common woodworking machines and are scaled to fit the basic blank floor plan in Figure 1.5. Use the templates as guides, but be sure to adjust them to match the equipment you have or intend to acquire. Scale: ¼" = 1'

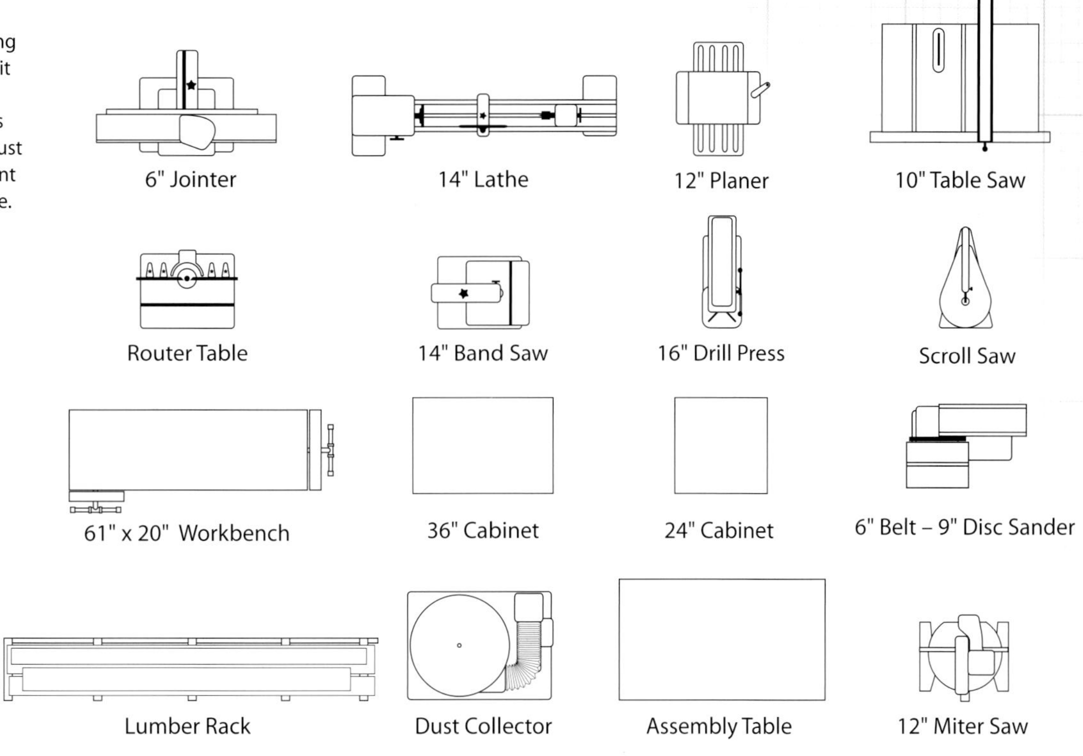

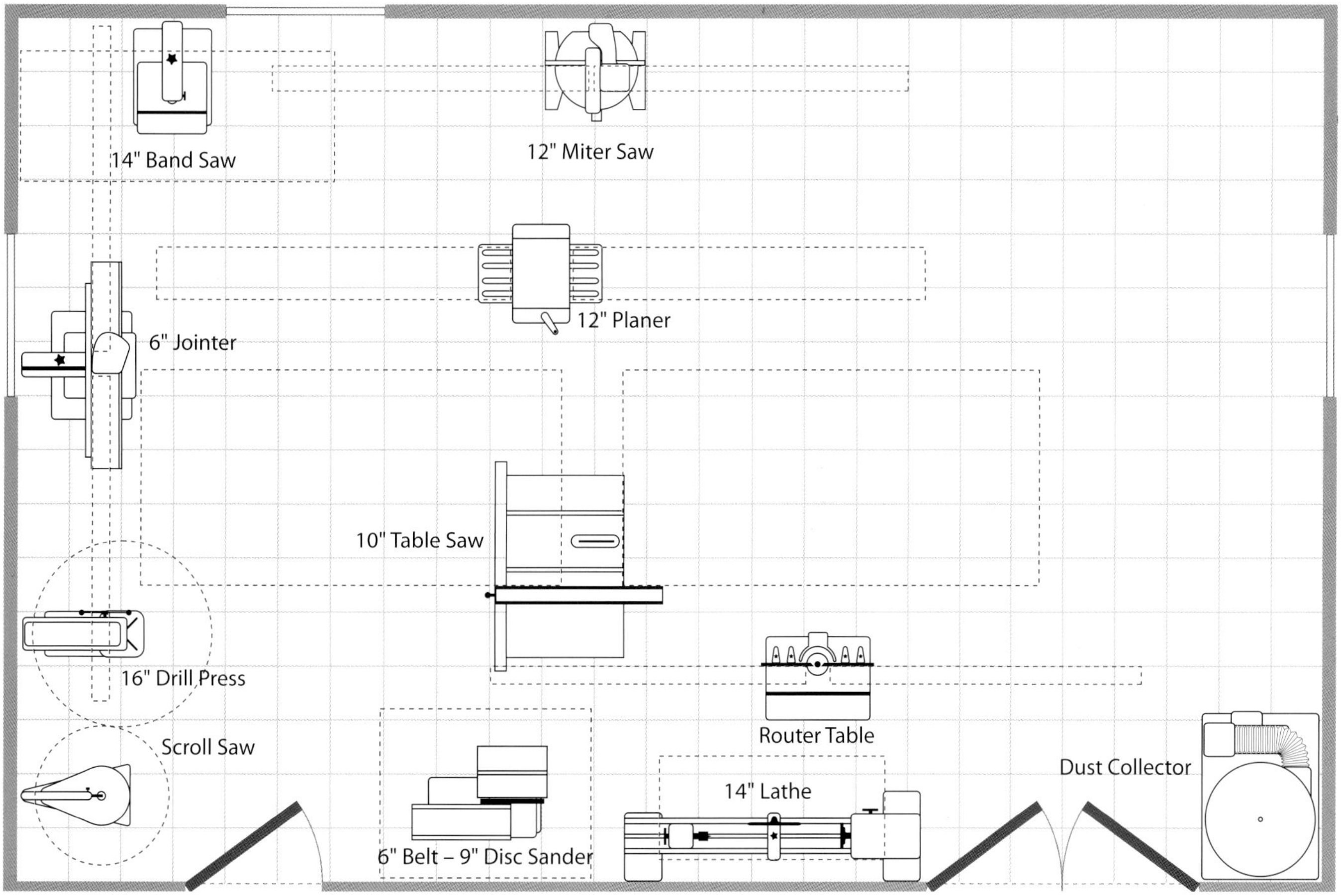

Figure 1.7. Once you have a basic floor plan, the next step is to explore what arrangements of machines might work in your space. Notice how this arrangement combines the machine footprints (black) with their larger useprints (red dashed lines). I can't stress enough how important it is to incorporate the useprint for each machine in your shop layout. Conflicts with other machines or obstacles when moving wood into or out of a machine can be very dangerous or severely limit the usefulness of a machine. Machines can share useprints.

Determining Useprint

To determine the useprint, you need to simulate cutting the largest piece of wood that you are likely to use in your shop. For some, that would be a 4' x 8' sheet of plywood; for others, it could be a 12' or 14' plank. Hustling a 4' x 8' sheet or a 14' board around a still-empty shop can be difficult and expensive, if you don't need the sheet for something else. Though you can make scale drawings and use colored paper cutouts on your floor plan, there's no substitute for moving around in the actual space.

Make cardboard templates to represent the outside dimensions (footprint) of a machine under consideration to help you decide if it will work in the available shop space.

Step 1: Start by making a simple frame to simulate the plywood. Construct it from 1" x 2" pine sold as furring strips, which are usually available in 10' or 12' lengths. This allows you to build a 4' x 9' frame to simulate the sheet plus a safety zone (the space you need to safely get a piece of wood into and out of the blade or cutter). Add a foot before and after the leading and trailing edges of a fully raised blade to create one.

Step 2: Check the space for various machines. When checking a machine with a moveable fence, be sure to place the mock-up in all fence positions and with its long axis parallel with and at 90 degrees to the blade. This is especially important if you want to be able to reduce that 4' x 8' sheet into smaller pieces directly on the table saw, which will require larger fence capacities in the 50" and above range.

Making a mock-up of a 4' x 8' sheet of plywood, often the largest single piece of wood you'll use, can be revealing. The useprint is much larger than the footprint, and you often do not have as much room as you thought.

Step 3: Consider your capacity needs. Working through this exercise might lead you to rethink the desire for a 50" fence and reconsider spending the extra money to get it. If you plan to produce a houseful of plywood cabinetry, a 50" fence capacity might be a good investment. (You will also need a place to store the incoming sheets and to stack and assemble the outgoing parts.) If you will only make a single cabinet or two, consider breaking down plywood sheets on the driveway with sawhorses and a portable circular saw, and then bringing the smaller pieces into the workshop to recut them to final size and squareness.

Working with long planks runs into similar limitations on space. If you want to crosscut a 14-footer on your chop saw, you'll need 15' on one side of the blade and at least 7' on the other. Here again, you might decide to make rough crosscuts on the driveway. Some woodworkers have been known to cut ports in the outside walls of small workshops so they can rip and plane long pieces of wood.

Step 4: Consider the path of the workpiece. In addition to space needed for machinery, consider how you will maneuver a plywood sheet or a long plank through the shop. You want it one way around for the table saw; then, you might need to turn it end-for-end for the jointer or planer. If you arrange the machines in the best possible way, you can probably eliminate obstacles that can make end-for-end turns difficult or even dangerous.

Remember to use the plywood mock-up with the fence set close to the blade and as far from the blade as it goes.

Choosing your overall layout

Once you have made templates for the machines you have or are thinking about buying, it's time to look at the overall scheme for your shop so that you can determine the best placement for your equipment. Oversimplified, shop layouts can be broken down into two categories: shops with fixed equipment and shops with mobile equipment. Shops with fixed equipment are generally more spacious or do not have to share the space with too many cars and other items. Shops with mobile equipment are often smaller or are spaces that must be shared with other needs. Given the varied nature of the work a hobby woodworker is likely to tackle and the limitations most folks have on shop space, mobile bases probably are a good idea.

Layout Considerations

Since everyone's workshop needs and plans are different, few generalities can be provided. But there are a few. Most of these apply to both fixed-equipment and mobile-base workshops:

- Most woodworkers put the table saw close to the middle of the workshop, occasionally with more space on the left side, from the operator's point of view, than on the right.
- Once you have placed the table saw, place the other machines according to the path the workpiece will take. The normal sequence is table saw to jointer to thickness planer. Thus, you will often see a jointer on the right side of the table saw, again from the operator's point of view, with the planer just a walking space away.
- If you plan to use a chop saw for crosscutting planks, put it along the wall directly inside the shop door where the wood will enter. That way the wood can go straight in through the door and onto the chop saw table, where it gets cut into shorter, more easily managed pieces.
- If you possibly can, put your workbench under a window or next to overhead doors that you can open on a sunny day.
- Somewhere near the workbench, you should plan to have a comfortable-height assembly table about 4' x 4' in size. That's where you can stack parts after sawing, build subassemblies, leave projects in clamps while the glue dries, and do finishing.
- A dedicated finishing area is a wonderful luxury, but it is not essential in the small workshop.
- Plywood can be stored on edge against the wall or against a lumber rack. But you have to be sure it is standing up on edge, not leaning, or it soon will take on the shape of a potato chip.
- Planks of wood can be stored lying flat or standing up on end, provided they are shorter than the shop ceiling. As with plywood, flat storage has to be truly flat and supported every two or three feet, and vertical storage has to be vertical, not leaning. It does not take long for wood to bend to match its storage conditions.
- A workshop soon needs more shelf and cabinet storage than you can possibly imagine, and twice as much if you have the pack rat gene. I'm talking about portable power tools, hand tools, cutters and bits, fences, nails, screws, finishing materials, sandpaper, jigs and fixtures, interesting mistakes, and half-finished projects. When the workbench becomes home to half-full cans of finish, you no longer have a workshop—you have an expensive storage locker instead.
- Decide where you will stash short ends of wood. While I have encountered hardy souls who say they always discard potentially useful scrap, I don't actually believe them. Decide where you will stash it, and vow to yourself that when the designated space is full, you'll at least throw away the pieces you knew were junk when you put them there.

Shops with Fixed Equipment

If you're lucky enough to have a large shop space that will allow all of your machines and equipment to have their own permanent places, carefully select a space for each machine (see **Figure 1.8**). When deciding on locations, make sure that there is enough room to operate the machine safely and that it has access to other necessities, such as power supply, dust collection, and lighting. Then, think about how the various machines relate to one another, and see if you can puzzle out the path that each plank or piece of plywood will have to follow, from the shop door to the assembly table where it joins up with the rest of your project.

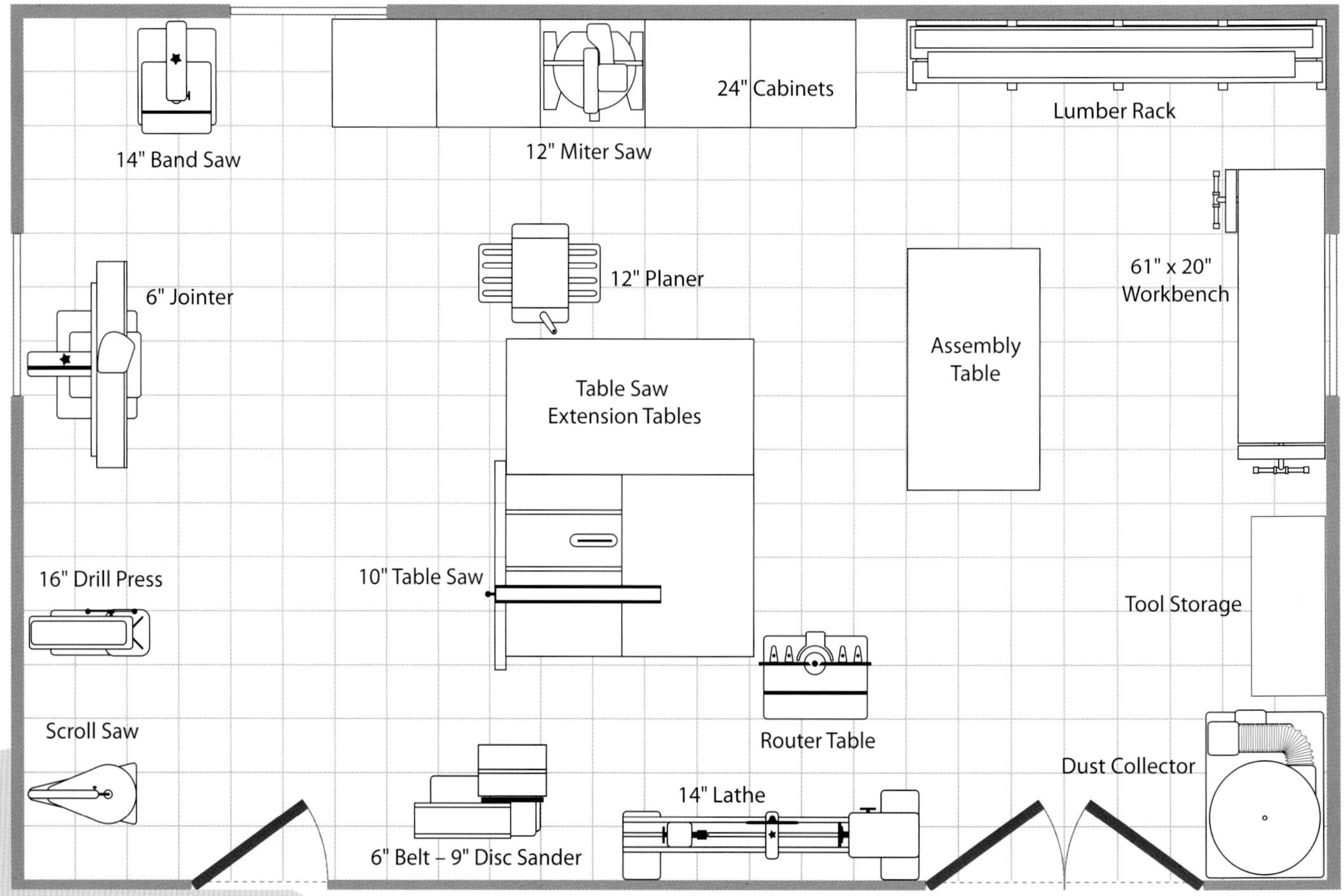

Figure 1.8. If your shop is large enough and doesn't share a lot of space with other items, you can use a fixed-equipment layout, which allows you to carefully choose a permanent space for each machine. As you try out different locations, be sure to consider the machine useprints and think about the machines' needs for lighting, dust collection, and power. In this layout, tables, cabinets, and other storage items have been added so that the path of the raw materials can be checked.

Shops with Mobile Equipment

If your shop space is limited, plan for an area in which to store equipment not being used so that you can have the maximum open space for working (see **Figure 1.9**). Since you'll most likely be moving machines into the open space with this style of layout, mobile bases for your tools will be important. Storage space for supplies and smaller equipment will also be needed. Knowing which wall spaces will be most accessible will help design and place freestanding or wall-mounted cabinets and racks in a way that will be most useful.

Mobile bases

Being able to reposition a machine can be useful regardless of the shop dimensions but can be essential in smaller shops. Even the table saw, traditionally the most-used machine in a woodworking shop, is needed for only a portion of a project. When not in use, being able to move it to an out-of-the-way parking area makes precious floor space available for other tasks (see **Figure 1.10**). When the shop space has to be returned to other service, like parking a car, mobile bases are even more important.

A machine on a mobile base can be positioned to take advantage of a clear path or corridor in the shop when cutting long stock. The ability for individual machines to use a common open area maximizes the workshop space. When not in use, the machines can be parked out of the way to maintain that free space for other procedures such as assembly, sanding, or finishing. More information on the different kinds of mobile bases can be found in Chapter 2, "Buying Tools," on page 33.

Outfeed Support

If a mobile worktable is in your plan, build it so its surface is at the same height as the surface of the table saw. That way, the mobile worktable can double as an outfeed support when cutting large pieces of lumber or plywood sheets.

Figure 1.10. Having most of my machines on mobile bases allows me to park them in part of one garage bay. This makes my shop seem larger than it is.

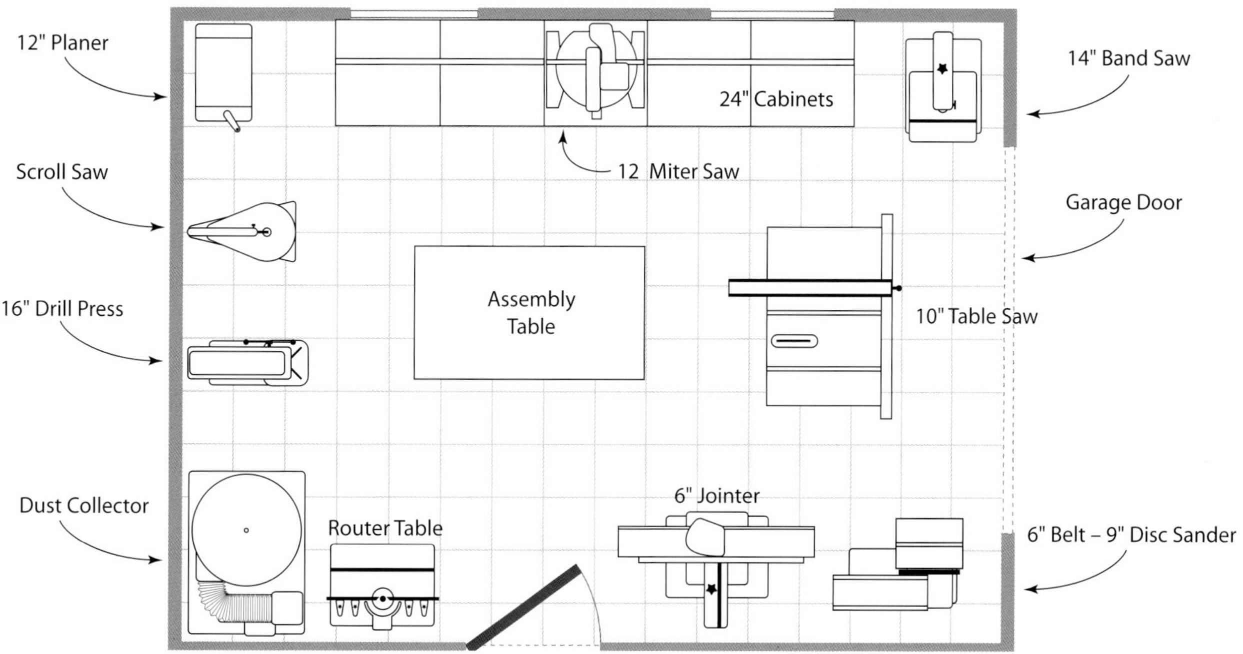

Figure 1.9. In a smaller shop or a shop that uses temporary space, using a mobile equipment layout often maximizes the space available. This type of layout means adding mobile bases to machines, storing the machines out of the way, and bringing them into the center of the shop for use.

Coming up with a base shop layout

Use the machine templates to block in the layout for your shop space. Keep in mind that this process is likely to involve several revisions, especially when you next take a hard look at the electrical situation (see the Electrical Service section on page 20). Developing a sensible layout that affords the necessary free space around all of the machines might not be as easy as it sounds, but it can be done (see **Figure 1.11**).

While working on the placement of freestanding machines and equipment, remember the workbench and wall cabinets. The space above a permanent bench is prime territory for wall-mounted storage cabinets, but there may be other options available, too.

Some woodworkers choose a knockdown or mobile worktable in place of a fixed bench, especially in smaller shops. Whatever your choice, its size and how it relates to the equipment surrounding it has to be figured into the layout plan. Making space for an assembly table is also a good idea.

Consider having full-length cabinets that rest on the floor (see **Figure 1.12**). Unless there is a spot that can safely be dedicated to such a cabinet, wait until the machine and equipment layout is at least roughed in before trying locations (see **Figure 1.13**).

Safety Over Efficiency

A good way to complicate the layout process is trying to minimize footsteps between frequently used machines. That may sound like a good idea but can make eliminating conflicts between useprints more difficult. Efficiency is nice, but safety has to come first. Walking a few extra steps is less time-consuming than driving to the emergency room.

Figure 1.11. My shop is surprisingly efficient now, but it did not start out that way. Guessing what should go where and what machines I would have in the future led to three major overhauls—so far.

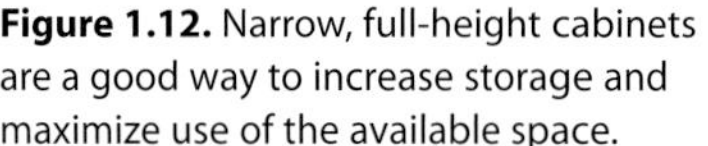

Figure 1.12. Narrow, full-height cabinets are a good way to increase storage and maximize use of the available space.

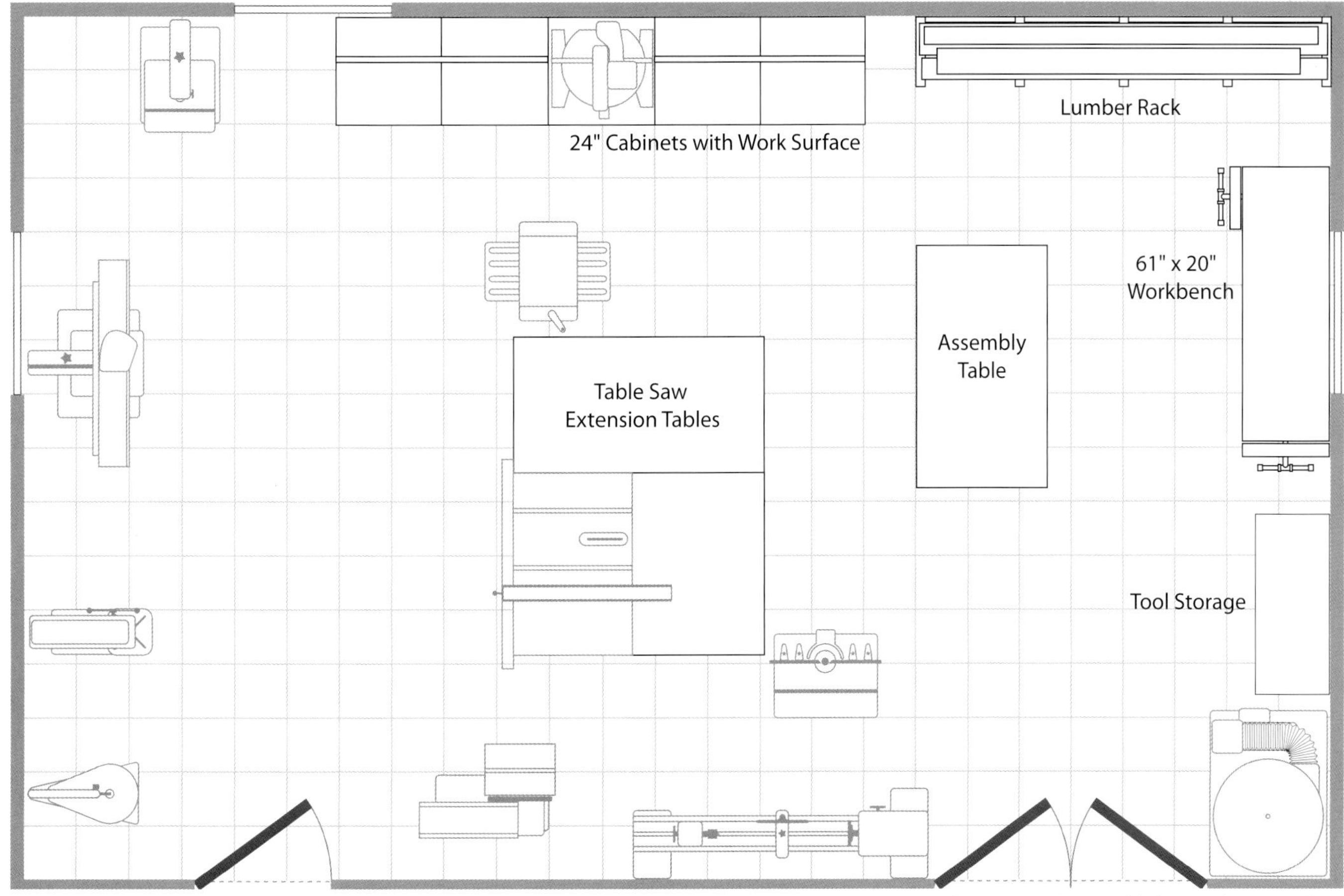

Figure 1.13. Once you have created a possible layout showing where the machines and work stations will be, you can begin to find places for floor and wall-mounted storage cabinets, tables, and other storage items. This way, you can ensure that they won't interfere with the useprints of the machines. Here, the machines are shown in gray and the worktables and storage areas are shown in black for clarity.

"While working on the placement of freestanding machines and equipment, remember the workbench and wall cabinets. The space above a permanent bench is prime territory for wall-mounted storage cabinets."

Electrical service

Now you have a good idea of what you want in your shop and where you want the equipment to go. However, before finalizing machine template locations, review the electrical situation in the shop space because the placement of outlets can influence where a machine can be located. Owning powerful machines can be a good thing, but it takes power to make power. Before springing for that 5 hp monster saw, make sure there is an equally huge electrical circuit. Extension cords are an option but should be last on your list of options: You think you won't trip on them, but you will.

Assessing Your Current Electrical Service

Take the time to add any outlets, lights, and other electrical fixtures to the diagram you created previously (see **Figure 1.14**). Be sure to note how many of them are on common circuits. If you can isolate a group of outlets on a circuit, you can find the breaker that operates it and see what its rating is. If you are in the basement, the electrical panel is probably nearby, making it easier to run new circuits. If your shop is in a garage, chances are you are not going to be overjoyed with what you find.

In garages, 15-amp circuits are common; you might have 20-amp if you are lucky. If you are living right and have been blessed by the woodworking spirits, there will be more than one circuit dedicated to the garage. Finding a dedicated 220-volt circuit and receptacle means the garage probably has been inhabited by a woodworker or someone with a race car. In either case, you lucked out big time.

In the real world, you found too few outlets, probably all on one 15-amp circuit. A new

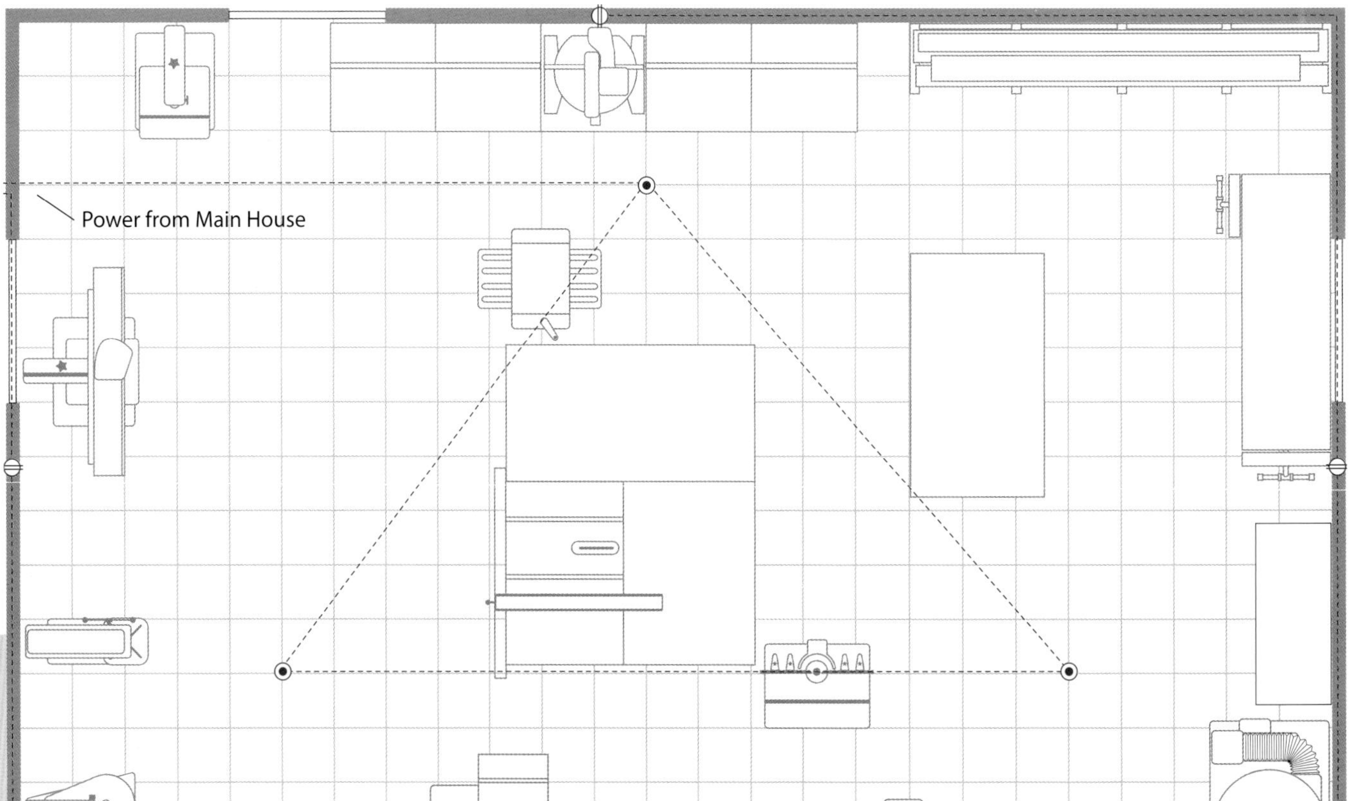

Power from Main House

Figure 1.14. After diagramming the machines and workstations, add the electrical outlets and lights. Be sure to separate them according to their circuits so that you can prevent a circuit overload. As you can see, the existing lights and outlets in this shop would not be nearly enough to provide light and power to all of the machines. The power is coming from the main panel in the house, so upgrading to include a service panel in the shop would be ideal. This diagram will be a big help when talking to an electrician about updating the electrical service to fit your needs.

woodworker may be able to live with one or two 15- or 20-amp circuits, but, as the inventory of equipment builds, so does the need for electrical capacity. Usually, both happen quite fast.

Before adding outlets, adding circuits, or calling an electrician, figure out what kind of electrical service is actually needed. Developing a rough idea of where outlets should go and what kinds of power should be available at each place in the shop will make the process much easier.

Powering Machines

Virtually every electrically driven tool or machine has its amp draw listed on a plate or sticker on the motor itself (see **Figure 1.15**) or in the information provided by the manufacturer. You can also find this information on the manufacturer's website or in the descriptions offered by many online retailers, and you should note it on your floor plan.

A complicating factor is the fact that a machine listing a 15-amp draw could exceed that for a short time during startup. To combat this, your electrician may suggest using circuit breakers with a short built-in delay that prevents them from tripping during these startup spikes.

Compiling a list of the power draws of the machines you have and those you plan to have in the future will help determine if your shop has adequate power. If it doesn't, you have the information necessary to talk to an electrician who can fix that.

Remember that the shop's electrical need is not the same as the total current draw of all the machines. It would be the total if you were a commercial operation where all the machines might be humming at once. But you aren't. Except in unusual situations, you can't possibly be using more than one machine at a time when working alone. Even if you run your dust collector, plus the lights, plus the boom box, the current draw will add up, but not to the total of all the machine motor plates.

110 Volts Versus 220 Volts

Many machines are capable of being converted to operate on 110-volt or 220-volt power. Most of these machines are wired for 110-volt power at the factory but can be converted to run on 220-volt rather easily. Larger machines with motors in the 2 hp and up range generally run on 220-volt power only. In most cases, you can do the conversion yourself. It involves switching a couple of wires inside the motor's electrical box, following the diagram you'll find pasted inside the box. You'll also have to change the machine's power cord and plug to match the 220-volt outlet you'll be using.

There is a misconception that converting a motor from 110-volt to 220-volt operation increases its power output. Not true. The motor may run a little cooler, in part because it draws fewer amps, but the power it generates remains essentially the same. One benefit of converting a large machine to 220 volts is that it runs on a circuit that is independent of others in the shop. That means while running a 220-volt table saw, turning on the 110-volt dust collector will not trip circuit breakers or dim the lights in the house, making your family wonder if you just executed a neighbor who asked to borrow one of your tools.

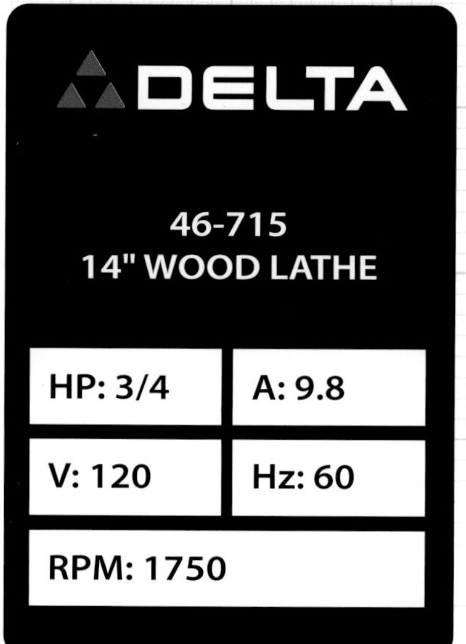

Figure 1.15. Before you upgrade the electrical service in a shop, you need to determine how much power you need. An information plate listing the amp draw should be affixed to the electric motors on the machines.

"There is a misconception that converting a motor from 110-volt to 220-volt operation increases its power output. Not true. The motor may run a little cooler, but the power it generates remains essentially the same."

Planning Lighting

A common pitfall in woodshop design is inadequate lighting. It is difficult to have too much light, but very easy to have too little. If you find yourself undecided between a smaller or larger number of lighting fixtures, go for more. Spreading the light over the entire shop area makes expanding work areas or placing new machines easier because there are no dim spots to avoid.

Designing a layout for light fixtures is rather easy in most shops. The goal is good light everywhere with minimal shadows and dim spots. It's smarter to give the entire shop good coverage, rather than concentrate fixtures over individual machines or benches, because equipment is likely to get moved as new machines and tools are introduced. In addition, with multiple fixtures spread over the ceiling, virtually

Figure 1.16. When installing lights above a bench, keep them far enough from the walls so that cabinets do not cast a shadow on the work surface below. Spreading light fixtures across the ceiling is not only easier on the eyes, but also safer because there are fewer shadows and dark spots in which to have accidents.

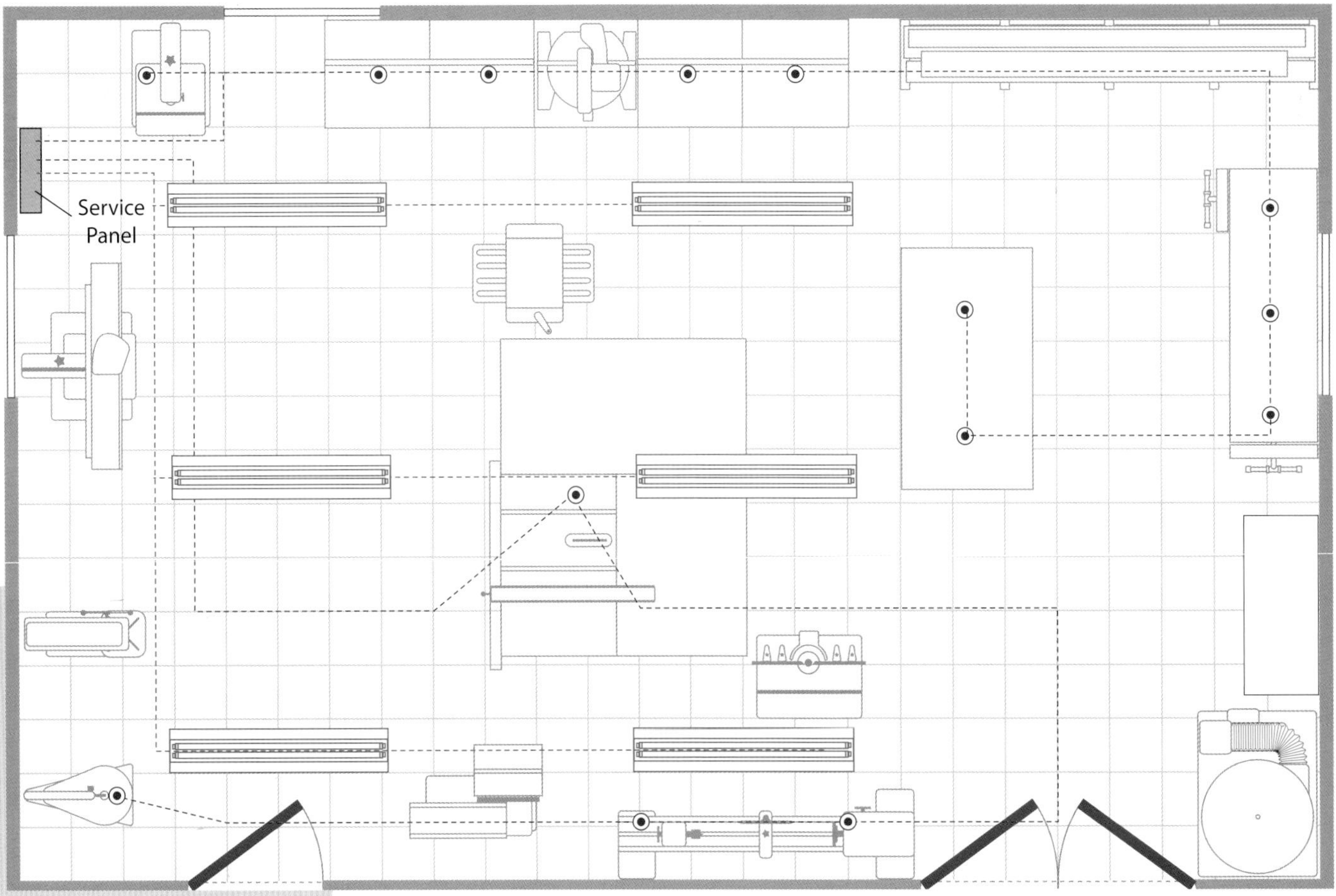

Figure 1.17. Whether it includes incandescent lights, fluorescent lights, or a combination of the two, a good lighting scheme will illuminate the shop in general and will have more focused light where needed. This lighting layout has task lights over specific workstations and machines, augmented by generalized lighting that will combine to eliminate dim spots. Notice that there are two incandescent lighting circuits (red) and one fluorescent circuit (blue). Separating these lighting schemes to individual circuits is a very good idea to prevent overloading a circuit when a machine is turned on.

every spot in the shop will be lit from more than one direction (see **Figure 1.16**). That helps prevent you from standing at odd angles trying to keep your shadow off the layout lines.

A way to plan lighting is to make a copy of your shop floor plan or lay a sheet of tissue paper over it. Draw the existing lights and the lights you would like to add on the copy or overlay (see **Figure 1.17**). Think about how the lights will be located near the perimeter of the shop. Workbenches and machines are often put against the walls, making it important to light these areas properly. Hanging cabinets on the wall will block the light if the fixture is too close to the wall.

The two most common types of lighting for woodworking shops are fluorescent tube fixtures and incandescent bulbs. Regardless of which type you choose, all of the fixtures should be on one or more circuits that are separate from those supplying the outlets around the shop. Otherwise, your machine might trip the breaker and leave you in the dark at the same time.

Power Strips

Don't be tempted to cheat the electricity gods by increasing the number of outlets with a power strip or two. The problem is that all of the outlets on the power strip draw current from the one outlet it is plugged into. If that outlet is wired into a circuit that doesn't have enough power to begin with, all you have done is add more ways to trip the circuit breaker. Things are getting worse, not better.

I have two power strips in my shop, both located where I commonly use smaller power tools. Though I leave a few things plugged into the strips, I only use one tool at a time. Turning on a second tool would exceed the circuit capacity. Power strips can bring some convenience to a work area, but they are not the answer to an underpowered electrical service.

A more serious problem created by adding power strip outlets, or otherwise intentionally overtaxing a circuit, is overheating, possibly causing a fire. If there is a weak spot or problem anywhere in the circuit, the firefighters you might have to call will not be enthused about what you did to ignite the blaze. The only happy person in this situation could be your homeowner's insurance carrier, who may have a "stupid" clause in the policy that frees them from having to write a big check.

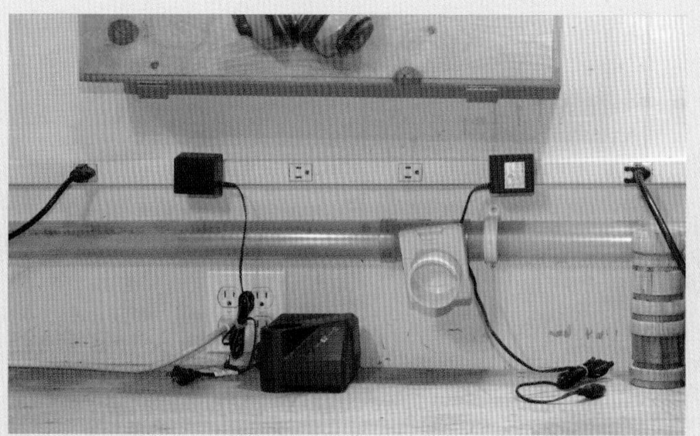

Power strips are handy but should not be used to increase the number of outlets in the shop. I have power strips in two places where I commonly use small, handheld tools, but only one at a time.

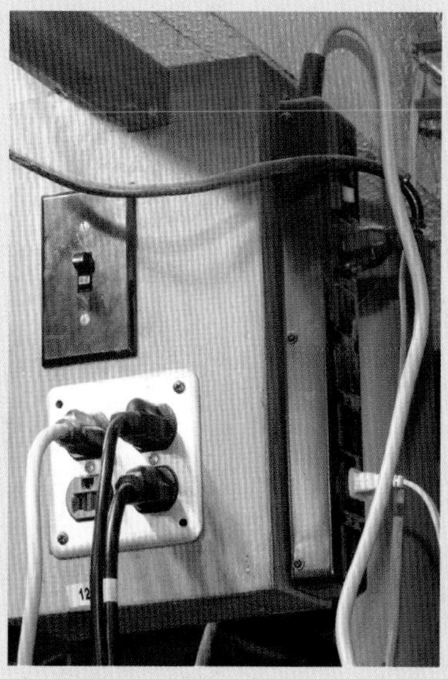

Adding two more outlets to a box that only had two to start just increases the load on a weak circuit. Add in a power strip and things can get out of hand quickly.

Fluorescent tubes

Fluorescent tube fixtures are generally arranged in rows spaced 4' or 5' apart to provide consistent lighting over the entire shop area (see **Figure 1.18**). Small or oddly shaped spaces may require the fixtures to be arranged differently, but the goal remains the same—light the entire space adequately and evenly. When you do it this way, the light coming from all directions tends to knock out shadows.

Fluorescent fixtures can be disappointing in the life of the tubes and in the trouble they have starting up in cold weather. As you might expect, cheap fluorescent fixtures and bulbs cause the most trouble. Buying commercial-grade fixtures and bulbs tends to eliminate these problems and a bunch of cash at the same time.

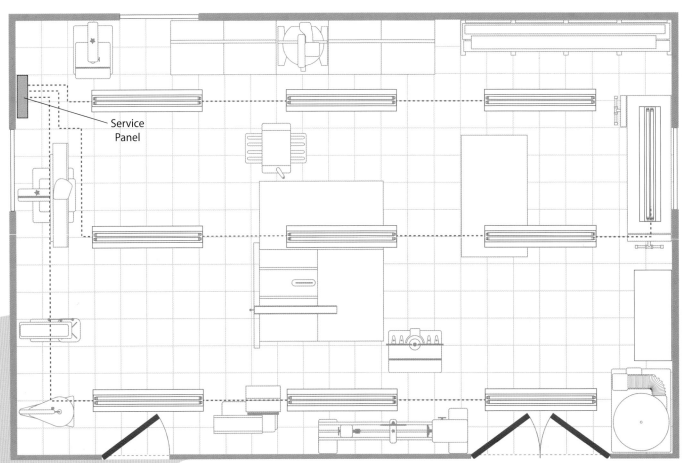

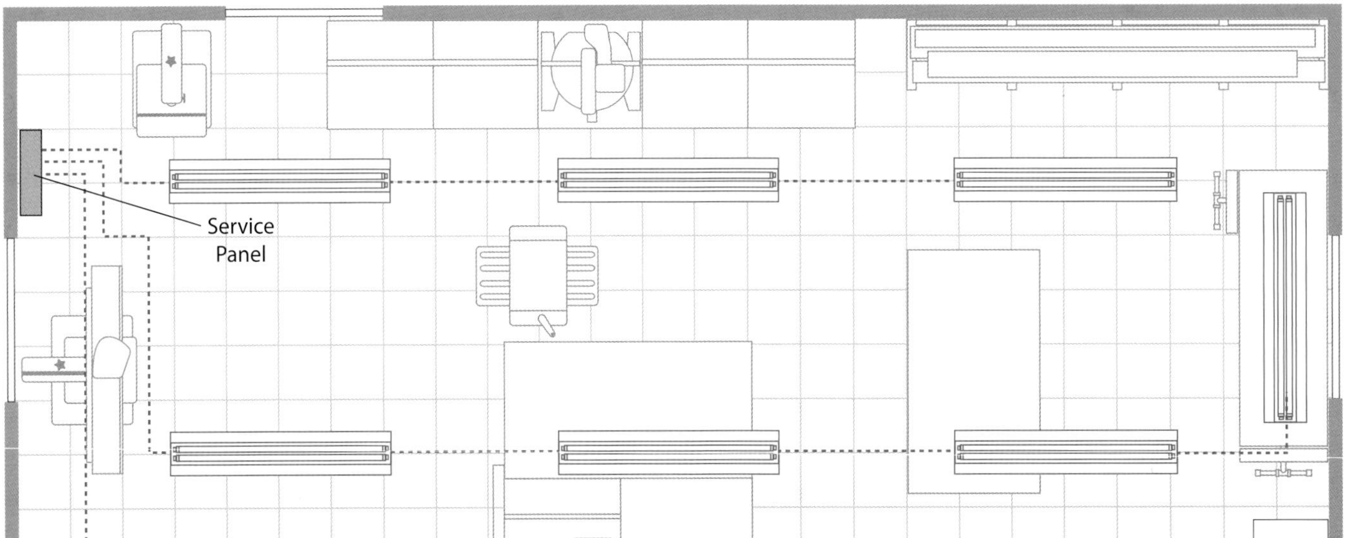

Service Panel

Figure 1.18. This lighting layout shows how you might light a shop using only fluorescent lights and features three fluorescent circuits. Properly spaced fluorescent fixtures can provide good light throughout the shop. The key is spacing the lights so that the light from each fixture overlaps that of the one next to it.

Incandescent bulbs

Incandescent bulbs and fixtures can be a good alternative to fluorescent lighting. In some shops, placing an incandescent fixture to properly light a machine or workspace can be much easier than trying to put a 4' fluorescent fixture in the same space (see **Figure 1.19**).

Take the time to determine the number of fixtures you need before talking with a local electrical supplier about the types of fixtures available, and you will get a more definitive cost estimate.

I recently changed to incandescent bulbs after a lengthy and occasionally loud battle with fluorescent fixtures that were plagued by startup and bulb life issues. Since the change, my lighting problems have disappeared.

I replaced four, 4' fluorescent fixtures with four, two-bulb incandescent fixtures, each with two 100-watt bulbs. The fixtures are regular fixed boxes. It was easy to do and cost less than $100.

While a large number of fixtures may be needed to provide full coverage with incandescent bulbs, the wide range of outputs available makes fine-tuning the light for an area of the shop as simple as screwing in a few new bulbs. It is also easier to install incandescent fixtures in smaller shop spaces. Remember that you want to minimize lights hanging down off the ceiling, especially if you carry around long boards in your shop.

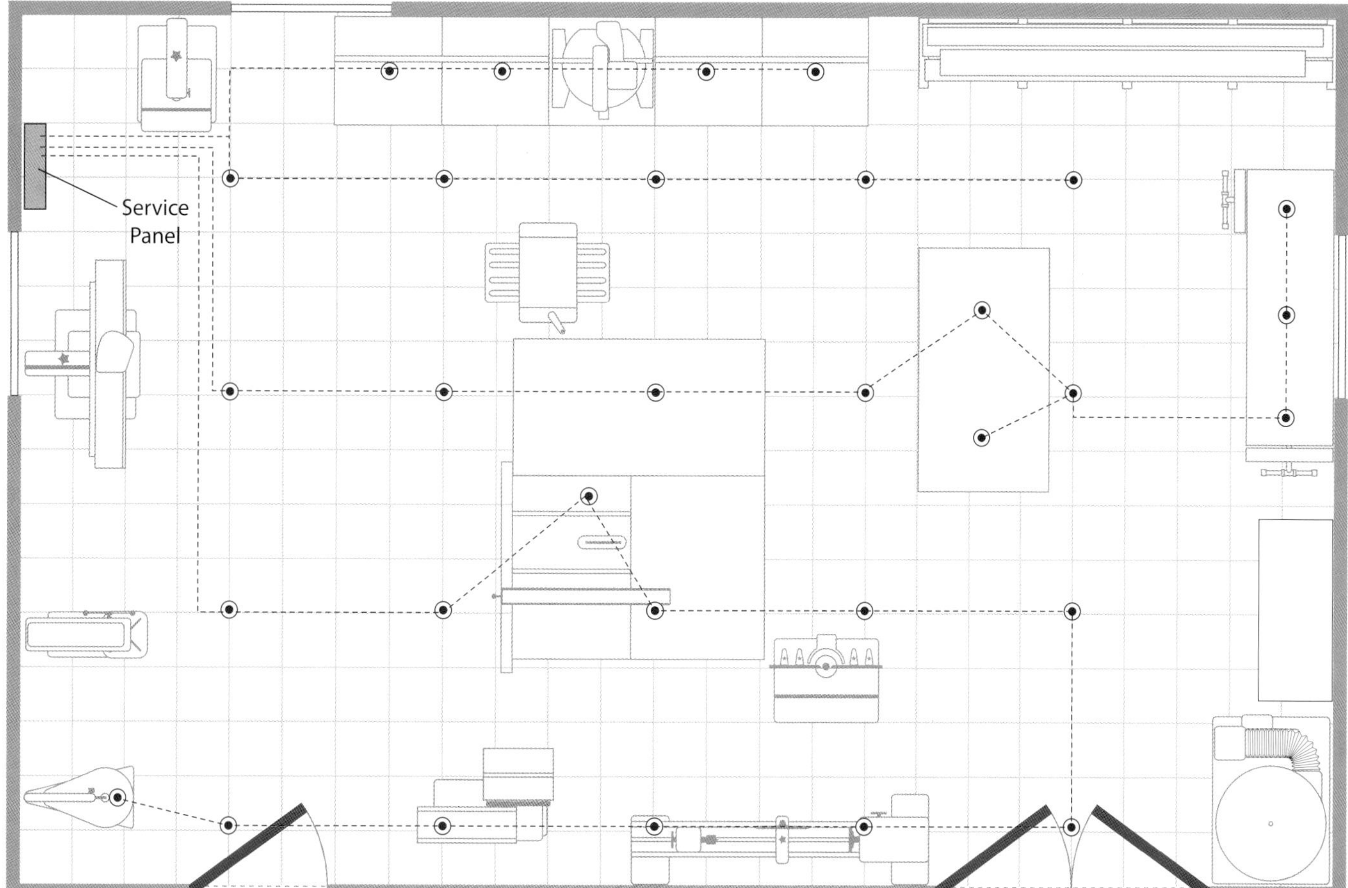

Figure 1.19. This lighting layout shows how you might light a shop using only incandescent lights and features three incandescent circuits. Saturating the shop with incandescent bulb fixtures can be cheaper than using fluorescent fixtures even though the incandescent numbers are greater. Also, being able to regulate output with the various-watt incandescent bulbs available can make tailoring the light at specific spots easier without having to replace fixtures.

Upgrading the Electrical System

The only sane approach to correcting electrical inadequacies in the shop space is to contact a qualified electrician who is licensed to work in your community. If you can describe what you want to do and provide the base power draws of the equipment under consideration, the electrician can design a safe, efficient electrical system that adheres to local building codes (see **Figure 1.20**).

While hiring an electrician to upgrade the shop is not cheap, you can make it even more expensive by not anticipating future power needs as the number and size of machines increase electrical demands. Having the electrician build in extra capacity in the form of additional circuits, sockets, and breakers will save money in the long run.

Electrical System Checklist

Are you ready to implement your electrical plan? Before you put your plan into action, make sure you have completed the following steps:

- Mark any existing outlets, lights, and other electrical fixtures on your basic floor plan, and note how many are on common circuits.
- Compile a list of the power draws of your current and future machines.
- Decide where to add new outlets and how much power must be available at each.
- Create an overall lighting plan, keeping all light fixtures on circuits separate from those supplying outlets.
- Determine whether the amperage of your current electrical service can handle your shop needs.
- If you need to upgrade your service, call an electrician who is licensed in your community.

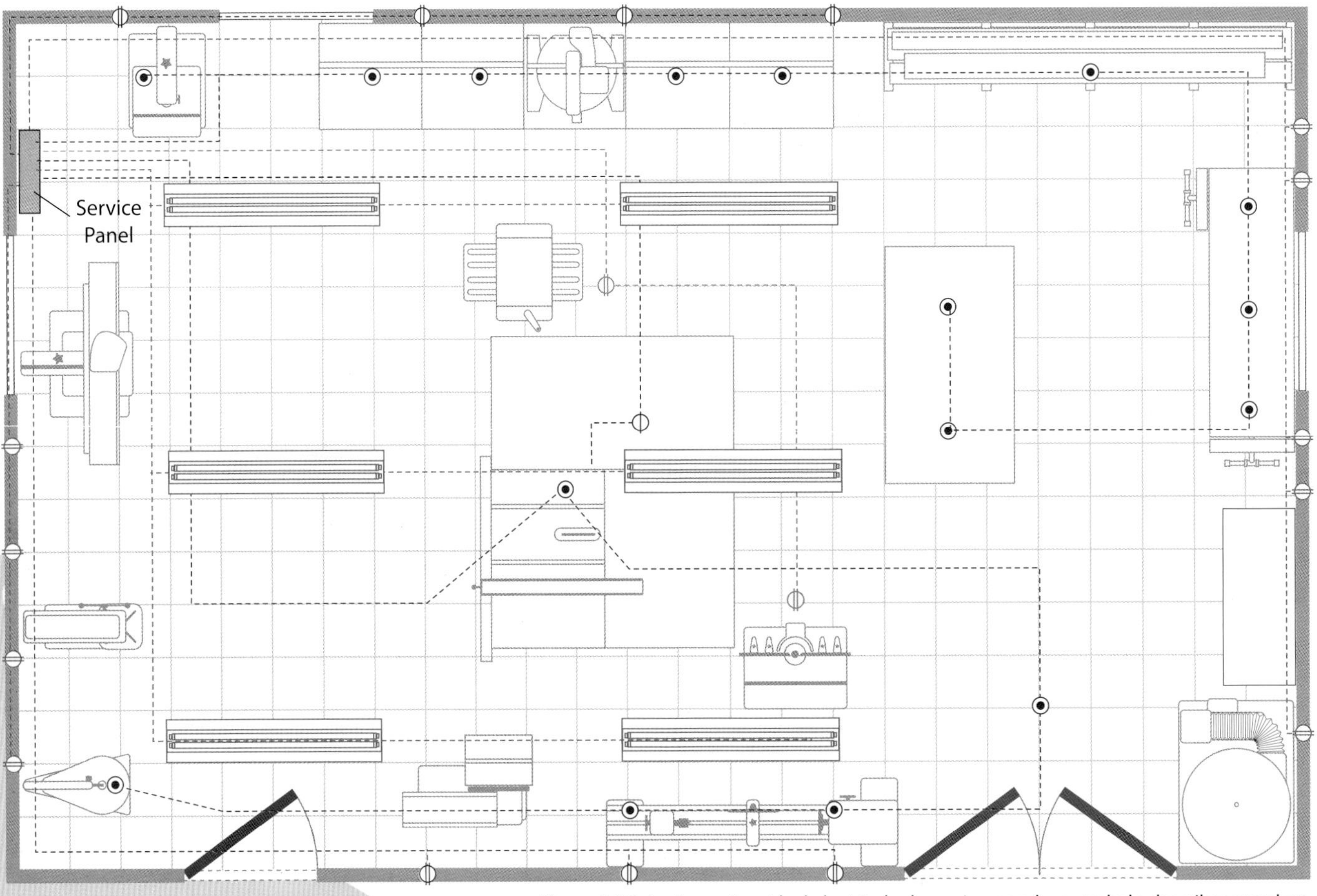

Figure 1.20. Laying out an ideal electrical scheme is a good way to help describe your shop to a qualified electrician, who can then make suggestions and put your plan into action. This electrical and lighting layout meets current needs and also provides for future expansion. Building in extra capacity is much cheaper the first time around than adding it later will be.

Safety considerations

While working out the layout of your shop, you should also be sure to incorporate the safety basics: fire protection and dust collection devices, as well as a good first-aid kit.

Fire Extinguishers

Have at least one fire extinguisher with an ABC rating in the shop (see **Figure 1.21**), keeping in mind that even large handheld fire extinguishers are for dealing with exceptionally small fires. Fire trucks, and the equipment they carry, should handle everything else. Even if you think you have put out the fire by yourself, you should call the fire department. Stuff can smolder for a long time; let the professionals be sure it is out.

When installing a fire extinguisher in your shop, resist the urge to put it near materials or places you feel are most likely to catch fire. That kind of placement means that, should a fire start, you will not be able to get to the extinguisher, and it will be one of the first things to burn up. Hang fire extinguishers next to exits that will be your primary avenues of escape. That way, you can get out in the event the fire gets out of hand.

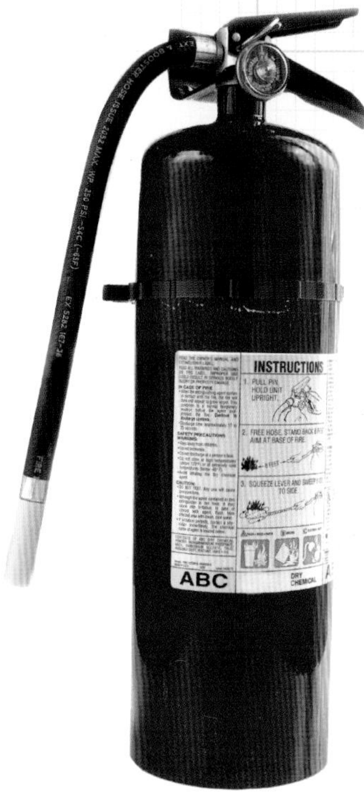

Figure 1.21. Choose at least one fire extinguisher with an ABC rating for your shop. This type of extinguisher can be used on almost any type of fire that might occur in a woodshop.

The ABCs of Fire Extinguishers

Fire extinguishers have letter designations related to the type of materials they are designed to work with. Successfully putting out each type of fire requires using the proper fire extinguisher for the type of fuel that is burning.

- **Class A fires** involve ordinary combustibles, such as wood, paper, cloth, trash, and plastics.
- **Class B fires** involve flammable liquids, such as gasoline, petroleum oil, and paint, and flammable gases, such as propane and butane.
- **Class C fires** involve energized electrical equipment, such as motors, transformers, and electrical appliances. Remove the power and a Class C fire becomes one of the other two classes of fire.

The most widely used type of fire extinguisher today is the multipurpose dry chemical extinguisher that is effective on Class A, B, and C fires. This type of extinguisher can be used on virtually any fire that might occur in the shop.

Fire extinguishers are sized according to the weight of the dry chemical they contain. For a workshop, a 5-pound extinguisher is the minimum size to consider.

Smoke Alarms

Install a smoke alarm, even if the law in your area doesn't require it (see **Figure 1.22**). It can alert you to a fire early in its development. Install it according to the manufacturer's instructions, taking care not to mount it directly above an area where you routinely do something that generates smoke or the combustion gases that detectors often sniff for (like branding projects or decorative woodburning).

If the smoke detector goes off when you are using the table saw or other woodworking equipment, do not disable the detector. You have problems with the machine or tool generating the smoke. Very often, a dull or dirty blade or cutter, sometimes augmented by a misalignment of the machine, is the cause. In any case, those problems need to be fixed, not the smoke detector.

Figure 1.22. It is a good idea to clean smoke detectors located in a woodworking shop once a month as they can become contaminated by the dust. After you put it back together, give the test button a push.

Sprinkler System

If you are building a new woodshop, adding a sprinkler system could be more cost-effective than you think. Not only can it save the building and its contents, it often qualifies the structure for a substantial discount on insurance.

Five Things to Minimize Fire Risk

- Keep your shop and machines clean.
- Sweep up sawdust from the floor and clean it from your machines often.
- Be cautious when using heated tools, like branding irons.
- Store flammable materials away from sources of ignition.
- Place fire extinguishers near exits.

Basic safety equipment, such as a first-aid kit, smoke alarm, and fire extinguisher, are cheap insurance that could pay big dividends if something goes wrong.

Dust Collection

Having a good dust collector is all but mandatory to keep the shop as healthy a place to work as possible. Whether you want to install permanent tubing around the shop that hooks to the dust collector or use flexible hose to reach the machines, try to find a central location for the unit (see **Figure 1.23**). Most smaller shops do not have enough room to keep moving the dust collector from machine to machine without compromising free space or safety.

Dust collectors usually work by mounting an air filter bag above a container that actually catches the dust and chips. They move a lot of air, and they tend to be tall, so check the specs and make sure the collector you choose will fit under the ceiling in your workshop.

Sizing a dust collector can be complicated, especially if you are trying to minimize the investment by purchasing the minimal amount of capacity needed for the machines you might have connected at one time and by minimizing the length and turns in the tubing. Here again, buying the most dust collector capacity you can afford (and fit in the shop) will ensure good performance and save money in coming years when it does not have to be replaced to keep up with your new machines. There's more on dust collectors in Chapter 2, under Managing Dust and Chips on page 66.

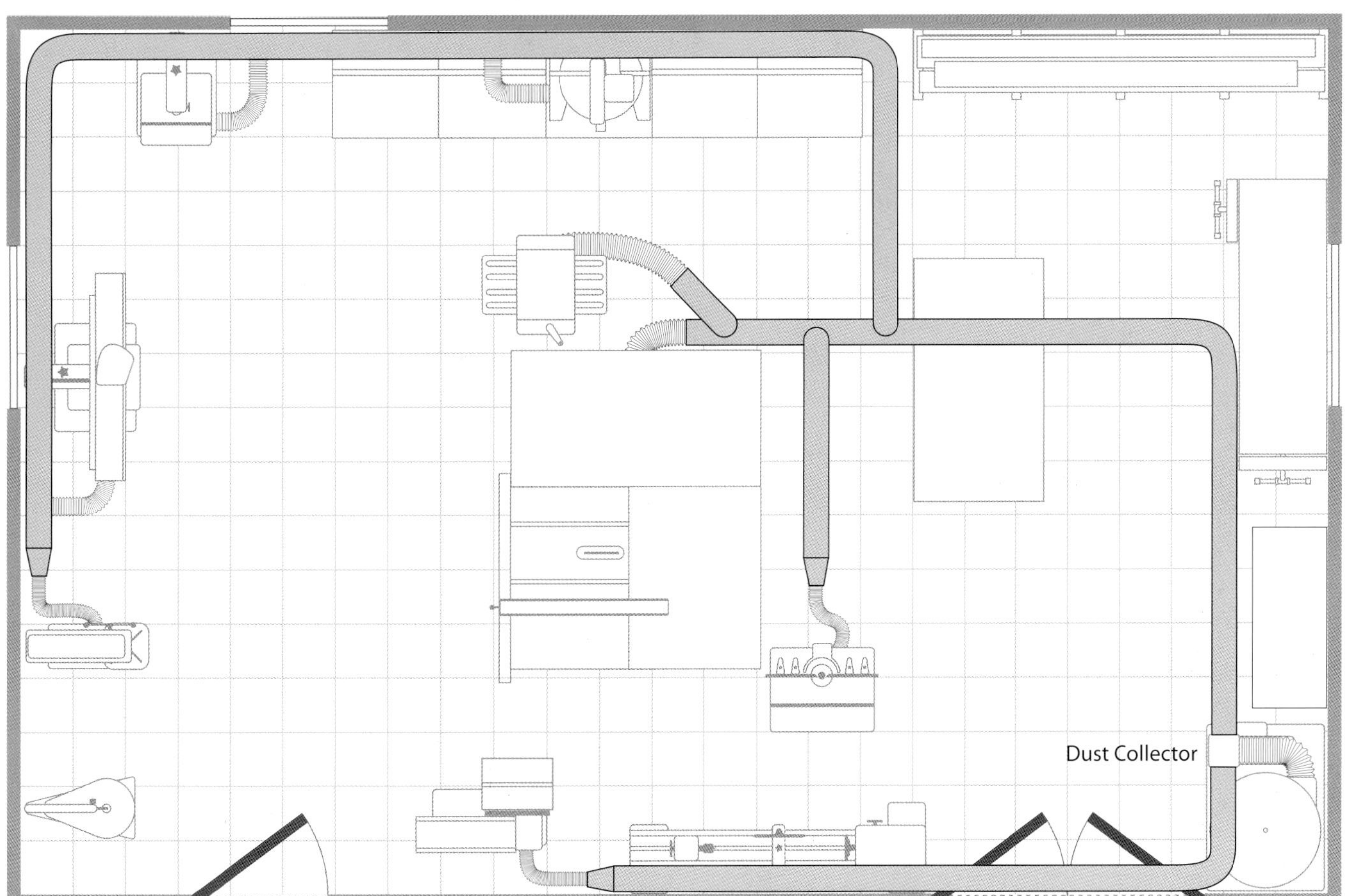

Figure 1.23. Installing permanent dust collection tubing is convenient, but sufficient capacity to suck the dust through it is mandatory. Having too much dust collection capacity is nearly impossible, but having too little is very easy and cheaper to start with. Buying the most dust collection capacity you can afford will save money in the long run. This workshop has dust collection tubing installed to each machine.

First-Aid Kit

Most woodworkers never do themselves serious harm in the shop, but the tools they use are capable of inflicting major injuries, usually the result of an equally serious lapse in judgment or concentration. Having a comprehensive first-aid kit nearby can help mitigate pain, bleeding, and infection should an injury occur.

My shop has an industrial/construction-rated first-aid kit hanging near the main exit. It contains everything needed to provide initial treatment for cuts, bruises, burns, breaks, and eye contamination (see **Figure 1.24**). Unfortunately, it has nothing to prevent brain fade, which most commonly occurs right after meals and late in the evening, and which generally causes the need for the supplies.

This first-aid kit, purchased at a local home center for less than $25, came in a plastic case that has a gasket around the cover to keep dust out. It also has slotted holes in the handle from which to hang it on the wall.

Figure 1.24. A box of bandages is not a first-aid kit in an environment with potential for serious injury. I bought this industrial-rated kit at a local home center for less than $25.

Can I go shopping yet?

Once satisfied with the layout plan (see **Figure 1.25**) and understanding that it will need some tweaking along the way, you are ready to go out and buy tools! Almost. But first turn to Chapter 2, "Buying Tools," on page 33, to find out what you should know before you start shopping. Then, I promise, you can go buy stuff!

A Checklist for Your Shop Layout Plan

Before finalizing your shop layout, be sure you have taken all of the following steps:

- Using graph paper, draw your basic floor plan to scale, including doors, windows, and other physical features.
- Choose the best locations for your machines, keeping in mind the footprint and useprint of each as well as your workflow.
- Decide where to put your workbench, cabinets and other storage, and possibly an assembly table.
- Assess your current electrical service, including circuits, lights, and outlets.
- Determine what additional electrical requirements your shop needs, and consult an electrician if necessary.
- Incorporate a high-quality dust collection system.
- Add fire extinguishers and smoke alarms; if building a freestanding shop, consider a sprinkler system.

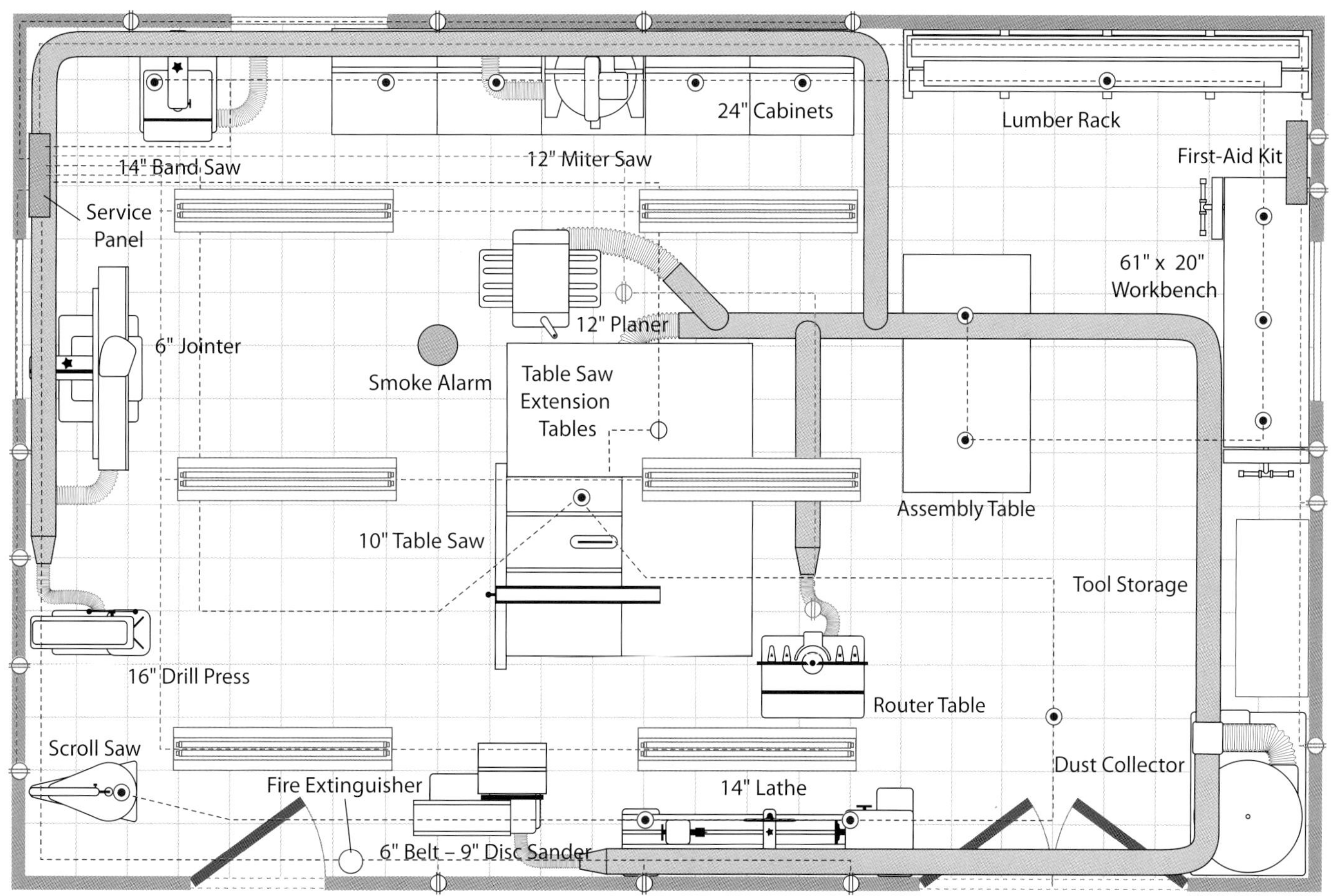

Figure 1.25. Here is a complete layout showing machines, storage, wall outlets, lights, dust collection, and basic safety equipment. Armed with this layout, you are well on your way to setting up a workshop to suit your needs. The next steps will involve making any changes to your space, such as changes to the electrical system, and purchasing tools. Be sure to read on to the next chapter for the information you need to know before you buy tools.

Chapter 2

Buying Tools

For most woodworkers, even after thoroughly surveying the workshop space and its electrical service, buying tools is complicated by two things: deciding what to buy and trying to respect the budget. For most of us, budgetary constraints mean buying tools and equipment over an extended period of time. It can be tough to make choices on what to buy now, what to buy later, and what to continue dreaming about.

For the new woodworker, tool purchase decisions are further clouded by uncertainty about what will be on the project list six months from now. It is common for new woodworkers to seriously underestimate their skill level and what they will be building a few short months in the future. The result can be buying small tools and machines that fill today's needs, only to discover in a few months that you have outgrown the capabilities of your equipment. Much of the time you will be able to make do, but sometimes you'll have no choice but to sell or junk the inadequate equipment and buy the piece you could have acquired in the first place.

In this chapter, you will find all of the information you need to avoid making purchasing mistakes. I'll show you why cheaper tools may cost you more in the long run, take a look at five general categories of tools, and provide a handful of wish lists for beginning woodworking tools all the way up to dream tools. When you've finished reading this chapter, you'll be well versed in the types of tools that are available and more confident in your buying decisions.

Cheaper costs more

Until the corporations that manufacture tools and machines free themselves from the bonds of overhead and of having to show a profit to exist at all, there will be no free lunch in woodworking. Wail if you want, whine if you must, but, upon your return to the real world, realize that better (more expensive) equipment will, in the long run, cost less than the cheap stuff.

When it comes to woodworking tools and machines, when there is a substantial difference in the cost of two similar products, there are reasons for the disparity that run deeper than the color. Buy it cheap now, and most likely you will be buying the better version soon.

Getting a good deal on a tool or machine is something we all strive for and is a smart way to stretch your tool dollars. However, giving price more weight than function and quality is dumb on more than one level. An eye-catching low price should at least make buyers suspicious. Often, markedly low prices forewarn of equivalent reductions in performance or capability. You can also be reasonably certain that a bargain-priced piece of equipment will not be the poster child for durability.

Having to replace a dud piece of equipment can lead to one of the tougher tasks in woodworking: explaining to whomever else has budgetary input why the dollars spent on the money-saving tool have more or less evaporated and why more dollars are needed to buy the piece you originally decided against.

Let's say you saved $400 by purchasing a $600 version of a $1000 machine, only to discover that the bargain is more disappointing than useful. By purchasing the better model in the first place, you could have thrown $600 in cash out of the car window on the way to the machinery dealer and still have been gas money ahead of what you will ultimately have invested. Incidentally, if you killed any wood while trying to make the first machine work, or if you paid to try to fix it, that money also goes out the window.

The most consistent way to save money is to buy the best-quality tool or machine that you can afford, even if that means saving up for a while. Postponing a tool purchase is difficult, but life will be far less complicated when you do not have to buy it twice.

When you actually go tool shopping, take your time, remember your space and electrical limitations, and do not leave your common sense at the door. If a deal looks too good to be true, it probably isn't true. If a tool or machine is too big for your shop at the store, it will be too big when you get it home. Do not let your ego or your lust for new cast iron get ahead of your common sense.

Pace yourself

Buying everything you need to set up a woodworking shop in one trip simply is not feasible for most new woodworkers. Concentrate on the machines and accessories needed most, particularly those involving safety. Then, fill in the rest as your budget allows (see **Figure 2.1**).

Spreading these purchases out allows you to benefit from experience in your shop. No matter how well you plan it, actually working in the shop space will reveal special needs as well as clarify decisions on the size and style of future equipment. Besides, it is easier to sneak this stuff into the shop one piece at a time.

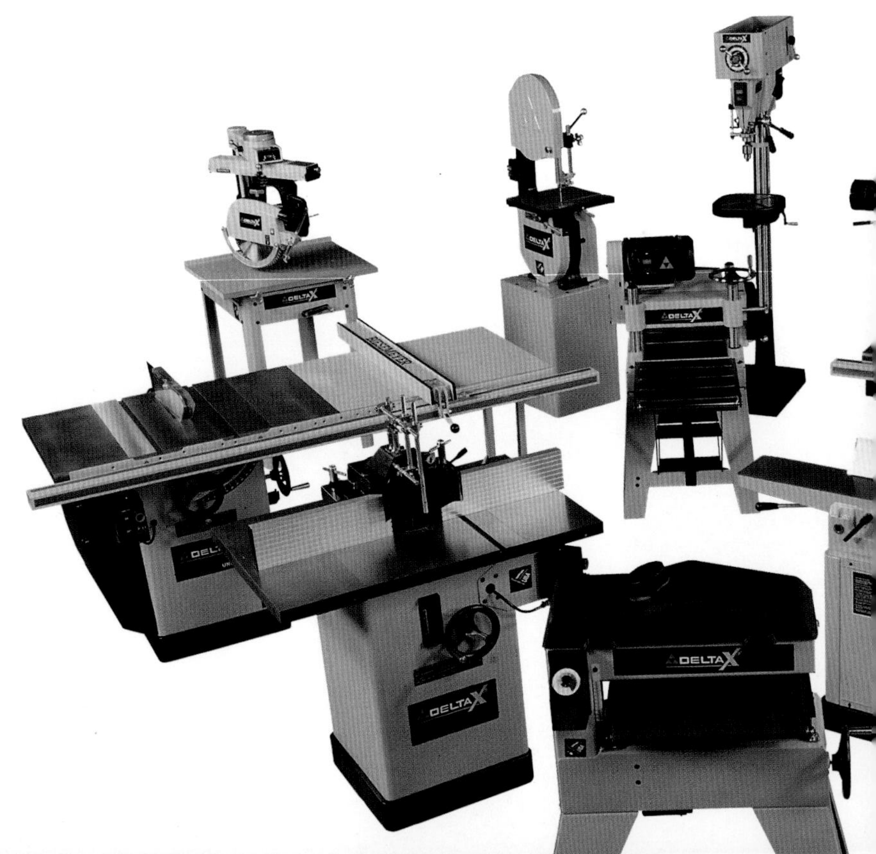

Before you use your tools

As a veteran tool buyer, I know all too well the urge to get a machine or tool out of its packaging, plugged in, and cutting something. That rush to powering up a tool can be dangerous for a couple of reasons.

First, you need to be sure that the tool or machine is assembled correctly, properly set up, and adjusted (see Chapter 3, "Tool Setup, Alignment, and Maintenance," on page 81). Second, you need to know everything you can about a new piece of equipment to avoid making a mistake that could damage it, your materials, or you.

Finding your way

In the following pages, we will look at the more common tools and machines used in home woodworking shops. We'll look at:

- General shop tools that are common to all forms of woodworking
- Table saws, the heart of the modern shop
- Other stationary/portable machines such as jointers, planers, and lathes
- Portable power tools like drills and routers
- Hand tools like chisels, planes, and saws.

The order in which they are presented here may not reflect your individual needs. Read about them and decide which best fit your shop and woodworking interests as you know them now, remembering that your interests are likely to grow.

Figure 2.1. Buying every tool you need to set up shop is not feasible for most woodworkers. Instead, decide which ones you need the most, and spread out the rest of the purchases over time.

Tools, Cars, and Your Back

The downsizing of the car you drive can turn the glee of buying a piece of equipment to frustration when it becomes obvious there is no way to get it into the car. When dealing with machines like table saws, jointers, and lathes, the weight alone may exceed the safe loading limit of most cars. Concentrating all of that weight behind the rear wheels will not make the springs and shocks happy either.

If a pickup or large van is not available, consider renting a suitable vehicle or having the machine delivered. I know this adds to the price, but that amount pales when compared to having the car repaired or dropping your new machine on the highway at 60 mph.

After hustling several large machinery cartons off the backs of semi-trailers, I can attest that lifting 300 pounds 4' off the ground is nothing to take lightly. The machines and my back survived, but not by much.

I lucked out when my Delta Iron Bed lathe (an honest 300 pounds in the box) was delivered. Having been through this before, the shipping company insisted on using a truck equipped with a lift gate rather than a normal semi. Though initially frustrated over having to wait a couple extra days, I got over it as soon as the driver lifted the gate to reveal a coffin-size crate that refused to move when I yanked on it.

The driver used his pallet jack to roll the crate onto the lift gate, down to the driveway, and then into my shop. I was able to handle opening the crate and assembling the lathe from there, but I would have been in big trouble without that lift gate.

The point is to be aware of transportation when buying larger equipment. A little planning can prevent turning what should be a fun day into a memorable disaster. A sturdy hand truck, which won't cost you more than $35, can help you jockey loads up to 500 pounds. If you can't get a truck with a lift gate to make the delivery, make a wooden ramp out of 2 x 10 planks and skid the boxes down. And ask your friends to come over to help. You might have to let them play with your new toy, but at least they won't be able to "borrow" it away.

General shop tools

While you have a great many choices to make in equipping your workshop, there are some general shop tools that you will need no matter what else you buy, whatever you decide to make. These include a workbench and vise, measuring and layout tools, hammers, screwdrivers, wrenches, clamps, a sharpening setup, and safety basics such as a fire extinguisher and a first-aid kit (see Safety Considerations on page 27).

Workbench

Function: Surface on which to work and organize your tools
Features: Solid, flat surface; sturdy; storage areas such as tool trays, drawers, or shelves
Price: $300 to $1500

You will want a sturdy workbench with as large a working surface as you can fit in your shop without compromising needed free space for using other equipment (see **Figure 2.2**). I am not going to get into whether you should build your bench or buy it—you should do what you want. Let me just say that making a really good bench is a big project that can mean making mortise and tenon joints that might still be a bit out of your skill and tool range. If you choose to build a bench, concentrate on making it solid and stable. Later, as your skills and needs evolve, you may want to replace it and can then apply the joinery skills you have learned along the way. Buying a bench can get you started quicker, and you can still build a fancier bench that is more tailored to your shop and needs later on.

The key feature of a good bench is a solid, flat surface, and, whenever possible, you should lag the bench to the wall to prevent movement during use. You want to be able to clamp to it and pound on it without it flexing or skidding away from you, and, since you may clamp project assemblies to it, you want it to be flat so they will come out flat and square.

Figure 2.2. Buying a good workbench can be a good way to get started and to learn what you really want in this important piece of woodshop furniture. Like anything else, a good commercially made workbench is not going to be cheap. This European workbench has two built-in vises and an array of storage underneath.

New Tools!

General Shop

The choices get tough when the price tags get big—that is, when you start to buy table saws and other stationary machines and special-purpose power tools. Your choices depend on budget and what you currently plan to make, and each choice affects the ones that come next—as does each mistaken purchase.

No matter which set of machinery choices you make, there's a basic set of general shop tools you're going to need no matter what. Assembling this basic set of tools can also be a good way to prepare your significant other for what is to come.

My short list:

- Workbench or worktable
- Hammer, screwdrivers, set of wrenches
- Cordless drill and bits
- Clamps
- Layout and measuring tools
- Sandpaper
- First-aid kit and fire extinguisher
- Dust brush, broom, and dustpan
- Handsaw
- Small hand plane
- Basic set of chisels
- Sharpening setup
- Dust collector (preferred) or shop vacuum
- And more clamps

> "You want a sturdy workbench with as large a working surface as you can fit in your shop without compromising needed free space for other equipment."

Many benches have a tool tray alongside the top surface. Its purpose is to provide a place for the small tools you're using at the time, without having them catch underneath the work or fall on the floor. The tray also is a great place for sawdust, scraps of wood, dead sanding belts, and stray nails and screws to accumulate. If you think you would be better off without all that stuff, you're certainly right.

Whether your bench has drawers or open storage space underneath is a matter of personal preference and work style. Clamping operations are common at the workbench, making an overhang around its perimeter for installing clamps a good thing. Remember that during clamping operations, at least the upper tier of drawers can be obstructed.

You can pay anywhere from $300 to $1500 for a nice workbench, depending on size, construction, and features such as built-in vises, bench dogs (surface clamping), and more.

Vise

Function: Secures work-in-progress during sanding, planing, or cutting
Features: Adaptable to any bench design
Price: $35 to $300

While not an exotic tool, a good bench vise is a necessity in any shop and can make many operations easier and safer (see **Figure 2.3**). Being able to secure a piece of wood for sanding, planing, or cutting is far safer than trying to hold it with one hand and shape it with the other—a step away from a nasty cut.

A woodworking vise usually has wooden faces (often made by the user) that enable it to grip workpieces without damage. While there are many styles of vises, you need not get fancy for the first, basic shop vise. The one in Figure 2.3 works great and can be adapted to nearly any bench design, including adding it to an existing bench. You do want to be sure that the metal jaws are below the bench surface and that the wood faces are flush with it.

Most right-handers prefer to mount the vise on the front of the workbench near its left end. Some people like a second vise mounted on the opposite end of the bench.

Wood vises run between $35 and $300, depending on how fancy you want to get.

Figure 2.3. A good woodworking bench vise is essential in any shop. Being able to hold pieces securely while drilling, cutting, or shaping makes those operations easier and safer.

Layout and Measuring Tools

Unless you are determined to randomly make short boards out of long ones, a way to locate and then draw cut lines accurately will be exceedingly handy. Keep in mind that whatever you draw on the wood has to come off again, so perish any thoughts you may have had about ink or any kind of felt-tip markers. You also will need tools that help draw straight, square, and angled layout lines accurately. In some cases, such as when marking the shoulders of a tenon, you may want to incise the layout line with a sharp knife or layout scribe.

Tape measure

Function: Measures dimensions
Features: Accurate, some have a scale to find a piece of wood's center
Price: $10 to $20

The most-used measuring tool in most shops, the tape measure is frequently not afforded the importance it deserves. Most good-quality tapes are very accurate, so you need not buy the most expensive one in town, nor the cheapest—expect to spend between $10 and $20.

Most woodworkers deliberately use one tape measure for everything in the shop—it's always on the belt or in the apron pocket. If a tape measure is off a little—and few are these days, but it does happen—using it for all measurements makes everything off by that same amount. The result of that consistency is that projects still come out square, though they might be 1/64" taller or shorter than anticipated.

I use a Centerpoint 16-foot tape measure (see **Figure 2.4**). While it is accurate, in addition to the normal markings along its top edge, it has another scale along the bottom for finding the center of a piece of wood. Just measure the piece with the top scale and locate the same dimension in the bottom scale to find the center.

Straightedge

Function: Measures dimensions, assesses surface flatness, helps set up machines
Features: Comes in different lengths
Price: $15 to $50

A metal straightedge is very helpful in assessing the flatness of surfaces as well as for measuring dimensions without the encumbrance of the tape measure's case. It's also a help in setting up machines. A good length is 24" to 36" and will cost between $15 and $50, depending on materials and quality.

The Little Tab Moves

I get e-mails all the time asking why the metal tab on the end of the tape is loose, occasionally from someone who recently hammered the rivets tight to secure it. The tab, meant for hooking over the edge of a piece of wood, is purposely free on the tape and moves just enough to equal its own thickness. That way, when the tape is hooked over an edge and you pull it tight, the tab slips out and the scale is actually reading from the edge of the board. When the tape is placed against an object to take an inside measurement, the tab slides in, canceling out the thickness of the tab.

The amount of movement is small but specific, making it a bad idea to retract the tape and let the tip slam against the case. The holes will eventually be hammered out of shape, making the tape inaccurate, usually shortly before the tab breaks off altogether.

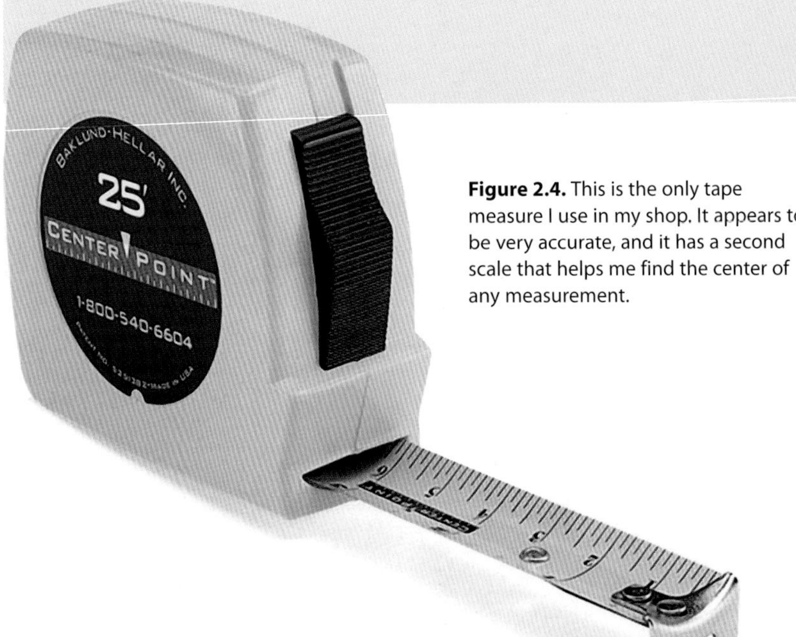

Figure 2.4. This is the only tape measure I use in my shop. It appears to be very accurate, and it has a second scale that helps me find the center of any measurement.

Square

Function: Aids in precise layout and assembly, checks alignment of machines and cuts
Features: Different lengths
Price: $15 to $150

A good square is invaluable in a woodworking shop. In addition to precise layout and assembly, squares in various forms are useful for checking the alignment of machines and the cuts they produce.

I have high-precision 90- and 45-degree squares that I often use for tool setup (see **Figure 2.5**). They also are used to check the accuracy of smaller cuts and to check for squareness during assembly. Squares of this quality are made exceptionally well, are dead-on accurate, and will stay that way. At around $40 each, they certainly are not cheap, but with minimal care (meaning don't ever drop them on cement) they will last forever.

For the beginning woodworker, good-quality combination squares in 6" and 18" lengths will handle the majority of alignment, assembly, and layout tasks with reasonable accuracy. The most common size is a 12" combination square, which will cost anywhere from $15 for a useable one to $150 for the very best.

Combination squares are available at any woodworking shop and most home centers, but stay away from the bargain-priced versions because the blades are often made from aluminum or other relatively soft material that can bend or distort rather easily. The mechanism that locks the blade in place can be inconsistent, holding the blade slightly out of square to the frame.

In addition to traditional woodworking squares, other types can also be useful. One I find especially helpful is a 14" artist's triangle, or square. Cheap and accurate, the artist's square is great for aligning miter guides, assembly, and layout tasks. A good drywall square with a 4'-long blade comes in handy for marking full sheets of plywood for cuts. A 12" speed square, the kind carpenters favor, has a lip along one side. This means you can use it as a fence for the portable circular saw to make square crosscuts.

Figure 2.5. Good-quality squares are invaluable for laying out cut lines and checking the alignment of tools and machines. Too many woodworkers think that a $3 square is as accurate as a $30 one. I have never found this to be true.

How Square Is That?

A simple way to check the accuracy of a 90-degree square, including combination squares, is to hold the square on the top of a straight piece of wood or MDF (medium-density fiberboard), its short frame leg pointing to the left and the blade down the board. Draw a line along the full length of the blade. Flip the square so the frame leg points to the right, and align the blade to the line. If the blade follows the line precisely over its entire length, the square is properly aligned and is truly square. If it's not aligned, there's nothing simple you can do about it except get another square.

This same test can be used to check virtually any type of 90-degree square including framing and speed squares.

Pencil

Function: Draws layout lines for better accuracy
Features: Sharp point to create a fine line
Price: $1 to $12 per dozen

The type of pencil used to draw layout lines can make a difference in overall accuracy. Flat carpenter's pencils may be okay when building a deck or shed, but in woodworking, the lines they make are too wide. In addition, their flat shape makes it easy to space the line away from a straightedge if the pencil rotates at all while drawing the line.

Most woodworkers use a standard No. 2 pencil for layout (see **Figure 2.6**). Keeping the point sharp produces a fine line that can be drawn with precision along a straightedge. Fine pencil lines, drawn only dark enough to be seen easily, are much easier to remove during preparation for finishing.

Figure 2.6. This photo shows (from left to right) a mechanical pencil, a No. 2 pencil, and a carpenter's pencil. Most woodworkers use a No. 2 pencil because it easily creates fine lines and stays close to a straightedge.

Marking knives

Function: Lays out joints, sharpens pencils
Features: Flat on one side, beveled on the other
Price: $15

A sharp marking knife will be a help for laying out joints as well as for sharpening your pencil. It should be flat on one side and beveled on the other (see **Figure 2.7**). The cost is about $15.

Figure 2.7. Marking knives can be useful when laying out cut lines and are flat on one side so they can follow the square accurately. They make very fine lines and slice the surface grain to help reduce chipping and splintering when the cut is made. They should not be used for general layout lines that have to disappear later.

Erasing the Lines

No. 2 lead pencil lines can be erased with a cloth dampened with plain rubbing alcohol. When the alcohol does not remove the lines completely, what remains can be sanded away very easily.

"Choose a No. 2 pencil over a flat carpenter's pencil for drawing layout lines. The lines from a flat carpenter's pencil are too wide for woodworking projects, and the flat shape may force your line to be farther away from your straightedge than needed."

Specialized layout tools

One of the recent advances in layout technology that I find very useful is the line of Incra rules (see **Figure 2.8**). These innovative devices use precisely located slots to guide the pencil, substantially enhancing accuracy and ease of use as a result.

One of the problems with drawing a straight line parallel to an edge is the grain deflecting or guiding the pencil away from the straightedge. The slots in the Incra rules are sized to fit the thin lead of a mechanical pencil (included in Incra rules sets) or that of a sharp No. 2 pencil. With the pencil point trapped in the slot at the dimension desired, the Incra rule can be slid along the edge of the wood to draw a perfectly straight line that is absolutely parallel to the edge, as shown in **Figure 2.9**. This can be especially important when other layout lines are based off the first. The traditional way of doing this is with a marking gauge, which actually digs a line into the wood rather than drawing one on it.

Another favorite layout tool is the Woodpeckers T-square with precisely drilled holes that fit a sharp pencil lead (see **Figure 2.10**). The head of the T-square fits over the edge of the wood firmly and allows drawing precise layout lines and square cut-off markings. These high-quality squares cost around $90.

Tool	Function	Features	Price
Incra Rule	Draws a perfectly straight line parallel to wood's edge	Slots to guide pencil	$10 to $50
T-Square	Draws accurate layout lines and square cut-off markings	Holes that fit pencil	$90

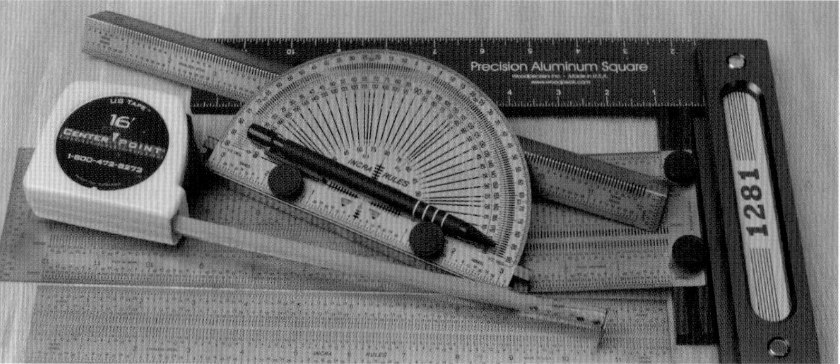

Figure 2.8. Tools that help you be precise when laying out projects and cut lines can have a huge impact on how a project turns out. If the lines are not thin, crisp, and in the right place, you will make erroneous cuts, bad-fitting joints, and out-of-square projects.

Figure 2.9. This marking square from Incra encourages extreme precision. The holes in the square guide the pencil lead so it draws a perfectly straight line without wandering or being deflected by the grain of the wood.

Hammer

Function: Drives nails, drives chisels
Features: Slightly crowned striking face and nail-pulling claw
Price: $20 to $30

A common nail-driving claw hammer should handle most of the pounding needs in a woodworking shop. While certain types of chisels must be struck with a wooden or composite mallet, many wood chisels have a metal striking heel that is compatible with a common hammer. The packaging or instructions that come with the chisels should specify this.

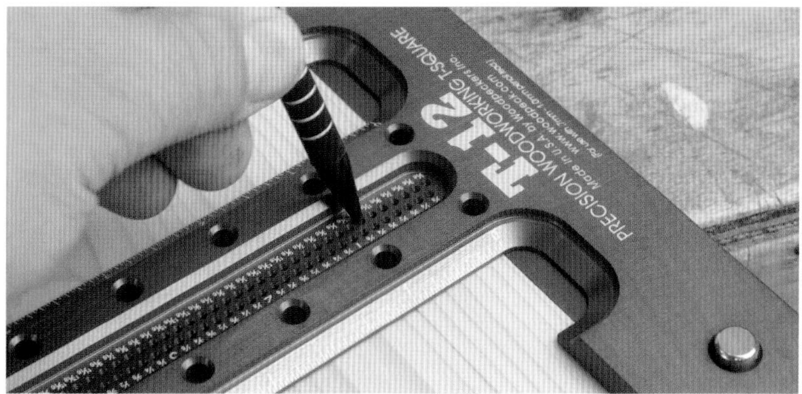

Figure 2.10. This T-square from Woodpeckers has holes to guide the pencil. The heavy aluminum construction and high-tech computerized numerical control (CNC) machining ensure a level of accuracy that was unavailable just a few years ago.

Screwdrivers and Wrenches

Function: Tighten screws, bolts, and other hardware
Features: Must be shaped and sized to fit the fastener
Price: $10 to $20

While not strictly woodworking tools, you will need screwdrivers with tips shaped to fit the kind of screws you choose. The choices are straight slot, cross slot (Phillips), and square drive, big and little in each. You'll also need wrenches for assembling equipment and for driving lag screws and tightening bolts in large constructions. Keep in mind that most fasteners you will use have U.S.-style heads, while many of the machines use metric fasteners and adjustment screws. This means you'll need metric tools as well as American ones.

Clamps

Clamps are for holding pieces of wood together while glue dries, for holding parts together while you mark the next cuts, and for securing the workpiece while you work on it. There is a proverb in woodworking that predicts you will never have enough clamps. While there are enough clamps in the world to make this untrue, I have yet to encounter anyone with enough money to buy them. Complicating the quest for clamp nirvana are the many styles available and your need for some of each. Your preference in clamps and projects will influence the selection but somehow never seems to limit how many you need. The best plan is to buy all you can to start with, and then add to the collection whenever possible.

Tip!

Clean Your Pipes

Black iron pipe for clamps has a black protective coating on it that will get all over everything it gets close to. Before installing the clamp heads, wiping the pipe down with lacquer thinner or other cleaner will prevent lots of frustration later on. Or try galvanized pipe.

Pipe clamps

Pipe clamps are so common because they work well enough for edge gluing pieces of wood together and for assembly, and they are cheap (see **Figure 2.11**). You buy the clamp heads and install them on a length of ¾"- or 1"-diameter black iron pipe. The tail piece slides and locks along the pipe to regulate width. The head piece has a coarse screw that drives the clamping face. This pipe is available at any home center in many different lengths, plus it can be cut and threaded at whatever length you want. Pipe clamp head sets cost $12 to $20, depending on size and style. The pipe is under $2 per foot.

Figure 2.11. Pipe clamps are cheap, rugged, and work well, and you get to decide how long they are.

Bar clamps

Bar clamps are the best and the worst (see **Figure 2.12**). Bar clamps work similarly to pipe clamps except that the moving head adjusts the capacity and has a built-in screw that applies pressure. The bar has a serrated edge into which the moveable head locks when pressure is applied. The bad news is that the bar material is not available locally, so it must be purchased as part of the clamp.

Since the heads are square to the bar, bar clamps are a big help in making glue-ups come out right. They're also useful for holding the workpiece down on the bench or on a jig, for holding groups of parts together while you make layout lines on all of them, and for holding project assemblies against something immoveable.

Figure 2.12. Bar clamps are either really good (expensive) or really bad (cheap). The good ones help glue up square and tight assemblies.

It should come as no surprise that the best bar clamps are really expensive and the worst ones are really cheap. The best have a heavy, rigid bar with hefty clamping heads that work smoothly, fit squarely, and hold fast. The cheap versions are easy to spot because the bar is noticeably small and the clamping heads look cheesy.

Bar clamp prices vary considerably according to length, but in the very useful 24" to 48" lengths, the cheap ones you should avoid can be under $10, and the ones you want start at $25. Some 8" or 12" or 18" ones will be very useful also.

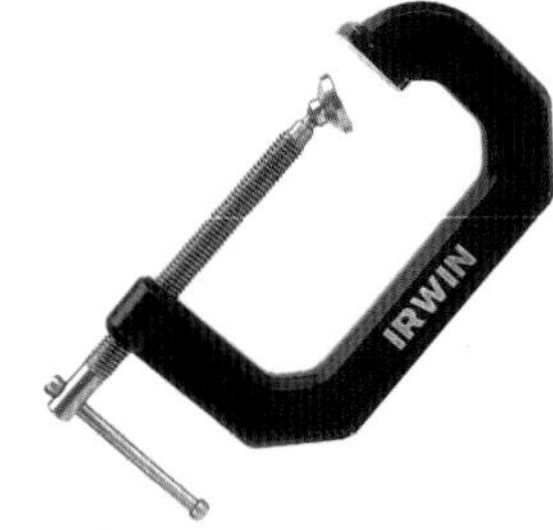

Figure 2.13. C-clamps are cheap but effective. For clamping across small distances, a good C-clamp is often the easiest clamp style to use. They are also good for holding fixtures and tools to benches.

Tool	Function	Features	Price
Pipe Clamp	Holds wood together for edge gluing and assembly	Clamp heads are installed on ¾"- to 1"-diameter black iron pipe	Head sets—$12 to $20; Pipe—under $2 per foot
Bar Clamp	Holds wood together for glue-up or making layout lines; holds wood against jig or something immovable	Works similar to pipe clamp; different lengths; jaws are square to bar	Under $10 to more than $25
C-Clamp	Holds wood together for glue-up; secures material or jig to table and fence	Different sizes	A few dollars to $15 or $20
Speed Clamp	Holds material to do low-impact tasks, to attach heavier clamps, and to keep hands free	Operated with one hand; different sizes	Under $10 to $50
Specialty Clamp	Makes assembly easier	One for securing corners; one for squaring one board to the middle of another; one for clamping miter joints	$13 to $35

C-clamps

Don't forget these ancient clamps. C-clamps work well and are rather cheap (see **Figure 2.13**). Their gripping range is limited, but in addition to holding pieces for gluing, C-clamps are great for securing material or jigs to the bench and fence. C-clamps are really for metalworking and are overbuilt for most woodworking uses, so the main features to check are that the screw works easily and that the swivel end of the screw is free.

Prices for C-clamps run from a few dollars for 3" or 4" sizes to $15 or $20 for 10" versions. When the clamping job requires over 10" of reach, I use pipe or bar clamps.

Speed clamps

Speed clamps get their name because they can be operated with one hand. Each time you squeeze the handle, the jaws close a little (see **Figure 2.14**). While these clamps do not have the power of pipe or bar clamps, they are great for securing pieces for low-impact tasks, keeping pieces in place while you install heavier clamps, or just holding a piece to free your hands to fasten it permanently.

Speed clamps are available in a wide range of sizes from 12" to 48" (and more) and cost from under $10 to around $50.

Specialty clamps

Specialty clamps designed for specific tasks are making assembly easier for mere mortal woodworkers with only two hands. They also bring a new level of accuracy to common jobs that seem so simple but can be very difficult in the real world. Clamping two pieces of wood to form a truly square corner is just one of those very common but equally deceptive little tasks that can have you pulling your hair out (see **Figure 2.15**).

Woodpeckers has come up with a group of clamps for securing corners, for joining one board square to the middle of another, and for clamping miter joints with precision.

Specialty clamps cost between $13 and $35 but are worth their weight in gold when you run out of hands and the glue is setting.

Figure 2.14. Speed clamps are popular because of their one-handed operation. They offer good clamping pressure and usually have a protective pad on the jaws that will not mar a wooden surface.

Figure 2.15. Corner clamps are designed to help woodworkers achieve a truly square corner.

> "There is a proverb in woodworking that predicts you will never have enough clamps. The best plan is to buy all you can to start with, and then add to the collection whenever possible."

Sharpening Machines

Function: Sharpens tools with cutting edges
Features: Able to sharpen a variety of edge types, variable speed grinding wheel, fine grit
Price: $50 to $400

Many of the tools used in woodworking, like chisels, hand planes, and jointer and planer knives, have cutting edges that need sharpening to perform correctly. In fact, many chisels and plane irons actually need sharpening before they are used the first time. If woodturning or woodcarving is in your future, you'll need to sharpen your tools often.

There are woodworkers who are proficient at sharpening their tools by hand, and enjoy it. Using everything from sandpaper on glass to power sanders, stones of all descriptions, and common grinders fitted with commercial or shop-made jigs, many folks can achieve edges rivaling those made on a dedicated sharpening machine. For others, a dedicated machine does the best job because it makes sharpening more accurate, easier, and perhaps faster. While sharpening machines may have a high initial cost, that investment looks very smart to me in the long term.

A dedicated sharpening system will need a table where it can live permanently. Its footprint and useprint will be the same size, with space at the front where you stand.

I have two powered sharpening systems in my shop and use both frequently. One is a single speed (3450 rpm) grinder fitted with 6"-diameter wheels and a Wolverine sharpening system (see **Figure 2.16**). The other is the Tormek system (see **Figure 2.17**). Both are highly regarded in the woodworking community. New to the dedicated sharpening machine world is the Jet Wet Sharpener that is in many ways very similar to the Tormek but adds variable speed to the grinding wheel. The Jet Wet Sharpener is quickly gaining favor with woodworkers.

Do you really need two sharpening systems? No, either one can be made to do the whole job. I like having both because of the wide range of edges they allow me to sharpen quickly and easily.

Figure 2.16. This Wolverine grinding jig works with a normal grinder to produce very sharp edges in remarkably little time. Though most frequently associated with turning tools, the Wolverine can also manage many other edges.

Wolverine system

The Wolverine system, when combined with proper grit wheels, does a very good job of sharpening tools with exceptional speed. Once the Wolverine support arm is properly adjusted, a woodturning bowl gouge can be sharpened in seconds.

Specialized jigs are available that allow complex cutting edges to be sharpened quickly and accurately. There's also an adjustable flat table for sharpening chisels and plane irons. The table ensures grinding a consistent angle, but it is up to the operator to keep the cutting edge square to the grinding wheel.

A very attractive feature of the Wolverine system is its price: $94 for the basic system plus $30 to $50 for specialized jigs.

Wet sharpening systems

The Jet and Tormek systems use a large 10"-diameter by 2"-wide, slow-speed (90 rpm on the Tormek, 90 to 150 rpm on the Jet) grinding wheel, turning in a water bath that eliminates heat buildup in the tool being sharpened. The Jet and Tormek machines, combined with specialized jigs, can create a highly refined edge with remarkable precision, and can be reset to very specific angles in the future.

The 2"-wide grinding wheel gives the Jet and Tormek machines a distinct advantage over other systems because it can handle a huge array of cutting tools, including jointer and planer knives as well as most carving tools. These machines also sharpen kitchen knives and scissors exceptionally well, capabilities that more than a few woodworkers have used during the justification process with their significant other.

With the slow speed, accuracy, and relatively fine grit of the Jet and Tormek wheels, cutting edges can be highly refined with very little loss of material. That translates into a significantly extended tool life. Once a bevel is established, freshening it on the Jet and Tormek machines is very fast.

The basic Tormek costs around $400 with jigs priced from $12 to $150, depending on their complexity. The Jet runs about $300 with jigs costing slightly less than many of the comparable Tormek versions. While these costs are not insignificant, being able to perform these sharpening tasks yourself, whenever needed, is a convenience that I think is worth the expense.

> "There are woodworkers who are proficient at sharpening their tools by hand, and enjoy it. For others, a dedicated machine does the best job because it makes sharpening more accurate, easier, and perhaps faster."

Figure 2.17. The Tormek system is admittedly pricey but can sharpen everything from bench chisels to turning tools, kitchen knives, scissors, jointer knives, and planer knives. Jet recently released a similar machine that adds variable speed capability to the grinding wheel.

Table saw:
heart of the workshop

The table saw is the heart and anchor of most woodworking shops and often represents the biggest single investment in a machine. Beyond the cost of the saw itself, there may be jigs and attachments that extend its capabilities that you'll need to consider. Consequently, this purchase should not be done hastily.

There are four popular types of table saw:

- Cabinet saw
- Contractor saw
- Job site saw
- Benchtop saw

Table Saw Or Not Table Saw?

While most woodworkers would consider the table saw to be the heart of the workshop, those who are forced to work in exceptionally small areas sometimes opt to use a sliding compound miter saw for crosscutting and a band saw or portable circular saw for ripping. While using these tools in place of a table saw does involve compromises, for some, they can be the only real choice, and this combination is considerably safer than a table saw. To be sure, I have seen beautiful projects made with this set of machines by folks who developed appropriate techniques. You can make junk on the best table saw by using poor technique. The person operating any machine will always be the most important factor.

All four have their place in modern woodworking shops, with the choice usually based on the amount of money, space, and electrical power available. Some new woodworkers base their table saw decision on their current project list, thinking that they simply do not need more capacity or features. Remember that most woodworkers progress quickly in terms of skills and the type and size of projects they build. Buying a smaller or less capable saw at the onset can save a few bucks but frequently ends up costing more when you outgrow it and need to purchase a full-size or more capable machine.

The vast majority of woodworking table saws use a 10"-diameter blade, though 12" and larger models are available and are used more frequently for industrial purposes. Fortunately, the 12" machines come with a steep enough price tag to make mere mortal woodworkers get over that idea quickly. Aside from bragging rights in a "who's got the biggest blade" conversation, a 12" table saw brings little added benefit to the average shop.

I discussed the space a table saw needs in Chapter 1, under Making Templates on page 12. To recap here, all table saws need space fore and aft that exceeds the longest workpiece you're likely to encounter, plus space on each side for crosscutting planks and plywood. When you consider this useprint rather than just the physical size of the saw, even benchtop models can lose their perceived space-saving advantage except in storage requirements.

Choosing a table saw is an important decision that will have long-lasting effects on your shop. Be realistic about the available shop space and budget, and be careful about underestimating the size and style of projects you soon will build. While I have heard from hundreds of woodworkers who felt they had outgrown a piece of equipment, few have complained about a machine being excessively capable.

In the following sections, I'll discuss the four kinds of saw; then, I'll go into features and accessories common to all table saws.

Tool	Function	Features	Price
Cabinet Saw	Rip, crosscut, miter, and bevel solid wood and plywood; all-day use in professional shop	Built-in dust collection; motor enclosed in cabinet; 1½ to 5 hp; extensions allow working with large materials; holds alignment well	$900 to $2000
Contractor Saw	Rip, crosscut, miter, and bevel solid wood and plywood; intermittent use in shop or on jobsite	Open cabinet with exposed motor; roller base to change locations in shop; 1½ hp; accurate alignment; no dust collection	$300 to $2000
Job Site Saw	Rip, crosscut, miter, and bevel solid wood and plywood; portable saw for jobsite use	Lightweight and compact; portable; can be stored; short fences; excellent dust collection	$200 to $600
Benchtop Saw	Rip, crosscut, miter, and bevel solid wood and plywood; light hobby and craft work	Sits on an existing table or workbench; 10" or 8" blade	$100 to $400

Errata

This corrected version of page 47 includes a more complete description of cabinet saw features. We apologize for any inconvenience the missing material may have caused.

Cabinet Saw

Cabinet saws are at the higher end of the table saw spectrum and, as you might suspect, have the motor and other mechanicals inside a full-length cabinet, as shown in **Figure 2.18**. Cabinet saws generally feature built-in dust collection, sophisticated blade height/tilt mechanisms, and higher-powered motors than are available on other styles of saws. While a bunch of power may sound nice, remember that 2 hp to 5 hp motors require 220-volt electrical service. Some manufacturers do offer cabinet saws in the 1½ hp range that can run on 110-volt power with the option of being rewired for 220 volts.

Cabinet saws were originally designed for all-day operation in professional cabinet shops but have become a favorite of serious hobbyist woodworkers. They can be equipped with table extensions and fence systems to manage full sheets of plywood.

Cabinet saws are often easier to align and tend to hold alignment better than other saw designs. On most cabinet saws, the table itself is moved to align the miter slot with the blade, rather than moving the blade mechanism as on most other saw designs.

Cabinet saw: pro and con

In terms of pure footprint and useprint, cabinet saws aren't much different from contractor saws. When cutting wood, virtually the same amount of floor space is needed for a cabinet saw as is needed for a contractor saw. Materials and workmanship can tell a lot about the overall quality of the machine. The smoothness of the blade tilt and height mechanisms can be revealing as well.

Nearly all cabinet saws come with cast-iron extension wings that should be flat and flush with the main saw table. Cabinet saws with extended fence rails may have a laminate-covered, wooden table extension on the right side, extending to the maximum capacity of the fence. Laminate extensions should also be flat and flush with the primary cast-iron table.

Large-capacity fence systems are probably the most popular option on cabinet saws and can have a significant impact on the purchase price. However, remember the space limitations of your shop before being seduced.

For many new woodworkers, the downside to cabinet saws is the price. Count on spending from $900 to $2000 (or more), depending on the overall quality, power, and features.

New Tools!

First Big Buy!

What's the minimum list of stuff you need to be able to build projects in your workshop after you've obtained the general shop tools listed in New Tools! on page 36? Here's my personal rock-bottom must-have list:

- Table saw with blades
- Portable circular saw
- Pair of roller work supports
- Router and a basic selection of bits
- And more clamps

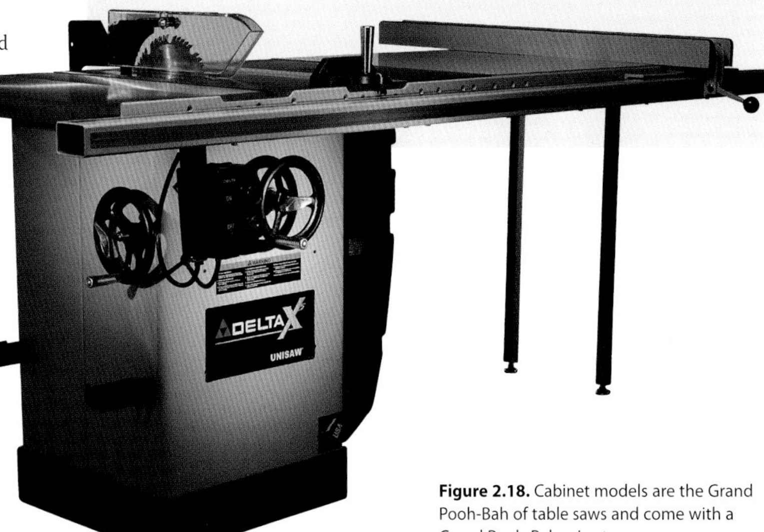

Figure 2.18. Cabinet models are the Grand Pooh-Bah of table saws and come with a Grand Pooh-Bah price tag.

on 110-volt power with the option of being rewired for 220 volts.

Cabinet saws were originally designed for all-day operation in professional cabinet shops but have become a favorite of serious hobbyist woodworkers. They can be equipped with table extensions and fence systems to manage full sheets of plywood.

Cabinet saws are often easier to align and tend to hold alignment better than other saw designs. On most cabinet saws, the table itself is moved to align the miter slot with the blade, rather than moving the blade mechanism as on most other saw designs.

Cabinet saw: pro and con

In terms of pure footprint and useprint, cabinet saws aren't much different from contractor saws. When cutting wood, virtually the same amount of floor space is needed for a cabinet saw as is needed for a contractor saw. Materials and workmanship can tell a lot about the overall quality of the machine. The smoothness of the blade tilt and height mechanisms can be revealing as well.

Nearly all cabinet saws come with cast-iron extension wings that should be flat and flush with the main saw table. Cabinet saws with extended fence rails may have a laminate-covered, wooden table extension on the right side, extending to the maximum capacity of the fence. Laminate extensions should also be flat and flush with the primary cast-iron table.

Large-capacity fence systems are probably the most popular option on cabinet saws and can have a significant impact on the purchase price. However, remember the space limitations of your shop before being seduced.

For many new woodworkers, the downside to cabinet saws is the price. Count on spending from $900 to $2000 (or more), depending on the overall quality, power, and features.

New Tools!

First Big Buy!

What's the minimum list of stuff you need to be able to build projects in your workshop after you've obtained the general shop tools listed in New Tools! on page 36? Here's my personal rock-bottom must-have list:

- Table saw with blades
- Portable circular saw
- Pair of roller work supports
- Router and a basic selection of bits
- And more clamps

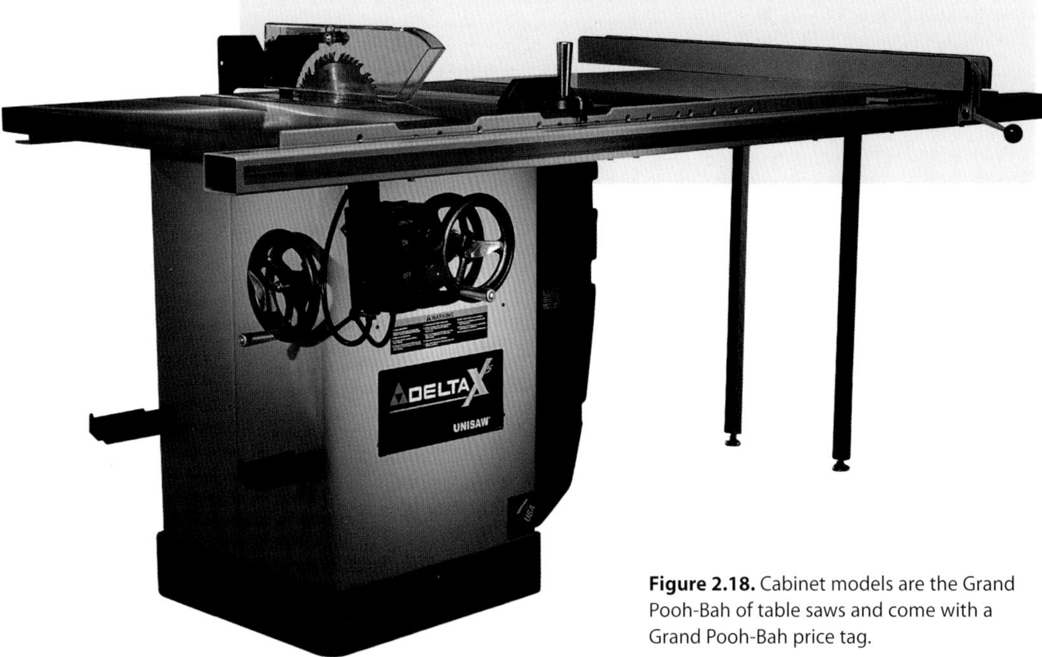

Figure 2.18. Cabinet models are the Grand Pooh-Bah of table saws and come with a Grand Pooh-Bah price tag.

Contractor Saw

Probably the most popular in home woodshops, contractor-style saws (see **Figure 2.19**) embody the general size and capacity of cabinet saws with a price tag that is less likely to put the budget on life support. Contractor-style saws have a short, open cabinet attached to an open leg base. A dominant feature of contractor saws is the motor hanging outside the rear of the cabinet on a hinged mount. That hinge allows the weight of the motor to apply tension to the drive belt.

Contractor saws were originally designed to be taken to the job site by carpenters and cabinetmakers. Despite that reputed portability, contractor saws are too heavy to be easily moved by one person. A roller base cures that problem in the home woodworking shop.

Contractor saws are generally equipped with 1½ hp motors. Some come ready for 110 volts but can be rewired to run on 220 volts, which is more efficient and may also help distribute the electrical load among the available circuits.

While more power may seem desirable, it is more luxury than necessity for many hobbyist woodworkers. A properly aligned contractor saw, equipped with a sharp blade, will handle home woodworking cutting tasks with ease.

Contractor saw: pro and con

The blade height and tilt mechanism is mounted on the underside of the saw table, with fasteners that are not always easy to get at. This can make blade alignment a chore, but the good news is that it can be done with accuracy. Better yet, this alignment is not a frequent task.

Dust collection on most contractor saws consists of letting the dust fall onto the floor through the open-bottomed cabinet and then sweeping it up (see **Figure 2.20**). Being the industrious types, woodworkers have been known to close off the cabinet with wooden panels and attach a dust collector unit. I have done this myself and still am not convinced it was worth the effort. It didn't catch all the airborne dust, and I still had to sweep the shop anyway.

Most of the fence systems found on cabinet saws are available for contractor saws as well. Adding a good fence can bump up the price a few hundred dollars but can have an equally significant effect on how the saw performs.

Prices for contractor saws range from around $300 to over $2000. However, getting the biggest bang for your tool budget dollar means shopping within the $500 to $1000 range. Spending more than that should at least cause you to look at cabinet saws and compare the features to see which represents the best deal for your needs.

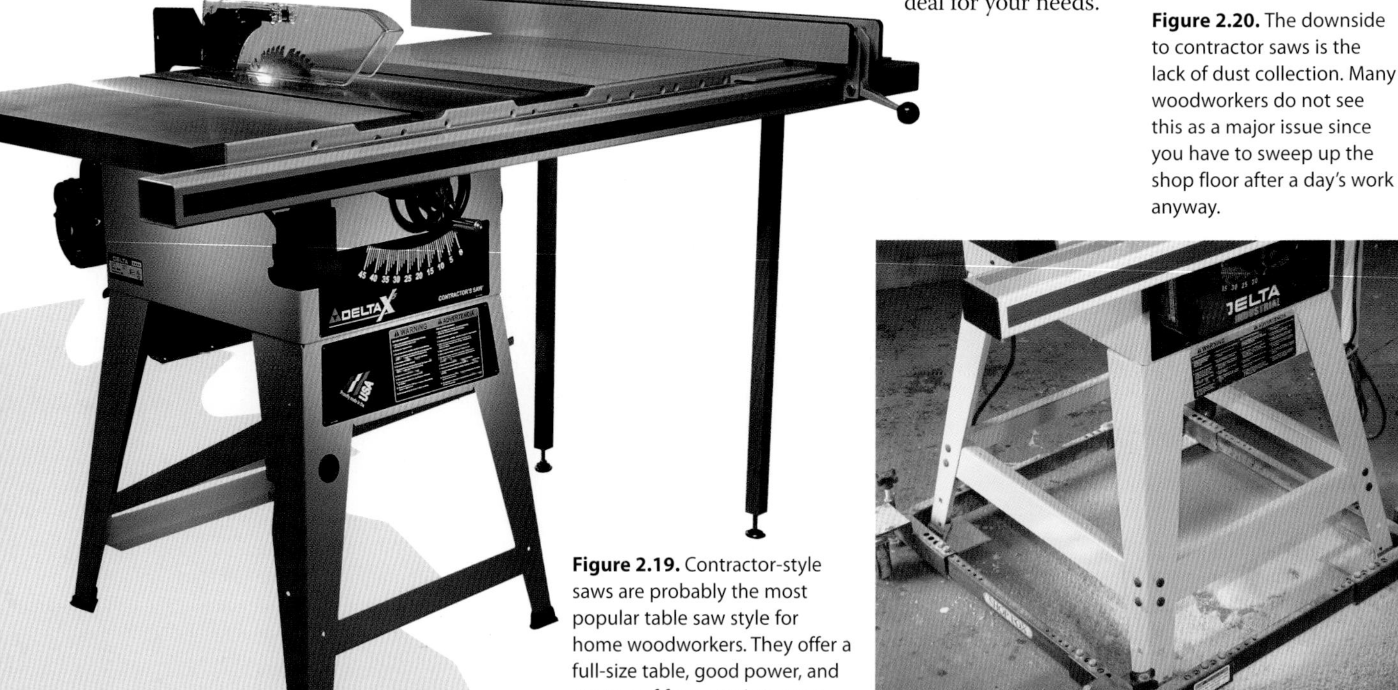

Figure 2.20. The downside to contractor saws is the lack of dust collection. Many woodworkers do not see this as a major issue since you have to sweep up the shop floor after a day's work anyway.

Figure 2.19. Contractor-style saws are probably the most popular table saw style for home woodworkers. They offer a full-size table, good power, and a range of fence options at an affordable price.

Job Site Saw

A more portable version of the contractor models, job site saws are designed to be lightweight and compact but retain the core features, as shown in **Figure 2.21**. Reducing weight and physical size forfeits some accuracy and power, especially with the lower-priced models. In recent years, high-quality job site saws have come on the market with better components to make them more accurate and user friendly. Job site saw tables are usually cast from aluminum and therefore are less susceptible to the humidity and rust than their cast-iron brothers. Despite the lightweight materials, the better job site saw tables are flat and stay that way.

Job site saws originally were designed for trim carpenters and tradesmen who would be coming into the home or commercial site for some specific repair or renovation. That's why the best of them have high-quality fence systems and excellent dust collection hook-ups. The better ones are not simply benchtop saws with a stand.

One of the most attractive features of job site saws for small shop owners is the folding stand that many of these machines either come with or have available as an accessory. Some of the stands have wheels (or they can be added easily) that make moving the saw to where it is needed simple and safe. When folded into the storage configuration, the footprint needed to store the saw and cart is dramatically smaller than cabinet or contractor saws (see **Figure 2.22**). This roll-and-fold capability can be especially important in small shops and in those that must be shared with cars or other family-oriented needs.

Job site saw: pro and con

Job site saws have smaller motors than contractor saws, usually mounted inside the short cabinet. Motors with a 15-amp rating are common, but the advertised horsepower ratings vary wildly. Whatever the true horsepower is, all of the job site saws I have tried cut well with a good-quality, sharp blade. Feed rates may be a bit slower, but they get the job done. Though some job site saws are direct drive (the blade mounted on the motor shaft), many of the better ones use a form of belt and pulley system.

Figure 2.21. Job site saws used to be purchased primarily by contractors, but a growing list of improvements, capabilities, and features has made them attractive to home woodworkers, particularly those with small or shared workspaces.

Fence systems on job site saws were notoriously unstable in the past but have improved substantially in recent years, particularly on the more expensive models. With mobility a priority, the fences are relatively short, often no longer than the table. However, modern clamping and alignment systems make these fences easier and more accurate to use.

Another compromise is the length of the blade arbor. Though more than sufficient for normal blades, job site saw arbors might be too short to install a stacked dado set at its full width.

Some of the best on-board dust extraction systems I have seen are built into job site saws. Some models enclose the blade below the table in a shroud that traps and directs much of the sawdust to a port at the rear of the cabinet. The shroud greatly reduces the amount of air movement required to evacuate dust, enabling a good shop-style vacuum to handle the task surprisingly well.

Job site saws carry price tags from \$200 to \$600 with the most popular in the \$400 to \$600 range. While the job site saw can be an economical way to get started, many woodworkers keep these machines after buying contractor or cabinet saws. The job site saw makes a good backup or second machine that many find useful when the big saw is set up for a particular operation and another cut must be made, or when it's necessary to set up a temporary work station elsewhere.

Figure 2.22. An important feature of some job site saws is the small footprint they require in the stored configuration. This Bosch model shrinks to 28½" wide by 30" deep and 45" tall when folded up.

Benchtop Saw

The cheapest and smallest of the table saw varieties, benchtop saws are more suited for light hobby and craft work than for woodworking (see **Figure 2.23**). However, more than a few woodworkers use benchtop saws and produce very nice work with them. Using a benchtop as the primary saw will require some compromises and ingenuity.

Figure 2.23. Benchtop table saws lack the size and power of larger machines, so woodworkers who use them have to be creative in designing jigs and fixtures that extend their capabilities.

Benchtop saws: pro and con

Some benchtop saws can take 10" blades, while others are limited to 8" blades. This affects the depth of cut you can make. The small overall size of a benchtop saw may seem like a good idea in a small shop, but to maximize the saw's usefulness, you'll have to invest considerable effort and ingenuity in jigs and table extensions. I have seen remarkable rolling cabinets built around benchtop saws that, while effective, make me wonder if the investment had not brought the actual price to where buying a job site or contractor saw would make more sense.

Benchtop saws range in price from $100 to $400 and more. While the more expensive models may have a bit more power and better features, they remain small, a fact that should be considered. If you are thinking about a benchtop saw, be sure to consider all of your options before making the investment.

Drive System

There are two primary drive systems used in table saws: belt drive and direct drive. The belt system (see **Figure 2.24**) is more desirable (and popular) because it reduces vibrations, runs smoothly, and is very quiet.

Some feel belt drives are safer because the belt can slip on the pulleys should the wood become jammed at the blade, stopping the saw. While this may be true, it is definitely not a safety factor to depend on, since getting into such a predicament means you have done something seriously wrong.

Direct drive systems have the blade mounted directly on the motor shaft and are found primarily on benchtop and low-priced job-site-style saws. The blade and motor are usually mounted directly to the saw cabinet, increasing sound and vibration substantially as compared to contractor and cabinet saws. The motor housing may also limit how high you can raise the blade. Higher-quality job site and benchtop saws use a short belt system between the motor and blade, which helps control sound and vibration.

While belt drive is preferred, budget constraints could dictate a saw with the direct drive system. Used properly, direct drive saws are capable of handling most home woodworking chores. There are more than a few woodworkers using direct drive saws to produce high-quality projects.

Figure 2.24. Belt drives are smooth and tend to make a saw quieter than direct drive. Most belt drives are maintenance free, aside from occasionally checking the wear on the belt and making sure nothing is rubbing on it inside the saw.

Figure 2.25. Given the option, most woodworkers prefer a blade that tilts away from the saw fence. That lets the cut-off piece drop to the table rather than on the blade. Unfortunately, not many table saws below the cabinet saw level offer a choice of which way the blade tilts.

Figure 2.26. The most common table saw motor has 1½ hp to 2 hp. With a sharp blade and moderate feed rate, that's plenty of power to cut nearly any material you are likely to encounter.

Left or Right Tilt

The blades on the majority of contractor and cabinet saws tilt to the right for bevel cuts (see **Figure 2.25**), with the left tilt being an extra cost option on some models. Nearly all benchtop and job site saws are right tilt as well. Choosing which way to tilt the blade is largely a matter of personal taste, though it can involve a safety issue: It is a bad idea for the waste (uncontrolled) piece to be trapped between the tilted blade and the rip fence, where it can be pinched and kicked back at the operator. So you would move the fence to one side or the other to prevent trapping the waste piece.

Motors and Horsepower Ratings

Motors used on most table saws are engineered to work in a less-than-spotless environment. The better motors carry the TEFC designation: Totally Enclosed Fan Cooled. These motors are sealed to keep dust and debris from contaminating the inner workings and bearings.

Veteran woodworkers are increasingly skeptical of advertised electric motor power ratings. Terms like "maximum developed" or "peak" used in conjunction with a horsepower rating make people suspect these claims are fudging on the actual power developed. Electricians explain that the amperage draw is the limiting factor in developing horsepower, so they use the amperage to judge how much power a saw actually has.

Once I had a manufacturer's representative go to great lengths explaining how horsepower measured at the blade can be more than what the motor itself develops because of different pulley sizes on the motor and saw arbor. Others say that only torque can be increased by way of different pulley sizes. Other critics contend that the "maximum developed horsepower" claim had to be measured just before the motor fried.

Lacking a reliable way to test actual horsepower, you are forced to rely on experience. I have owned three different saws, each rated at 1½ hp by the manufacturer. In use, all three seemed to have different amounts of power. However, it is most important to note that all three, equipped with sharp, quality blades, easily handled my needs in the shop (see **Figure 2.26**). When a motor seems to have less power, slowing the rate at which the wood is fed into the blade usually eliminates that problem.

Table Saw Fences

Few things can affect the accuracy of a table saw as much as the rip fence system. Job site and benchtop saws are usually limited to the fences that came with them, but contractor and cabinet saws are more standardized in terms of table size and how the fence rails mount. That opens the door for aftermarket inventors and the original manufacturers to develop a range of fence systems that will fit a large number of machines (see **Figure 2.27**).

The important qualities of a fence are rigidity, ease of alignment, and how well it holds that alignment in use. Stability and alignment are important not only to performance but to safety as well. A misaligned fence can make kickbacks far more likely.

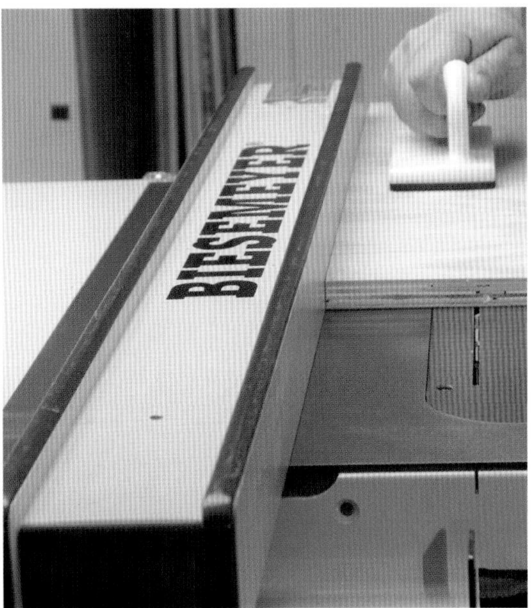

Figure 2.27. Table saw fence systems are critical to the accuracy and performance of a table saw and remain a favorite option or upgrade. This Biesemeyer commercial fence is known for its rigidity, accuracy, and simple adjustability.

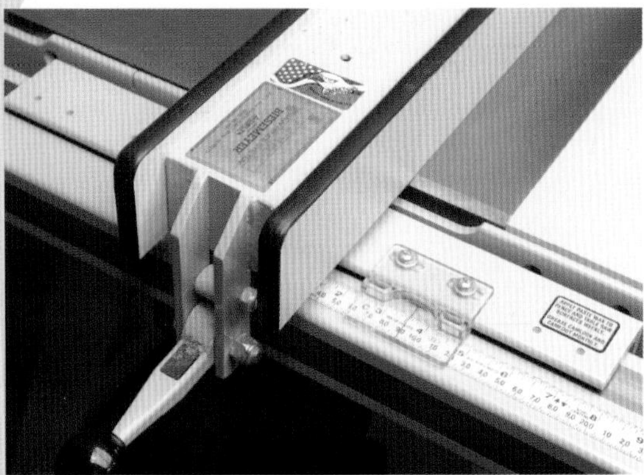

Figure 2.28. The built-in scales on table saw fences can be extremely accurate when assembled and adjusted properly, though most woodworkers habitually double-check with a tape measure.

The shape of the fence itself can be important since woodworkers frequently build jigs and fixtures that fit over it or clamp to it. Many of the better fences are square or rectangular, which makes building and attaching jigs easy.

Fences have built-in scales that, when adjusted correctly, indicate the distance from the fence face to the edge of the blade. While this scale is useful, most woodworkers double-check the fence-to-blade distance with a tape measure. I used to be one of those non-believers, but since getting my current saw with a Biesemeyer commercial fence, I am learning to have faith and to rely on the built-in scale (see **Figure 2.28**).

Adding a high-quality fence system when buying a new saw can be surprisingly cheap. Buying these fence systems to upgrade an existing saw can run $300 or more, depending on the brand, style, and rail length.

Table Saw Guards

All table saws come with a blade guard that has some kind of anti-kickback mechanism, but not all saw guards are created equal. Saws made for the European market often have better standard guards than saws made for the U.S. market. Heft, plus the presence of an arbor-mounted riving knife in back of the blade, makes them better. The riving knife, which looks like a shark fin, helps prevent kickback by keeping the just-sawn wood from turning into the saw teeth at the back of the blade (see **Figure 2.29**).

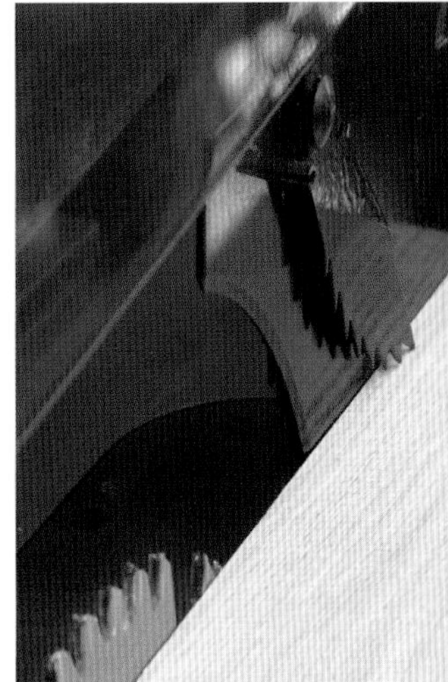

Figure 2.29. The riving knife mounted behind the table saw blade is an important safety device for preventing kickback, as are the saw guard and the anti-kickback pawls mounted on it.

Aside from helping prevent kickback, the guard's primary purpose is to keep your fingers away from the saw teeth. It provides a physical barrier as well as a visual reminder of where the blade is.

It is always dumb to remove the guard from your table saw. If you can't make the cut because the guard is in the way, you're probably doing it wrong or doing it on the wrong machine. If you lack faith in the standard guard, consider adding an aftermarket guard system such as the Biesemeyer or the Brett. Both are excellent.

Table Saw Blades

Most table saws come with a carbide-tipped blade, but don't be surprised if its performance declines relatively quickly. The manufacturer wants the saw to perform well but also has to keep the price down so you will buy it in the first place. Expect to be shopping for more and better blades very soon after acquiring your saw (see **Figure 2.30**). Expect to pay between $50 and $125 for good-quality 10"-diameter table saw blades.

Figure 2.30. Nothing can ruin the cut quality of a properly aligned table saw like a cheap or dull blade. In recent years, blade design and quality have improved considerably, giving the woodworker a large number of options.

Carbide versus carbide

Not long ago, a blade with carbide-tipped teeth was at the high end of the technology range. Today, there are several grades of carbide being applied to table saw blades, with an equal number of price points that generally reflect their quality.

Micro-grain carbide is the newest formulation meant to produce sharper edges that last longer. The silicon carbide in the sharpened tips is very consistent, making the blade stronger and better able to resist the impacts of cutting wood.

Tooth design

Just wanting to buy a good-quality blade is not enough. The number, design, and layout of the teeth give each blade specific characteristics that make it best suited for particular cutting jobs.

The most common tooth design has the top of each tooth ground at an angle that helps it slice across the wood fibers and cuts a clean edge without chipping or splintering. The top angle, often 20 to 30 degrees, alternates left and right with the pattern repeating around the blade. These blades are called Alternate Top Bevel (ATB). Sometimes there is a single flat-topped tooth, called a raker or planer, in between each set of angled teeth to help clean up the cut.

Each tooth has a hook angle, the degree to which it tilts forward or backward when viewed from the side. Higher hook angles make the blade cut more aggressively, while smaller hook angles reduce chipping and splintering. Table saw blades usually have a positive hook angle—the top of the tooth tilts forward. Miter saw and radial arm saw blades may have small positive or negative hook angles, with the top of the tooth tilted backward, to reduce their tendency to creep forward while cutting.

How many teeth

The number of teeth on a blade has a lot to do with how it cuts and the intended purpose. A ripping blade may have as few as 24 teeth (see **Figure 2.31**), while a finish blade can have 50 or more teeth. Blades designed to cut veneer plywood or melamine board can have 70 or 80 teeth.

A popular compromise is the combination blade that has 40 or 50 teeth ground in an ATB pattern with a hook angle around 20 degrees. These blades produce good-quality cuts in most types of wood. Woodworkers with more specific needs and a budget to match may own dedicated rip, crosscut, and plywood blades.

Figure 2.31. Specialized ripping blades (top) augment equally special crosscut versions to produce ultra-smooth surfaces. Most woodworkers begin with a good-quality combination blade and then add to their collection as their needs and budget allow.

Stationary woodworking machines

Now that you have figured out which table saw you want, and perhaps have already bought it, you can move on to consider some of the other stationary machines common in woodworking shops. In addition to such general-purpose accessories as dust collectors, work supports, and mobile bases, these include:

- Miter saw
- Band saw
- Scroll saw
- Jointer
- Planer
- Lathe
- Drill press
- Sanding machines

> “Populating your shop with big tools like a band saw, a planer, or a drill press can be traumatic to your budget. Exactly which machines you need depends a lot on what you intend to make.”

Populating your shop with these big tools can be traumatic to the budget, and you may not need them all, but no doubt many will tempt you, and you will end up owning some. Exactly which machines you need depends a lot on what you intend to make, so I'll discuss the capabilities and features of each in this section.

Miter and Sliding Miter Saw

The advent of sliding compound miter saws (SCMS) has complicated life for those considering standard compound miter saws (CMS) and even the radial arm saw (RAS). However, the big difference in price between slider and non-slider saws will make this an easier decision if the budget is tight. Miter saws use the same ATB carbide blades as table saws (see Table Saw Blades on page 53).

Miter saws and sliding miter saws need space to each side and a place for the operator to stand in front, but they differ in the space required to the rear. A sliding miter saw has a mechanism that protrudes to the rear as the saw is moved through its motion. Consequently, the slider function requires more free space to the rear than a non-sliding version. While stands can be bought for them, many woodworkers build them into a bench with a lowered center section for the machine itself and work-supporting wings that are level with the saw's table. They're also quite portable.

One of the more recent—and occasionally controversial—features on both types of saws is the laser cut line indicator. While this sounds like a great idea, not everyone is convinced, particularly those who use these saws in the sunlight, which makes the laser lines difficult to see.

If you have a good table saw, you don't really need a miter saw. However, if you have both machines, you'll almost certainly find yourself doing much of your crosscutting and mitering on the miter saw, limited by its width capacity. This can leave the table saw free for other operations including ripping solid wood and cutting plywood sheets.

Figure 2.32. Compound miter saws make it easy to cut clean, true crosscuts and angles. Their biggest limitation is in the width of stock that can be cut.

Compound miter saw

Compound miter saws (CMS) are great for making square and miter cuts in relatively narrow stock, especially molding and trim stock (see **Figure 2.32**). Modern manufacturing has increased the accuracy considerably, and, when combined with a quality blade, crosscutting perfectly square and clean ends and tight-fitting miters can be easier than on a table saw.

The blade on a CMS is usually mounted directly to the motor shaft. That creates more noise when cutting, but more importantly places the motor at the center of the blade where it can limit the depth of cut, even at relatively shallow bevel angles.

The major shortcoming of a non-sliding miter saw is the limitation in the width of the stock it will cut. A 10" compound miter saw at 90 degrees often has a maximum crosscut of about 5½ inches. Prices for good compound miter saws run between $100 and $250.

Sliding compound miter saw

A 10" sliding compound miter saw (SCMS) (see **Figure 2.33**) can crosscut up to 12 inches at 90 degrees and cut a 45-degree miter completely across an 8"-wide board. In addition to the substantially greater cutting range, SCMS are generally more sophisticated, with detents for cutting crown molding to the right or left and expanded miter capability that can reach up to 60 degrees. These machines excel at making square crosscuts and in solid wood can entirely replace the table saw for that task.

Rather than direct drive, some SCMS have the motor mounted high on the saw and drive the blade with a belt. That results in a smoother running saw with greater depth capacity, especially when cutting steep bevels.

Figure 2.33. A sliding compound miter saw (SCMS) will cut much wider material than a non-slider, plus it has more features and more preset detents for commonly used angles.

Features to look for are solid locking in the detents (see **Figure 2.34**) and smooth travel both vertically and in the sliding motion. Some SCMS have a depth stop that allows them to cut dados, but they have to use the standard-width blade. Specialized dado cutting blades cannot be used on a miter saw. Adjustable handles are a popular feature on SCMS and make it easy to cut to the left or right of center regardless of the operator's dominant hand.

Better sliding compound miter saws cost between $400 and $550.

Figure 2.34. This Bosch sliding compound miter saw features up-front controls, a wide angle capability, fine-tuning of the angles, and more.

Tool	Function	Features	Price
Compound Miter Saw	Makes square and miter crosscuts in narrow stock like molding and trim	Limited width of cut	$100 to $250
Sliding Compound Miter Saw	Makes square and miter crosscuts in narrow and wider stock	Smooth running; greater width capacity; detents; sliding motion	$300 to $550

Band Saw

Band saws (see **Figure 2.35**) are a favorite of woodworkers because of their versatility and the wide-ranging capabilities they bring to the shop: They can rip wood, saw curves, slice veneers off boards, and make boards out of small logs. Band saws make cutting small pieces much safer, and with commercial or shop-made jigs, they can handle many odd cuts including sawing circles and finely detailed scrollwork. Band saws take their name from their unique blade: a continuous band of steel with teeth cut in one edge.

Figure 2.35. Band saws are highly versatile and augment virtually all other cutting machines in the shop. They can saw straight lines, curves, and circles, and they also can resaw boards, make veneers, and saw small logs into planks.

Kinds of band saw

There are three common band saw designs: benchtop, open stand, and enclosed cabinet models, with size and price increasing in that same order. Key features of floor models include a heavy-duty cast-iron frame, a large cast-iron table that tilts to 45 degrees, and overall quality construction.

Band saws are classified primarily by the distance from the blade to the frame, called the throat width. Commonly used sizes in the wood shop range between 10" and 18", with the 14" saw being most common, and with considerably larger machines found in industrial settings. Benchtop models, sized at 6", 8", and 10", are also available.

Most woodworkers also consider resaw capacity, the distance from the bottom of the blade guard to the table surface. Riser kits that increase this vertical capacity are available for many band saws, increasing their normal resaw capacity from 6" to almost 12", as shown in **Figure 2.36**. That is a huge jump in capacity, and not all saws have the motor power to match.

The floor space a band saw needs depends very much on what you intend to do with the saw. It doesn't need any space to the operator's left, since the column interferes with workpieces that are wide in that direction. It needs space to the front, rear, and right according to the dimensions of the workpiece you intend to cut. Band saws are very easy to mount on mobile bases and trundle around the workshop.

Figure 2.36. Resawing, or cutting thin slices from the faces of boards, is one of the operations band saws handle better than any other machine. When equipped with a riser kit, a typical 14" band saw can resaw boards almost 12" wide.

Tool	Function	Features	Price
Benchtop Band Saw	Hobby and light woodworking; sawing curves in small work	6", 8", or 10" throat	$100 to $300
Open Stand Band Saw	General woodworking; sawing curves and light resawing	Cast-iron frame; table tilts to 45 degrees; 10" to 18" throat; able to use blade up to 1" wide; can often be enhanced with a riser block to increase resaw capacity	$300 to $2000
Enclosed Cabinet Band Saw	General woodworking; sawing curves and straight cuts; deep resawing	Cast-iron frame; table tilts to 45 degrees; enclosed motor; 10" to 24" throat; able to use blade up to 1" wide; better dust collection	$1500+

Band saw features

The width of the blade a band saw is designed to use is quite important. While many band saws will handle narrow blades ⅛" to ¼" wide, it is the maximum width that gets the woodworker's attention. Wider blades are essential for resawing and, to a lesser degree, making straight cuts in thick wood. While 10" to 12" band saws may be limited to ⅜"-wide blades, 14" models can often use blades up to ¾" wide, and larger machines up to 1" or wider, a substantial advantage. Also important is the quality and type of blade guides a band saw has. Precisely adjusted guides are crucial to how a band saw cuts. Guides range from full ball bearing rollers on the high end to solid rubbing blocks made from metal or various composites. Aftermarket guides are available to upgrade most saws.

The quality of the wheels on which the blade runs contributes to how smoothly a band saw runs and to the stability of the blade. The wheels are fitted with slightly crowned rubber or vinyl tires stretched around their outside rim, on which the blade actually runs. The upper wheel has a tracking adjustment that tilts it slightly so various-width blades will run in the center of the tire.

Band saw blades must run under a specific amount of tension to work correctly. The upper wheel is mounted to a spring-loaded block that moves up and down to regulate tension, traditionally by turning a knob. While that type of system works, it's time consuming to relax the tension on the blade when not in use. That is the politically correct way of saying woodworkers don't do it. Leaving the blade under tension all the time can shorten its life. A recent innovation in band saws is a quick-release lever mechanism that makes applying and relaxing blade tension nearly instantaneous (see **Figure 2.37**). Consequently, it is more likely to be used, resulting in blades and wheel bearings that perform better for longer.

Power is important, but there are few options on band saws in terms of the motor, though many can be rewired to run on 220 volts. Nearly all band saws are belt-driven, and some have two blade speeds, changed by moving the drive belt from one set of pulley grooves to another.

> "Key band saw features include a heavy-duty frame, a large table that tilts to 45 degrees, and overall quality construction."

Dust collection on most band saws is marginal at best. Having the blade running around two wheels in separate cabinets and through a table in between makes directing even a majority of the dust toward a single collection port more engineering than most woodworkers want to pay for. Band saws mounted on an enclosed stand tend to have somewhat better dust collection, but count on needing a broom and a shop vac anyway.

Benchtop band saws cost $100 to $300 while floor model prices range from $300 to $2000, depending on capacity, features, and quality. You can do quite well in the $600 to $1000 price range.

Despite its usefulness and versatility, unless you intend to resaw planks or small logs and make your own veneers, a band saw is not an essential machine. A portable jigsaw will do fine for the occasional curve. A scroll saw is better for fine fretwork, in part because it can make an inside cut using a starter hole, something a band saw can't do.

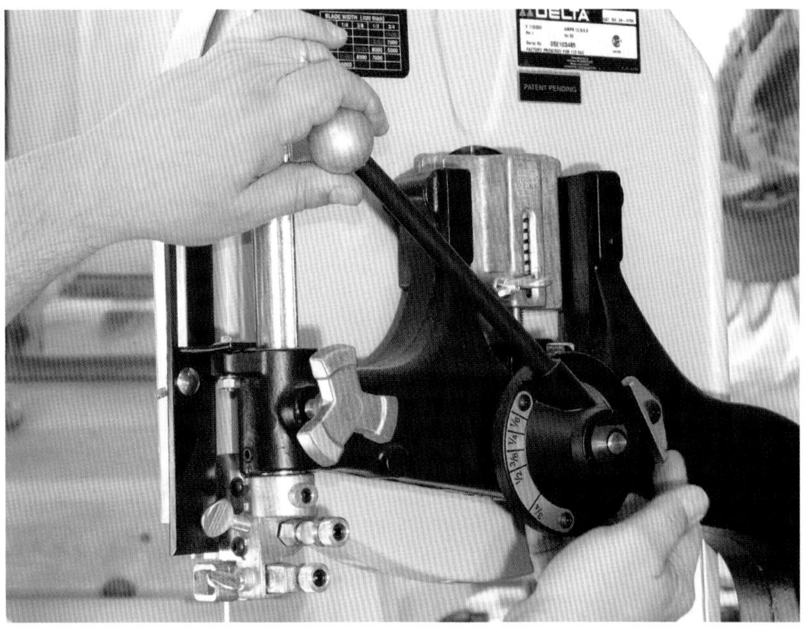

Figure 2.37. Band saw blades must be tensioned to cut correctly. However, that tension can shorten their useful lives if not relaxed when the saw is not being used. This saw has a lever that makes applying or relaxing the necessary tension quick and easy.

Scroll Saw

Function: Makes fine, intricate cuts for fretwork, plaques, ornaments, intarsia, and more
Features: Exterior and interior cuts with threadable blade, variable blade control, easy to clean, accurate, requires little space
Price: $100 to $500

Figure 2.38. Scroll saws have a dedicated following but are frequently found in general woodworking shops as well. They can cut odd shapes, inside and out, as well as decorate large-scale pieces with appliqués or fretwork.

Designed for fine, intricate cutting, a scroll saw (see **Figure 2.38**) is a nice complement to the woodworking shop for making decorative pieces on larger projects. It also excels at making fretwork and stand-alone decorative plaques, ornaments, and more. The scroll saw uses a short, slender blade that moves rapidly up and down. Unlike the band saw, the scroll saw blade can be threaded through a starter hole to make an interior cutout.

Intarsia, based almost exclusively on the scroll saw, is rapidly growing in popularity as an art form unto itself. It's the art of making inlays and pictures using small pieces of wood. Intarsia is closely related to marquetry, the art of making pictures by sawing pieces of veneer that fit tightly together.

Scroll saw features

Scroll saws are rated by throat depth from the blade to the frame, often in the 16" to 20" range. Also important are blade controls, blade mounting, and the overall quality of the operating mechanism. The better machines produce less vibration and have blade movement systems that make them easier to use, cleaner cutting, and more accurate.

Scroll saws do not require much space, they can back into a wall, and they are easy to move around. Most machines have a footprint about 18" wide and 3' deep, with the operator sitting or standing at the side or end.

Prices vary widely for scroll saws, from under $100 to well over $500 for professional-level machines. They are not essential machines, until you catch the scroll sawing bug. Then you will have to have one.

Scroll Sawing Is Fun!

You can make a lot of very neat projects with a scroll saw, including decorative accent pieces for other projects, intarsia pictures, fret sawn decorative accessories, and toys for your kids. You'll be shopping for:

- Scroll saw
- Spindle sander

Jointer

The jointer has two flat tables flanking a cylindrical cutter head containing two, three, or four long knives, with a fence alongside the tables.

The jointer excels at straightening and flattening one face and one edge of a board in preparation for gluing pieces together to make a panel (see **Figure 2.39**). Straightening edges and faces is necessary to prepare wood for use in frames or other project parts. The jointer can also make two adjoining faces square to each other or cut them at a specific angle. However, remember that the jointer cannot make any two surfaces parallel to each other. That is the job of the planer and table saw.

Jointer capacity

Jointers are rated by the width of the knives and the length of the tables. The most common knife lengths are 4", 6", and 8", though wider models are common to industrial settings. Benchtop jointers are usually limited to 4" or 6" knives while floor (stationary) models commonly have 6" or 8" knives. A jointer's face-flattening ability is limited to widths that do not exceed its knife length.

An important difference between benchtop and floor model jointers is the length of the tables and the material from which they are made. Benchtop models often have machined aluminum tables, usually under 36" in length. Floor models have cast-iron tables that can run 40" and longer, and are correspondingly wider too. Table length is important because it dictates the length of stock that can be accurately trued. A commonly used rule of thumb for maximum stock length is double the length of a jointer's table, though that is not a strict limit.

A jointer needs space left and right to match the longest wood you expect to straighten, but no space is needed on the back side and only enough room for the operator to stand is needed on the front side. It can happily go against the wall.

Jointer features

Most jointer outfeed tables have a rabbeting ledge machined into them that few owners seem to use. Both stationary jointers that I have owned had rabbeting ledges, and I cut exactly one rabbet on each of them just to try it—I think a router equipped with a rabbeting bit or a table saw fitted with a stacked dado set is easier and faster.

Jointer fences are generally made from the same material as the tables, and while fence length is important, it is not crucial. Jointer fences have stops at 90 degrees (straight up) and 45 degrees, as shown in **Figure 2.40**. Higher-priced machines may have additional stops and fences that tilt both in and out in relation to the table.

The number of knives, their adjustment, and how sharp they are determine the quality of the cuts a jointer produces. Most floor model jointers have three or four knives while benchtop and bargain-priced models may have two. Fewer knives cut slower, wear faster, and generally produce a less refined surface on the wood. On the other hand, more knives may be more difficult to align, which matters because, if one knife is set higher than the others, it does most of the work, and not too well either.

The power of a jointer's electric motor is seldom a major issue. This is a good thing since increasing motor power is not an option without moving up to a larger, more expensive machine. Of course there is nothing to stop you from thinking that machine is underpowered also. In that case, your best remedy is to take a lighter cut.

Most jointers have a dust chute that helps direct the large volume of debris these machines create away from the cutter head. Where benchtop models frequently just dump the dust on the bench, most stationary models include a hose adapter so

Figure 2.39. A jointer makes gluing up panels and cutting clean-fitting joints possible. Straightening one face and one edge of a piece of stock is the first step to accurately squaring it up. Nothing helps woodworking more than straight, square stock.

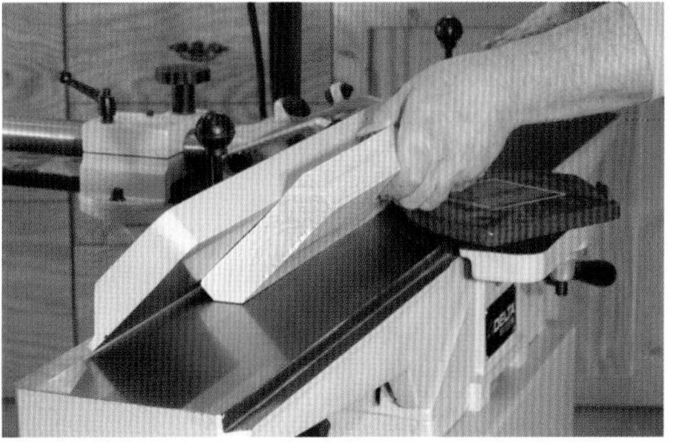

Figure 2.40. Jointers can also bevel stock with an accuracy that is difficult to beat. The jointer keeps that edge straight as well.

Tool	Function	Features	Price
Benchtop Jointer	Straightens and flattens one face and one edge of a board; used in panel assembly and to prepare project wood	Two 4" or 6" knives; aluminum tables under 36" long; stops at 90 and 45 degrees; dust chute	$120 to $300
Stationary Jointer (Floor Model)	Straightens and flattens one face and one edge of a board; used in panel assembly and to prepare project wood	Three or four 6" or 8" knives; 40" and longer cast-iron tables; rabbeting ledges; additional stops and fences; dust chute with hose adapter	$500 to $1000

Jointer or Planer or Both?

Having a jointer and a planer in the shop allows perfect preparation of the wood for your projects. You can machine wood to be perfectly flat and straight, and to very specific dimensions, capabilities that add considerable design freedom and accuracy to the process of building projects. In addition, you can process cheaper rough-sawn lumber, which can save money. However, you will have to process a lot of lumber before you save enough to actually pay for the machines. Predicting large savings to a significant other as justification for the purchase is not a good plan because those savings will be slow in coming and often spent on more tools in the meantime.

If the budget allows purchasing both a jointer and a planer at one time, you avoid one of the more perplexing decisions in tool buying. Most of us have to choose the one to buy now and must wait for the tool budget to recover before buying the other. That decision often makes you more aware of not having the other and can inspire you to save the money.

If you have a jointer but no planer, you can be sure of having straight edges and one flat side on your wood. And if you have a planer but no jointer, while it's no problem to make one surface parallel to the other, you can't necessarily make either of them flat. If the board goes in bowed from end to end, it'll come out with the same bow in it. Chicken or egg? To me, it would make the most sense to get the jointer first and the planer second, but your mileage may vary, and it really won't be long before you have to own them both.

the chute can be connected to a dust collector. A dust collector, rather than a shop vac, is needed to handle the large volume of debris a jointer creates, particularly when jointing the wide face of a board.

Owning a jointer (and/or planer) often causes the woodworker to buy a dust collector. Sweeping up the impressive pile of chips a jointer spits out gets old fast.

Benchtop jointers vary in price from $120 to $300 while stationary models cost from $500 to well over $1000, depending on quality and capacity.

Figure 2.41. Thickness planers work with the jointer when preparing lumber. Where the jointer straightens one edge or face, the planer makes the opposing face true and parallel. Planers can also reduce the thickness of stock to the exact dimension needed and produce an exceptionally smooth surface at the same time.

Planer

Often called a thickness planer or surface planer, this machine uses a set of long knives in a rotating cutter head, mounted parallel to a flat but short bed on which the wood slides (see **Figure 2.41**). Unlike other common machines, the planer moves the wood by itself with a pair of rollers that both hold

Figure 2.42. Most better planers have two speeds. The faster speed is used when reducing wood to a specific thickness. The slower speed is used for the final cuts to produce an ultra-smooth surface.

Tool	Function	Features	Price
Lunchbox Planer	Flattens opposite side of a jointed board	Handles 12"- to 15"-wide stock; fast and slow speed rate	$200 to $600
Stationary Planer	Flattens opposite side of a jointed board	Handles stock up to 24"; fast and slow speed rate	$700 to $1500

the stock against the table and keep it traveling at a consistent rate.

If the bottom surface of the wood is flat, the knives will cut the top face flat and parallel to the bottom surface. However, if the board has a twist or bow along its length, the planer will try to duplicate that in the upper surface. Its tables and rollers are too small and close together to do anything more than that. If the board is cupped, the planer won't do much about that either—the feed rollers will press the cup flat, but it springs back. This is why a planer works best in conjunction with a jointer. The jointer flattens one surface, and then the planer can flatten the opposite face while making it parallel to the jointed side at the same time.

It is possible to hand plane the surface of a plank of wood so it ends up smooth and flat, but it is very hard and tedious work. Many are not willing to use hand planes when there is an alternative, such as buying surfaced wood, owning your own thickness planer, or going fishing instead. Another machine that can do the same job is the drum sander (see Sanding Machines on page 64).

Features and capacities

Planers are rated primarily by the width of stock they are capable of cutting. Most semi-portable planers, sometimes called lunchbox planers, handle between 12"- and 15"-wide stock. Larger planers can accept stock up to 16", 20", and even 24" wide, but the price and power requirements jump accordingly.

Many planers have two feed rates (see **Figure 2.42**) that help speed the process and control the quality of the surface produced. The faster speed is used when reducing the wood close to the thickness wanted, a process called dimensioning. For the final one or two cuts, the operator should change to the slower feed rate to increase the cuts per inch (CPI) and obtain the smoothest finish possible.

Lunchbox planers, by far the most popular, run between $200 and $600 while the larger stationary machines may cost $700 to $1500 and more, depending on capacity and power. As with table saws, when the motors produce over 1½ or 2 hp, 220-volt power is required.

Like the jointer, a planer needs space fore and aft to match the length of the wood being processed. It needs space on the right or the left only for the operator to move about safely. Because jointers and planers complement each other, they often are positioned side by side.

Woodturning Lathe

Sometimes considered a type of woodworking all its own, woodturning is growing in popularity. The lathe is the only woodworking machine that spins the wood against a handheld tool supported by a stationary rest. The lathe can produce all manner of wooden plates, bowls, and vases, plus stair balusters and newels, pens, toys, peppermills, knobs and handles, walking sticks, and decorative furniture parts (see **Figure 2.43**).

One of the attractions of woodturning is the range of lathe sizes and projects that make it possible to add a lathe to virtually any shop. The other attraction is speed: You can go from raw wood to a finished and polished piece in a very short amount of time. Be forewarned: Many woodworkers find woodturning to be somewhere between engrossing and outright addictive.

Figure 2.43. Woodworking lathes are capable of producing finished turnings and decorative parts for dressing up other projects. This 14" Delta Iron Bed Lathe is in the most popular range for the home shop.

Tool	Function	Features	Price
Benchtop Lathe	Turning small projects like pens and jewelry	3" to 5" swing range	$175 to $300
Stationary Lathe	Turning larger projects like table legs and salad bowls	12" to 14" swing range; 40" bed capacity	$300 to $1500 plus

> **“Many woodworkers find woodturning to be somewhere between engrossing and outright addictive. Virtually any shop has space for a lathe, and you can go from raw wood to a finished and polished piece in a short amount of time.”**

Lathe capacity

Lathes are rated primarily by the swing and bed length. The swing is the diameter of the largest piece of wood that can be turned, or double the distance from the center of the spindle to the bed. Bed capacity is the maximum length of material that can fit between the spindle and tailstock. The most common swings for home woodturning are 12" and 14". Bed capacities of these lathes are around 40".

Smaller benchtop lathes with 3" to 5" swings (see **Figure 2.44**) are popular for turning pens, jewelry, and many other small projects. Remember that small projects can be turned on large lathes, but large projects cannot be turned on small lathes.

The lathe's useprint is hardly bigger than its footprint. You need very little space to each side, none in back, and enough for the operator to move around in front.

Lathe features

Horsepower is a consideration with lathes but seems to be more of a worry on the bargain-priced machines. Machines in the mid to upper price ranges come with 1½ to 2 hp motors that are adequate for all but the most unusual turning jobs.

Controlling spindle speed is important in turning, and most of the popular lathes have five or six speeds, regulated with a lever on the power head. In most cases, speeds can only be changed when the machine is running.

In the past, to change spindle speeds, the turner had to move the drive belt from one set of pulleys to another. Today, a variable-diameter pulley system called a Reeves drive is very popular. As the speed handle is moved from one position to another, the two-piece pulleys open or close, allowing the belt to run higher or lower, simulating larger- or smaller-diameter pulleys, and causing the lathe to turn faster or slower. Oddly, some of the higher-end lathes still have the multi-pulley system that requires physically moving the belt to change speeds. However, moving the drive belt between pulley stations is not a difficult task and with a little practice can be done rather quickly.

Lathes with 12" to 14" swings range in price from $300 to well over $1500, depending on features and quality. Benchtop lathes cost from $175 for single-speed models to $300 for more feature-rich, multi-speed versions. In general, heavier is better because mass dampens vibration.

Do you need a lathe? Of course, if you are fascinated by the art of woodturning. Otherwise, in general woodworking, you will use it once in a while for knobs and legs, and you probably can do without it.

Figure 2.44. Benchtop lathes are popular because of their small footprint and price. They are capable of turning many types of projects, including pens, small bowls, toys, peppermills, and decorative pieces.

New Tools!

Woodturning Is Fun!

You took a class or watched a DVD and you're hooked. Woodturning is fast, is fun, and doesn't use vast amounts of wood. The details of woodturning are beyond the scope of this book, but at a glance here's what you're in for:

- Lathe
- Turning tools, lots of different ones
- Lathe chuck
- Sharpening upgrade
- Band saw

Drill Press

Function: Drills straight holes in wood
Features: Benchtop or floor model, multiple speeds, tilting table, ½"-capacity chuck, adjustable table height, depth limiting system
Price: $125 for benchtop, $800 plus for floor model

Though not specifically a woodworking tool, a drill press makes it easy to drill straight holes in wood (see **Figure 2.45**). With simple jigs, the drill press can produce shelf pinholes or be converted to a workable drum sander.

Though benchtop models are relatively common, a decent floor model drill press is more versatile. The extra vertical capacity of a floor model allows it to make holes in the ends of longer pieces of wood, which you might need for dowel joints.

Features to look for include a ½"-capacity chuck, multiple speeds, a tilting table, and a table height adjustment system that locks solidly. A depth limiting system is very handy in the woodshop and comes standard on most drill presses, but check for it, too.

A drill press has a small footprint, though it does need space from side to side to accommodate the workpiece. The operator stands in front of the machine. It can go against a wall. Storage for drill bits and accessories should be close at hand.

Drill press prices run from about $125 for a good benchtop model to $800 or more for a floor model with all the bells and whistles. A basic machine is not expensive and will prove very handy to have.

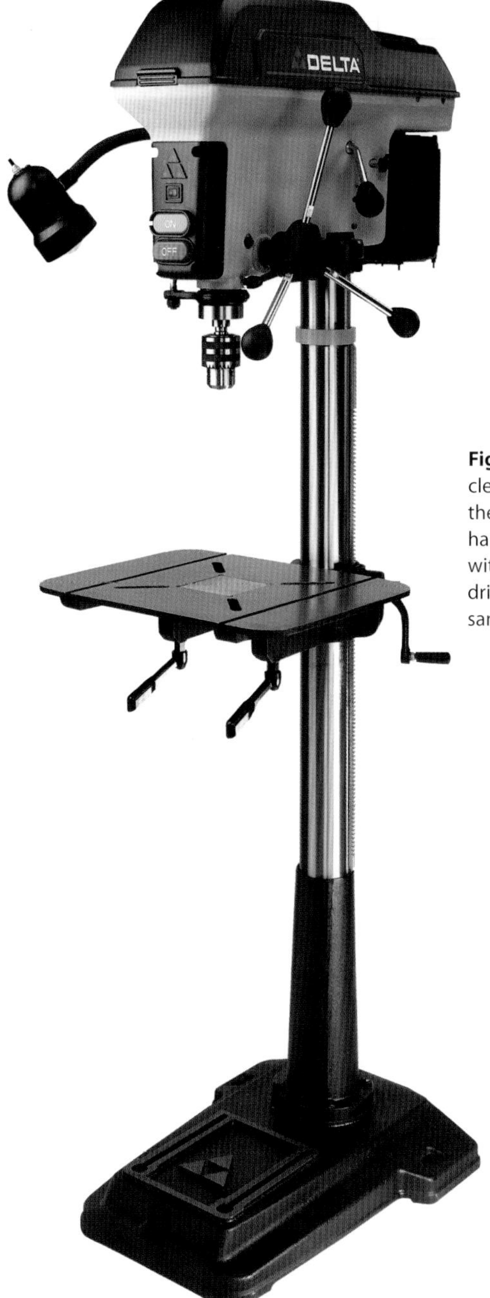

Figure 2.45. Drill presses drill clean holes that are square to the surface much easier than handheld drills. Equipped with a sanding drum, the drill press also makes a good sanding machine.

"Woodworkers continually expand the capabilities of drill presses with shop-built jigs and fixtures that make repetitive and specialty drilling tasks fast and accurate."

> “Sanding machines are helpful but not essential. Buy one once you are more familiar with woodworking because the type of projects that interest you may change and alter your need for one of these machines.”

Sanding Machines

While sanding machines are popular with woodworkers, the styles they like vary considerably. The range of sanding machine configurations available allows woodworkers to choose one with a set of capabilities that most closely matches the projects they build and the needs of their shop. Sanding machines help shape and smooth the wood, and some, such as pneumatic spindle sanders, can work with contoured shapes.

The sanding machines discussed here have small footprints and useprints and are not too heavy, so they can be dragged around the shop as needed.

Sanding machines vary in price considerably according to the quality of construction, capacity, and features. You can spend as little as $100 on a benchtop belt/disk sander or several thousand dollars for a wide belt or drum sander. Most home woodworkers will find a machine to handle their needs for between $300 and $500.

Sanding machines are very helpful, but they are not essential. My best advice is to wait until you get more familiar with woodworking because the type of projects that interest you most may change. Getting some experience under your belt will make choosing the right sanding machine easier, if you need one at all.

Belt and disk sander

Belt and disk sanders, including combination machines (see **Figure 2.46**), are most common. Most belt sanders, including the belt portion of a combination machine, are made so the belt can be horizontal, vertical, or at any angle between.

Figure 2.46. Belt and disk sander combinations are versatile and useful for shaping and finishing small flat parts.

Tool	Function	Features	Price
Belt and Disk Sander	Shapes and sands wood with flat surfaces	Adjustable belt angle; 8" to 20" disk; table square to disk; slot for miter or jig	$100 to $300
Spindle Sander	Shapes and sands wood with flat or contoured surfaces	Cylindrical sanding drum rotates and oscillates; pneumatic drum	$125 to $400
Horizontal Drum Sander	Removes wood from top surface, making it flat and uniformly thick	Two speeds or variable speeds; open end can sand wood twice as wide as the drum	$400 to $1,000+

Figure 2.47. Oscillating spindle sanders, which can be fitted with pneumatic drums, will help shape and smooth curved parts.

These sanders usually have two or more feed rates, and some have infinitely variable speeds. Along with the grit of abrasive paper being used, the feed and speed controls vary how quickly material is removed and how smooth the surface is.

An attractive feature of the horizontal drum sander is its open end. That allows for sanding wood that is nearly twice as wide as the drum. In fact, the sander's designation often reflects this, such as 22-44, indicating the drum is 22" wide, but, when reversed, a 44"-wide board can be sanded.

Figure 2.48. A drum sander can flatten panels and produce finish-ready surfaces on wide pieces of wood. The open-end design allows sanding one half of the piece, turning it around, and sanding the other half, effectively doubling the width capacity.

Most disk sanders have a table square to the face of the rotating disk, which can be anywhere from 8" to 20" in size. Some models have a slot in the table for a miter guide or other jig.

Spindle sander

The spindle sander has a cylindrical sanding drum that both rotates and oscillates up and down to increase its effectiveness and extend the life of the abrasive (see **Figure 2.47**). Some have a pneumatic drum that will flex to sand the curves and contours of the workpiece.

Horizontal drum sander

Also known as a thickness sander, the horizontal drum sander is similar to a planer in that it removes material from the top surface of the wood. Instead of knives, the drum sander has a wide driven belt that moves the material under a spinning drum wrapped with an abrasive strip that spirals from one end to the other (see **Figure 2.48**). Larger industrial models use a wide, continuous abrasive belt slung between two or more rollers.

Dedicated Mortising Machine

Function: Drills and chisels square holes
Features: Drill-chisel combinations for holes ¼", 5/16", ⅜", and ½" square; ½ hp motor; benchtop and floor models available
Price: $180 to $250 for benchtop, $900 plus for floor model

The sole purpose of a mortising machine is to drill and chisel square holes in one motion, and do it accurately (see **Figure 2.49**). A drill bit running inside a hollow square chisel actually removes most of the material, and then the chisel shaves the round hole to a square as it is plunged into the wood. The drill also lifts the chips out of the hole and ejects them through a slot in the side of the chisel. By drilling overlapping, square holes, a mortise of any length and width can be made.

Mortising machines usually come with a selection of drill-chisel combinations for holes ¼", 5/16", ⅜", and ½" square. Power is not a big selling point since most benchtop models have ½ hp motors, which are more than sufficient if you keep the chisels sharp.

Dedicated mortising machines cost between $180 and $250 for the better benchtop models, with some floor models that have more features running $900 and more. The benchtop machine can be placed on its own little table or can be used on a bench when needed and stored out of the way the rest of the time. It can go against the wall, with side-to-side space to match your workpieces, and some room in front for you.

Mortising machines make perfect sense, and owning one has made me far better at mortise and tenon joints, one of the fundamental ways for creating exceptionally strong joints in wood. However, you do not strictly need one. You can chop mortises by hand with a chisel and a mallet (a process I personally do not enjoy), you can chop them by machine with a drill press attachment (one of the more useless tool ideas in woodworking), or you can rout them with flat-bottomed, spiral-cutting router bits in a plunge router, guided by a suitable jig.

Figure 2.49. Mortising machines are very specialized in what they do, but once you use one, there is no going back to a mallet and chisel. Since getting one in my shop, I fear no mortise, nor project that needs one.

Shaper

The shaper is a production-level machine that does all the same things you can do on a router table, only quicker and with bigger cutters that are capable of removing more wood per pass. The size of a shaper itself and the cost of the cutters make it rather rare in the home woodworking shop.

Managing Dust and Chips

Woodworkers are wising up about dust in the shop and its potential effects on health. Dust may never be eliminated from the shop environment completely, but with a good dust collector, ambient air cleaner, and dust mask, it can be reduced to manageable levels.

In addition to protecting the woodworker, controlling dust in the shop helps reduce its migration into the living areas of the home. This certainly will improve the attitude of your significant other. However, do be clear that a shop vacuum, though very helpful, is not the same as a dust collector.

Shop vacuums move a relatively small volume of air at high speeds because the actual inlet opening through which they inhale is very small. Dust collectors move large volumes of air at somewhat slower speeds in order to suspend sawdust particles and move them to the catch container (see **Figure 2.50**). It is that large volume of air that gives a purpose-designed dust collector a major edge over a shop vacuum, especially when removing dust from woodworking machines such as table saws, jointers, and planers. I would consider dust collection and air filtering equipment essential, not optional.

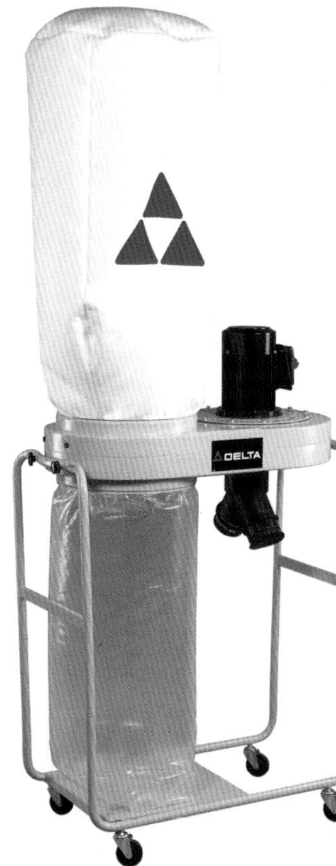

Figure 2.50. Real dust collectors designed for woodworking are so big because they have to pass a huge amount of air to be efficient at extracting sawdust from a machine and then carrying it to the bag or can for storage. Hoses to the machines attach to the black Y fitting on the right.

Dust collection systems

Real dust collectors are physically large but necessarily so. The exhaust bag must have a significant amount of surface area to exhaust the large volume of air and still filter efficiently. The better bags and cartridges filter out particles down to one micron in diameter. They may cost a little more, but the difference they make in the shop can be dramatic.

A good dust collector for small- to intermediate-size shops should move 1000 cfm (cubic feet per minute) or more. Most dust collectors come with a length of 4"-diameter hose and some kind of a stand or cart so they can be moved from machine to machine. If you want to collect dust from more than one machine at a time, a rare occurrence in a home woodworking shop, the cfm capacity may have to be much larger to work efficiently, and you should prepare yourself for the sticker shock of the connector hoses and control gates. Buying more flow capacity than needed is always a good idea if the budget allows. Your needs for collecting and filtering dust are certain to increase in the not-so-distant future.

A dust collector's useprint is the same size as its footprint, but in this case the critical dimension is height: some collectors are 8' or 9' tall. Prices range from $130 to over $500 for more capacity and filtering.

My first dust collector bag only filtered down to 30 microns, which meant it was knocking the big stuff out of the air but launching most of the dust back into the shop, only doing it more efficiently than the machines creating it in the first place. Consequently, the air in my shop was probably more contaminated with airborne dust than if that coarse-filtering dust collector wasn't used at all.

Air cleaners

A shop air cleaner is usually mounted on the ceiling, positioned so that the air moving through it circulates throughout the shop. A series of filter elements designed specifically for this task do a very good job of removing extremely fine dust particles from the air, provided the machine is properly maintained as described in its instructions. These machines do a very good job of removing dust under the one-micron size, often considered the most dangerous, from the air that dust collectors miss (see **Figure 2.51**).

Figure 2.51. Ambient air cleaners should be considered a safety item and consequently should be placed high on the "to buy" list. These trap the tiny dust particles that do the most harm.

The most obvious feature to consider is the cfm rating. As with the dust collector, more is better, especially if your shop area is larger than a one-car garage. A better machine has at least two speeds to help regulate its performance based on the conditions under which it is being used. A remote control is handy since reaching the on-off switch of a ceiling-mounted machine is not always easy.

Another nice feature is a timer that allows letting the air cleaner run a specific amount of time after leaving the shop to thoroughly clean the air. In addition to keeping the shop air purer, less dust-contaminated air migrates to other parts of the house.

Prices run from about $180 to $400, depending on capacity and features.

Shop vacuum

Even with a good dust collection system and your trusty broom and dustpan, you'll still need a good shop vacuum. You'll need it to clean accumulated dust out of the insides of machines, as well as to help you clean up the shop and to vacuum yourself off before you go in to dinner. Look for one that has a wide base; they're a lot less likely to tip over. Plan on investing $75 to $250.

Tool	Function	Features	Price
Dust Collector	Removes dust particles from the air and collects larger chips	Filters out particles down to 1 micron; moves 1000 cfm; attaches directly to various machines	$130 to $500
Air Cleaner	Removes invisible dust particles from the air	Mounts on the ceiling; removes particles less than 1 micron; multiple speeds; remote control; timed on and off	$180 to $400
Shop Vacuum	Removes larger particles from floor, surfaces, and machines	Handheld; wide base prevents tipping	$75 to $250

Work Supports

Function: Prevents long workpieces from falling or drooping
Features: Different roller styles, adjustable-height stand
Price: $20 to $75

Figure 2.52. Work supports can help feed work into machines and also catch it coming out the other side. They are mandatory for both efficiency and safety around table saws, planers, and most other machines.

Roller-topped work supports (see **Figure 2.52**) are often used to prevent longer pieces of wood from falling or drooping as they enter or exit a machine. Aside from preventing damage to the wood itself, a work support can prevent injuries caused by your trying to catch or grab the piece as it passes a blade or cutter.

Work supports have either one long roller or a line of ball-type rollers, both on an adjustable-height stand. While both styles work, the roller style can direct the wood to one side or the other if it is significantly out of line with the machine. The ball-roller type has no directional problems but can allow narrow stock to tip or drop between the rollers. Stands with two to four lines of rollers are also available.

Work supports will cost from $20 to $75, with the ball style and stands with multiple rows on the higher end of, or exceeding, that price range.

Mobile Bases

Function: Makes use and storage of equipment easier
Features: Pair of fixed wheels and pair of adjustable non-skid feet, recommended weight capacity, available in kits
Price: $50 to $150

Mobile bases make using and storing equipment in a small shop much easier. While most mobile bases roll easily, they are not off-road capable. None negotiate rough surfaces very well. Most shop floors, if they are in relatively good condition, do not pose a problem. Normal seams between concrete slabs pose no problem to a mobile base, nor do floor drains.

Figure 2.53. Mobile base kits are economical and will fit a wide range of machines. This one, from Rockler, has a removable lifting caster that can be used on other machines.

Many garage floors are flush with the driveway paving, which allows moving machines out of the shop entirely. This can be a big help for breaking down oversize lumber or just taking advantage of a nice day. However, if your garage floor is an inch or so above the outside paving, a mobile base cannot negotiate that step without some kind of ramp to smooth the transition.

Figure 2.54. All-metal universal kits are also available, usually in a few sizes that each fit a specific range of machine bases.

The only downside to using a mobile base is forgetting to lower it or to lock the wheels before using the machine. When you start pushing a piece of wood through a blade and the machine starts rolling away also, bad things can happen. The woodworker is expected to be smarter than the mobile base. That means taking your time and being sure the machine is ready for use, including having the base in the secured position.

Features and specs

Most mobile bases have a pair of fixed wheels on one end and a pair of adjustable non-skid feet on the other. A foot-operated lever pushes a swivel caster down to lift the end with the non-skid feet. With the machine riding on the caster and fixed wheels, maneuvering it in tight areas is very easy. When the actuator lever is released, the machine sits down on the stationary feet.

Figure 2.55. Fully welded steel bases, usually from the same manufacturer as the machine they carry, are the top of the line. They have large weight capacities, roll easily, and require little assembly. They are a bit more expensive but are virtually indestructible and work much better than the lower-priced options.

Mobile bases are assigned a recommended weight capacity by the manufacturer, which is usually listed on the package. While this generally exceeds the weight of most machines they fit, be sure to check. Remember to consider the added weight of the material being cut, jigs, fixtures, and you leaning on the machine. If the listed capacity of the base seems close to the anticipated overall weight, move up to a stronger base.

I like the mobile base kits from Rockler (see **Figure 2.53**), which use shop-made wooden rails to connect prefabricated metal corners. Aside from the initial cost savings, these kits can be sized to fit a wide range of machine base sizes. That also means they can be reused by making new rails to fit should a machine be replaced. Another nice feature is that the lifting caster can be used on more than one base by removing a pair of special finger-tightened bolts.

Another type of universal base uses perforated steel tubes for rails that bolt together (see **Figure 2.54**). These kits are usually offered in a few variations, each with rail lengths designed to fit a range of base sizes.

At the top of the mobile base list are fully welded, heavy-duty metal bases that require a small amount of assembly to complete. These bases are usually designed to fit a specific machine or leg pattern, as shown in **Figure 2.55**. Typical features are substantial weight capacities, large smooth-rolling wheels, and easy-to-use, foot-operated lifting casters.

Handheld power tools

Handheld routers, sanders, saws, and drill drivers have come a long way in the last decade. They perform better, have more capabilities, last longer, and in some cases actually cost less than they did several years ago. Many portable power tools are available not only with a regular electrical cord, but also as battery-powered cordless units and also as air-powered pneumatic units (but their air requirements mean an air compressor is needed to operate them). The bad news is that there are lots and lots of them from which to choose.

When choosing handheld tools, capabilities are important, but so are comfort and safety. Keep all three in mind when evaluating these tools because you are likely to use them often.

Cordless Drill

Function: Drives small screws and other small fasteners
Features: Powerful, long lasting, variable speed, adjustable slip clutches, one-hand keyless chucks, push-button reverse, batteries supply 12 to 24 volts, rechargeable
Price: $100 to $200

While the cordless revolution encompasses virtually all types of handheld power tools, the drill driver is by far the most prevalent in the woodworking shop (see **Figure 2.56**). It's probably the first power tool most people buy, homeowners as well as would-be woodworkers. Advances in battery and motor technology over the last decade have made the new breed of drill drivers powerful and long lasting. Add variable speed, adjustable slip clutches, and one-hand keyless chucks, and corded drills pale by comparison.

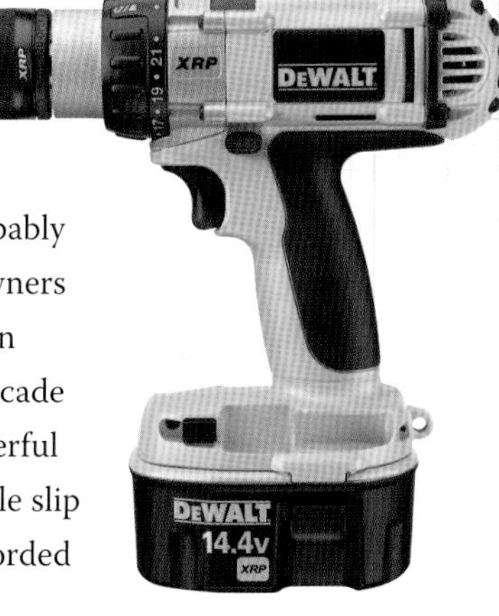

Figure 2.56. Cordless drill drivers have made corded versions nearly obsolete. Increased battery power, fast chargers, and a full range of useable features make them easy to use and very effective.

Drill drivers come with batteries packing anywhere between 12 volts and 24 volts, but the most popular seem to be in the 14- to 18-volt range. The 14- to 18-volt batteries offer plenty of power and run time without the excessive weight of higher voltage packs. Excessive battery weight can throw the driver out of balance and make it tiring to use. The chargers packaged with drill drivers usually recharge the battery packs in an hour or less.

Features and specs

Standard features include a no-tools chuck, variable speed trigger, push-button reversing, and dual speed ranges. The high-speed setting is used for drilling and most screw driving. The slower power setting develops lots of torque that drives large screws or lags with ease. In fact, when used in the slower power range, you must take care to avoid twisting weaker fasteners in half or stripping out the hole.

Features to look for include a ½"-capacity chuck, fast charger, two battery packs, dual speed range, and a decent price. The values for the money appear to be in the mid to upper price ranges where the driver and batteries tend to live longer and perform better.

If you are going to make outdoor projects and do light carpentry work with 2 x 4s and 1 x pine lumber, glue and screws will be your basic joinery technique. It won't be long before you own two cordless drills, one for pilot holes and the other for driving screws.

Prices for drill driver kits are about $100 to $200.

Impact Drivers

Function: Drives large screws, lag screws, and other big fasteners
Features: Cordless
Price: $150 to $250

While pneumatic impact drivers have been around for ages, the cordless electric versions are relative newcomers to woodworking (see **Figure 2.57**). They are gaining popularity quickly because of their tremendous fastener driving and extracting power.

Figure 2.57. The newest cousin of the drill driver, cordless impact drivers deliver a huge amount of power that comes in handy when installing cabinets or driving large fasteners.

Woodworkers tend to use large screws when building benches and other big-scale projects. Lag screws are also popular for installing cabinets and fixtures around the shop and home. Cordless impact drivers handle these big fastener chores without a whimper, making it easier to be accurate as well.

New Wood-Words: Chuck, Collet

Chuck: Apparatus on a drill that locks the drill bit in place and adjusts in size to accommodate different bits. Older chucks and drill press chucks are tightened with a toothed key. Newer chucks are keyless, tightened by hand.

Collet: Apparatus on a router that locks the router bit in place. Collets work by squeezing a split sleeve; they cannot be adjusted in size but can be replaced with one of a different size. The predominant collet sizes are ¼" and ½". Older collets tighten with wrenches; some newer ones hand tighten.

Impact driver kits with a spare battery and charger cost between $150 and $250. It's not an essential tool since you can do the same work with a cordless drill and a set of socket wrenches, but it sure does save a lot of work on big projects.

Router

Function: Shapes joints, moldings; cuts decorative edges, grooves, chamfers, etc.
Features: Fixed, plunge, or D-handle base; adjustable bit height; ¼" and ½" collets included; variable speed control
Price: $180 to $250

Probably the most versatile tool in the shop, the modern router can shape parts for many types of joints, shape moldings, and cut decorative edges, grooves, chamfers, and more. These little machines are smoother running, quieter, and more powerful than ever (see **Figure 2.58**).

For most woodworkers, a multi-base router kit provides extensive capabilities at a very good price. Most of these kits have a fixed base and a plunge base (see **Figure 2.59**), with some adding a third, D-handle base. A single motor, usually 2¼ hp, can be installed in the base that is most appropriate for the task. Some manufacturers offer special table-mount bases (see **Figure 2.60**) that use the same motor as their kits. This provides lots of versatility.

A fixed base permits adjusting the depth of cut, but only before starting the machine. A plunge base permits starting the router, then pushing the bit into the wood to one or more preset depths of cut. A D-handle base is essentially a fixed base with a built-in handle and an on-off trigger. The D-shaped handle is preferred by some for following templates or for use on dovetail and other jigs.

Figure 2.58. Routers may be the most versatile power tools for shaping edges, cutting grooves, and making joints. The router's range of power and capabilities make it indispensable.

On any router base, the bit height mechanism should be checked (see **Figure 2.61**). Is it easy to adjust? Are very small changes easy to make accurately? If you plan to use any of the bases in a router table, is there a provision for adjusting bit height through the table?

The good news is that the better router kits carry price tags between $180 and $250, with some kits that contain additional bases or features running a little higher.

"The modern router is probably the most versatile tool in the shop. It can shape parts for joints; shape moldings; cut decorative edges, grooves, and chamfers; and do a whole lot more."

Features and specs

Most routers come with ¼" and ½" collets, though bits with ½"-diameter shanks are favored because of their stability, superior cut quality, and safety.

An important feature of modern routers is a variable speed control (see **Figure 2.62**). Left uncontrolled, most unloaded routers will spin up to 20,000 to 23,000 rpm. When bit diameter exceeds 1", that speed must be reduced for safety. Controlling bit speed can also contribute to making better cuts. The manufacturer should specify a maximum rpm for the bit and whether it is designed for use in a handheld or table-mounted router.

Figure 2.59. Most router manufacturers offer router kits that include fixed and plunge bases, collets for bits with ¼" and ½" shanks, and related tools. These kits are very popular with new woodworkers.

Figure 2.60. This under-table mounting plate unit accepts the very popular Porter Cable router motor. Its regular base is at the right.

Router Table

Router tables, fitted with your regular router or with a larger, 3-plus hp router, are very popular with woodworkers because of the accuracy, capabilities, and safety they bring to the shop. Instead of the router itself being steered on top of the workpiece, the table puts the router underneath, with the bit protruding through a hole. The big advantages are you can have a fence to guide the workpiece and you can see what you are doing. Most larger-diameter bit designs, such as panel raising and door making bits, are made to be used in a table where it is much safer to control the wood rather than trying to control a handheld router with a large-diameter bit installed.

Whether you build or buy a router table, important features include a solid, flat table surface, a sturdy, easy-to-adjust fence, and a good-quality mounting plate or lift for fitting the router to the

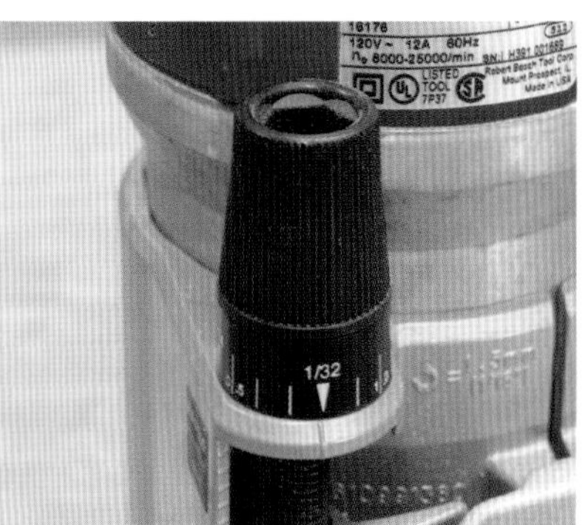

Figure 2.61. The new breed of routers includes ultra-precise bit height adjustment mechanisms that make fine corrections much easier. These adjustments are also handy when the router is installed under a table.

Figure 2.62. Variable speed control has become standard equipment on better routers. The outer edges of a large, 3¼"-diameter bit (right) will reach dangerous speeds at the same rpm at which a ½"-diameter bit (left) can be safely operated. The only safe answer is to slow down the router.

table. Mounting plates depend on the router base for bit height changes. Lift plates (see **Figure 2.63**) have their own height change mechanism that is accessible from above the table and makes ultra-precise height changes easy. Some router and lift plate combinations allow above-table bit changes, a definite time and labor saver.

There are almost as many router table fence options as there are routers and tables. Fences range from a board clamped to the table to ultra-precise, multi-function aftermarket assemblies that can help cut everything from simple rabbets to complex decorative dovetail joints. Some fences have a built-in dust collection port.

Routers in the 3 hp range (see **Figure 2.64**) usually have a variable speed control, but check before buying. Without the speed control, big horsepower routers are all but useless to woodworkers. Expect to pay between $175 and $300 for a 3 to 3½ hp router. Simple router mounting plates run from $40 to over $100. Lift plates can cost between $150 and $300. Fence systems vary between free for a length of wood clamped to the surface to $300 or more.

The router table itself can be cheap if you build it yourself to well over $300 for commercially made tables with lots of features. Most have a footprint around 24" x 30", with a useprint extended to each side according to the length of the parts being routed and to the front to accommodate the operator. Do you really need a router table? If you find yourself using your handheld router a lot, the answer is a definite yes since the table will make it safer, more accurate, and more versatile.

Router Bits

Buying cheap router bits can be a great way to waste money if features besides price are not taken into consideration. This kind of fiscal shortsightedness can also turn your shop into a combat zone: You'll be spinning a cheap hunk of metal with cutters cheaply brazed to it at up to 20,000 rpm directly in front of your soft body.

With all good-quality routers capable of using ½"-shank bits, there is no reason to use the older ¼" shanks except for a few tiny profiles that are not otherwise available (see **Figure 2.65**). The ½" shanks are far stronger and more stable, making them safer. They also produce better cuts because they resist deflection, vibration, and chatter. With their popularity growing rapidly over the last few years, ½"-shank bits have become a good value as well (see **Figure 2.66**).

Many bits have guide bearings mounted on top of the cutter (see **Figure 2.67**). The guide bearing steers the router (or the workpiece in a table setup) along a template or the uncut portion of the edge, or the adjacent face, of the wood. These bits can often be used without a router fence or other guide. Bits without guide bearings must be steered along a fence. Old-style bits with a solid pilot instead of a bearing are very likely to scorch the wood, and I hope you never have to learn just how deep into the wood a router scorch can go.

Figure 2.63. Lift plates, like the Woodpeckers PRL shown here, make changing bits and bit height easy while holding powerful routers absolutely still.

Figure 2.64. Routers in the 3 hp range are often dedicated to a table mount for use with large-diameter bits like those used to make raised panel doors and larger moldings.

Anti-kickback design in a router bit means that the body of the bit extends most of the way around the bit rather than just having the cutters hang out in the open. Extending the body helps prevent taking too deep a cut, one cause of violent kickbacks (although anti-kickback design reduces the risk, it does not eliminate it).

Generally, bits larger than 1¼" in diameter must be used in a router table. They're too big to control safely in a handheld router.

Router Bit Speed Chart

Bit Diameter	Maximum Speed (rpm)
Up to 1"	24,000
1¼" to 2"	18,000
2¼" to 2½"	16,000
3" to 3½"	12,000

Router Bit Speed Chart courtesy of Infinity Cutting Tools, www.infinitytools.com

Sets of bits

While buying a set of router bits may sound like a good way to save money and jump-start your collection, many sets include bits the manufacturer cannot sell otherwise because nobody uses them, just as you won't. However, there are starter sets available that are made up of bits most woodworkers will use frequently. The eight-piece professional set from Infinity Tools, for example, is a well-balanced bit set. It includes small and large round-over bits, a cove cutter, a chamfer bit, a rabbetting bit, a pattern-following straight bit, and a flat-bottomed straight bit, all guided with high-quality ball bearings (see Figure 2.67).

Before buying a set, look closely at the included profiles and consider your need for them. It only takes one or two duds to make buying them individually more cost effective.

Don't dismiss groups of bits designed for specific processes such as panel raising and door making (see **Figure 2.68**). These sets have matched bit profiles designed to work together. In most cases, these task-specific sets save money without slipping a dud into the deal.

Quality ½"-shank router bits range in price from $20 to well over $100 each, depending on size, materials, and complexity of the profile. Sets, such as those for making raised panel doors, can run $100 to over $200 but will last a long time. Do you really need a lot of router bits? Yes, ultimately, but, if you buy them as needed, you'll hardly notice the pain. As you build your collection, you'll also need to provide storage. You'll want to be able to find the one you need without any of them banging their sharp edges together.

Figure 2.65. While many routers come with both ¼" and ½" collets, most woodworkers buy bits with the larger shank whenever possible. The additional metal in the shank makes the bit far more stable in operation, thus safer.

Figure 2.66. Woodworkers develop a collection of router bits that is limited only by imagination and budget. The adage "cheap costs more" definitely applies to router bits; high-quality ones last longer, cut better, and are safer.

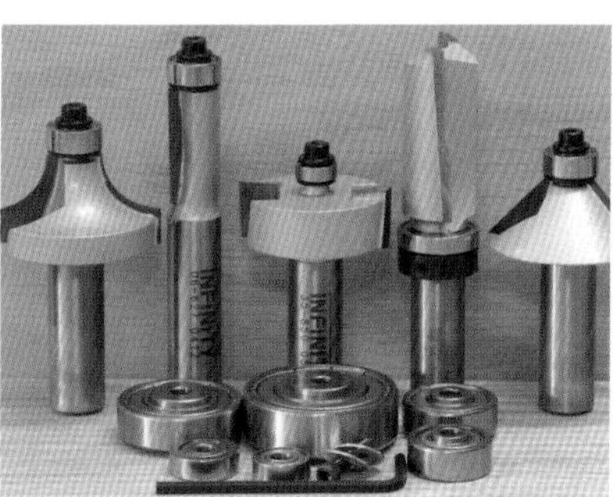

Figure 2.67. I am not a fan of router bit sets because they usually contain some designs woodworkers will never use, but this eight-piece set from Infinity Tools is an exception to that rule. This is a well-thought-out group of bearing-guided bits, all on ½" shanks.

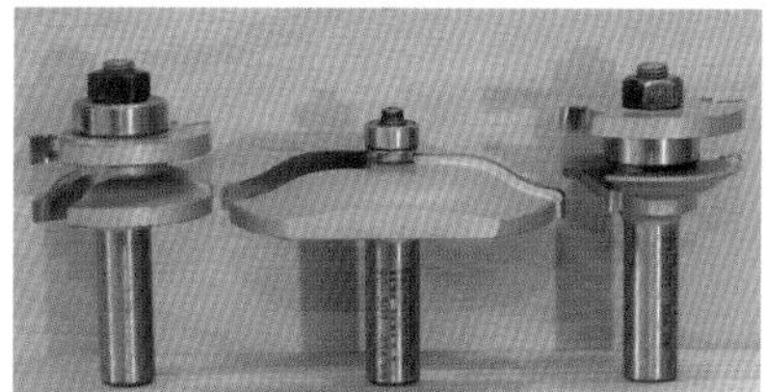

Figure 2.68. Special-use sets of router bits, such as this raised panel door set, are designed to work together with one cutting the rails (right), one the stiles (left), and one the raised panel (center).

Keeping Track of Bits

Because router bit profiles are the opposite of the shape they cut in the wood, selecting them can be confusing. Most bit manufacturers offer catalogs and websites with illustrations of the bit and the shape it cuts. These resources will help eliminate buying the wrong bit and are helpful when looking for the right profile for a project.

Portable Circular Saw

Function: Makes accurate rips and crosscuts
Features: Comfortable grips; base plate that is parallel to blade, with adjustable stops; available in right- or left-bladed versions
Price: $120 to $200

A good handheld circular saw, equipped with a quality blade, is more useful than many realize, especially in smaller spaces when you need to break down large pieces of material (see **Figure 2.69**). Being able to make these cuts with reasonable accuracy reduces the waste generated by making final cuts on the table saw. Guided by a clamped-on fence or a straight board, a circular saw can make rips and crosscuts with accuracy.

The qualities to look for in a circular saw are comfortable grips and a well-made, straight-sided base plate or sole that is parallel to the blade. The base plate should have adjustable stops at 90 and 45 degrees, with easy-to-use depth and bevel locks.

Power is not an issue because nearly all of the better circular saws are equipped with 15-amp motors that generate plenty of power on common electrical circuits.

Some circular saws are available in right- or left-bladed versions; which you choose is a matter of personal preference and comfort. I like left-bladed saws because I see the blade and the cut line better. Others like right-bladed ones for the same reasons.

The better circular saws cost between $120 and $200. Prices have come down in recent years, making it easier to get a good circular saw without breaking the tool budget.

Figure 2.69. A good circular saw can be a key component of small woodworking shops. Cutting large stock into pieces closer to the dimensions needed for a project can be done outside with the circular saw, and then the smaller pieces brought into the shop for final sizing and other operations.

Jigsaw

Function: Cuts curves, inside cuts; removes waste wood
Features: Balanced motors; quiet blade driving systems; top strap or barrel grip handle styles; fast, easy blade change; speed control; dust blower; adjustable base plate
Price: $125 to $175

Too often thought of as a small replacement for a band saw, the portable jigsaw does more than cut curves. These versatile saws can make inside cutouts and small cuts and are handy for cutting away the waste before finishing a template-based job with a router. Between blade stabilization and modern blade technology, the handheld jigsaw is more useful than ever before, though it is not much good for cutting a perfectly straight edge.

Better jigsaws have powerful, balanced motors and blade driving systems that virtually eliminate vibration. When fitted with a quality blade, jigsaws are easy to use accurately. There are two handle styles, the top strap and the barrel grip (see **Figure 2.70**). There is usually little difference in price and no difference in their effectiveness. The choice is purely a matter of what you like.

A good jigsaw will have fast and easy blade changing (see **Figure 2.71**), stroke control, speed control, a dust blower, and an adjustable base plate. As the overall quality and the price of the saw go up, so do its accuracy and ease of use.

A good-quality jigsaw will cost between $125 and $175. Beware of imitators with markedly lower prices because, in this case, what is inside really does count. If you fall for the low price, those insides are likely to count against you.

Do you need a jigsaw? It depends on what kind of work you do. If you already have a band saw or a scroll saw, maybe not. Many woodworkers use a good jigsaw frequently for small cuts, curved or not, especially on larger pieces of wood that can be difficult to handle at the band saw or table saw.

Figure 2.70. The two main styles of jigsaw are the top strap grip (rear) and the barrel grip (foreground). The handle style has nothing to do with how well the saw cuts, but woodworkers do differ in which style they like best.

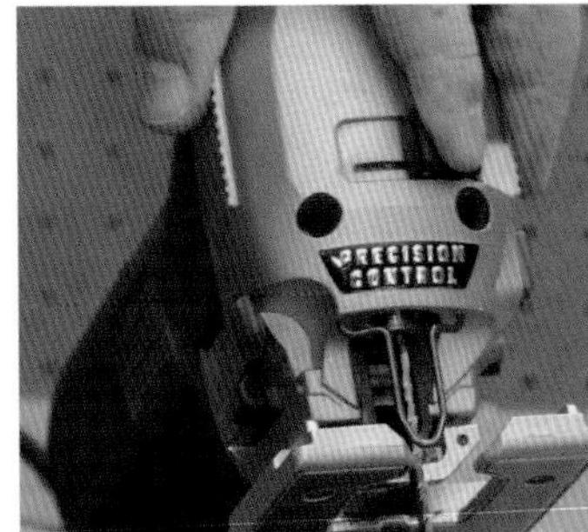

Figure 2.71. This jigsaw has a slider button that, when pushed, pops the blade out onto the bench. Installing a new blade is as easy as pushing it in until it clicks.

Sanders

Sanding projects may not be your favorite part of woodworking, but it makes a huge difference in the quality of whatever finish you apply. The type and quality of the sander will affect how tough that sanding job will be.

Random orbit sander

The new kid on the block, the random orbit sander (ROS) (see **Figure 2.72**) has quickly become a favorite of woodworkers because it strikes a good balance between removing material rapidly and creating a finish-ready surface.

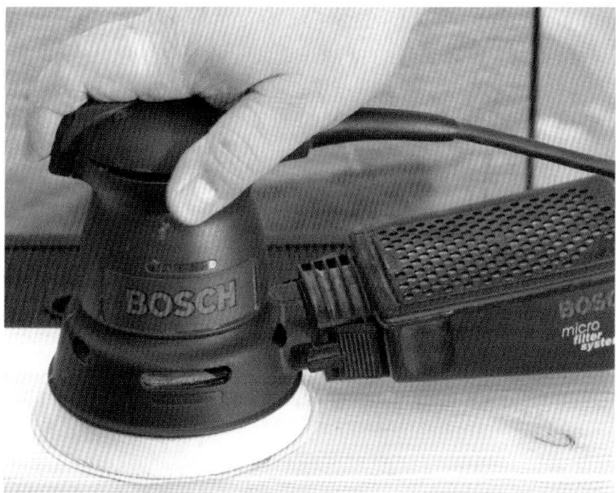

Figure 2.72. Random orbit sanders are the workhorse sanding machines in most shops. They can remove material quickly or polish the wood, depending on the grit of the disk attached.

The sander is so effective because its round pad spins and moves in an elliptical orbit at the same time. This dual motion eliminates the straight-line action that causes noticeable scratches in the wood.

You will have to choose between stick-on sanding disks and disks that mount with a hook and loop system. The hook and loop ones are better because you can remove and reuse the disks. With 80-grit to 150-grit disks, the random orbit sander can remove surprising amounts of wood very quickly, though nothing like a belt sander. Equipped with 320- or 400-grit paper, the ROS is capable of producing silky smooth surfaces on all types of wood.

A good ROS has a comfortable grip, hook and loop pad, and dust collection; some also have variable speed. Expect to pay between $50 and $150 for a good 4" or 5" (pad diameter) model.

Do you need a random orbit sander? Yes, it should be the first power sander you buy because it can do rough sanding almost as well as a belt sander and finish sanding almost as well as a palm sander.

Belt sander

Used almost exclusively for rough work, belt sanders are designed to remove lots of material quickly (see **Figure 2.73**). That makes them useless for finish sanding. The need for a belt sander seems to lessen as a woodworker gains experience and fewer joints have to be sanded flush.

For most woodworking shops, a belt sander with a 3"- or 4"-wide belt will handle all of your heavy

Figure 2.73. Belt sanders are handy for flattening large glued-up panels with joints that did not come out as level as you might have liked. Even with a fine-grit belt, these machines remove material very quickly.

Tool	Function	Features	Price
Random Orbit Sander	Creates fine finishes	Rapid material removal; creates a finish-ready surface; stick-on or mounted sanding disks; accepts up to 400-grit paper; dust collection; variable speed	$50 to $150
Belt Sander	Used for rough sanding work	Removes lots of material quickly; 3" to 4" belt; dust control	$100 to $200
Palm Sander	Light sanding with fine grits just before finishing or between finishing coats	No visible scratches; dust control; variable speed; easy paper changing	$40 to $100

sanding needs. The better belt sanders have effective dust control, good belt tracking, and easy belt changing systems. Expect to pay between $100 and $200 for a good belt sander.

Do you need a belt sander? Yes, if you find yourself trying to sand parts flush after assembly. Otherwise, it probably will stay in the drawer for extended periods, but it might save the day when you do need it.

Palm sander

A long-time favorite for finish work, vibration-based palm sanders (see **Figure 2.74**) remain best suited for light sanding with fine-grit paper just before finishing and in between finish coats. Modern palm sanders do not vibrate in a straight line but incorporate a small orbiting action that helps eliminate visible scratches. Nearly all palm sanders feature some form of dust control that is most efficient when connected to a vacuum.

Good palm sanders have a comfortable grip and easy paper changing. Some now offer variable speed as well. Expect to pay between $40 and $100 for a good, long-lasting model.

Do you need one? Newer and more versatile random orbit sanders have all but replaced these older machines. However, if you contemplate a lot of finicky finishing, the palm sander is best in between coats.

Figure 2.74. Palm grip sanders, equipped with fine-grit paper, excel at refining the surface of wood. Many woodworkers depend on a palm grip sander for the final sanding before finishing and often between finish coats.

Biscuit Joiner

Function: Cuts biscuit joints
Features: Adjustable fence, depth control, carbide-tipped blade
Price: $150 to $200

Figure 2.75. Biscuits are popular as an alternative method of joining wood. They also help align the parts. A biscuit joiner is easy and fast, and the biscuits themselves are relatively cheap.

Biscuit joiners came from Europe to America more than 40 years ago, but they are still news to many woodworkers. Simply put, they give you an alternate approach that can solve most joinery problems. The machine consists of a motor turning a small saw blade that is concealed inside the housing. When you press the machine's housing against the wood, the blade emerges a measured amount and cuts a crescent-shaped groove (see **Figure 2.75**).

To make a joint, you cut mating grooves in both pieces of wood. Then, you coat a flat, football-shaped biscuit made of pressed hardwood with glue, insert it into the slots, and clamp the joint to dry. The wood grain runs diagonally across the biscuit, making it very strong. The compressed wood expands to fill the slot when the moist glue hits it.

When you are edge-gluing boards, the biscuit is as much for alignment as for strength. When you are making frames and boxes, it is as strong as any other form of joint, and is much quicker to make. Biscuits come in three standard sizes, and you also can get hinges that mount in biscuit slots.

A good biscuit cutter has an adjustable fence that allows centering the biscuit slot on various wood thicknesses and making slots in the angled ends of miter joints. A depth control regulates blade exposure for cutting slots to match the various-size biscuits, and the cutter is equipped with a carbide-tipped blade. Expect to pay between $150 and $200.

Do you need a biscuit joiner? Some woodworkers consider them essential; others consider them a novelty. It's possible to make biscuits your primary joint for everything, putting you in the "essential" camp. If you already have good techniques for making panels, frames, and boxes, you can do without one.

Air Tools

Air nailers and staplers are very popular in woodworking, though they do require a small compressor for power. However, a compressor sized to run an air nailer efficiently may be inadequate for running other air-powered tools like drills, sanders, and impact drivers that require many times the amount of air for proper operation. You'll also be able to use the compressor for blowing dust out of machines and off your clothes, and into your breathing air.

Do you need air tools? No, but they are a reasonable choice in many situations, and having the ability to shoot brads makes fastening plywood backs on cabinets and many other "tacking" jobs much faster than pounding nails in by hand.

Compressor

Pancake-style and other small compressors (see **Figure 2.76**) are popular in woodshops because they take up little room but develop plenty of air for brad and finish nailers. They also have enough air power to blow up tires, balls, and mattresses and to make a simple nail gun dangerous if you are not paying attention. If you anticipate spraying finishes, even a little, you need a much bigger compressor because spray guns and other air-powered tools like drills and sanders require huge amounts of air.

Figure 2.76. Small air compressors are capable of powering most air nailers plus can be used with a blowgun to clear dust from large areas. They also earn brownie points when someone needs a tire, ball, or air mattress inflated.

Air tools have a label on them or their packaging that tells the amount of air they use. Compressors have a similar label listing how much air they make. Both are shown as cfm (cubic feet per minute) or scfm (standard cubic feet per minute). Use these labels to be sure the air tools you buy work with your compressor or the compressor you are buying produces enough air to operate your tools.

Shop-size air compressors cost between $125 and $400 depending on their cfm rating. Some manufacturers sell their nail guns in kits with a compressor, which assures you that you have a correct match and may even save you a few dollars.

Nailer

Nail guns are available for shooting anything from ½"-long brads to spikes that woodworkers should never consider using. Finish nailers are as big as you need (see **Figure 2.77**).

Figure 2.77. Good-quality air nailers are safe, are easy to use, and last a very long time in a home woodworking shop. However, trying to cheapen this purchase with a bargain nailer can be very disappointing.

Better nailers have adjustable depth settings that actually work and an aimable air exhaust. A relatively new feature is easy jam clearing in the form of a swing-open door on the front of the gun that exposes the fastener path. I have noticed that if you buy a good-quality gun with an effective jam-clearing feature, it won't jam. I have opened the jam-clearing door only to show someone how cool it is.

Tool	Function	Features	Price
Compressor	Supplies air for brad and finish nailers, spray finishes, drills, and sanders	Attaches directly to your tools	$125 to $400
Nailer	Shoots nails ½" long and longer	Adjustable depth settings; air exhaust; jam clearing; oil-free or oil versions	$75 to $200
Stapler	Shoots small staples; used for tacking wood or upholstery	Depth control	$75 to $200

Air nailers are available in oil-free and oiled versions. The oil-free models do not require you to do anything but supply air. The others require adding a few drops of oil to the air inlet before using it that day. I use the kind needing oil because they seem to have a little more power. A few people have warned me that oil-type air nailers will spread oil all over my projects, but in seven years of using them, that has not happened once.

Air nailers vary widely in price, depending on the size of fastener they handle, features, and quality. Expect to spend between $75 and $200 per gun, and remember the gun/compressor package deals.

Stapler

Air staplers shoot small, resin-coated staples instead of nails. They are great for tack-clamping pieces of wood together while glue dries—if you look inside upholstered furniture, you'll probably see gazillions of little staple scars.

Like air nailers, air staplers vary in price according to quality: $75 to $200. Do you need one? Air staplers are growing in popularity in part because of their increased versatility and the much-improved depth control on the better models that makes attaching thin plywood backs to cabinets simple and reliable. Air staplers are not for everyone, but their sales are growing rapidly, so somebody besides me is buying them!

> "You need chisels, planes, and handsaws. Even though power tools may be what really float your boat, hand tools will be necessary."

Hand tools

Even though power tools may be what really float your boat, hand tools will be necessary. There are plenty of occasions when you need to remove a little bit of wood from a location where the machine cutter just can't go. You need chisels, planes, and handsaws. Some woodworkers enjoy using hand tools more than their powered cousins, while others cringe at anything without a cord. Most woodworkers fall somewhere in the middle.

Chisels

Function: Removes small amounts of wood to make joints and mortises
Features: Quality steel, ¼" to 1" wide in size, available in sets
Price: $50 to $100

Chisels are for paring off small amounts of wood when making joints and other parts you want to fit neatly together. You can also use regular bevel-edged chisels for making hinge mortises, though for making deep mortises for joints, you'll want a special mortising chisel.

For most woodworkers, a set of good wood chisels with sizes from ¼" to 1" wide will handle common needs (see **Figure 2.78**). However, it is worthwhile to buy a set made from quality steel because the chisels will take and hold a sharp edge and last longer overall. Expect to spend between $50 and $100 for a five- or six-piece set that will last decades.

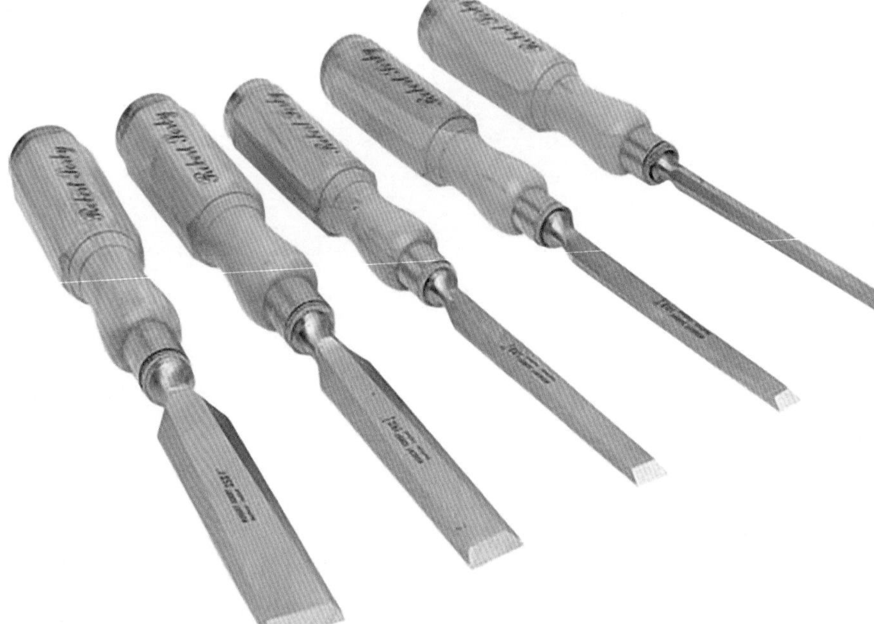

Figure 2.78. For most woodworkers, a set of good wood chisels will work for common tasks. Be sure to choose a set made from high-quality steel so that your tools last.

Mallet

Any pounding needs not met by the hammer can be taken care of by a good dead-blow mallet. Certain chisels must be hit with a wood or composite mallet, information that should be mentioned in the chisel's instructions. Many woodworkers prefer a wooden mallet, versions of which can be purchased or made in the shop. If you have a lathe in your shop, I'm pretty sure it is illegal to buy a mallet.

Planes

There are dozens of different kinds of planes for woodworking, but you only need a few (see **Figure 2.79**). Planes have a sharp blade like a chisel set in a cast-iron body with a flat sole so only the very edge peeks out through a slit in the sole. There's an adjustment for how much sharp edge sticks out, and also for tilting the edge to the right or left. They are for peeling the surface of the wood a shaving at a time to make it level, straight, and smooth. They do have to be perfectly sharp, and they do take some skill and practice to use. But when you get it right, they are delightful. You can take a smooth-planed surface directly to finishing, without any sanding, if you want.

Most woodworkers find plenty of good uses for a block plane, which is about 7" long and fits easily in one hand. You can use a block plane for paring end grain and for beveling or chamfering the sharp corners off a piece of wood to make it hand friendly. A cheap one will cost about $15, and a good one about $35.

You'll also find a smooth plane to be useful. It's a little larger than the block plane, about 10" long, and you hold it with two hands instead of one. It's for leveling and smoothing the surface of a piece of wood to make it ready for finishing. The disadvantage is using a smooth plane does require practice and skill. The advantage is you won't be breathing as much sanding dust. A cheap smooth plane costs about $30, while a good one is $50 or more.

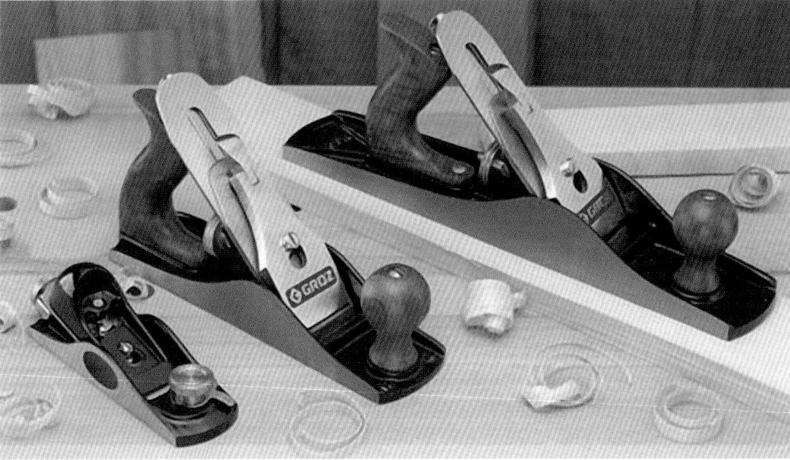

Figure 2.79. The longer the plane, the longer the surface it can flatten. Here are a 7" blade plane, a 10" smooth plane, and a 15" jack plane.

If you don't have a jointer and you do want to make perfectly straight and square edges for gluing together, try a jack plane (about 15" long) or a fore plane (about 20" or 22"). The long sole allows the plane to cut away hills and valleys in the edge; a shorter one would just follow the contours. It's hard to find a cheap one; a good one costs $100 and up.

Handsaw

Function: Removes wood that can't be removed with power tools
Features: Available with fine teeth or coarse teeth for crosscutting and ripping
Price: $20+

Handsaws may not be high on the must-have list, but they do come in handy on occasion. Fine-toothed ones have 12 to 16 teeth per inch and are best for cutting across the wood grain. Coarser teeth, around 6 or 8 to the inch, are for ripping with the grain. If you're a machine woodworker like I am, you'll get most of your sawing done with power tools. But there will be a time when you have to remove a notch of wood or cut something after assembling it to other parts, and you won't have any choice but to hand saw. A good handsaw will cost at least $20.

Tool	Function	Features	Price
Block Plane	Pares end grain; bevels or chamfers off sharp corners	7" long; fits in one hand	$15 to $35
Smooth Plane	Levels and smoothes wood surface for finishing	10" long; used with two hands	$30 to $50 or more
Jack Plane or Fore Plane	Makes edges straight and square for glue-up	15" long (jack plane); 20" or 22" long (fore plane)	$100 or more

Chapter 3

Tool Setup, Alignment, and Maintenance

Most woodworking machines require you to set them up and align them properly before they can work for you. It's your chance to learn more about how the machine works and how it is set up so you can restore those settings periodically. Setting aside time to go over the adjustments and alignments of your equipment on a regular basis will head off problems that could damage the equipment, the work, or you. You paid good money for the equipment in your shop, and staying current on the maintenance will go a long way toward protecting your investment and your safety.

The time saved by not checking them over could cost you dearly in premature repairs or replacement. Left misaligned, power tools will wear themselves out at an ever-increasing rate. In addition to performance, setup and alignment are important for safety. If a machine is working improperly, you risk doing something dangerous trying to get the wood through it. Nothing good will come from trying to overcome a setup or alignment error with bad technique. Machines that are properly tuned produce straighter cuts, smoother finishes, and less scrap. Machines that are properly aligned work easier and last longer.

In this chapter, we'll review the particulars of tool alignment as they apply to common shop tools like table saws, jointers, and drill presses. Then, we'll take a look at the myths and facts of tool maintenance and address some basic troubleshooting issues.

Tools and accuracy

Woodworkers disagree over the level of accuracy necessary when performing setup or alignment. Some shoot for perfection, while others stop at close enough.

I am on the perfection side; I like accuracy. To me, there is logic in spending money on a well-made machine and then using high-resolution tools to align it as perfectly as possible (see **Figures 3.1** and **3.2**). I enjoy shaving a few thousandths of an inch off the manufacturer's specs. When the spec says 0.005" is the acceptable tolerance, dialing the machine in to 0.002" or less makes my day. Besides, accurately aligned machines run better, cut cleaner, and wear less on things like $60 blades. I enjoy that part of it also.

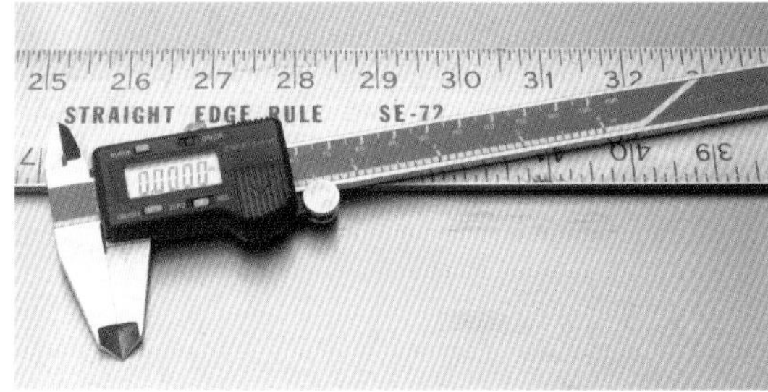

Figure 3.1. Fine-tolerance tools for alignment, measuring, or layout help adjust your machines closer to perfect and your layout lines and measurements spot on, making your projects that much better. Here are a precision digital caliper and a steel straightedge.

Figure 3.2. Buying good alignment tools is a wise investment that will help keep your equipment performing as it was designed. An out-of-alignment machine works harder and cannot produce good results.

Safety Tip: Setup Safety

Get in the habit of unplugging tools and machines whenever they are being worked on. Unless you are actually cutting wood, there is no reason to take the risk of leaving a tool connected to the electrical power. While you are leaning into its guts, you very easily could bump into the on button. An accidental startup may be rare but will almost certainly cause devastating injuries when it does occur.

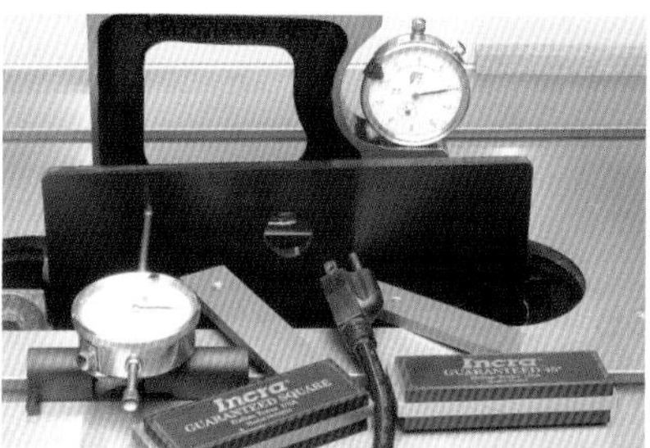

Alignment and adjustment put your hands close to the blade and other workings of a machine. To be safe, unplug the machine. Get in the habit of laying the plug on the work surface where you can see it.

Setup and alignment of new machines

Manufacturers generally do a good job with the alignments that can be set prior to packaging. We have to remember that the folks performing these alignments are just as human as we are, which makes at least checking their work a good idea.

The manufacturer's setup parameters, along with instructions on how to achieve them, are included in the literature supplied with the tool or machine. They should be read (and understood) before assembling anything.

While you most often think of setup and alignment as being for equipment like table saws and jointers, it is equally important on smaller tools. If it has a blade or cutter and a way to adjust the cut in any way, there is an alignment that should be at least checked.

Perfect Versus Close Enough

When I set up my machines, my alignment tools give me tolerances of 0.001", that's one-thousandth of an inch, which I consider "close enough." Other people use simpler tools with tolerances closer to 0.01", or one-hundredth of an inch; that's ten times more slop. How do they get away with it?

They'd say that woodworking is inherently inexact, the tiniest speck of sawdust will throw you off by more than 0.01", and the wood can expand that much in response to humidity changes.

I still think it makes sense to get as close as you can. You will have to decide what makes most sense to you.

Sequence and Points of Reference

Sometimes setup and alignment are part of the assembly process as described in the instructions. Other times these procedures are to be done after the machine is fully assembled. In either case, make sure you go through the complete setup and alignment process before using the machine. You've waited this long; a little longer won't hurt you, while rushing just might.

Setup and alignment procedures usually must be done in order. That's because the alignment of one part creates the basis for aligning the one that comes next. If the manual specifies a sequence, follow it exactly and double-check each setting to be sure it is correct before moving on to the next step.

Reading through the entire procedure before starting will help give you a better understanding of how to do it, especially if you are new to the tool or machine. Unfortunately, it may be necessary to read some manuals a few times just to understand what is loosely called a translation. Fortunately, there are pictures to help puzzle it out.

Alignment tools

Like anything else, setup and alignment tools come in a variety of styles, qualities, and prices. You can do "close enough" alignment with simple layout tools you may already own (see Layout and Measuring Tools on page 38). But I think this is a good place to invest the extra cash to buy the best tools your budget will allow. These tools are not used constantly and, with a little care, will last forever. I used cheaper alignment tools in the past, and the frustrating experiences with them are largely responsible for my owning the much better ones I use now.

There are people who can achieve remarkable accuracy with sticks, screws, and feeler gauges (see Sticks and Screws on page 88). I am not one of those people. Judging by the number of e-mails I receive on this subject, neither are many of you. I rely on the dial indicator devices discussed in New Tools! at right.

New Tools!

I achieve great accuracy with these measurement tools, but there are other tools made by other manufacturers similar to those described here that you might like just as well.

SuperBar and MasterPlate—The SuperBar and MasterPlate are for aligning the table saw blade and fence. The square MasterPlate, $49, is installed in place of the blade and provides a thick, extremely flat, non-flexing surface from which to measure. The SuperBar, $69, can be adjusted to fit in the miter slot without play and comes with a dial indicator mounted on top for measuring the distance to the blade or fence anywhere along the miter slot.

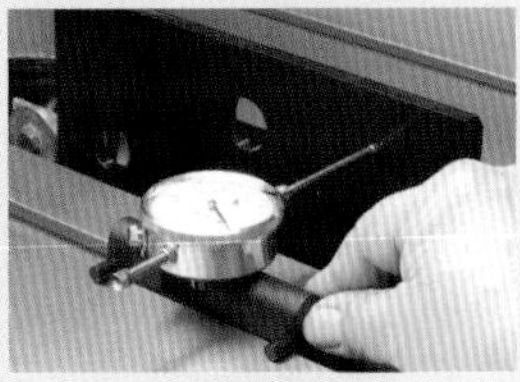

The SuperBar and MasterPlate bring a high degree of accuracy to aligning the blade and the fence to the miter slot. Getting these alignments right makes your saw cut cleaner, easier, and safer.

Multi-Gauge—The Multi-Gauge frame has three sides machined square that can be used for checking fences or blades to be sure they are actually square to the table. The fourth side houses a built-in dial indicator. The Multi-Gauge, $80, can set blade and bit heights to an exact dimension above the table with amazing precision. Probably most impressive is its ability to compare the height of one surface to another, invaluable when adjusting router plates, table saw inserts, planer knives, and jointer knives.

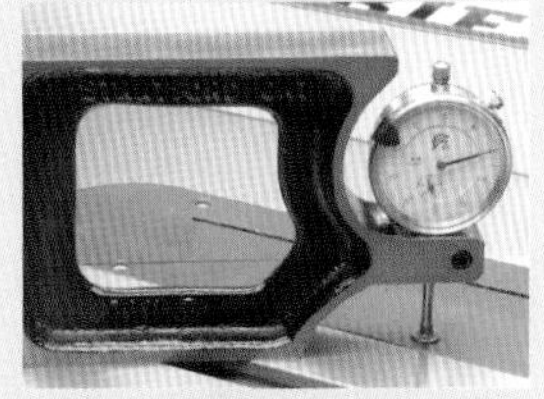

The Multi-Gauge is another simple but ingenious and highly accurate measuring device for setting bit, blade, and knife heights. It also works great for aligning jointer knives and for leveling table saw inserts and router lift plates.

Incra Square—Small squares, big squares, 90-degree, 45-degree, and sliding combination squares all have multiple uses in a woodworking shop and are invaluable for setting up machines. I keep a specific few squares in padded boxes and bring them out only for fine work and machine setup. Made by Incra, these $40 squares are pricey but are exceptionally accurate and will stay that way as long as I don't hit them with the car. Starrett is another great brand for accurate squares.

Using high-precision 45-degree and 90-degree squares allows me to dial in my machines very precisely. If the cuts are not right, the project cannot come out square.

Table saw alignments

All table saw alignments are based on measurements taken from a single spot on the flat face of the saw blade just below the gullets between the teeth, or from the SuperPlate installed in the blade's place. A correctly aligned saw will have its blade and fence parallel to the miter gauge slots in the table. Many woodworkers tail the fence away from the blade slightly (0.001" or 0.002") to help prevent the wood from rubbing against the teeth on the back side of the blade. The blade's 90-degree and 45-degree stops should also be set very accurately. The miter gauge should be set exactly 90 degrees to the miter slot. Some recommend setting the miter gauge so it is square to the blade, but, unless the blade is exactly parallel to the miter slot, you are simply transferring any error there to the miter gauge, thereby ensuring the cuts made with it will not be perfectly square. Following are a few alignments and adjustments with which you should be familiar.

Assembly

During assembly, most table saws require aligning the pulley on the motor to the pulley at the blade so the belt runs true. If the pulleys are out of alignment, the belt will wear quickly and could come off during operation. This is true of all belt drive machines.

For this alignment, hold a straightedge against the sides of the pulleys, as shown in **Figure 3.3**. Usually one side of the pulleys will be in line with each other when the motor is positioned correctly, and the straightedge gives you a clear picture of how close that alignment is.

Some table saw fence systems have rails that may require adjusting to properly locate and support the fence in relation to the table surface. This will be described in the manual, including how to adjust them if they are not correct when assembled.

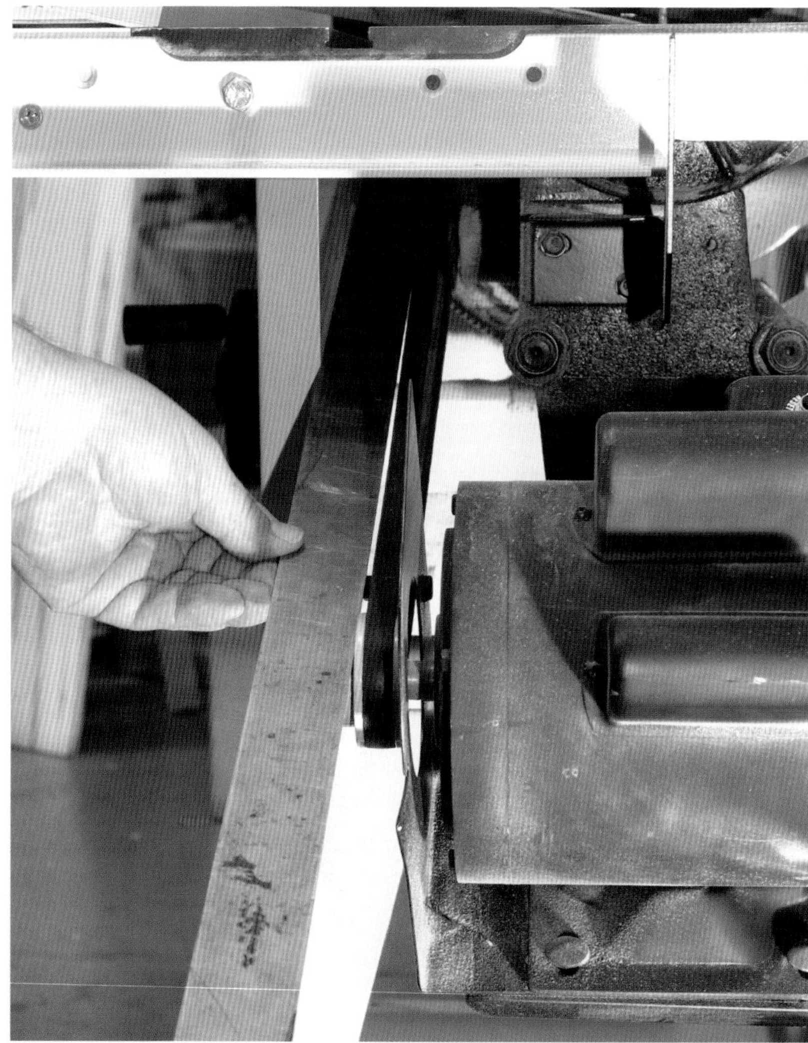

Figure 3.3. An aluminum yardstick makes it easy to align a motor pulley with the one at the saw's arbor. The machine may run if the pulleys are not aligned, but the belt life will be shortened considerably and it could jump off.

Tip!

Tailing the Fence

Many, including myself, like to tail the fence away from the blade at the rear by 0.001" or 0.002". This tiny amount of angle away from the blade at the rear ensures that the wood is released from the blade as the cut is completed, not squeezed into it. If the fence angles toward the blade, even just several thousandths of an inch, the wood is pushed against the teeth as they come up from the table. This greatly increases the chance of the stock lifting and being thrown, an occurrence better known as kickback.

Aligning Your Table Saw

1. Check the pulley alignment.
2. Determine if there is any blade runout.
3. Determine if there is any arbor runout.
4. Make sure the blade is parallel to the slots milled in the table surface.
5. Set the rip fence so it is parallel to the miter slot.
6. Square the miter guide to the blade.

Figure 3.4. When checking blade runout (saw unplugged!), put the indicator tip slightly below the deepest gullets between the teeth, and slowly turn the blade by hand with the belt. Pushing anywhere on the blade itself—including with a stick as in this photo—will make it flex, confusing the readings.

Blade Runout

Once the saw is assembled, the first thing you'll want to do is determine if there is any runout (wobble) in the blade or the arbor to which it mounts. Excessive runout will cause errors in adjustments made later. While runout in a new table saw is unusual, getting in the habit of checking for it can prevent problems later. Typical manufacturing tolerance is 0.001" per inch of blade diameter for runout. If you find runout greatly exceeding that in a new machine, you probably should return it to the dealer. Follow these steps to check for runout:

1. Raise the blade fully and place the dial indicator probe just inside the gullets near the front of the blade, as shown in **Figure 3.4**. Make a dot with a felt-tipped pen where the probe touches the blade.
2. Zero the scale on the dial indicator and slowly turn the blade using the motor pulley or belt. Do not touch the blade itself. Turn the blade a full revolution while watching the dial indicator. If there is more than 0.003" of change, I look for the reason.
3. If runout is discovered at the blade, remove the blade and place the dial indicator probe on the edge of the arbor, as shown in **Figure 3.5**, and zero the scale. Rotate the arbor using the motor pulley or belt and watch the indicator face. If the arbor shows any runout, call the manufacturer to discuss it.

   If the arbor appears to be good, try cleaning the arbor and washers before reinstalling the blade. Small bits of sawdust or other buildup can make a straight blade wobble. If that does not eliminate the runout, try another blade.

Figure 3.5. If you measure excessive runout at the blade (most manufacturers allow 0.001" per inch of blade diameter), remove the blade and place the indicator tip on the inside arbor washer and repeat the test. A few specks of dust between the blade and the washer can cause bad runout readings.

Blade Parallelism

You want the face of the blade to be parallel to the slots milled in the table surface. To check parallelism using the blade, you first must eliminate deviations in the blade itself or the arbor. To do that, make a dot just below one of the gullets between the teeth. Rotate the blade so that the dot is toward the front of the saw. Set up the dial indicator (or whatever you are measuring with) so that the probe is on that dot and then zero the scale, as shown in **Figure 3.6**.

Rotate the blade so the dot is at the rear of the saw, slide the indicator to the rear of the blade, place the probe on that same dot, and note any difference (see **Figure 3.7**). The difference between the front and rear readings shows what corrections are needed to make the blade parallel to the miter slot.

When using a purpose-designed testing fixture like the MasterPlate in place of the blade, parallelism readings can be taken over a much wider area, making them more accurate. I can get blade parallelism within 0.001" or less. I spent a half hour setting the blade parallelism on my new Delta contractor saw and finished with no measurable error. It came from the factory at just over 0.002" out of parallel—I have a hard time leaving well enough alone.

Adjusting for parallel

On cabinet saws, you generally make this adjustment by loosening the table from the base and shifting it slightly to make the needed correction. On contractor saws, the blade mechanism will be attached to the underside of the table, so you have to loosen the bolts and shift the mechanism itself. Three of the four bolts are easy to access, but usually one of the front bolts is very difficult to reach. Looking up from under the saw and using socket wrenches on an extension or two is often the only way to get at that bolt.

Loosening the bolts and then snugging them down lightly will make it easier to bump the assembly into alignment. To avoid damage, I tap on the undercarriage mounting boss with a piece of wood and a dead-blow hammer. Be sure to recheck the alignment after tightening the bolts because it can change. I had a contractor saw that always changed by 0.005" in the same direction when I tightened the bolts. After fighting this with different washers and lubricants, I simply overadjusted the blade mechanism by 0.005" before tightening the bolts. Then, it lined up perfectly.

Figure 3.6. When using a dial indicator on the blade to measure parallelism to the miter slot, use one spot on the blade to eliminate any runout. Make a dot below a gullet, and turn the blade so the dot is as far forward as possible.

Figure 3.7. Turn the blade so the dot is as far to the rear as possible, place the dial indicator on the dot, and take another reading. The difference between the readings at the front and rear represents the current blade parallelism.

Rip Fence

I also use the SuperBar to set the rip fence so it is parallel to the miter slot. Here again, the process is extremely accurate, which is a good thing. A fence that is off by as little as 0.01", especially if it is tailed toward the blade at the rear, can cause the wood to rub against the back half of the blade, leaving rough edges and making kickbacks more likely.

To check the fence, lower the blade completely below the table surface to get it out of the way. Install the dial indicator in the left miter slot near the front of the table, slide the fence over until it depresses the indicator probe about ½", and then lock the fence down. Zero the dial indicator scale, and then slide it to the rear of the table, noting the difference in readings (see **Figure 3.8**).

Adjust the fence as necessary and repeat to check the new alignment. On most fences, you make the adjustment with a couple of readily accessible bolts or screws; check the manual to find them. While you are at it, make sure the fence locking mechanism works easily and holds securely.

Remember, it is better to have the back end of the fence tailing minutely away from the blade rather than toward it. If the fence angles toward the blade at the rear, even a little, it squeezes the wood against the spinning teeth, and that's how kickbacks begin. With the rear of the fence tailing away from the blade, the wood is released at the end of the cut.

I have been able to keep my fence within 0.002" of parallel with that little bit of error showing that the fence tailed away from the blade at the rear.

Figure 3.8. Use the dial indicator to set the saw's rip fence parallel to the blade. I use the SuperBar to set up my rip fence. With the blade lowered below the table surface, slide the fence over to the SuperBar, lock it down, and carefully slide the SuperBar the full length of the miter slot, noting any change along the way.

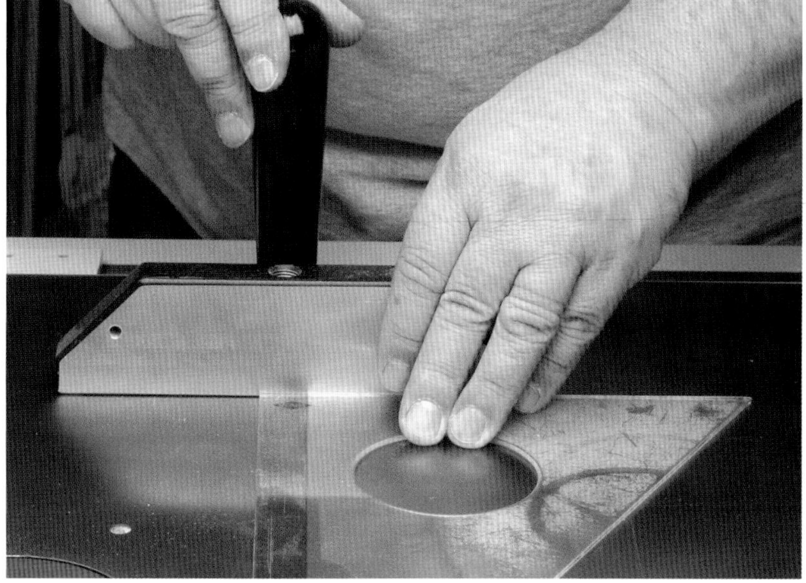

Figure 3.9. Use a drafting triangle to align the miter guide fence to the miter slot. It is more accurate than using a square against the blade.

Squaring the Miter Guide

Manufacturers sometimes advise squaring the miter guide (also called a miter gauge) to the blade. This is the simple way of doing it, and, if the blade is exactly parallel to the miter slot, it is accurate. However, if the blade is not exactly parallel to the miter slot, squaring the miter guide to it just replicates that error. I prefer to square the miter guide to the miter slot instead of the blade. That way, if the blade is slightly out of parallel, it will cut a slightly wider kerf, but the edge of the wood being cut will be square.

I use a plastic, 14" drafting triangle that has a 90-degree corner on the long leg; any accurate square with a 12" leg can be used. Place the base of the square against the miter guide fence, as shown in **Figure 3.9**, and align the long side to the edge of the miter slot. Adjust the miter guide fence until the square is even with the miter slot over its entire length, and set the stop on the gauge so you can return it to this setting. That's it. This is an accurate (and easy) way to align the miter guide.

New Wood-Word: Kerf

Kerf: The width of material that is removed by the saw blade. Most common blades are ⅛" thick, so when perfectly aligned, they will remove ⅛" of wood.

Sticks and Screws

If a dial indicator setup is not in the offing, you can make a stick and screw device for table saw alignment (see **Figure 3.10**); that is much better than eyeballs alone or wishful thinking. Some folks are able to do a very good alignment with this seemingly primitive (and cheap) device, though I have never been able to approach the accuracy of a dial indicator.

One thing that concerns me about the stick and screw method is the flexibility of the table saw blade. You often think of blades as rigid, but, in reality, pressing near the outer edge of a 10" blade will produce small deflections that can compromise the accuracy of the stick and screw device with surprising ease. Keep in mind that regardless of what is used to take the measurement, pressing on the side of the blade can seriously compromise accuracy. That's why I like the MasterPlate—it can't deflect.

Some folks slide a feeler gauge between the screw and blade to measure the gap. I have done this with a dial indicator on the opposite side of the blade and noticed deflections up to 0.007" without noticeable resistance to the feeler gauge. That kind of error makes trying to get a blade within a few thousandths of parallel all but impossible.

To build a stick and screw fixture, follow these steps:

1. Cut a 6" piece of hardwood sized to fit your miter slot as closely as possible. If it turns out undersize, apply strips of masking tape until it fits the slot without any wiggling.
2. Cut a piece of ¼" or ½" plywood to the shape shown in **Figure 3.11**. It should be long enough for the screw to reach the blade, and it should extend across the miter slot a few inches for stability. Using glue and a couple brads, secure the plywood to the runner strip.
3. Next, make a small block with a hole for the screw, and drill a pilot hole close to its bottom. Glue the block to the end of the plywood arm, and, when it's dry, thread a screw into the hole.

Figure 3.10. Some folks can align the table saw very satisfactorily with this simple shop-built jig plus an automotive feeler gauge. I have never been able to equal the precision of a dial indicator with devices like this.

Figure 3.11. When making this jig, be sure the runner fits the miter slot snugly so the whole thing cannot wiggle. Any side play at the miter slot makes attaining an accurate setup impossible.

4. To use the stick and screw device on either the blade or the fence, adjust the screw so it is close to the surface being measured and then slide it along, watching the gap to find the closest point. Adjust the screw so it just touches at that point, slide it back to the other end, and use feeler gauges to measure that gap. Make small adjustments to the blade or fence, and repeat the process until there is no difference at each end.

When using the stick and screw device to adjust the fence, leave a tiny gap at the rear. A good set of feeler gauges will have a leaf in the 0.002" range. If you can adjust the gap at the rear of the fence to fit that thickness, it will be tailed away from the blade sufficiently.

Safety Tip: Unplug It Already!

By now, I should not have to remind you to unplug a machine before working on it, and better yet, throw the breaker it's connected to. This eliminates any risk of accidental startup with your hands in the works. Just do it.

The instruction manual may suggest tools that can be used to complete the alignment and setup procedures. If you do not have dial indicators and such, follow those suggestions, take your time, and be as accurate as possible. Investing a little extra time will be more than worth it when the machine runs smoothly and performs well afterward.

> “The circular saw is a must-have, but it’s also one of the most dangerous tools. When properly aligned, the circular saw cuts cleanly with little tendency to kick back.”

Portable circular saw alignments

Portable circular saws have come a long way in terms of design, quality, and cut capabilities. It is a must-have tool, especially in smaller shops, for reducing large materials to more manageable sizes. There are only three alignments to check.

Something to keep in mind is that in terms of overall injuries sustained, the handheld circular saw is one of the most dangerous tools in existence. That is due in large part to the huge number of occasional users who have virtually no experience with the tool and the fact that they have no concept of what it takes to align it properly. When properly aligned, the circular saw cuts cleanly with little tendency to kick back. Here are the steps for aligning a circular saw:

1. Unplug the saw and adjust the shoe so it’s parallel to the blade face.
2. Extend the blade fully and lock it in that position.
3. Place a combination square against the outside edge of the shoe, and extend its rule until it just touches the blade body (not a tooth). Lock the rule and slide it across the blade, keeping the shoulder of the combination square tight against the shoe (see **Figure 3.12**). The end of the rule should stay against the blade as it slides. If it does not, the shoe has to be tweaked until it does.

   Some circular saws have provisions for adjusting the shoe so it is parallel to the blade. If yours does, it will say how to do that in the manual. If this adjustment is not present, you may have to bend one of the shoe mounts slightly. Be careful that bending a mount does not affect the bevel mechanism. On some saws, you can place thin shims under the shoe plate mounting screws at the saw housing to correct parallelism.
4. Adjust the shoe so it is 90 degrees to the blade, according to its scale indicator. Use a good square to check that, and adjust as needed (see **Figure 3.13**).
5. Set the shoe to 45 degrees, verify the shoe-to-blade angle, and make any adjustments needed. Return the shoe to 90 degrees and recheck that. Better circular saws have adjustments for correcting the 90- and 45-degree settings, so check your manual.

Keeping the shoe aligned helps the saw cut cleaner, makes it easier to follow the layout line, and makes the saw safer to use.

Figure 3.12. Use a combination square to check whether the circular saw blade is parallel to the edge of its guide shoe.

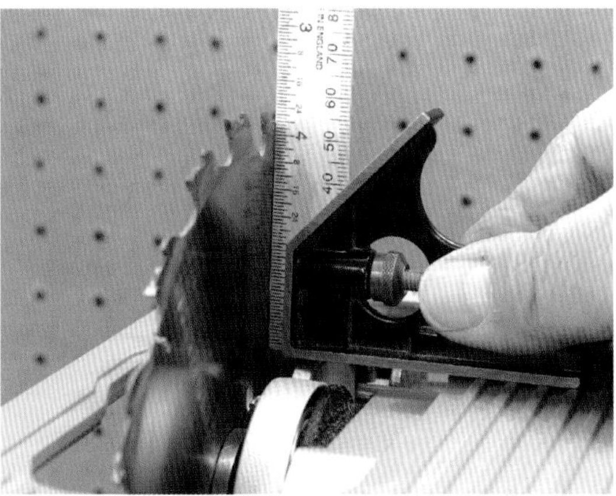

Figure 3.13. Portable circular saws usually have adjustable stops at 90 degrees and 45 degrees. Take the time to get those stops perfect.

Jointer alignments

While the jointer is an old machine that has changed little over the years, it can be tough to align if you do not understand it. When it's not aligned, the workpiece can develop scallops and tapers that you didn't intend.

Like the shaper and router table fence, the jointer's table surface is divided into an infeed side and an outfeed side, with the cutter head in between them. The infeed and outfeed tables have to be aligned with each other on two planes: left to right and front to back. When the tables are properly aligned on both of these planes, they are said to be coplanar. All of the jointers I have had in the shop arrived from the factory with the tables perfectly aligned. Many of the better jointers have their tables assembled to the bases and then have a final truing cut taken across their surfaces to ensure they are coplanar. However, if you do not check this, the woodworking spirits will make sure the tables are out of alignment, and the resulting cuts will make you crazy. Though unlikely, it is possible to knock one of the tables out of alignment.

Align the Tables

All you need to do a basic check of the jointer tables is a pair of accurate framing squares. Follow these steps:

1. Disconnect the power supply and get the fence and guard out of the way. Then, rotate the cutter head so none of the knives are pointed up.
2. Put the long leg of each square on one of the tables and butt the vertical legs against each other. If there is no gap anywhere along the edges of the squares that are touching, chances are good that your tables are in line side to side (see **Figure 3.14**).
3. If a gap develops when you slide the squares from the rear to the front of the tables, something needs adjusting. Jointers vary in how to do this adjustment, so check the instruction manual. If directions are not shown there, contact the manufacturer for specific instructions on how to adjust the tables on your jointer. Nearly all jointers have adjusting screws along the keyway where the tables meet the base. In most cases, these gib screws adjust the play between the table and the keyway, not the attitude of the table. Most often, shims must be added between the table runners and the keyways to correct table misalignments. Getting specific instructions from the manufacturer for making this kind of correction on your jointer is strongly advised.
4. The jointer works by having its outfeed table parallel to the cutter head and level with the knives at the top dead-center position. Though some outfeed tables have a height adjustment, there are few reasons for the average woodworker to use it. When I get a new jointer in the shop, I make sure that the outfeed table is flush with the knives, lock it down, and leave it alone. Controlling cut depth is made by adjusting the height of the infeed table.

Set the Knives

With the tables in the same plane, you can set the jointer's knives so they are parallel to the outfeed table and level with its surface at top dead center. This is the same procedure used when installing new

Aligning Your Jointer

1. Make sure the infeed and outfeed tables are aligned left to right and front to back.
2. Set the knives so they are parallel to the outfeed table and level with its surface.
3. Adjust the fence so it is at a 90-degree angle to the outfeed table.

Figure 3.14. A pair of framing squares set on the jointer tables will show how well those tables are aligned to each other.

Safety Tip: Protect Your Hand

Adjusting jointer knives usually involves loosening and tightening a row of fasteners that hold each knife in its pocket. If a fastener breaks free unexpectedly, you're liable to slice your hand on the knife. Positioning the wrench so you are pulling away from the knives or covering them with a piece of scrap plywood will help keep your day blood-free.

knives or after sharpening the old ones. Smaller jointers may have two knives while larger and better-quality machines have three or even four. The owner's manual will show what system should be used to retain and adjust the knives.

The key to setting jointer knives correctly is getting them all flush with the outfeed table surface over their full length. That allows all of the knives to cut equally to produce the best finish and distribute wear evenly. There are a number of tools designed to make aligning jointer knives easier and more accurate. I use the Oneway Multi-Gauge (see New Tools! on page 83) and find it the easiest way to get all the knives perfectly level and even with the outfeed table. Here's how to get the knives level using the Multi-Gauge:

1. Set the dial indicator to read zero with the probe on the outfeed table (see **Figure 3.15**).

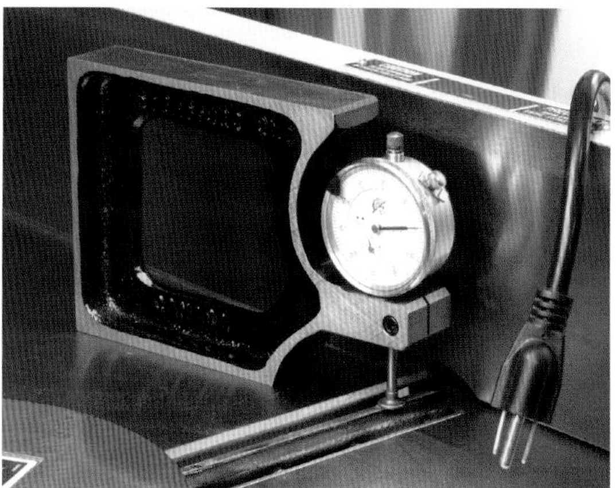

Figure 3.15. An indicator like this Multi-Gauge makes it easy to set the height of jointer knives so they are even with the outfeed table across their full length.

2. Move the probe so it rests on the edge of the knife currently at top dead center, and adjust the knife in its pocket so the indicator reads zero again. Check the setting at both ends of each knife to be sure it is parallel to the table surface. This can be a tedious process but is much easier with a tool like the Multi-Gauge that shows tiny changes in knife height very clearly.
3. Repeat the process on the remaining knives.

Some use a straightedge or a straight piece of wood held on the outfeed table surface and over the knives, and they adjust each knife to it. With practice, you might be able to get the knives close with this technique, but achieving the level of accuracy made possible by a good dial indicator is unlikely. If you are like me, using the Multi-Gauge saves lots of time and even more frustration. Ensuring that all of the knives are working equally delays having to replace them, which ends up saving money.

Adjust the Fence

Start by checking the fence in its 90-degree position. Using a good square, be sure the fence is exactly 90 degrees to the outfeed table (see **Figure 3.16**). Once that is set perfectly, slide the square down the fence to be sure the rest of the outfeed table and then the infeed table are also square to the fence. If a gap develops between the square and the fence or the table, look at both surfaces to see if one has a twist or warp. This kind of defect is very rare and seldom can be repaired by an adjustment. Warps and twists have to be ground out of the surface, an operation that can be done by most machine shops.

Figure 3.16. Since the jointer is the basis for squaring wood, take the time to be certain the fence is actually 90 degrees to the table.

Drill press alignments

A major reason to have a drill press is drilling holes that are straight and square to the surface of the wood. Rather than assume the drill press table angle indicator is accurate, check it yourself. Here are the steps:

1. Install a large twist drill in the chuck and tighten it down.
2. Set the table so your square can rest on the table surface with its leg against the side of the drill without contacting the chuck (see **Figure 3.17**).
3. Check the table angle to the drill front to back and side to side. Side-to-side adjustments are usually easy, made by loosening a locking bolt commonly found under the table or at the rear of it. When you get it right, tighten the locking bolt and zero the scale or pointer.
4. If the table is out of square to the drill front to back, check the manual, but there probably will be no adjustment. Contacting the manufacturer may be the only course of action. The good news is that this is a rare problem and one most often found on bargain-priced machines.

Figure 3.17. The drill press must be aligned if you expect holes to be drilled square to the surface of the wood.

Tool maintenance and troubleshooting

After a new tool is set up and aligned, its need for periodic care is only beginning. Even though everything is operating as expected, taking the time to maintain the machine will extend its life, ensure it continues to operate properly, and, in more ways than you might suspect, keep your shop safe.

Get in the habit of checking the alignment of your tools on a regular schedule. How frequently depends on how often the tools are used. I try to check most of my machines once a month if nothing bad is happening. If problems develop in the performance of a machine, I check the alignments first. It is far more common to find an alignment issue than a failure of the machine.

Sawdust

Like it or not, woodworkers generate lots of sawdust that has to be cleaned up—and not just to keep the shop looking spiffy. The longer sawdust is left lying around, the better chance it has to find its way into places where it can do the most harm, such as the inner workings of motors and switches. Gears and slides all function much better without sawdust being packed into them.

Using an air gun to blast sawdust from your machines is fun but may drive it further into bad places rather than out of them. Using a brush or a vacuum is safer for the machine as well as for your eyes and lungs (see **Figure 3.18**).

Regular Maintenance Checklist

Check and realign tools as necessary.

- Use a brush or a vacuum to remove sawdust from machines.
- Clean router collet parts and the receptacle machined into the spindle.
- Lubricate working machine parts.
- Remove rust spots from cast iron and apply paste wax.
- Clean blades and cutters.
- Sharpen edge tools.

Figure 3.18. If you use compressed air to blow the sawdust out of the mechanism, you may actually just drive it in deeper. Brush it off and vacuum it up.

Clean the Collet

Sawdust and other contaminants normally found in wood can pack up inside router collets, hardening into a shiny residue that interferes with gripping on the cutter. Cleaning the collet parts and the receptacle machined into the spindle into which they fit is an important bit of regular maintenance. WD-40 and a round brass-bristle brush, which you might have to buy from a gun store, can make the job easier.

Figure 3.19. Here's a useful array of products, none containing any silicone, for cleaning and lubricating woodworking machinery.

Lubrication

The fact that woodworking tools and machines generate large amounts of wood dust complicates their lubrication needs. Too often, a lubricant such as white grease that would seem best suited for making gears or shafts operate freely is exactly the wrong material for the job. In addition to their ability to make things slippery, most lubricants also attract and then hold dust. Another problem with common lubricants is that many contain silicone. While high in lubrication capability, silicone is even more effective at preventing finish from sticking to wood that has become contaminated with it. Silicone also migrates from one surface to another and then onto yet another, and ultimately onto your workpiece. Fortunately, the science of modern lubrication provides dry lubricants that contain no silicones and, when applied correctly, do not attract significant quantities of wood dust (see **Figures 3.19** and **3.20**).

Lubricating the moving parts of your tools and equipment is almost a no-brainer. Before applying a new dose of lubricant to a gear set or slide, clean the surface thoroughly. Even the best dry lubricant may attract and hold some amount of dust, particularly very fine dust. Applying a new layer of lube over that will not make it go away.

Figure 3.20. A spray-on dry lubricant will keep this pulley mechanism running freely without encouraging sawdust to build up.

Rust

Cast iron has been the favorite material for saw and jointer tables as well as many other parts of woodworking machines. While it is heavy, durable, and stable, it rusts very easily. Nothing makes a woodworker sound as if somebody just kicked his puppy more than finding a rust spot on a saw table.

Aside from humidity, prime causes of rust in the wood shop are unnoticed drops of sweat, condensation from a soft drink, and even dust from cutting a piece of wood with a high moisture content. Once rust begins, it must be removed before anything can be done to prevent it from happening again.

There are commercially prepared concoctions such as TopSaver (Empire Manufacturing) that I have found to be particularly good at dissolving, neutralizing, and then preventing rust. With a little rubbing, they seem to get all the rust out. Other people use more common materials like WD-40 or other thin, non-silicone lubricants. With steel wool or ScotchBrite pads and some elbow grease, a rust spot can usually be removed (see **Figure 3.21**). Keep in mind that even though the rust itself is removed, a visible spot will remain because a small amount of the metal is lost as rust forms. If you catch these spots early enough, the cleaned-up area will be barely noticeable. After removing the rust, clean the surface thoroughly.

Figure 3.21. TopSaver does a good job of removing rust from cast-iron surfaces, so long as you add elbow grease with steel wool or a plastic abrasive pad.

Car Wax?

I know it is tempting to use up that half-bottle of car wax on the saw table, but it probably contains loads of silicone that could migrate onto wood and haunt you for years. At least read the list of ingredients carefully.

Wax and Other Preparations

The traditional favorite for protecting cast-iron tables is Johnson's Paste Wax (see **Figure 3.22**), the same as you would put on wooden floors. It does not contain silicones and does a very good job of shielding cast iron from the elements if applied regularly. A side benefit of paste wax is that it makes the table surface slick so wood slides over it easily. This improves safety since, on a dry table, wood can feel as though it is trying to stick to the surface. On a slick table, the wood is predictable in its movement, allowing the operator to be in control.

Figure 3.22. Regular paste wax does a fine job of making machine tables slick and smooth, and it also will help prevent rust. Whatever wax or preparation is used on woodworking machines, be sure it does not contain silicones.

Cleaning Blades and Cutters

An inescapable consequence of cutting and shaping wood is contaminating the cutter with resins, pitch, and other natural components of wood (see **Figure 3.23**). Manufacturers apply stick-resistant coatings that reduce or delay the onset of contamination, but it will happen eventually.

Nothing will compromise the performance and safety of an otherwise perfect table saw like a dull or dirty blade. Reducing cutting efficiency increases the force needed to continue a cut, reducing the quality of the cut and increasing the safety risks.

When a blade, bit, or knife is contaminated, it holds heat longer, which makes it build even more heat. Performance can suffer to the point that you might think it has gone dull. In many cases, cleaning away the contamination will restore performance and postpone sharpening or replacement.

Today there are a number of purpose-designed materials that clean cutters safely. Even household cleaners like Simple Green (see **Figure 3.24**) can be used without endangering the integrity of the cutter. In addition to using sensible cleaning agents, it is important to scrub or scrape cutters with non-marring tools like plastic scrapers and brass-bristled brushes (see **Figure 3.25**). Anything that is hard enough to scratch the surface will also dull the cutter or damage the brazing.

Apply the cleaning agent, allow it to soak in a few minutes, and then scrub the contamination away with a brush or a rag. If the cutter has a lot of buildup, more than one cleaning may be required.

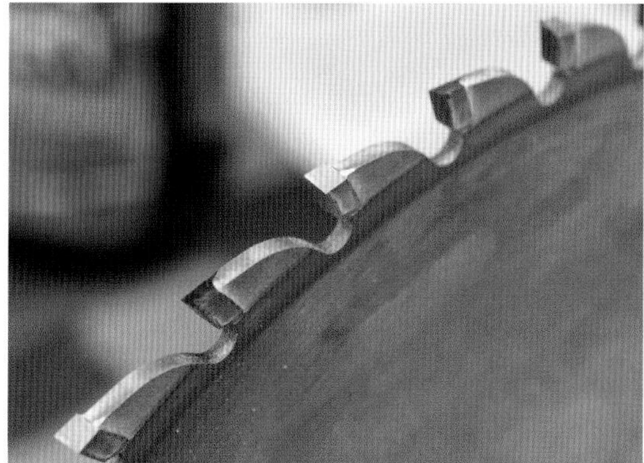

Figure 3.23. This blade is not very dirty, but I have learned to clean them before the residue gets cooked on.

Figure 3.24. Simple Green is one household cleaner that does a good job removing built-up crud from blades and bits. Use it with a soft brass-bristle brush.

Figure 3.25. After spraying the cleaning material on the blade, scrub it with a brass-bristle or plastic-bristled brush. These soft brushes won't damage the carbide or the blade body.

When the cutter is clean, rinse and dry it to remove any traces of the cleaner, and then wipe it down with a non-silicone oil or special blade-protecting compound.

Remember that even a dull blade or cutter remains sharp to your fingers. Be careful when scrubbing or wiping a blade so you do not have to wash away blood in addition to the contamination.

Forget the Easy-Off

Woodworkers have used all sorts of products to clean cutters, including flammable liquids like gasoline, kerosene, thinners, and even caustic oven cleaners like Easy-Off. However, any of these substances may also affect the high-tech brazing material used to weld carbide cutting tips onto blade and cutter bodies. Choose a cleaner formulated for use with woodworking tools or a non-caustic household cleaner like Simple Green.

Sharpening Edge Tools

Tool maintenance includes sharpening edge tools. You can, and should, sharpen your own chisels, plane irons, kitchen and marking knives, scissors, turning tools, and carving tools. With a power sharpening setup, you probably can sharpen your own jointer and planer knives as well, though many woodworkers prefer to send them out to a sharpening service.

Two of the more frequent discussions related to sharpening focus on flat versus round sharpening mediums and edge refinement. While the goal is to create a sharp cutting edge, how that is achieved can vary widely. Some firmly believe that sharpening nearly any cutting tool on a flat surface makes for a better edge, in part because the bevel remains absolutely flat, whereas sharpening on a stone wheel creates some degree of a concave shape. While everyone agrees that this difference exists, there is little consensus on its effect when the tool is used. Personally, I see no difference between flat and the tiny concave shape a round grinding wheel creates in bevels.

I have tried many sharpening methods and am able to get a relatively sharp edge on a common flat sharpening stone. However, I was less impressed with the time it took and the difficulty of sharpening nearly any edge correctly (see **Figure 3.26**). It's especially difficult to hold the tool at the correct angle and square to the stone throughout the process, even using a simple jig. If the tool tilts, it can round or alter the angle of the cutting edge in relation to the rest of the tool. Of course, this same problem can occur on a powered machine if it is set up incorrectly, but that is less likely to happen.

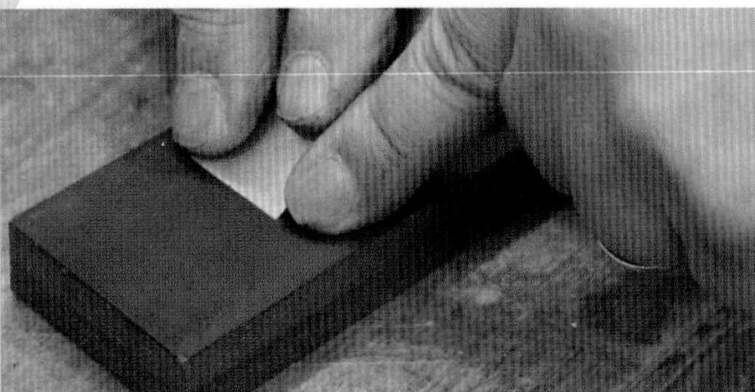

Figure 3.26. Some folks can sharpen almost anything on a flat stone and do it perfectly. I can sharpen virtually nothing that way, and if my e-mail is at all representative, neither can many of you.

For me, the big problem with flat sharpening is the time required to do it correctly. Some enjoy this type of sharpening and consider it part of woodworking. There is nothing wrong with that, and you may enjoy it as well. As for me, I enjoy the speed and accuracy of powered sharpening machines (see **Figure 3.27**).

Since sharpening is intended to create an edge that cuts wood easily, it should be no surprise that those same edges will cut your fingers or hands even more easily. So be especially careful when performing this maintenance task.

Figure 3.27. The powered wet sharpening systems have a wide water-cooled grinding wheel on one side and a leather honing wheel on the other.

Setting a bevel

When setting up any sharpening jig or machine, the first step is to match the existing bevel angle to the stone—unless, of course, you have decided to change the bevel for some good reason. You can come very close by eyeballing it. To minimize the sharpening time and reduce the amount of material removed, you will want to get that angle as perfect as possible before you begin sharpening. The only additional tool you need is a permanent marking pen. Follow these steps to set a bevel:

1. Clean any residue from the bevel to prevent contaminating the grinding medium.
2. Color the entire bevel with the marking pen (see **Figure 3.28**). This provides a clear visual indicator of your progress.

3. Install the tool in the jig or machine, and set the angle as close as possible by eye.
4. Lock the tool in place, hold it against the stone, and move the tool across the handheld stone or, on a powered machine, turn the grinding wheel by hand.
5. Look at the bevel. The coloring will be scraped away where the bevel was in contact with the stone (see **Figure 3.29**). If the mark does not run all the way across the bevel, adjust the angle needed, color in that scratch mark, and repeat the process until you achieve a full scratch pattern.

It is most important to get the scratch pattern at least centered on the bevel front to back. Deformation of the cutting edge may prevent the scratch pattern from covering the entire bevel, but you want to know the bevel is as centered against the grinding stone as possible. That makes the sharpening operation go faster because less material has to be removed to freshen the entire bevel.

Figure 3.28. Color the original bevel with a marker so you can use it to set the angle of your sharpening system.

Refining the edge

A few quick passes on a regular grinding wheel or coarse stone may restore a worn cutting edge. However, going the next step and refining that edge with fine-grit stones or honing it on a machine reduces the scratch pattern and polishes the bevel. There is more to this than appearance.

If you look at an unrefined cutting edge under magnification, the scratch marks create distinct peaks along the edge that, while sharp initially, do more tearing than cutting and can go dull very quickly as they break off or bend. These peaks involve small amounts of unsupported metal, making them inherently weak.

Honing removes the scratches and makes the cutting edge more uniform. When the bevel and cutting edge are refined, there are fewer individual peaks and more of a continuous edge that is stronger and resists bending and breaking far more than those little peaks. The result is an edge that cuts very cleanly and stays sharper longer.

Creating this highly refined, uniform cutting edge is something at which the powered wet sharpening systems, such as the Jet or Tormek, excel. Because the grinding wheels can be changed from 220 grit to 1000 grit, they grind a remarkably smooth edge to begin with. The stones do not actually change grits; rather, the surface texture is altered by a grading stone to approximate the different grit properties. Move to the leather honing wheel on the other side of the powered sharpeners, and that edge can be refined to a mirror finish (see **Figure 3.30**).

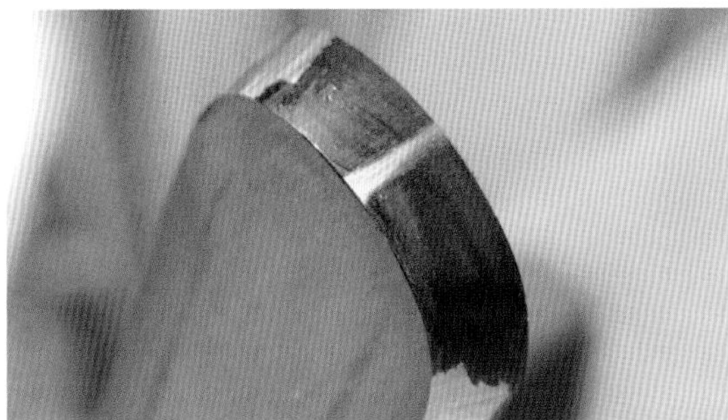

Figure 3.29. Hit the stone with the colored bevel, or set it against the machine and turn it by hand. When the scratch pattern is centered on the bevel (front to back), the bevel is correctly set in relation to the grinding stone.

Figure 3.30. After shaping the bevel and honing it on my powered wet grinding machine, each chisel has a mirror shine and a sharp edge that will last.

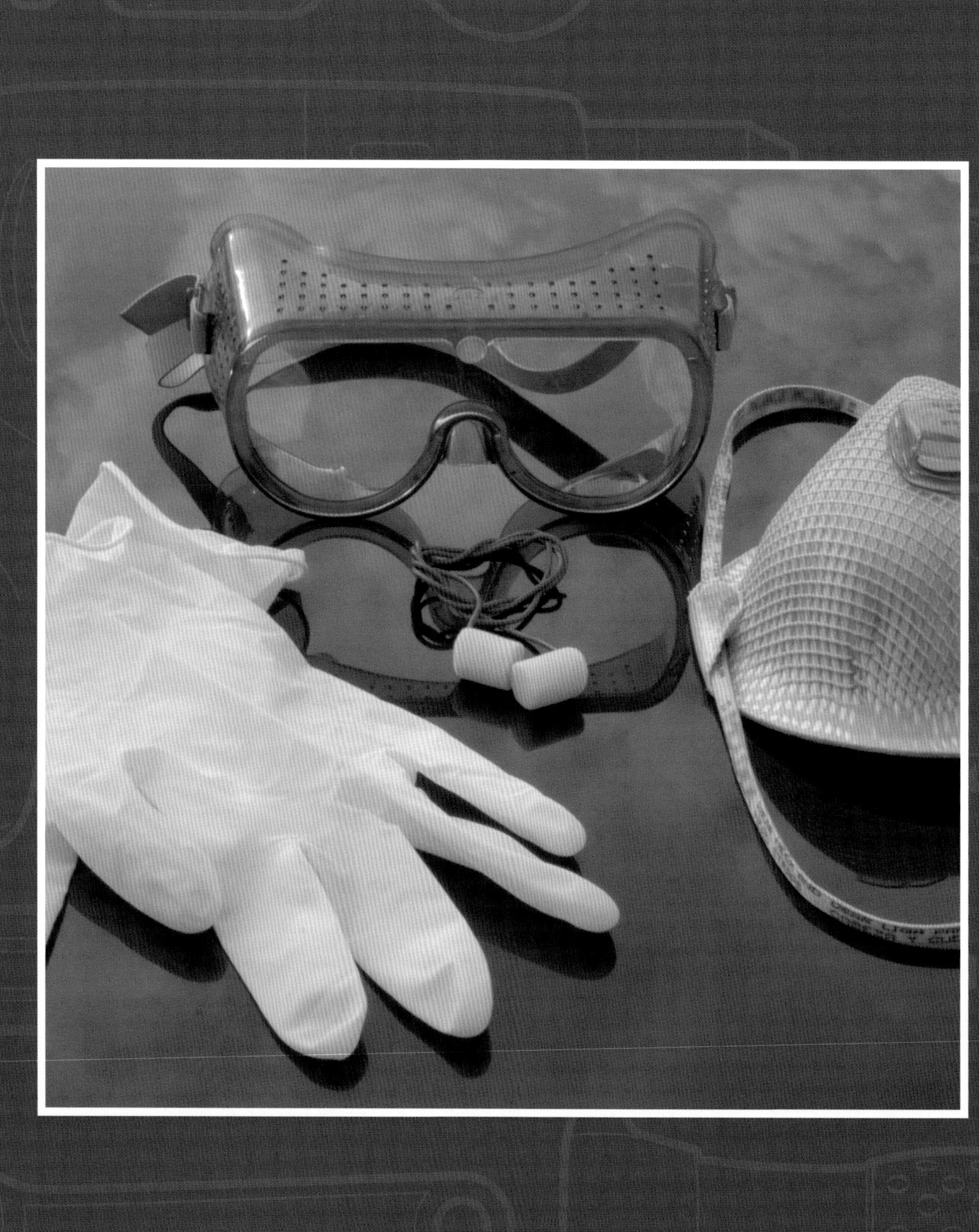

Chapter 4

Working Safely

Today's woodworking tools and machines are safer than ever because manufacturers continually refine their designs to reduce the chance of injury. The manufacturers know how their equipment should be operated and relate that information to the consumer through the instruction manuals packed with each tool and machine. Their biggest problem is coercing the woodworker to read and then follow those instructions.

This chapter focuses on the safety factors that you can control in your shop. I'll explain the common safety errors and present ways—concrete and commonsense—to keep you safe. I'll also point out specific safety hazards with shop tools like the band saw, the drill press, and the circular saw and tell you how to guard against them. You'll find that woodworking can be a safe hobby when the woodworker puts safety first.

The human factor

A few years ago, *NewWoodworker.com* conducted an online survey asking woodworkers if they had ever experienced a woodworking injury, and, if so, what caused it. The results were surprising. Less than 2% of those who were injured in accidents blamed the equipment. Of those, none could supply evidence of a contributing malfunction or design flaw. The remaining 98% flatly admitted their actions caused the incident.

Table saws are the most used power tools in woodworking, so their involvement in 167 of the 262 reported accidents was not a big surprise. Of those incidents, 113 involved direct contact with the spinning blade. That was a little surprising.

Those involved described their actions using the words "dumb" or "stupid" in 117 of 167 reports! They knew they were doing something wrong, but had done it before—often frequently—without a problem, so they continued until they had an accident.

What "dumb" and "stupid" things did they do? They disabled or removed safety features (see **Figure 4.1**), failed to read instructions, or both. Nearly all of these accidents could have been prevented had the woodworkers simply followed instructions.

Another big surprise was the amount of woodworking experience reported by those having the most accidents. Of the 262 accident reports submitted, 57% listed woodworking experience averaging just over 18 years. This loudly suggests that complacency can be a greater danger than lack of experience.

This statistical landslide reinforces the need to read and follow the manufacturer's instructions to learn how to use the equipment properly before bad habits set in. It also points out the need to remember and use those procedures all the time, not just until a level of comfort is achieved.

You need not fear woodworking machines, but you do have to respect them. Their ability to cut and shape wood effortlessly demonstrates their capability of inflicting serious injury if used improperly.

> "The most effective safety tool is your brain, providing it is used. Use your brainpower to pay attention to what is happening around you and to think through procedures."

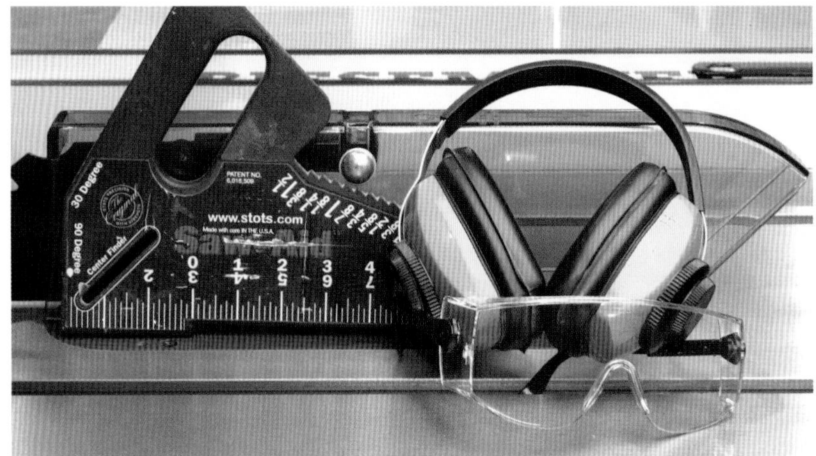

Figure 4.1. The equipment needed to work safely in a woodworking shop is neither expensive nor difficult to use. It is, however, difficult to understand the excuses woodworkers give for not using it.

The most effective safety tool

Even in the exceedingly rare woodworking shops with "cost-is-no-object" budgets, the most effective safety tool is your brain, providing it is used. Most woodworkers I have spoken with who have suffered an injury had some anticipation that it would happen. They knew they were doing something unsafe, but they continued until things went wrong.

Woodworkers tend to be smart people who should know better. Unfortunately, some use their intellect to work around safety devices, only to discover that the laws of probability are not to be denied.

Use your brainpower to pay attention to what is happening around you, and think through new cuts or procedures before trying them. If something seems dangerous, find another way of doing it. Seeking the advice of another woodworker or the manufacturer of the tool may add a little time to a project but could end up saving far more time plus a lot of grief.

Siesta Time

Some years ago, one of the major woodworking magazines conducted a similar accident survey to New Woodworker's, with very similar findings. It uncovered one more significant contributing factor: lunch. A very large share of woodworking accidents occurred in the two hours following a meal, a time when many of us feel the overwhelming desire to nap. So fit that fact into your woodworking weekend, and organize your work so you don't attempt potentially dangerous operations at siesta time.

Working Tired

The hectic schedule many of us maintain trying to balance a career, children, and keeping up with a home often leaves little time for hobbies. That can mean limited time in the shop, sometimes at odd hours.

Using powerful woodworking machines, or even handheld tools, can be extremely dangerous when you are tired or distracted. Tired woodworkers with years of experience have reached directly into a spinning saw blade to retrieve a piece of wood. It only takes a second or two of thinking about something else to get yourself into real trouble.

Even if you avoid accidents, the quality of your work will suffer. Save the project and your fingers for another day. When you get tired, or have too much on your mind, get out of the shop.

Read the manual

Reading instruction manuals (see **Figure 4.2**) is an excellent way for any woodworker to become familiar with a new piece of equipment, how it works, how to adjust it accurately, and then how to operate it safely. For the new woodworker, the instructions can be even more important. With little or no prior knowledge about woodworking tools and equipment, the information contained in the literature packed with the tool can help prevent disappointing results, accidental damage to the machine, and injury to you.

Most instruction manuals guide new owners through assembly, setup, and adjustment of a new machine in a specific order. Jumping ahead can result in a machine that may look fine, but which actually may be dangerously out of alignment. Safety devices on a machine that is incorrectly assembled may not function or may function at a reduced level of protection.

Save your instruction manuals, and find a safe place in your shop to store them where you can find them when you need them (see **Figure 4.3**). They will be invaluable references not only for answering any operating questions that may arise, but also for realigning and adjusting your equipment. Manuals also contain parts lists, exploded views, and resource information for obtaining replacement parts or service. Should you decide to sell a machine to make room for a newer model, having the original instruction manual is a good selling point.

Tape It to the Cover

Along with keeping the owner's manual, consider taping or stapling the original invoice to the cover. That way you will know when and where you bought the machine for warranty purposes, and you will know what you paid when it's time to sell.

Figure 4.2. Following the instructions that describe how to set up and align a new machine will yield a better-running piece of equipment and a smarter, safer operator.

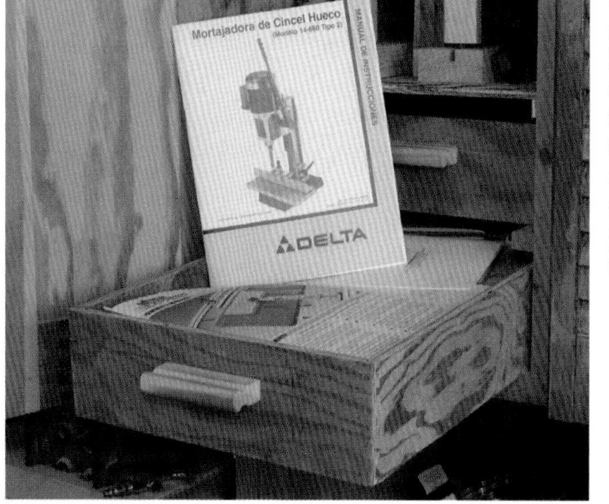

Figure 4.3. When I built my large shop cabinet, I included a drawer that holds nothing but the manuals and literature that came with my woodworking tools and equipment. When I have a question or need a phone or part number, I know where to go.

General protection

In addition to containing the obvious danger of fingers contacting blades or cutters, the woodworking shop should also be considered a hostile environment for the eyes and the ears. Any machine capable of cutting wood will throw some of the debris well beyond the person operating it. Also, the process of cutting and shaping wood makes noise, sometimes a lot of noise.

While it would seem that protecting your eyes and ears at all times in the shop is simple common sense, far too many woodworkers use inadequate protection or no protection.

Beware the Startle

When you are working intently at a shop machine, wearing your safety glasses and your ear protection, you're not likely to notice someone entering the shop and attempting to get your attention. So he or she taps your shoulder, or shouts. And you jump. You'll be lucky if the workpiece is the only thing that gets damaged.

Explain to your significant other, and to anyone else likely to visit unannounced, that you're not ignoring him or her out of curmudgeonly spite. You really don't know anyone is there. And he or she should please just wait quietly until you turn off the machine and look up.

Eye Protection

Though you most often think about sawdust being thrown around, wood is an inconsistent medium that may contain hidden cracks, knots, or other imperfections. When contacted by the blade or cutter, invisible weaknesses within the wood can unexpectedly generate wooden missiles capable of causing serious damage to eyes and the rest of the human body. Your eyes are at risk any time you are running a woodworking machine or portable power tool. Your eyes are also at risk whenever you strike metal with a hammer, whether another tool or a nail. The force of the blow can send a metal chip, or the nail itself, flying right at your face.

A good pair of safety glasses should be part of your standard shop wardrobe, regardless of what you are doing at the moment. If you normally wear corrective lenses, get prescription safety glasses. In addition to safety lenses, side shields should be part of all safety glasses. Dust and debris do not always fly in a straight line, and you are not always facing the source straight on. Those little screens or shields on the sides of good safety glasses can easily prevent an injury (see **Figure 4.4**).

As an alternative to expensive prescription safety glasses, find a pair of safety goggles, or a full face shield, that will fit right over your regular glasses. Of the two, you'll find the goggles less likely to fog up.

Hearing Protection

Manufacturers sometimes supply decibel ratings for a machine, but those should be considered guidelines only. The type of wood and the environment in which the machine is operated can have dramatic effects on the intensity of the sound produced, as can the distance and orientation of the ear in relation to it. The most serious hearing damage does not result from brief exposure to high decibel levels, but from prolonged exposure.

Some machines, like jointers or planers, are obviously loud, and woodworkers are more likely to use hearing protection when operating them. However, other seemingly quiet machines could also be generating potentially damaging sounds without you realizing it, especially if you are using the machine for many hours at a time. Permanent hearing damage can also be caused by sound frequencies that are not audible. You may not notice a problem at the end of the day, but in coming weeks or months, you may think everyone around you is mumbling.

Turn It Down

An MP3 or portable CD player blasting your favorite tunes loud enough to drown out woodworking machines is not hearing protection. By the time you get the music up loud enough to hear over the roar of the machines, you've just added to the burden on your ears.

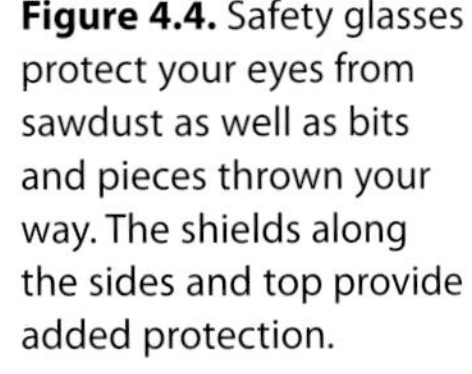

Figure 4.4. Safety glasses protect your eyes from sawdust as well as bits and pieces thrown your way. The shields along the sides and top provide added protection.

Figure 4.5. It may not be obvious when a tool is generating sound at levels that can cause irreversible hearing damage. Wear ear protection. These muffs are comfortable and filter out machine sounds, but you can still hear speech through them.

Effective hearing protection is available in many forms, from little foam earplugs to earmuffs equipped with sophisticated noise-canceling electronics. While something is better than nothing, this is an area where you should spend a little more now and save lots later. I habitually wear earmuff-style hearing protection every time I turn on a machine (see **Figure 4.5**), and I advise you to do the same.

Workshop fashions

Dressing safely and comfortably in the woodworking shop is important. Being stylish is not. Dressing safely may sound like a no-brainer, but I promise there will be thousands of emergency room visits this year caused by loose clothing, long hair, and jewelry becoming entangled in machines.

Clothing and Hair

Loose-fitting clothes and unrestrained long hair can easily become entangled in a machine and land you in the emergency room (see **Figure 4.6**). Common sense is your best indicator. If your clothes or hair seem dangerous to you, they probably are. If you can imagine that sleeve catching, roll it up and secure it. If you worry about your hair being close to something, restrain it.

Jewelry

The same goes for jewelry, notably necklaces that supposedly stay inside clothing. Dangling necklaces, bracelets, and wristwatches pose the same risks of getting caught in machines as loose clothing and hair. The danger of a ring is less obvious: That little band is entirely capable of getting snagged by a moving machine part or becoming crimped around a soon-to-be blood-starved finger by an unintentional blow (see **Figure 4.7**). One of your first projects should be a little shelf, box, or drawer to store these items while you are working in the shop.

> "Clothing, hair, and fashion accessories can be a danger in the workshop. Take care to keep all of them away from the operating parts of your woodworking machines."

Shoes

Solid shoes, particularly those with steel toes, are another good investment. While long planks and most projects are sufficiently heavy to do serious damage if dropped on a sneakered foot, a surprisingly small piece of wood can break bones if it lands on the edge, as they always seem to in my shop. Also, drop a cutting tool of any kind and by the time it reaches your feet, the edge you spent so much time sharpening will no doubt be pointed down.

Figure 4.6. Loose or dangling clothing can become entangled in a machine. You can be reeled in and injured before you realize what is happening.

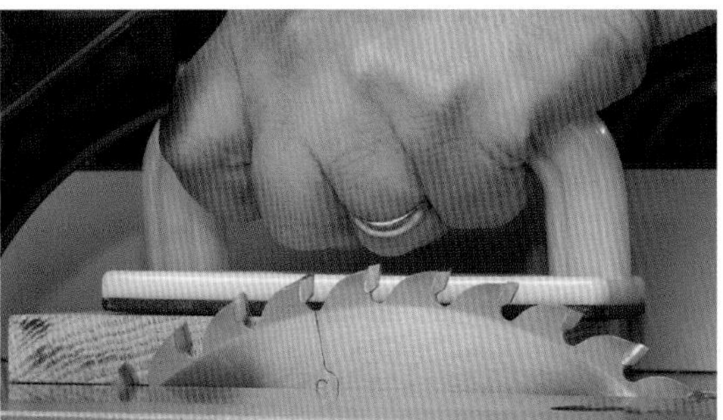

Figure 4.7. Rings, necklaces, and other jewelry can be snagged or otherwise grabbed by a machine. These injuries are seldom minor.

Machinery guards

The guards that came with your machines may not be the most user-friendly things ever invented, but they do serve a purpose. When set up and used properly, most table saw blade guard/splitter and anti-kickback pawl systems can be used effectively.

One thing I have noticed is that new woodworkers are far more likely to use the factory guard system without complaint than a veteran. Maybe the newer breed just understands the dangers better. Whatever the reason is, the newer crowd seems much less antagonized by the factory safety equipment. I can't see a thing wrong with that.

There are some common instances in which many woodworkers have removed their guards. We'll look at some of them here, and I'll give some solutions that don't involve removing the guards.

- **Cutting narrow strips** on the table saw has always been a problem. When the width of the piece gets too narrow for a push handle to fit between the fence and blade guard, you need another plan—or perhaps another machine. Starting with a large piece and moving the cut-off piece to the opposite side of the blade from the fence is a little more difficult in terms of laying out the cut, but it is a bunch safer. Safer yet is using a band saw.
- **Sawing smaller pieces** can be difficult. The smaller pieces get, the more dangerous they are on the table saw (see **Figure 4.8**). I try not to cut anything that is less than a foot long and that is not wide enough for a good push handle to maintain a solid grip as it passes the blade. Here again, the band saw is often a better choice for small pieces.
- **When using a dado set**, you must remove the blade guard. While it is obvious that the blade guard and splitter assembly has to come off to use a dado set in the table saw, it remains important to protect your hands. Too many woodworkers think that just because the dado blade is buried in the wood that their hand is safe. If a spinning dado set less than ½" below your hand is not frightening to you, you don't understand the problem. Push blocks, like those that come with many jointers, work great for controlling wood as it passes over a dado blade. I still try to place the push block somewhere besides directly over the dado blade, just in case.

> **"Manufacturers did not invent machinery guards to antagonize you. They are there for a purpose."**

Figure 4.8. Cutting a small piece of wood is always dangerous. On the table saw, it is foolhardy. If this piece is kicked out, fingers will be in serious danger and probably will thrust directly toward the blade.

Machinery danger zones

A key to the safe operation of woodworking equipment is keeping your hands out of the danger zone around the blade or cutter. While there is no set rule for establishing precise dimensions of danger zones, they are easy to understand: If your hands can get to the cutter should something unexpected happen, they are inside the danger zone (see **Figure 4.9**).

Woodworkers of all experience levels tend to underestimate what a safe distance is, particularly if it has been a while since they scared themselves. Thinking their hands are far enough from the cutter, some make matters worse by choosing not to use safety push devices.

I try to keep my hands and fingers at least several inches from a blade or cutter. That is not always easy, but using a good push device increases the safety margin in several ways: It keeps your hands farther from the cutter and puts sacrificial material (the wood and the push device) between you and the cutter. It also changes the path in which your hand will go, should the worst happen. In most cases, a good push device elevates the hand, so if something happens at the blade or cutter, your hand is not aimed directly at it. Push sticks, push handles, and push pads have probably prevented more injuries than any other safety devices this side of a clear-thinking brain.

Push Devices

Over the years, a wide range of devices has been developed for pushing wood through machines. Everything from long-handled sticks to flat, rubber-bottomed pads with elevated handles are available from just about any woodworking outlet (see **Figure 4.10**).

While many of these devices can be made in a woodworking shop, I encourage the new woodworker to buy commercially made devices to get used to how they work. Then, with a better understanding of their function, making versions to suit your shop needs will be easier and safer.

The most effective push devices can improve safety only when you use them. For veteran woodworkers, reconditioning themselves to use push devices consistently can be difficult, but it is worth the effort. Those just starting in the hobby have the advantage of learning good habits from the start. Automatically reaching for the push device when working at a machine is a great habit to have, and one that will go a long way toward keeping you safe.

Figure 4.9. Woodworkers tend to think the danger zone around a blade or cutter is smaller than it really is. When things go wrong, they happen fast, leaving your hands aimed directly at the danger. In this photo, you can see that my hands are far too close to the blade.

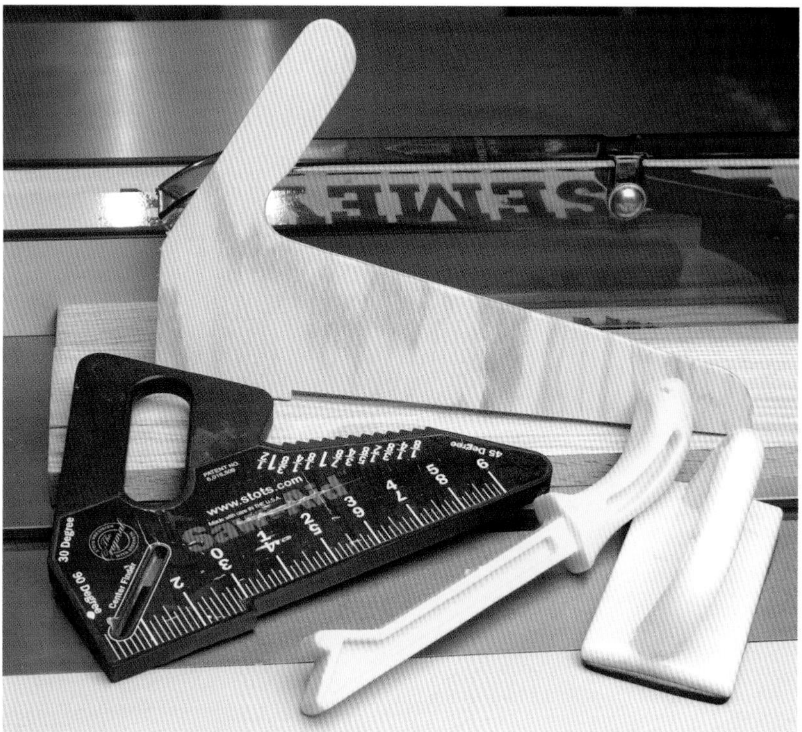

Figure 4.10. Push devices can make any operation safer. It is always better to ruin a push device than a finger or hand.

Push Sticks

In my opinion, basic push sticks are the least effective push devices because they offer little directional control over the wood. A notched end fits over the rear edge of the wood for pushing it, but there is nothing to help steer the piece to keep it against the fence (see **Figure 4.11**). If the wood begins to turn during the cut, there is little you can do other than hope the splitter and anti-kickback pawls that came with your machine are installed. If they are not, your day could be about to take a nasty turn for the worse.

A push stick can sometimes be used effectively in conjunction with a second stick fitted with a rubber end (see **Figure 4.12**). The rubber-tipped stick is positioned near the front of the wood to keep it against the fence while the notched stick pushes from the rear to move it across the blade or cutter. The problem is that at least one hand has to reach over the blade on a table saw. Even when the sticks are long enough to maintain several inches between the hand and the blade, it's not the safest technique.

I find this combination of sticks most useful at the router table when edging relatively narrow pieces of wood. The cutter is most often on the far side of the wood, and the natural line of pressure is against the fence, not the cutter itself.

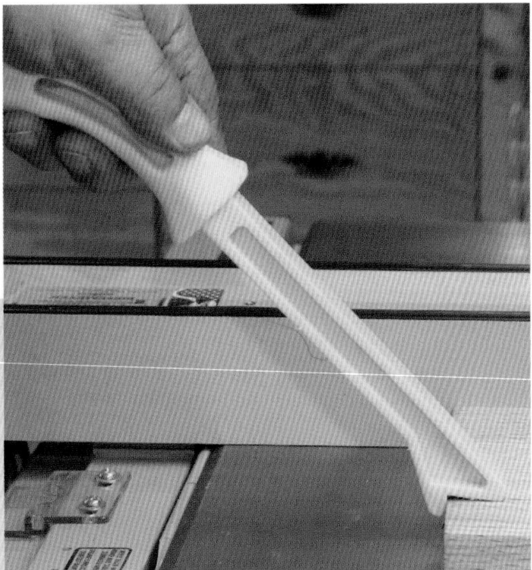

Figure 4.11. In my opinion, simple push sticks, when used alone, are worthless on a good day and dangerous the rest of the time. They afford no directional control. If the wood turns toward the blade, there is little you can do about it.

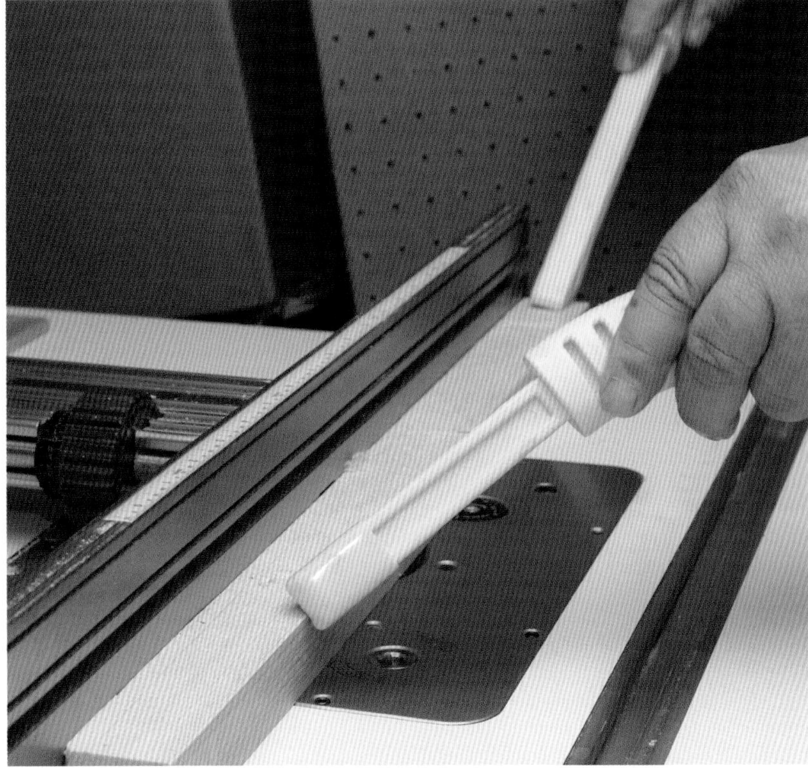

Figure 4.12. A simple push stick can be useful when used with another, particularly on a router table where you can guide both ends of the wood without reaching over the blade.

Push sticks are usually made from some type of plastic or composite material that will cut away easily, should they contact the blade or cutter. If you make your own push sticks, use plywood since it doesn't shatter as badly as solid wood can, should it contact the blade.

Push Handles

At the table saw, my favorite commercially made safety tool is the Stots Saw-Aid push handle (see **Figure 4.13**). Its relatively long foot protrudes forward, helping to grip the wood and provide good directional stability. The heel portion hooks over the rear edge of the wood to push it past the blade.

The Saw-Aid is only ½" wide, so it can be used when the blade is rather close to the fence. It is made from a resin-based material that, while strong, is soft enough to cut easily without shattering, should it contact the blade. The idea is to protect your hands, not destroy a blade, and the push device is a cheap sacrifice toward that end.

Shop-made versions of this device have been around for decades (see **Figure 4.14**). When making your own push handles, cut the handle high enough to position your hand several inches above

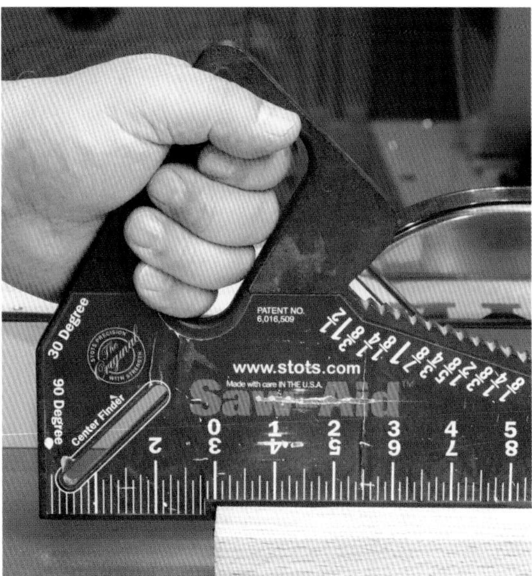

Figure 4.13. The push device I reach for most at the table saw is the Stots Saw-Aid. It is easy to use and grips the stock along its length, making it easy to keep the piece against the fence.

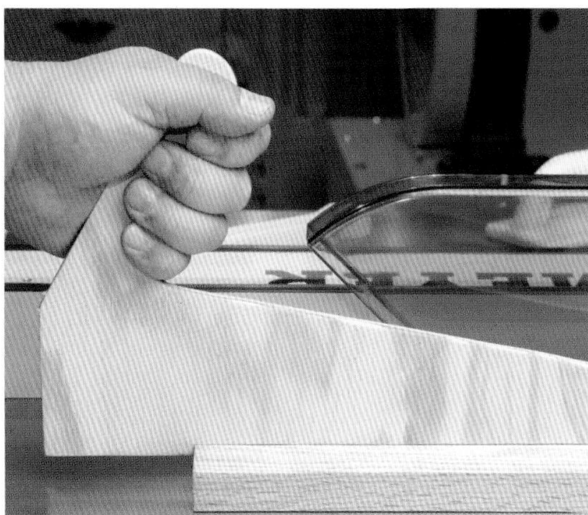

Figure 4.14. Making your own push handles is easy. You can design them for specific jobs. You soon will build a collection that can be used over and over.

the blade. The edge that will contact the wood must be flat for control. A step or heel hooks over the wood to push it. Nearly all of the push handles I make have a heel that extends downward ¼" to ⅜". That's big enough to hook the wood securely but shallow enough for thin wood.

Push handles should be made from ½" or ¾" plywood and can be cut out on a band saw or with a jigsaw. Solid wood can shatter. When using a good-size push handle with sanded edges around the grip area, accidental contact with the blade usually results in frayed nerves, but no frayed fingers.

Push Blocks

Rubber-soled push blocks, commonly supplied with jointers, also work well at the table saw and router table. Push blocks are particularly useful when handling material that is as wide as or wider than they are.

The rubber sole gets a good grip on wood for a solid feeling of control. In fact, I feel more in control of the wood with the push blocks than with anything else and use them even when cutting large pieces of stock that could be safely done with the hand alone (see **Figure 4.15**).

The push blocks are particularly good for cutting dados. Their flat, grippy rubber pad gives a good feel of control, but the handle keeps your hand spaced above the wood. They can also be useful at the router table and other machines. I usually choose them over other push devices.

Push blocks usually are not made in the shop because of the difficulty of finding and adhering the rubber pads. In the time it would take you to make them, you could have gone to the local woodworking shop, bought the push block and blown another $10 on shiny things you didn't need, and still come out ahead.

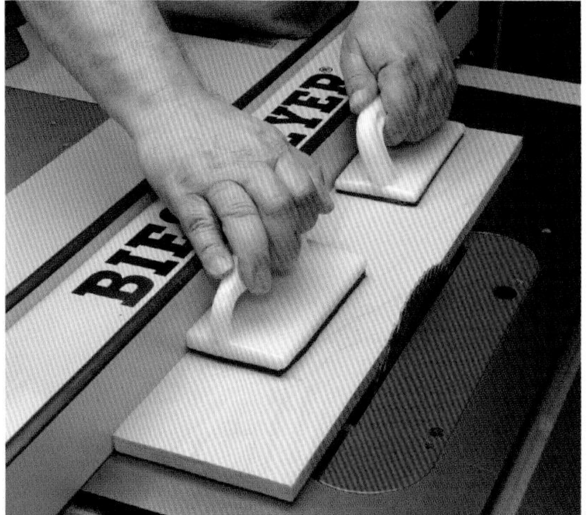

Figure 4.15. These push blocks came with my jointer but are also handy at the table saw and router table. The rubber sole provides an exceptional grip on flat stock.

Featherboards

Featherboards are simple devices that can be purchased commercially (see **Figure 4.16**) but are often made in the shop. A series of cuts in the angled end of a board creates flexible fingers that can apply pressure to the wood, holding it against the fence or table surface to ensure a consistent cut. In addition, the angle at which those fingers meet the wood reduces the risk of kickback.

Featherboards can be made with simple tools and in sizes to fit virtually any table saw or router table. They also can be made for special situations that would be difficult to match with a commercial design.

Figure 4.16. A featherboard can apply pressure right where you need it, converting a dangerous operation into a safe one.

Making Featherboards

Featherboards can be made from any wood, though pine and poplar are favored because the fingers are flexible. They can be made in virtually any length or width needed and can be clamped to a surface or secured in a miter slot with an expanding cleat (shown at right).

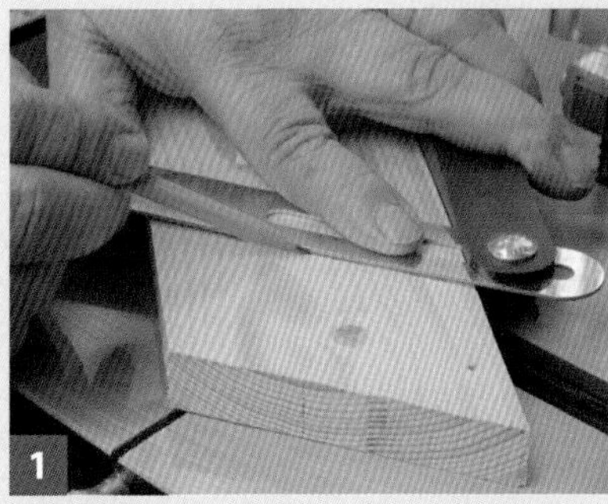

1 Start by cutting the featherboard blank; then, miter one end to 30 degrees. Draw a line, also at 30 degrees (parallel to the end cut), about 2½" in from the mitered end. This will be the stop line for the cuts to produce the fingers. The fingers should be about ⅛" wide and equally spaced across the width of the board. You may have to fudge the spacing slightly. If necessary, cut a narrower finger rather than one that is substantially thicker. Extra thickness will apply uneven pressure on the wood.

2 Cut the fingers on the band saw, with a handheld jigsaw, or with a small handsaw.

3 To make a locking featherboard, rout two slots parallel to its long axis and staggered at the finger angle. For the expanding cleat, cut a strip of hardwood wide enough to loosely fit the miter slot. The strip has to extend beyond the featherboard at least 1" on each side. Drill and countersink holes that match the slot spacing, sized for a countersunk ¼" x 20 machine screw. Drill a 5⁄16" hole an inch to each side of the screw holes.

4 To finish the cleat, use a jigsaw (or coping saw) to cut along the centerline between the 5⁄16" holes, passing through the bolt holes. Insert the bolts through the cleat and featherboard, and add large flat washers and finger knobs. When you tighten the knobs, the tapered heads of the bolts are drawn up into the cleat, expanding its sides against the sides of the miter slot, locking it in place.

Flying wood

Kickback and kickout are when the workpiece is kicked or thrown out of or off a machine. Both can cause injuries because of the speed and violence with which they happen. These injuries occur in two ways: You get hit or speared by the flying wood, and/or your hands, suddenly pushing on thin air, go into the blade or cutter.

Understanding how these accidents occur can help prevent them from happening at all. While kickback is most often associated with the table saw and kickout with the router table, both can happen on any machine that has a rotating cutter.

Kickback

One major cause of kickback is the wood turning toward the table saw blade during the cut, either from operator error (see **Figures 4.17** and **4.18**) or from stresses being released inside the material. The other major cause of kickback is trapping a piece of wood between the rip fence and the saw blade. The teeth at the back of the blade, which are rising from the saw table, can lift the wood, turn it, and then throw it. While the wood is definitely going to fly in the general direction of the operator, you can never be sure of the angle. The best plan is to prevent this accident from happening in the first place.

Kickback also can be caused or assisted by a misalignment of the machine, often combined with a loss of control, as described above. If the table saw fence angles toward the blade at the rear, rather than being parallel to it or angled slightly away, the wood gets squeezed into the side of the blade as you push it through. The misaligned fence is guiding the wood against the teeth at the back of

Figure 4.17. When this piece of wood was kicked back, it created an exceptionally clear track in the wood, clearly showing what happened. The deepest part of the cut is where the incident started. The blade was trying to continue the cut, but as the piece rotated and accelerated, it rode up on the blade and turned until it was ejected.

Figure 4.18. Even though I was using a very good push handle, the workpiece was just too small to be sawed safely. The handle apparently had rocked toward me, releasing the front end of the piece. With my pressure pinning the rear corner of the piece (B) to the table, it turned into the blade. As the piece turned, it accelerated, evidenced by the decreasing depth of the cut.

Safety Tip: Raise the Blade

You might think it is always safest to keep the table saw blade as low as possible, with just the gullets between the teeth breaking through the top surface. Actually, this is more dangerous than raising the blade. The reason is, when the blade is low, the teeth are moving almost horizontally in the wood, exerting horizontal forces on it and increasing the chances for kickback. When the blade is high, the teeth are moving almost vertically in the wood, exerting downward forces and decreasing the chances of kickback.

Safety Tip: Stand to the Side

A narrow ripping that kicks back can come at your soft belly like an Olympic javelin. Because kickback is always a danger at the table saw, train yourself to stand to the side of the path the wood will take if ejected. Which side depends on where you are most comfortable as well as on the size of the workpiece.

Safety Tip: Ripping Narrow Pieces

If you trap a narrow ripping between the blade and the fence, you dramatically increase the risk of a kickback. Whenever you want to rip narrow slices off a board, set up so the bulk of the workpiece is between the table saw blade and the fence, with the narrow ripping falling to the left side of the blade. If you want to rip a lot of narrow strips, adjust the fence for each one. Or band saw them.

the blade, and you once again are in the kickback zone, as described earlier. However, kickbacks can and do occur at the front edge of the blade as well.

Small pieces of wood are especially difficult to control on the table saw and can contribute to a kickback. It should be noted that if the splitter and anti-kickback devices that came with your table saw are properly installed, the risk of kickback accidents falls rapidly toward the rare end of the scale (see **Figure 4.19**). However, it would be best to avoid cutting small pieces on the table saw entirely.

Figure 4.19. Here is the same block of wood in the same settings but with the splitter and anti-kickback apparatus installed per the manufacturer's instructions. The wood is where it began rotating into the blade, and you can see that the splitter would have stopped it. The kickback was my fault in a number of ways. I was cutting a small piece of wood, I did not have the splitter in place, and my fence was out of alignment (slightly). Most important was that I knew I was breaking several safety rules but had reasoned that it was "just this one piece."

Kickout

Kickout frequently occurs at the router table when the woodworker mistakenly feeds the wood into the cutter in the same direction as its rotation, rather than against it. Another common cause is simply losing control of the wood. In either case, the cutting edges of the router bit become highly efficient feed dogs that grab, accelerate, and eject the wood in a fraction of a second (see **Figure 4.20**).

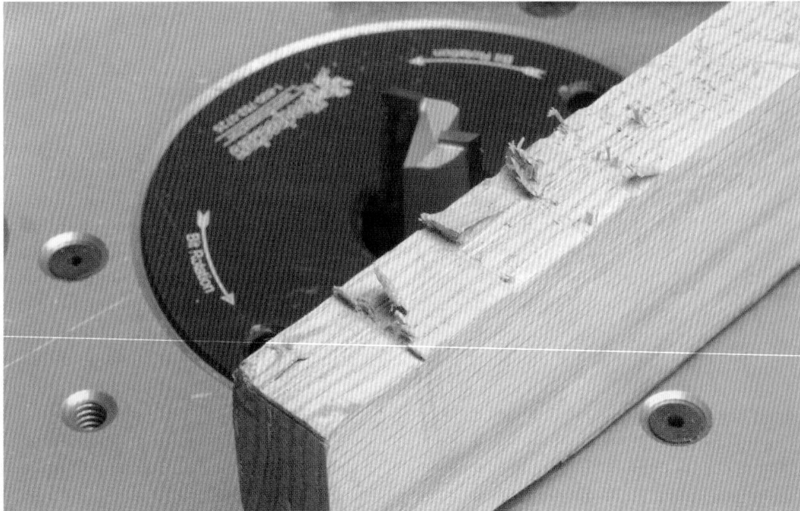

Figure 4.20. Here's the result of kickout on the router table. The cutter grabbed the wood and threw it.

Another frequent cause of kickout at the router table is the wood mistakenly being cut on the back side of the bit rather than the front. This also involves feeding the stock in the same direction as the bit rotation, but it can surprise even veteran woodworkers. Normally, you feed wood into the router bit (which always spins counterclockwise in a router table) from the right to the left, with the front side of the bit doing the cutting. The classic bad example is setting up the router table so the workpiece passes between the cutter and the fence. It is a mistake on two counts. First, feeding the stock in the normal direction means the back side of the bit will be doing the cutting, and you will be feeding with the direction of rotation instead of against it—inviting the cutter to grab the stock and throw it. The second mistake is that this setup is trapping the wood between the fence and the cutter. If there is any variation in its thickness, the workpiece is going to jam, chatter, or kick—or all three.

Problems occur when making a second pass, such as cutting a slot. Adjusting the fence even slightly toward the bit causes the cutting to happen on the back side of the bit. When the operator again feeds the wood in right to left, the cutter grabs it and bang—it's gone.

Even if you avoid direct contact with the cutter, just being hit by the kicked-out wood can be very painful, easily causing cuts, bruises, and even broken bones. I had one serious kickback incident a few years ago that left me with a half-dollar-size scrape in the middle of a grapefruit-size bruise on my side.

Other machines

The table saw and the router table are obvious candidates to be front and center in a safety discussion. But they are not the only dangerous machines in the workshop. Here's a brief rundown on safety issues with other common pieces of equipment.

Jointer

The jointer can kick back the same as the table saw, with the flying wood syndrome leaving the operator's suddenly empty hands pushing toward the cutter head. The solution is easy: Always use push blocks when you are face-jointing a piece of wood, and don't attempt to joint pieces shorter than 18". Joint while the wood is longer, and then crosscut to length. If chips clog the jointer's discharge chute, be sure you turn the machine off before you poke a stick in there to clear the jam. Don't ever put your hand in there without first unplugging the machine.

Thickness Planer

As you are reducing the thickness of the board, loose knots can lose their attachment, and hidden cracks or defects in the wood can shatter. Despite the relatively narrow opening, pieces of wood can still be thrown back toward the operator. Stand to one side. And wear your safety glasses. Also be sure that the planer is shut off before you poke a stick inside it to free a jammed piece of wood or clear a buildup of chips. Before you ever reach your hand inside, unplug the machine to be sure it is off.

Band Saw

Everyone thinks the band saw is safe, and it pretty much is, with three exceptions:

- When uncoiling a band saw blade, wear gloves and make sure the teeth are pointing away from your body. If you are lucky, you can get it uncoiled without serious injury. If you want to uncoil a band saw blade the truly safe way, take it outside, toss the coil on the lawn, and let it spring open out there. When it stops moving, go pick it up.
- When you are cutting off thin pieces, they can slip down into the slot in the band saw table insert. Shut off the saw before retrieving them, and then consider buying or making a zero-clearance insert for your band saw.
- When you are resawing a thick piece of wood, use push blocks placed on the sides of the wood, not on the end, to guide it over the blade. Pushing on the end of the wood is just asking to resaw a finger or two when the blade breaks through unexpectedly, as they do on occasion.

Drill Press

The most common accident at the drill press is when the bit grabs the piece being drilled (metal or wood) and begins spinning it. If your hands were holding it or are close, the speed and severity of the impact that is coming the next time around will amaze you and will cut you badly if the workpiece is sheet metal.

Get in the habit of clamping the piece being drilled to the table. Aside from preventing being whipped or cut, you can actually drill more accurate holes.

Portable Circular Saw

There are three things to keep in mind when using the portable circular saw:

- **The cord.** Drape it over your shoulder to help keep it from catching on the edge of the wood and stopping the saw when you are not expecting it. It is also bad form to saw the cord in half.
- **Work support.** The wood being cut should be supported so that it does not collapse on or pinch the blade, especially near the end of the cut. If the wood pinches the blade, the saw can kick back at the operator with the blade still spinning. This is one of the most common injuries because so many people use handheld circular saws and so few have much experience with them.
- **After the cut.** Take your finger off the saw trigger, and allow the blade to stop before you lift it away from the work; otherwise, you risk sawing into your own leg. Shut them off and allow the cutter to stop before lifting it off the wood. The same goes for the router and other handheld power tools.

Hand Tools

Remember that hand tools have sharp edges and you must not put your fingers in their path. Never hand hold the workpiece. Always trap it in a vise or with a clamp. It's not only safer, it's also more accurate: Now you have two good hands for steering the tool.

Chapter 5

Selecting Wood

For most novice woodworkers, choosing the type of wood for a project is a balance between cost and what can be found locally. Unless you are lucky enough to have a woodworking store or dedicated wood retailer in the neighborhood, the nearest home center chain store is likely to become familiar territory in the early stages of your woodworking experience. The pine, red oak, and poplar lumber you can buy there will most likely be the species with which you will learn woodworking.

Everyone develops his or her own taste about what species of wood he or she enjoys working with and what looks best to him or her in any project. Most important is remembering that these are your projects and you get to decide what wood will be used. Just because what you like does not follow the norm, does not mean you are wrong. You also get to decide how much will be invested in wood for learning. There are very few situations when pine or poplar simply will not work for a project. Your tastes in wood will develop naturally with the range of project types you build. The choice of species is a very individual part of woodworking, so unless you are bound by a contract with someone you are building the piece for, indulge yourself!

In this chapter, I'll introduce the basics of wood choice. You'll learn about the difference between softwoods and hardwoods, where to find wood, and how to store it. You'll also learn about the terms and formulas associated with choosing and buying wood.

Softwood and hardwood

Some things, like cutting boards, demand hardwood like maple because of their intended use. Other projects, like shop cabinets, might be better in a softwood like pine, which is cheaper. While each species has a unique set of traits, there are some generalities to consider, notably in price, availability, how they respond to machines, and how they take a finish. These differences generally divide between softwoods and hardwoods (see **Figure 5.1**).

Hardwood, from trees that lose their leaves in winter, is often easier to work with than softwood. Hardwood cuts, planes, chisels, and accepts finish more easily and more consistently than many softwood species. It's also more expensive, and some hardwood species may be more difficult to find locally.

Softwood, from needle-bearing evergreen trees, is readily available at the home center, but it also tends to chip, split, and fray during machine cutting, especially with a blade that is not clean and sharp. Softwoods can be downright frustrating to chisel, especially across the grain, because the fibers bend and collapse, though ultra-sharp cutting edges and patience will win out. Sanding softwoods is more difficult because of how quickly the wood is removed. It is much easier to sand errors into pine than it is into oak. While both can be sanded to a fine finish with proper technique, a softwood will succumb to lapses in concentration more quickly.

Hardwoods can suffer these same problems, but the density and consistency of the wood fibers generally hold up better. Open-grained (coarse-grained) woods, like red oak, are more prone to these problems than hardwoods with closed grain, but any cutting problems can be minimized by maintaining sharp, clean cutters.

Of the more popular hardwood species used in woodworking, poplar, walnut, maple, and mahogany are generally easier to machine than cherry and oak, both of which chip more easily (see **Figure 5.2**). Proper technique is required on all of them, but the more user-friendly properties of poplar can make learning basic techniques a little easier than with wood that is more sensitive.

Figure 5.1. Using a sharp chisel can be easier on hardwood like the oak on the left. Notice the rounded edge along the top of the cut in the pine on the right. Same chisel, same striking force, very different results because the pine is much softer.

Figure 5.2. Even when you do everything right, inconsistencies in the wood may cause problems. This dado was cut in red oak using a sharp, high-quality bit and a backer block to prevent tearout. Yet, when I removed the backer block, this chip fell out.

Lumber's little secret

Somewhere along the line, the word "nominal" was slipped into the lumber vocabulary. The relevant part of Webster's definition of "nominal" is as follows: "existing or being something in name or form only; of, being, or relating to a designated or theoretical size that may vary from the actual." Applied to wood, nominal simply means "less."

The dimensions listed on the sticker on a piece of wood are not what you get. A 2 x 4 is 1½" by 3½". A board sold as a nominal 1 x 6 actually measures ¾" x 5½". That nominal dimension is the size of the board when it was rough sawn, before it was planed to thickness and width. See the accompanying wood thickness chart for an expanded list of these disparities. In most cases, the advertised length is correct—in fact, it is usually rounded in your favor—but since this "nominal" deal snuck in, I check all dimensions frequently. Call me paranoid.

Calculating board feet

A board foot is the unit of measurement of lumber volume: One board foot is equal to 144 cubic inches. This unit of measurement is used when buying lumber because wood is typically priced by the board foot (Bd. ft.). Board feet are also used when determining how much wood will be needed for a certain project.

Calculating board feet often causes confusion for the new woodworker, but a simple formula will allow you to calculate board feet with ease. Multiply the thickness of the lumber by its width and length (all measured in inches), and divide that product by 144. Use the nominal measurements of the board when calculating board feet.

(Thickness" x Width" x Length") / 144" = Bd. ft.

For example, a 3' (or 36") long 2 x 4 is 2 board feet.
(2" x 4" x 36") / 144" = 2 Bd. ft.
A 10' x 1" x 8" piece of lumber is 6.67 board feet.
(120" x 1" x 8") / 144" = 6.67 Bd. ft.

If calculating board footage for a project, be sure to factor in additional footage to compensate for waste. Add an extra 15% if purchasing high-quality wood; add 30% or more if using lower-grade lumber, which contains more defects.

For example, if you need 3 board feet of high-quality lumber for a project, it would be wise to purchase 3.4 or 3.5 board feet to allow for flaws in the wood that you'll have to discard.

3 Bd. ft. x .15 = .45
3 + .45 = 3.45 Bd. ft.

If you chose instead to purchase lower-grade wood for the same project, you'd need at least .9 extra board feet, so buy 4 board feet.

3 Bd. ft. x .3 = .9 Bd. ft.
3 + .9 = 3.9 Bd. ft.

Nominal	Actual
1" x 2"	¾" x 1½"
1" x 3"	¾" x 2½"
1" x 4"	¾" x 3½"
1" x 6"	¾" x 5½"
1" x 8"	¾" x 7½"
1" x 10"	¾" x 9¼"
1" x 12"	¾" x 11¼"
1¼" x 4"	1" x 3½"
1¼" x 6"	1" x 5½"
1¼" x 8"	1" x 7¼"
1¼" x 10"	1" x 9¼"
1¼" x 12"	1" x 11¼"
1½" x 4"	1¼" x 3½"
1½" x 6"	1¼" x 5½"
1½" x 8"	1¼" x 7¼"
1½" x 10"	1¼" x 9¼"
1½" x 12"	1¼" x 11¼"
2" x 4"	1½" x 3½"
2" x 6"	1½" x 5½"
2" x 8"	1½" x 7¼"
2" x 10"	1½" x 9¼"
2" x 12"	1½" x 11¼"
4" x 4"	3½" x 3½"
4" x 6"	3½" x 5½"

Softwood plywood thicknesses		
Nominal	**Actual**	**Note:** Hardwood veneer plywood is often sized at "full" thickness, meaning ¾" is actually ¾". Check the actual thickness before buying any wood!
¼"	15⁄64"	
⅜"	13⁄32	
½	31⁄64	
⅝"	19⁄32	
¾"	23⁄32	

Quick Wood Primer

Hardwoods

Species: Alder
Features: Pale pinkish brown. Medium strength. Easy to work. Accepts glues, fasteners well.
Uses: Cabinets, toys, carving, turning, paneling, plywood veneers
Availability: Plentiful

Species: Ash, White
Features: Cream-colored with grayish brown streaks to light brown. Strong. Elastic. Accepts adhesives, fasteners well. Finishes well.
Uses: Fine furniture, furniture components, decorative veneers, tool handles
Availability: Plentiful

Species: Beech
Features: Pale tan with small, abundant dark rays. Strong. Requires considerable effort to work with hand tools. Accepts glues, fasteners well. Moderately fine texture. May not stain evenly.
Uses: Cabinets, furniture, turning, kitchenware, flooring, veneers
Availability: Plentiful

Species: Birch
Features: Grayish white. Strong. Accepts glues, fasteners well. Relatively easy to finish. Fine texture.
Uses: Cabinets, furniture, turning, plywood veneers, paneling, interior trim
Availability: Moderately plentiful

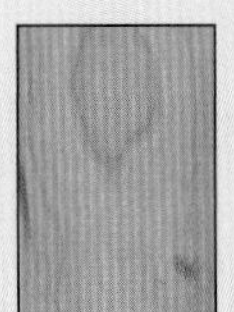

Species: Black Cherry
Features: Red brown. Strong. Fine texture. Works easily. Finishes well. Popular cabinet wood.
Uses: Cabinets, furniture, turning, carving, decorative veneers, interior trim
Availability: Adequate

Species: Hickory
Features: Whitish; darker-colored heartwood favored in cabinetmaking. Member of the walnut family. Strong. Coarse texture. Very elastic. Dense, difficult to work with hand tools. Difficult to glue. Takes clear finishes well.
Uses: Furniture, tool handles, sports equipment, plywood veneers
Availability: Plentiful

Species: Locust
Features: Creamy white to vivid yellow. Hard, heavy, extremely strong, ranks with hickory as one of the toughest woods native to North America. Dense. Used for pegs in 19th-century post-and-beam construction.
Uses: Furniture, turning
Availability: Plentiful

Species: Mahogany
Features: Red brown. Medium strength. Works easily. Accepts glue, fasteners well. Finishes well.
Uses: Cabinets, fine furniture, decorative veneers, turning, carving, model making
Availability: Becoming scarce

Species: Maple
Features: Creamy tan. Strong. Turns well. Accepts glue, fasteners well. Fine texture. Finishes nicely.
Uses: Cabinets, furniture, turning, decorative veneers, flooring, interior trim, plywood
Availability: Plentiful

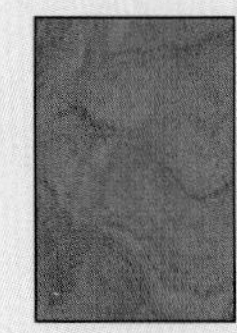

Species: Mesquite
Features: Reddish brown. Strong. Turns exceptionally well. Low natural luster. Coarse texture.
Uses: Cabinets, carving, turning, flooring
Availability: Plentiful (but difficult to find at retail outlets)

Species: Oak, Red
Features: Pinkish tan to reddish brown. May be streaked with dark brown stains or edged by pinkish yellow sapwood. Coarse texture. Strong. Works well. Stains readily. Accepts glue, fasteners well. Do not use with iron fasteners because of high tannin content.
Uses: Cabinets, furniture, trim, plywood
Availability: Plentiful

Species: Pecan
Features: Cinnamon tan. Machines well, difficult to work with hand tools.
Uses: Furniture, turning, veneers, tool handles
Availability: Adequate (but quality varies greatly)

Species: Poplar, Yellow
Features: White or yellowish brown, with streaks of green, purple, black, blue, red, or brown. Fine texture. Medium strength. Works easily. Accepts glue, fasteners well. Seal before staining. Paints well.
Uses: Cabinets, furniture, interior trim, plywood veneers
Availability: Plentiful

Species: Sassafras
Features: Pale brown to orange brown. Coarse texture. Not strong. Works easily with hand tools, but prone to splitting and checking. Accepts glue, fasteners well. Finishes well.
Uses: Boxes, turning, carving
Availability: Adequate

Species: Sycamore
Features: Light grayish yellow to reddish brown. Fine grain. Medium strength. Works easily with sharp hand tools. Finishes well.
Uses: Furniture, turning, inlay, decorative veneers
Availability: Plentiful

Species: Walnut, Black
Features: Dark brown, with magenta, purple, or gray highlights. Strong. Works easily. Turns well. Accepts glue, fasteners well. Finishes well.
Uses: Fine furniture, cabinets, boxes, carving, turning, decorative veneers, inlay, marquetry
Availability: Adequate

Softwoods

Species: Cedar, Western Red
Features: Reddish brown. Coarse texture. Low strength. Works easily. Accepts glue, fasteners well. Finishes well. Splits easily.
Uses: Lawn furniture, millwork, decking, siding
Availability: Adequate

Species: Douglas Fir
Features: Orange brown color. Linear grain pattern. Relatively strong.
Uses: Cabinets, furniture, paneling, siding, flooring, plywood, house framing
Availability: Plentiful

Species: Pine, Southern Yellow
Features: Coarse texture. High resin content.
Uses: Rustic furniture, flooring, decking, plywood
Availability: Plentiful

Species: Pine, White
Features: Light brown, often with red tint. Medium strength. Works easily, but deposits resins on tools. Holds fasteners well. Finishes well. Used for country-style furniture.
Uses: Cabinets, furniture, millwork, carving, toys, interior trim, model making
Availability: Plentiful

Plywood

There are many different kinds of plywood and other man-made boards. They have the advantage of being dimensionally stable, flat, and large, typically sold as 4' x 8' sheets in various thicknesses. Most home centers offer the following:

- **Softwood plywood in various grades,** rated for exterior or interior (cabinet) uses. It's mostly made of the same stuff as 2 x 4s, that is, Douglas fir and various other softwoods. Kitchen cabinets often are made from interior grade softwood plywood.
- **Hardwood plywood with various species** as the face veneer. The interior plies probably are poplar, birch, or alder. You can make fine cabinets with hardwood plywood.
- **Medium-density fiberboard (MDF),** a pressed board made of wood chips and glue. It usually gets covered with plastic laminate or veneer, but, in its raw form, it is good stuff for jigs and shop furniture.
- **Particleboard, a pressed board similar to MDF** but with bigger wood chips and a coarser surface. It's used in construction but usually not for cabinets.
- **Melamine board,** a fiberboard with white plastic laminate (melamine) glued to both surfaces. It's often used for cabinets and closets (see **Figure 5.3**).

Softwood plywood is not immune to nominal shrinkage. What used to be ¾" thick is now 23⁄32" thick (see **Figure 5.4**), though hardwood veneer plywood remains a full ¾" thick, in most cases. I check these dimensions too, though most plywood does carry its actual thickness on the label. This small reduction in plywood thickness means little in terms of strength. However, when cutting dados that rely on a snug fit to be strong, the nominal thickness becomes important and frustrating.

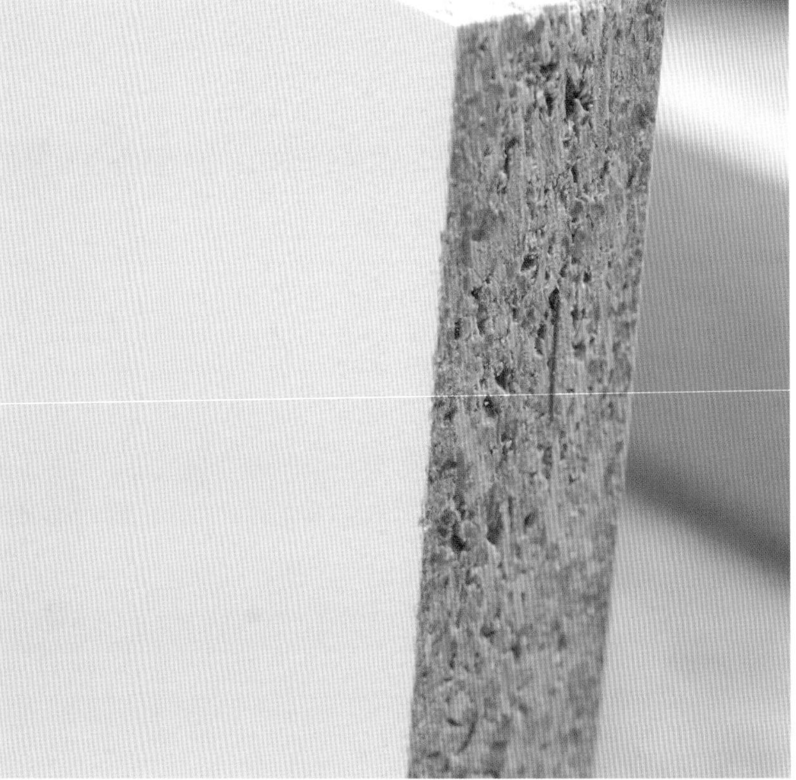

Figure 5.3. Another alternative wood type is manufactured melamine board, which is fiberboard or particleboard with a plastic laminate already applied. It's popular for cabinets and shelves.

Figure 5.4. In most situations, the difference in thickness between real ¾"-thick wood and 23⁄32"-thick plywood may have little impact. It becomes very important when you cut dados and rabbets because they should fit tight.

Finding good wood

A common question from new woodworkers is where they can find good wood. You can find a home center or a builder's lumberyard almost anywhere, and that's where most new woodworkers turn first. While most major cities have dedicated woodworking retailers and perhaps a hardwood dealer or two, many woodworkers have the good sense not to live in those areas. Living away from the city can mean long drives, mail order, or even cutting wood themselves. Rural woodworkers also have a better chance of finding (or knowing) a local sawyer, but that type of source is usually limited to local species (which some would consider a good thing).

Wood from the Home Center

Though hardwood offerings are typically limited to red oak and poplar—when they have any at all—home centers always have lots of pine, though you do have to look carefully to find straight boards you can work with. The large volume of pine is a plus because it allows you to sort through the split, twisted, knot-infested junk to find a few decent pieces. The red oak and poplar tend to be relatively high quality and are priced accordingly.

Pine is not everyone's choice, but if you look back at many of the classic Shaker and Craftsman pieces, you see that pine was frequently chosen for projects that have become time-honored classics. Though woodworkers tend to start out using lots of pine because of its availability and low cost, many do not forsake pine entirely when they move on to hardwoods. As your skills grow, that cheap, soft wood can be turned into projects of which anyone can be proud.

Poplar, though part of the hardwood family, is relatively soft, machines exceptionally well, and is moderately priced. Many large chain home centers have poplar that is dimensionally correct, dry, and straight. While certainly not cheap, poplar can be a reasonable alternative to other hardwoods. The final out-of-pocket

Cutters to Match

For a long time, woodworkers were forced to use undersize tools and make multiple passes to create dados that fit the skinny plywood properly. Recently, router bit manufacturers have designed dado-cutting bits with diameters matching the new plywood thicknesses. While using these new reality-size router bits is a huge step forward, you still have to check the wood because even small variances in thickness can mean sanding before everything fits properly. The moral of this story is that those who measure wood before cutting it are better off than those who assume they know the thickness.

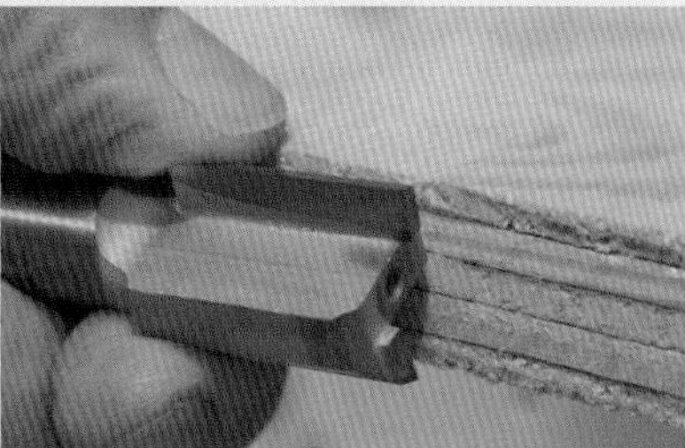

The advent of plywood-size router bits has made cutting dados for odd-size wood much easier. This $^{23}/_{32}$" bit is one of a set that handles the most common plywood thicknesses.

New Wood-Words:
Flat Sawn, Quarter Sawn, Rift Sawn

Remember that wood was sliced out of trees, which have annual rings. How the boards look depends on how they were sawn in relation to those rings, which you can determine by looking at the end grain.

Flat sawn or plain sawn: The log was sliced through and through. On the end, the rings are broad arcs running from edge to edge. On the surface, the wood figure tends to be whorls and long Vs. Most softwood lumber is flat sawn.

Quarter sawn: The log was sliced through its center, and the resulting half-logs again sliced through the center. On the end, the rings cross the thickness of the wood, making short arcs from edge to edge. On the surface, the wood figure tends to be long straight lines, and some species, like white oak, show lustrous patches called rays. Quarter-sawn wood moves less than flat sawn and is considered more desirable.

Rift sawn: The wood was sawn somewhere in between flat sawn and quarter sawn. On the ends, the rings make diagonal lines. On the surface, the figure tends to be straight, but some Vs and whorls may also form.

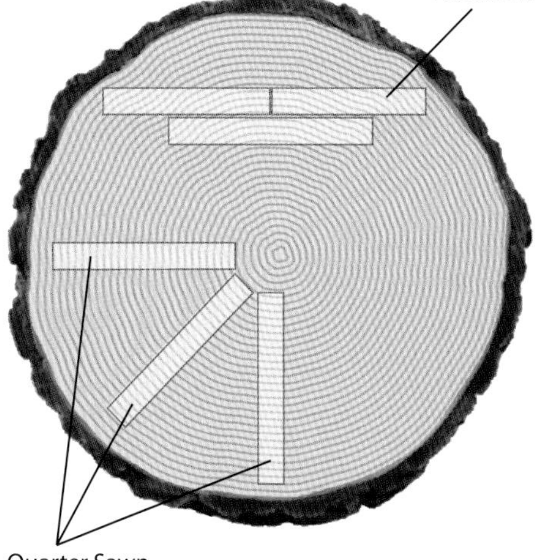

expenditure for ready-to-use poplar can be acceptable for many projects.

I like poplar because it machines better than virtually any other wood and can be a good foundation for learning to make joints. For painted projects, it is perfect. The downside to poplar is its predominantly greenish brown coloring (see **Figure 5.5**). You can use stain and transparent finishes to make poplar more visually appealing, but it is difficult even on a good day.

For an introduction to working with hardwoods, try red oak. It is medium hard, medium coarse in texture, and medium high in price. It machines well, but you have to be careful that it doesn't chip out as the cutter exits the wood. It also takes a clear finish nicely, but you may want to fill the open pores first. You'll probably be able to find some nice red oak at your local home center, and, if you enjoy working with it, you'll be encouraged to seek out other hardwoods to try.

More Wood Sources

Stand-alone lumberyards are increasingly difficult to find but can offer a wide range of wood species and services that make the search worthwhile. They'll also carry a better grade of pine than you'll find at the home center. If your shop lacks a jointer and planer, a good wood outlet can be your savior because they may offer jointing and planing services for a fee. As opposed to trying to learn joinery and proper building techniques with crooked wood, springing for basic preparation can be money well spent.

The best way to find good wood sources is local networking and on the Internet. If there are woodworkers in your area, they are getting wood from somewhere. Ask at the local woodworking shop (staff and other customers), and you may turn up a local source or two. Search the Internet and consult sites like *www.woodfinder.com*, and you can develop leads that will help track down wood sellers in your area. You may also find Internet forums that give you the chance to ask many woodworkers at once. Asking about a local wood supplier on a web resource may sound odd, but you may be surprised by how many woodworkers in your area respond.

Figure 5.5. The problem with poplar is applying stain and a clear finish. It is very difficult to make the greenish brown wood attractive. However, poplar takes paint exceptionally well and is a common choice for painted projects.

Wood and Water

When wood first comes off the tree, it contains a lot of water. By the time you buy it, most of that water has been dried off. As the wood dries, it also shrinks, just like a kitchen sponge. However, unlike a sponge, it shrinks mostly along the broad arc of the annual rings, somewhat less from one ring to the next, and hardly at all in length.

Why do you care about shrinkage if the wood is dry when you buy it? Here's the tricky part: The wood continues to swell and shrink in response to the humidity in your shop and home, a phenomenon called wood movement. Since many parts of the country have high humidity and are very damp in summer, the wood is at its largest dimension then. And where the climate is dry in winter, it shrinks to its smallest dimension then. Varnish and other finishes will slow down wood movement, but they won't prevent it.

So how much movement are we talking about? It depends on the species, but in a flat-sawn board, between ¼" and ½" per foot of width is typical. In a quarter-sawn board, maybe half that.

That's why woodworkers avoid gluing wide pieces face to face at right angles to one another, a no-no called cross-grain construction. It's very likely to break apart due to wood movement, no matter how much glue you use. That's also why woodworkers don't glue solid wood panels into frames; when the panel expands, it may break the frame apart.

Sawing Your Own Wood

Cutting your own wood may seem like the cheap way to supply the woodworking habit, but that illusion evaporates quickly when the equipment needed to produce even rough slabs of wood is considered. The cost of this kind of machinery can make having wood delivered by limo seem fiscally appropriate.

Even if you are blessed with a portable mill, jointer, and planer, you must find trees you can convert to useable wood. That is seldom cheap or easy. Trees that fall over on their own are riddled with rot, bugs, or both.

Assuming you have the truck and the machines to get the wood home and sliced into boards, you need to dry the wood before you can use it. A large shed or similar shelter will be needed to protect the wood from the elements, along with a considerable amount of patience. After the wood is cut and properly stacked, you can sit down and take a break while it dries, or seasons, for roughly one year per inch of wood thickness.

If you have a good moisture meter, you can augment your daily exercise routine with running out to the drying shed to check the drying process. It will still take around a year or so per inch of thickness, but when the wood finally does dry, you will be in great shape to carry it to the shop.

Storing Wood

Seasoned wood can be stored in flat piles in the workshop or out in the garage. Put down cross pieces of scrap wood to lift the pile off the floor, and make the pile level and tight. When you are ready to use the wood, bring it into the workshop a few weeks early to let it acclimate. Instead of piling the wood close together, put ¾"-thick sticks between each layer. Arrange these sticks, called stickers, every 2' or so along the pile. That way air can circulate all around the wood.

When you are trying to dry fresh-sawn wood, stack it with stickers in the garage or under a lean-to. It should be exposed to the outdoor air, but not to direct sun, rain, or snow.

Rough-Sawn Wood

If you are lucky enough to have a hardwood outlet or woodworking store that sells lumber, you may be able to get rough-sawn wood, often at a reasonably good price. You'll find it sold in several different conditions:

- Green, meaning sawn from the log into boards but not dried
- Air dried, meaning stacked outdoors under cover to dry
- Kiln dried, meaning cooked in an oven to dry
- Rough sawn, meaning as it came off the log
- S2S, meaning planed smooth on both sides
- S4S, meaning planed smooth on both sides and both long edges
- FAS, meaning Firsts and Seconds, high-grade wood sold at a premium price
- No. 1 Common, No. 2 Common, meaning wood with a lot of defects

Because this wood is intended to be finish machined by the woodworker, it usually is close to the nominal size, and sometimes it is even larger. This is a good thing if you have a jointer and a planer in the shop, or know someone who does. In addition to saving money on the initial price of the wood, being able to handle rough-sawn material can make more species available to you locally. Retailers that cater specifically to woodworkers, including local sawyers if you can find them, tend to offer at least some of their wood stocks in rough-sawn form.

Rough-sawn wood is usually ⅛" to 3⁄16" over the standard ¾" thickness to allow the woodworker room to refine the surface with a planer and end up with true ¾"-thick stock.

Using Cheap Wood

The cheapest wood probably will be found in your own pile of scraps and short ends (see **Figure 5.6**). You already paid for it, and you probably were going to burn it, so mine the pile for practice and test pieces, extra parts, and even whole projects.

The cheap pile at the local lumberyard is likely to have relatively straight wood in it if you are willing to dig for it. Taking the time to look down the edges and flat sides to see if the wood is straight (or close) is worth the time it takes. It's also a skill you will need later when digging through the piles of expensive hardwoods. Being more expensive does nothing to diminish their capacity to warp and twist.

Look for cracks, splits, and especially knots. A tight knot in the middle of a board can be attractive. Any knot, tight or loose, near the edge can become a missile during cutting or shaping. Given the option, find another board without a dangerous edge.

Figure 5.6. One of the first things a woodworker develops is an ever-growing pile of scraps. This pile is a source of wood for test pieces, extra parts, and at times, entire projects.

Salvage Wood

Woodworkers tend to be resourceful when it comes to finding wood to work with. Everything from discarded pallets to piles of wood from demolition can be attractive and cheap. While reclaimed lumber can be free, or close to it, preparing it for use can be labor intensive and not without expense.

The primary concern with used wood is unseen metal within it. Anything from bullets, staples, nails, or screws can destroy saw blades and the cutters inside jointers and planers. In addition to damaging cutters, hitting a bit of metal could damage a blade or knife sufficiently for pieces to fly off at dangerous speeds.

Visually inspecting wood may be free, but it is only effective if the metal is at or above the surface. Old wood also can have metal buried within it. The only reliable way to find these hidden dangers is with a metal detector. A metal detector will cost between $30 and $200 or so, but considering the cost of replacing a saw blade or knife set (you won't nick just one), the expenditure makes sense.

Wood from old buildings can be a real find because it often was harvested back when trees were real trees, not the speed-grown and cut-early versions that dominate wood supplies today. You will need to pull all the nails, then scrape, sand, and plane it, but the old wood can be spectacular when cleaned up.

Another good thing about old wood is that it was cut and sized before the era of nominal dimensions. Old boards can be well over ¾" thick, even thicker if they were used as flooring. That gives the woodworker plenty of room to refurbish them and still have ¾"-thick or better material.

A word of caution: Just because a building is being torn down and the wood is piled up on the side does not give you license to fill up the pickup. Someone still owns it and may have plans for it and you, should he or she witness what the police might consider outright thievery on your part. Ask first; load later!

Defects in Wood

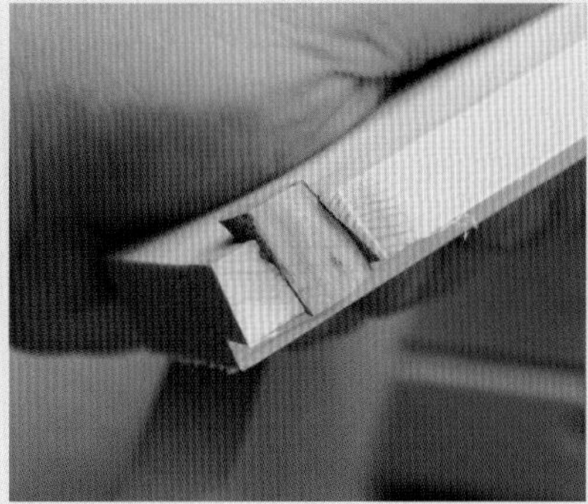

This knot felt and looked tight on inspection, but as the rabbet was cut beneath it, the knot came loose. Fortunately, the knot was not thrown out, though that can and does happen. Laying out cuts to avoid knots, cracks, and other defects is as much a safety issue as it is a matter of appearance.

Another important woodworking skill is choosing wood that doesn't work against you. Warped or twisted wood makes things tougher than they need to be. Good joints are all but impossible if the wood itself is not straight.

Wood is graded and priced according to how much usable material you might expect to cut from in between its various defects. When you get a bargain on wood, you're probably buying a lot of defects along with whatever clear cuttings you might obtain. Typical defects include:

- Knots, where a branch was anchored. You can't cut joints in knots, so you have to crosscut around them.
- Splits, where the wood grain has come apart in a lengthwise crack. The crack usually extends farther than you think. You have to rip the plank for what usable width there is.
- Wane, an edge with bark still on it. You'll have to saw it off, unless you are going for the natural-edge look.
- Pith, the center of the tree, unstable wood. If you have a wide plank containing the pith, saw on each side of the pith to make two narrower planks.
- Bow, wood with a curved surface from end to end, like an archer's bow. Spot it by looking down the surface from one end. Crosscut the bowed plank into shorter pieces.
- Crook, wood with a curved edge, like a kid's drawing of a rainbow. Joint the edges to remove crook.
- Cup, wood that's curved across its surface. Joint the surface to remove cup.
- Twist, wood that's like a potato chip. You can't do much to remove twist, except to saw the board into little pieces, so try to avoid buying it.

Figure 6.4. It's another chicken-and-egg proposition: to make a straight edge, you have to start with one. So make a sled by ripping a 4"-wide piece off a ¾" sheet of plywood, screw it onto a wider piece of ¼" plywood, add a couple of hold-down clamps, and use that. Clamp the board to be straightened onto this sled, and guide the long edge of the plywood against the fence to saw one edge of the workpiece straight. Because the wood is suspended on the jig, it is best to take the smallest cut possible to straighten the edge. Then, remove it from the jig, put the newly sawn edge against the fence, and make a pass to cut the opposing edge parallel to it, again taking the minimum cut needed to do it. Turn the board around and rip it to final width, squaring the edge originally straightened on the jig at the same time.

The traditional face edge mark is another looping lowercase *L* with the end of the stroke pointing toward the face side or a simple *V* with the vortex pointing toward the face side. But here again, you can use any mark you like.

Figure 6.3. The jointer is the best tool for creating a straight and square face edge on a board. As soon as the leading edge of the workpiece crosses the cutter head, transfer downward pressure to the outfeed side.

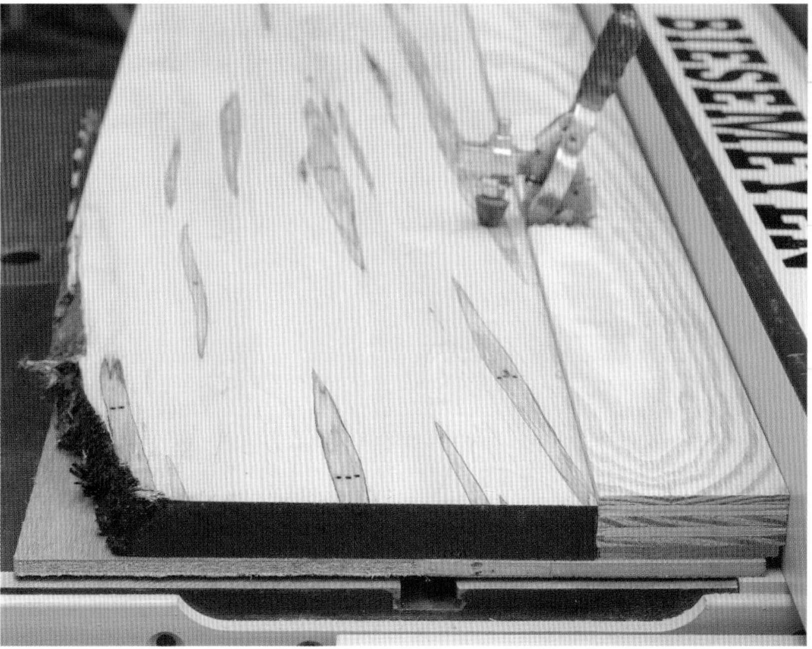

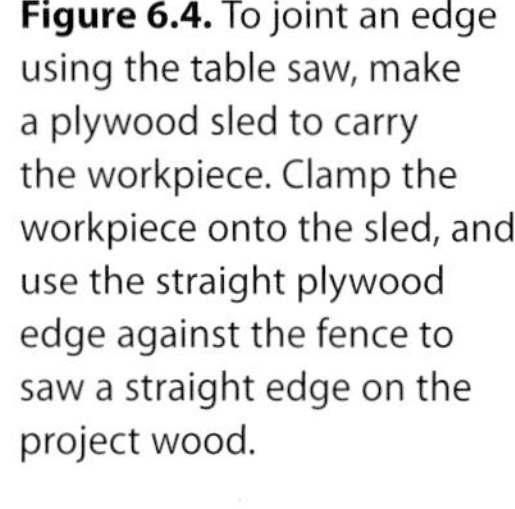

Figure 6.4. To joint an edge using the table saw, make a plywood sled to carry the workpiece. Clamp the workpiece onto the sled, and use the straight plywood edge against the fence to saw a straight edge on the project wood.

Ripping to width

Once you have a face side and edge, ripping to width is easy. On the table saw, just set the saw fence to the width you want, hold the face edge against the fence and the face side down on the saw table, and cut, as shown in **Figure 6.5**. Be sure to saw all the parts that are to be the same width at the same time. Even small differences in width will affect how your project comes together. With a portable circular saw, clamp a straight board to the workpiece to guide the cut. The little rip guide that comes with some circular saws just follows the edge whether it is straight or not.

Figure 6.5. Once you have made a face edge, or have straightened one edge, place that edge against the saw fence to rip the board to width, making the opposing edge parallel to the straightened edge at the same time.

Planing to thickness

The next step in preparation is planing the wood to thickness and simultaneously making the second side parallel to the face side. Planing the wood now prevents having to feed short lengths of wood into the planer, something that is dangerous. The planer instruction manual usually gives a minimum stock length for that machine, commonly around 18". If you are using planed wood from the home center, it has already been through a thickness planer, so you can skip this step if it is at the thickness desired. However, you will often get a smoother surface if you do plane off a little bit yourself (see **Figure 6.6**).

Remember that the planer keys off the surface of the wood that is facing down on the table. The cutter head is above the wood, parallel to the table, and is separated by only several inches from a pair of rollers, one before and one after the cutter head. Even if the bottom face of the wood is flat across its width, if the board has a bow or twist along its length, the planer will duplicate that defect. The top face will be flat side to side and parallel with the bottom face, but the long axis twist or bow will remain.

The length of the planer tables is only important to supporting the wood as it enters and exits the planer and to helping prevent snipe. Snipe is a slight dishing of the ends of the board. Usually snipe is confined to just a few inches, equal to the distance between the rollers and the cutter head. If the wood is not supported adequately by the planer tables or a work support outside of the planer, the board tries to tip up into the cutter head while it is controlled by only one of the rollers.

Planing across the full width of a board creates considerable stress that can lead to chipping and other small irregularities. Taking light cuts in the 1⁄32" range helps minimize these defects plus is easier on the planer and its knives.

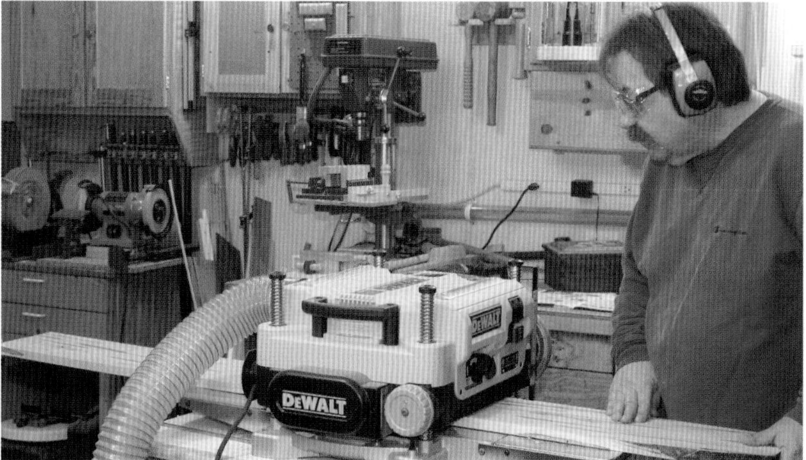

Figure 6.6. Plane the wood to final thickness, and smooth the surface using a thickness planer.

Crosscutting to length

The length of project parts is very important. In a square or rectangular project, the opposing sides (front/back or left/right) must be identical in length for the project to come out square. Identical length parts also allow the ends that will be joined to mate perfectly, making full use of the available contact area.

First, crosscut one end square, and, if there are a lot of parts, crosscut one end of all of them. Then, cut them all to finished length. Even small differences in length will force you to make compromises during assembly. Using a stop or gauge block (see Using a Gauge Block on the next page) is a cheap, effective way to make identical cuts whenever more than one is needed. Many aftermarket miter guides are equipped with adjustable stops that make cutting identical-length pieces easy.

A sliding compound miter saw is a good choice for this job (see **Figure 6.7**), but a properly adjusted table saw will also do a very good job. For multiple parts, you can clamp a stop block to its fence.

Marking the wood

After the machining of the wood is complete, take the time to look over the pieces and choose the sides that will face outward (presentation), and then mark them clearly. You wait until after all of the machining is complete because that process will remove those marks anyway and the figure often looks considerably different after even small amounts of wood are removed.

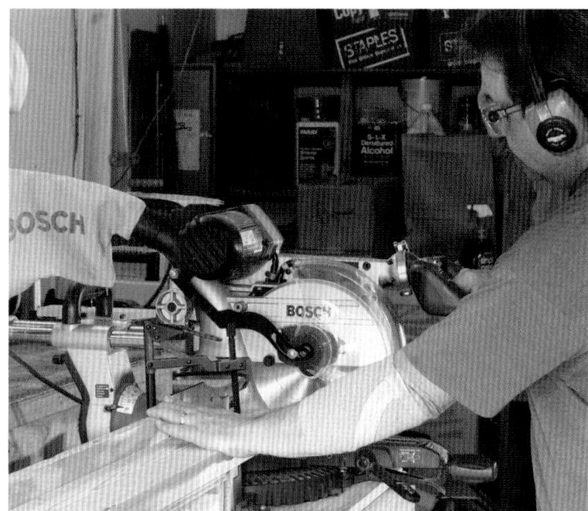

Figure 6.7. The sliding compound miter saw is a good choice for crosscutting wood to length. A properly aligned table saw and miter guide will also do a very good job.

However you decide to mark project pieces, be sure those marks are clear and easy for you to understand—then be consistent. Develop your own marking scheme and then stick to it (see **Figure 6.8**).

Choosing and marking the presentation sides of the wood will help prevent cutting the joint on the wrong side, something that is exceptionally easy to do for veteran and novice woodworkers. For the new woodworker who is concentrating on learning to make the joint or to use a joinery jig, mistaking in which side the joint is to be cut is easier yet. Taking the time to mark the stock can help make sure that any uglies like odd-looking knots or other defects will wind up on the inside of a box rather than front and center if you accidentally machine the joints on the wrong side.

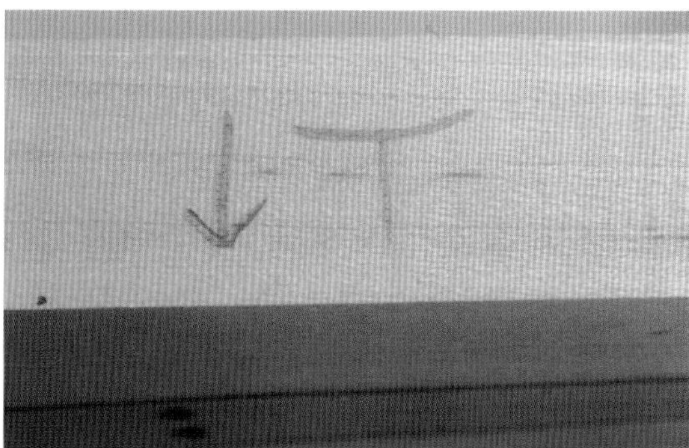
Figure 6.8. Marking the wood clearly to show which is the good, or presentation, side will prevent major mistakes later when doing the joinery. Use any marks that make sense to you. Being consistent with the marking scheme will make life easier in years to come.

Using a Gauge Block

Crosscutting to length on the table saw using the miter guide and rip fence simultaneously is a major no-no. That is because it is a great way to trap the cut-off piece between the blade and the fence and initiate a violent kickback. To prevent this and still make accurate, repetitive cuts, you have to create a gauge block that forces space between the wood and the fence before the wood reaches the saw blade.

A gauge block is nothing more than a piece of wood clamped to the fence, close to the forward edge of the saw table. If the fence-to-blade distance is measured from that block, rather than from the fence, you can make accurate repeat cuts using the miter guide without having to duck flying wood. Be sure to stop the saw before retrieving the cut-off pieces between cuts.

Set the Fence. To set the fence-to-blade distance, temporarily clamp the block to the table saw fence, even with the blade, and measure from the gauge block to the blade. Remember to measure to the correct side of the blade! For cutting off a piece, measure to the side of the blade facing the gauge block. When making a shoulder cut, dado, or rabbet, use the side of the blade facing away from the gauge block. Lock the fence down.

Move the Block. Move the gauge block close to the operator's edge of the table, and clamp it securely to the fence. The gauge block has to be far enough from the blade so the wood will not be in contact with it and the blade at the same time. If the stock being cut is too wide to clear the gauge block before contacting the blade, you need to devise another method.

Make the Cut. To use the gauge block, place the wood against the miter guide fence, and slide it over until it contacts the gauge block. Hold the wood tightly against the miter guide fence while you slide it forward off the gauge block toward the blade, and make the cut.

Scrap Falls Free. Using a gauge block allows the scrap to fall free without becoming wedged between the fence and the blade. After the cut, shut off the saw, wait for the blade to stop, and then remove the cut-off piece.

Chapter 7

Adhesives and Fasteners

A major part of assembling woodworking projects is fastening the parts together in a way that is both attractive and strong. Woodworkers today have many new glues to help with this process. The science behind the many types of adhesives woodworkers use has made them stronger, more predictable, and easier to use—provided that you choose the right glue for the job, learn good gluing techniques, and follow the manufacturer's directions.

We will also consider mechanical fasteners such as screws, nails, and staples. In some situations, a fastener can be used to hold the parts in place while the glue dries. In other situations, the fastener is essential to reinforce the joint, which ultimately will be held together by the combination of glue and fastener.

Keep in mind that glues and fasteners are essential to your project, especially if it needs to stand the test of time. Let's take a look at what's available.

Modern glues

There are six primary types of glue used in woodworking, all of which form strong bonds when used as directed. There are others you will hear about as you progress in the hobby, but the six covered here will be the ones you use most.

Modern glues can be applied in a wide temperature range. Probably most important is the lower end of that range, around 50 degrees Fahrenheit. With many woodworking shops located in garages and other unheated spaces, this can be a very important characteristic. It is relatively easy to bring these spaces into the 50-degree range using temporary heat sources, and you can always wrap the wood itself in an old electric blanket for an hour or so before gluing.

Glued joints do occasionally fail. When analyzing the cause of those failures, you seldom have to look farther than the woodworker who made the joint. If the parts being assembled are clean and fit well, the bond created by modern adhesives is nearly always stronger than the wood itself. When a properly made glue joint is stressed to failure, you will see glue and wood together in the break, indicating the wood around the joint failed, not the glue itself, as shown in **Figure 7.1**. If the glue were to fail, the broken joint would have glue on both pieces with no broken wood.

By understanding when and how to use which glues, you will be giving your project lasting stability.

Figure 7.1. Notice how this cyanoacrylate glue joint failed. Though the break occurred at the joint line, the glue itself did not break. The wood embedded in the glue shows that the wood fibers gave up, not the adhesive.

Glue name	Common name	Function	Features	Cost
Aliphatic Resin	Yellow Glue	Any project, wood to wood without exposure to moisture	Water-soluble in liquid state for easy cleanup; some are water resistant; no harmful vapors or strong odors; non-toxic	$
Polyurethane	Polyurethane	Any project, including outdoor	Nearly invulnerable to water; slow setting; easy cleanup; high strength	$$
Hot-Melt Polyurethane Glue	Hot-Melt Polyurethane Glue	Any project, especially outdoor applications; old style best for tacking	Waterproof; strong; fast setting	$
Two-Part Epoxy	Two-Part Epoxy	Attaching metal to wood	Water resistant; strong; various setting times; must be mixed	$$
Contact Cement	Contact Cement	Bonding plastic laminates to fiberboard and plywood	Forms instant bond; flammable; noxious fumes	$
Cyanoacrylate Glue	CA Glue or Super Glue	Tacking small pieces in place; permanent bonds; stiffening soft sections of wood; filling cracks	Very short setting time; forms quick, hard bond; variety of types	$$$
Key: $ = inexpensive; $$ = moderately expensive; $$$ = expensive				

Aliphatic Resin

Usually called yellow glue, aliphatic resin adhesives are by far the types most commonly used in woodworking (see **Figure 7.2**). Increases in the strength and versatility of aliphatic glues in recent years have expanded their range of uses.

Within the aliphatic family are formulations with varying open times (length of time the parts can be repositioned before the glue begins to set), moisture resistance, and other characteristics that allow woodworkers to choose the most appropriate one for the task.

Figure 7.2. Aliphatic resin (yellow) glues are the most commonly used in woodworking. Until recently, these glues were not suitable for moisture-prone applications. Now, several aliphatic formulations are suitable for outdoor projects. Check the label.

Though aliphatic resin glues are water soluble in their liquid state, some versions are now water resistant and can be used in non-submerged outdoor applications. Being water soluble makes them easier to clean up if you do it before they set. A damp rag or sponge is usually all that is needed to wipe up excess aliphatic glues.

Another reason aliphatic glues are so popular is that they do not produce harmful vapors or strong odors. Using them in basement or shared-space shops does not create health dangers to the woodworker or other occupants. Aliphatic glues are also non-toxic, though, as with all adhesives, you should minimize direct contact with the skin.

Polyurethane

A relative newcomer to the woodworking scene, polyurethane glues initially gained acceptance because of their near invulnerability to water. Woodworkers began using polyurethane glues for outdoor projects, but quickly found their slow setting (long open time), easy cleanup (after drying), and high strength useful on many other projects as well (see **Figure 7.3**).

Figure 7.3. Polyurethane glues gained their initial popularity because of their ability to resist water. However, their strength and relatively long open time make them right for many indoor and joinery applications as well.

Polyurethane adhesives cure in the presence of moisture. Most container instructions call for applying the polyurethane to one piece and wiping the other piece with a damp rag before assembling.

Polyurethane glues expand three to four times in volume as they begin curing. This makes them self-spreading, to an extent, though counting on this expansion for coverage is not a good plan. I have found that taking the time to apply a thin coat over the entire surface is still the best way to ensure a complete bond.

As polyurethane glue cures, it foams where it is not contained within the joint. While this foaming action will fill gaps, the foam has no appreciable strength, so it cannot be relied on as a crutch for sloppy joints. If allowed to cure completely, the foam that emerges from the joint can be scraped and sanded away easily without contaminating the surrounding wood (see **Figure 7.4**). I find this characteristic especially useful for tasks such as gluing dovetail joints in woods that reveal stray

Figure 7.4. When polyurethane glue oozes from a joint, it foams up and can be scraped or sanded away easily, as shown on the right half of this joint.

Figure 7.5. Being able to remove excess polyurethane so easily and completely is one reason I use it to secure dovetails in exotic woods. Since I started using polyurethane glues, finishing these projects with no glue-related light spots is simple.

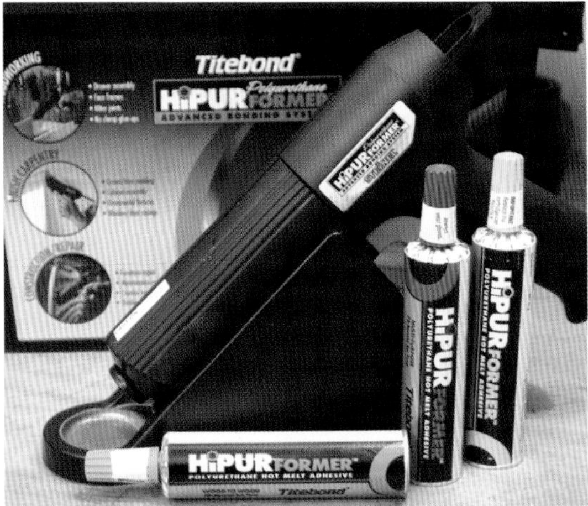

Figure 7.6. Hot-melt polyurethanes are new and show considerable promise for woodworking. Available in several set times, these glues retain most of the bond strength associated with their liquid cousins, but set quickly.

spots of glue through the finish, such as walnut and cherry, as shown in **Figure 7.5**.

The downside to using a polyurethane adhesive is that if you get it on your skin, it is going to be with you for several days. Being careful when using it is good; wearing protective disposable gloves is better. Like most glues, assemblies must be clamped while the polyurethane dries.

Hot-Melt Glue

Even newer are the hot-melt polyurethane glues (see **Figure 7.6**) that retain the strength and waterproof qualities of liquid polyurethane but have much shorter open times. So far, I have limited my use of hot-melt polyurethane to tack parts in place while I apply other glues or fasteners and to secure smaller parts, such as moldings. However, a growing number of woodworkers are using hot-melt polyurethane as a primary adhesive for many projects. I suspect hot-melt polyurethane will grow in popularity as woodworkers become more comfortable with its properties.

Older hot-melt glues are mostly based on polyvinyl acetate, the familiar milky-clear plastic from which Tupperware is made. While they are convenient and quick for tacking mock-ups and jigs together, they do not have much strength. This is the glue favored by many craft experts for sticking various parts of their projects together.

Epoxy

Before the advancements in aliphatic resin glues and the introduction of polyurethane, two-part epoxy adhesives were frequently used by woodworkers because of their high strength and water resistance. Epoxy is also formulated in a wide range of set times, making it good for complicated assemblies with many parts and also good for quick jobs that will set in a few minutes.

Epoxy remains the best glue for jobs like attaching metal to wood. If you want to permanently set a metal stud in wood, you should use epoxy. I have yet to find anything that holds as tightly and as well. Unlike most other glues, it remains strong when thickly spread to fill gaps and holes.

Most epoxies require mixing equal amounts of the two parts (see **Figure 7.7**). For small quantities, you can mix on a chunk of scrap wood or on a piece of paper. For larger quantities, use disposable

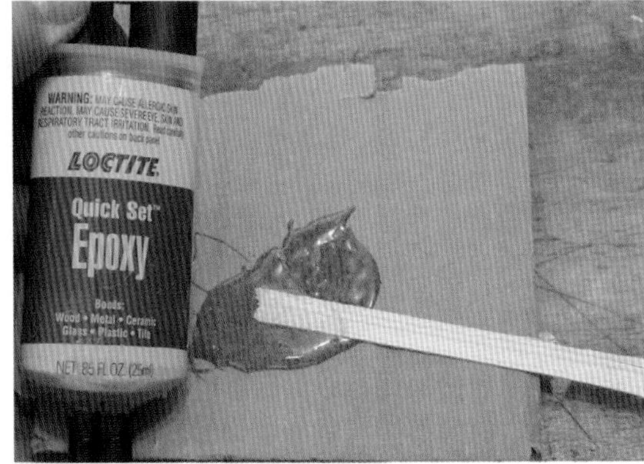

Figure 7.7. Epoxy has been around for decades and is a trusted friend of woodworkers. This two-part glue is available in formulations with a variety of set times, but all of them are very strong and waterproof.

plastic cups. Be sure to mix thoroughly, following the manufacturer's directions, and don't attempt to cheat the setting time by varying the proportions of the mix; it won't work.

In addition to the minor hassle of mixing the two parts, epoxy is less than user friendly when it comes to cleanup and to sanding away any excess after it begins setting up. Manufacturers will correctly point out that epoxy is at least as easy as any other adhesive to apply in the correct amount. Like polyurethane, it is very difficult to get off your fingers once it has begun to set up, so wear disposable gloves.

Contact Cement

Primarily used for bonding plastic laminates to fiberboard and plywood, contact cement remains part of most woodworkers' glue arsenals because no other adhesive works as well for this application. Some woodworkers do not like contact cement because, as the name suggests, it is very unforgiving during assembly. Once the parts touch together, there is no going back.

Contact cement has other drawbacks as well. Nearly all contact cements are based on volatile materials that are flammable and release noxious fumes. This is improving, due to increasingly restrictive laws being enacted that eventually will eliminate solvent-based contact cements. A few water-based versions are now on the market, and these eventually will replace solvent formulations (see **Figure 7.8**).

Whenever using contact cement, it is crucial to read, understand, and follow the instructions and warnings on the container. Breathing the fumes can be very dangerous to humans and pets. Good ventilation is mandatory. Contact cement is nothing to play with if you are not willing to follow the instructions.

Contact cement is usually spread with a roller or a flat piece of scrap laminate. However you spread it, a uniform coating on both surfaces is important. Woodworkers have devised many strategies for positioning laminate on cabinets before allowing it to touch and stick. The simplest method is to put long dowels or sticks of wood on the wood the laminate is being applied to, spaced a few inches apart. With the laminate correctly positioned on the dowels, you can remove the dowels one at a time while you press the laminate into place.

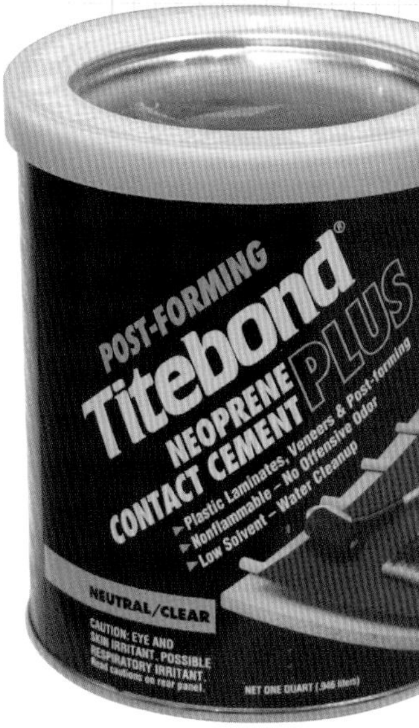

Figure 7.8. Contact cement is commonly used for adhering plastic laminates to wood substrates. Though most contact cements are solvent based, new latex-based formulas are appearing, like the Titebond shown here.

Cyanoacrylate

Cyanoacrylate glue, also called CA glue or Super Glue, is the newest adhesive in woodworking, and woodworkers are steadily finding new ways to use it. The open time is dramatically short, but the advantage of these glues is their ability to set hard almost instantly. CA glues come in a variety of thicknesses, from water-thin formulations to gooey gels (see **Figure 7.9**).

The most common use for CA glue is tacking small pieces in place while another, more traditional glue dries. Some woodworkers use CA glues for permanent bonds of small, low-stress pieces, as well.

Woodturners may be leading the hobby in CA glue use. Bowl turners have found thin CA glue to be helpful for stiffening soft and punky sections of wood, and thick CA useful for filling cracks. Some turners use CA glue to create a hard finish on small projects, like pens.

Once set, CA glue does not come off easily, and it will glue your fingertips together if you are not careful. Solvents for it are available, as are spray-on accelerators that will cause it to set in a flash.

Figure 7.9. CA (cyanoacrylate) glues are making the transition from other hobbies to woodworking. Woodworkers use CA glues for tacking small pieces in place, while turners have found them to be useful for stiffening soft wood, and even for some finishing. I suspect the use of CA glues in woodworking will slowly continue to grow.

Glue and wood grain

Wood is essentially a bundle of fibers, often compared to a fistful of soda straws. The fibers that run up and down a tree as it stands are what give wood strength. For adhesives to form the strongest possible bond, they must be able to grip those fibers. The orientation of the wood fibers to a glue joint is very important to the strength of the bond.

When you try to join the ends of two boards together, forcing the glue to grasp the ends of the grain, it is a short-grain-to-short-grain situation. Adhesives applied to end grain have little to lock onto. The bond is very weak, if it will bond at all.

The strongest wood joint comes when you glue long grain to long grain (see **Figure 7.10**), such as when you edge glue boards together to make a panel. A joint that runs parallel to the wood grain allows the adhesive to grip around the fibers.

A combination of grain orientations in one joint (long grain to short grain), such as attaching non-profiled rails to stiles when building a door frame, is no stronger than trying to bond two end-grain sections. The short-grain side of the joint remains the weak spot (see **Figure 7.11**). However, when this joint is profiled, such as when cut with a contoured router bit, parts of the profile cut into the end grain actually expose short sections of wood fiber that afford the glue a better bond. That, along with the increased surface area of the profiled joint, makes this a strong joint.

When simple, non-profiled long-grain-to-short-grain joints cannot be avoided, the only alternative is to reinforce the joint mechanically. Screws, biscuits, or dowels are all popular methods to increase the strength of these joints (see Chapter 8, "Joining Wood," on page 149).

Figure 7.10. When long-grain sections are being glued, the glue alone is enough, and mechanical help usually is not required.

Figure 7.11. When end grain is part of the joint, the glue bond is going to be weak and will need some form of mechanical reinforcement.

Drying Tips

- Consider the manufacturers' open times to be maximums.
- Consider the manufacturers' drying times to be minimums.
- Increase setting and drying times if humidity is high.

Directions and drying times

Adhesives are tested under very specific, controlled conditions. This allows the consumer to use the information provided to judge the properties of one glue against another with reasonable accuracy. However, you must recognize that your workshop does not have the high-dollar environmental controls found in testing laboratories. The variable temperature and humidity in which you use adhesives affects their performance, particularly their open times and setting, or drying, times.

Like many woodworkers, I have learned the hard way to consider the open times listed on the container to be the maximum in my shop and all set or dry times to be a minimum estimate. The manufacturers try to provide legitimate times, but unforeseen glitches in the assembly of your projects can delay that process, putting you in the danger zone where the glue can begin setting up before you are ready.

Similar problems can plague clamping and drying times. If your shop is anything like mine, humidity automatically goes up whenever I am doing a lot of gluing. If the directions suggest two hours of clamp time, I try to allow four. If the glue-up is large, overnight is the only safe bet. Twenty-four hours is even better.

Practice the Assembly

With any glue assembly, and particularly with complex jobs that have many parts, it will pay off to do a practice run before applying any glue. Get out all the clamps you expect to need, clear the work zone, and proceed as if you were using real glue. You will discover not only all the things you forgot to have at hand, but also how to get it done efficiently, giving you a fighting chance of completing the job before the glue begins to set up.

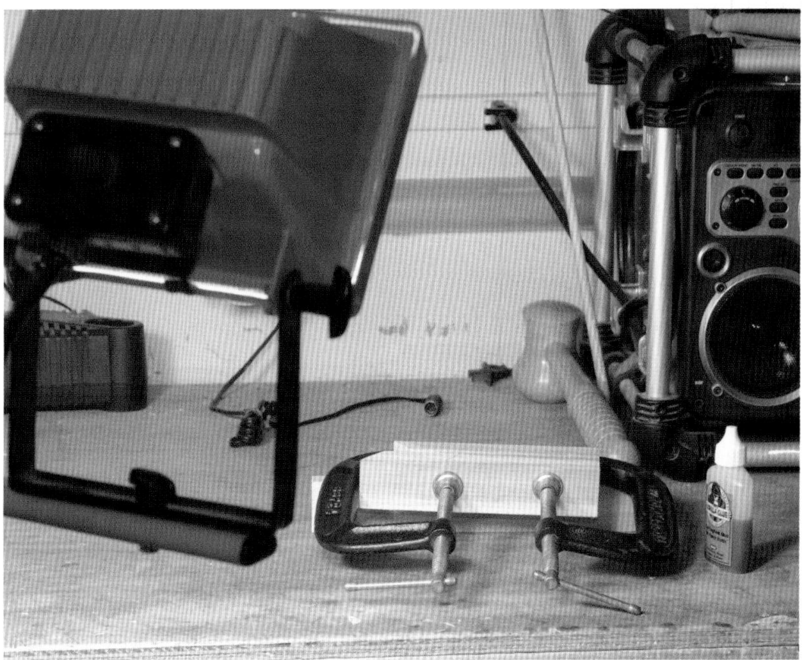

Figure 7.12. By aiming a halogen light at the glue joint and keeping it just close enough to gently warm the air around that joint, I can bring the assembly into the proper temperature range for the glue to cure properly.

Cheating Drying Times

Trying to accelerate the drying of glue by applying heat can be counterproductive because some glues actually soften when exposed to heat. If the room and material temperatures are above the minimum specified on the label, leave well enough alone and wait a little longer.

In a marginally heated shop during the winter months, introducing a small amount of heat to the general area of the joint can be helpful. However, all that is necessary is to gently warm the wood around the joint, not get it hot.

I can quickly raise the air temperature in my shop to comfortable levels, but the wood usually remains chilled much longer. I use a pair of halogen work lights on a stand, positioned a few feet from the joint, to gently warm it (see **Figure 7.12**).

If, after warming for a half hour or so, the wood does not feel cold or warm, it is probably just right. If your 98.6-degree hand feels warmth in the wood, it is logical to assume the wood is warmer than you are, putting it in the 100-degree range, and you should let it cool before gluing up.

Cold temperatures dramatically increase the setting time of epoxy glues but may prevent other types, aliphatic resin in particular, from setting properly at all. If you are using yellow glue and you see a chalky white residue on the glue line, it indicates the temperature of the wood was too low and the glue probably has failed. The only remedy is to take the piece apart, clean it up, warm it up, and try again.

How much glue?

Learning to apply the correct amount of glue to a joint is an acquired skill. Joints made with too much or too little adhesive are both weaker than one using the proper amount of adhesive. The ideal amount of glue is sufficient to grasp the fibers of both pieces of wood, without creating a pad of excess glue that holds the pieces apart.

Most adhesives are supposed to be applied in a thin coat to both pieces to ensure a complete bond. However, coating both pieces also makes it easy to use too much glue. As you gain experience making glue joints, it gets easier to resist the idea that more is better.

It is also important to keep the glue film consistent in thickness over the joint. If more glue is applied to one part of the joint than the other, clamping the pieces evenly will be very difficult. The pieces will also be more apt to slide out of alignment during clamping because they will float on the excess glue. Clamping pressure does not redistribute excess glue enough to even out the film thickness. More often, it holds the pieces out of alignment while the glue oozes out at the nearest joint line. Then, as the excess glue exits the joint, the clamping pressure can relax if you don't come back around to tighten it up.

Application Tools

Everything from brushes to rollers, roller bottles, and pieces of cardboard or scrap wood can be used to apply glue to the various types of joints you make. The goal is to achieve complete coverage of the joint area with a thin, consistent film of glue.

Flux brushes, which cost maybe 25 cents at the hardware store, make applying glue easy and quick on complex joints with multiple surfaces, like box or dovetail joints, as shown in **Figure 7.13**. These throwaway brushes have plastic bristles and a round, tin handle. Any brush will work, but trying to clean painting brushes for future use can be a lost cause.

For larger, flat surfaces, a piece of cardboard or a thin scrap of wood can help smooth a layer of glue quickly, as shown in **Figure 7.14**. Roller bottles, specifically designed for applying glue, are also popular.

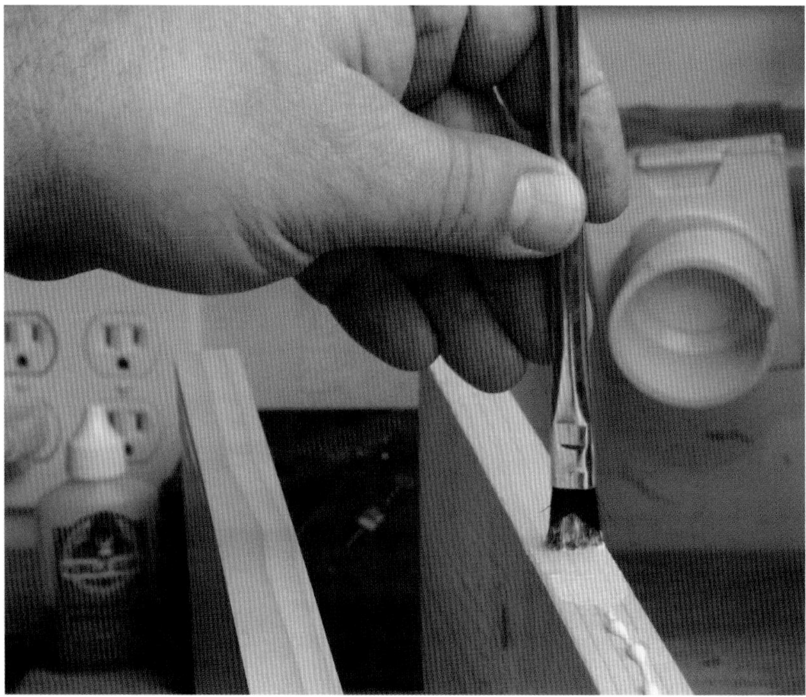

Figure 7.13. Cheap flux brushes are good for spreading glue on the edges of boards and in complex joints like dovetails.

Figure 7.14. For large, flat areas, a thin piece of scrap wood or cardboard makes a good spreader. Make sure there are no puddles or thick overlaps.

Tip!

Application Tips

- Thinly coat both pieces of wood.
- Keep the glue film consistent.

When spreading glue over a large surface, such as when bonding plastic laminates to sheets of plywood, a disposable short-napped paint roller may be the best tool. Regardless of the tool used, you have to avoid the thick lines of glue virtually any applicator can leave along the edges of each stroke. To ensure the best possible bond, those lines must be leveled out so the surfaces can make full contact and not trap the excess glue when assembled. In the case of plastic laminates, those ridges of trapped glue can become irregularities in the shiny surface after assembly. Once the glue sets up and the laminate has been installed, you can roll, press, or do whatever you like to remove the ridge, but it will remain.

Clamping

Regardless of the type of glue used, the joint must be clamped securely to achieve a solid bond, as shown in **Figure 7.15**. While pressing a joint together sounds like a simple task, it eventually gets all woodworkers in trouble, usually more than once.

Taking the time to do a test fit, including applying clamps, can reveal small problems that can be remedied before you apply the glue. Test fits also allow you to figure out how the clamps are best applied, so you can then have them laid out accordingly to speed the assembly process.

While it is impossible to use too many clamps, using too few is very easy. The idea is to apply consistent pressure over the entire joint surface. I have found it easiest to apply the clamps (lightly) that hold the pieces in alignment first, then fill in the gaps with more clamps, and then snug them all down to even out the pressure.

Most of the clamps used in woodworking are capable of applying more pressure than necessary. You only need enough pressure to hold the pieces together firmly. Cranking the clamps down too tightly can squeeze much of the glue out of the joint, dramatically reducing its strength.

Apply Clamps in a Sequence

- Apply clamps to hold pieces in alignment first.
- Fill in the gaps with more clamps.
- Snug down all the clamps.

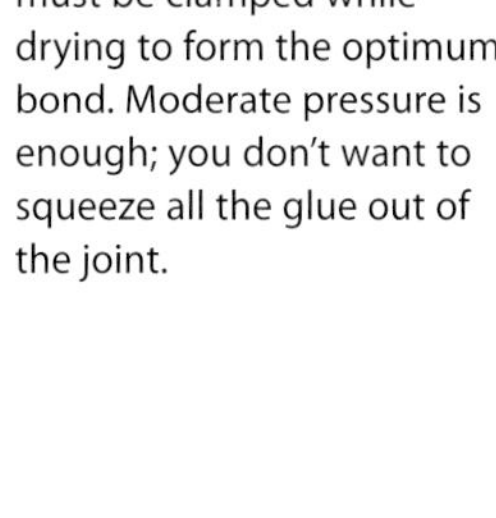

Figure 7.15. Nearly all glues must be clamped while drying to form the optimum bond. Moderate pressure is enough; you don't want to squeeze all the glue out of the joint.

Glue squeeze-out

When a joint fits correctly and the pieces are coated with the proper amount of glue, moderate clamp pressure will raise small beads of glue along the seam, as shown in **Figure 7.16**. If too much glue was applied, these beads quickly become puddles or streams that, without fail, will head for the most visible part of the project to make finishing as difficult as possible. How to deal with this squeezed-out glue has always been a point of contention among woodworkers. Some favor letting the excess glue dry, and they scrape it off later. Others prefer to clean it up immediately. I let it dry and scrape it later. I am right, but only because it works for me.

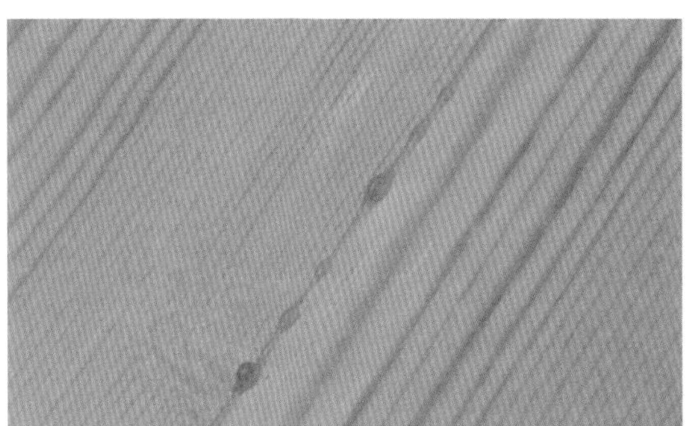

Figure 7.16. Learning to apply the correct amount of glue is a rite of passage in woodworking. Ideally, when the pieces are clamped, a line of small beads will rise from the joint.

When you allow the excess glue beads to dry, scraping them off prevents rubbing the glue into the pores of the wood with the damp rag (see **Figure 7.17**). However, if large amounts of glue emerge from the joint as it is clamped, it will run all over the project, so cleaning it up right away is the only good choice.

Figure 7.17. Some woodworkers like to wipe off squeezed-out glue with a damp rag. Others, myself included, believe that the best idea is letting the glue dry and then scraping it away with a simple painting scraper.

The directions on glue containers specify how to clean it up. Aliphatic glues can be cleaned up with a rag dampened with water. Other types of glue often require some kind of solvent, so be sure to read the directions and have the appropriate clean-up material available before making joints.

I have had a problem contaminating the pores of the wood when I have wiped off excess glue while it was still wet. Even small amounts of glue left on the wood or in the pores will be glaringly visible under most finishes. When using water or the appropriate solvent to remove the excess glue, it thins out, and a thin film can be all but invisible until applying the finish reveals it. At that point, lots of sanding and earnest hoping are your only real alternatives.

Fasteners

New woodworkers tend to use mechanical fasteners more frequently than they will after learning more about making joints and after developing more confidence in those techniques. Most woodworkers recognize that a well-placed and properly installed fastener may provide the essential strength needed to hold joints and projects together (see **Figure 7.18**).

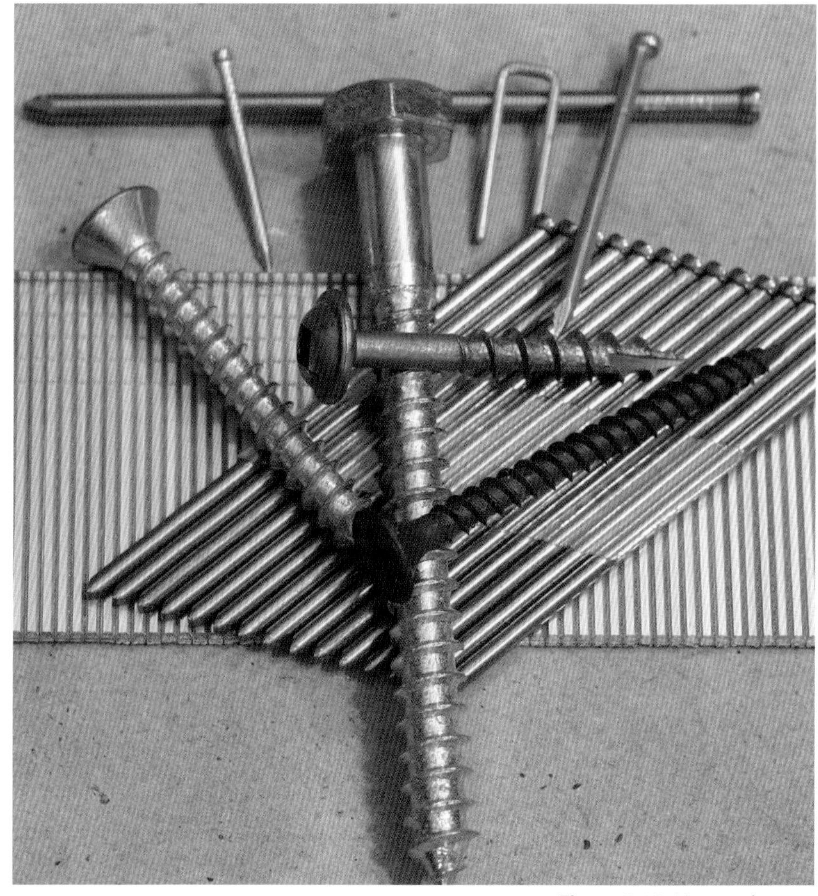

Figure 7.18. Many styles of mechanical fasteners, in as many sizes, are used in woodworking. As your joinery skills increase, the need for fasteners is reduced, though it never fades completely.

The tricks to using fasteners are choosing the right type for the job, installing them properly (including drilling pilot holes to maximize their effectiveness), and, in some cases, hiding them. I do not consider the concealment of fasteners to be subterfuge, but rather a legitimate aesthetic technique to enhance viewer appreciation. In other words, I am hiding them more professionally these days.

One pitfall with fasteners is using too many. I discovered this early on when nailing a workbench together. Since three nails would hold a joint, I decided that six or eight would be even stronger. I failed to realize that while a bunch of fasteners could generate lots of holding power, shredding the wood with so many in one area gave them little to hold onto. The joint grew looser as I drove more nails into it. This is true for screws as well: Rare is the situation where two or three screws are not enough.

Once you identify the need for a mechanical fastener, you have three primary types from which to choose. Screws, nails, and staples each have qualities that could make them the best choice for a particular circumstance.

Screws

Screws are easily the strongest of the three primary types of fasteners because of their large shaft diameter and the grip their threads generate. These qualities allow screws to resist both pull and shear loads very well. When used with a properly applied adhesive, screws help to make a very strong joint. That's why this combination is often favored in high-load situations.

Lay a wood screw next to a bolt or machine screw, and the difference in their threads is obvious, as shown in **Figure 7.19**. The threads on a machine screw are formed low and fine to fit mating threads in a nut or tapped hole. Wood screw threads look like a thin strip of metal wrapped around the shaft, thin and tall compared to those on a machine screw. Wood screw threads cut their own path into the surrounding wood to generate tremendous holding power.

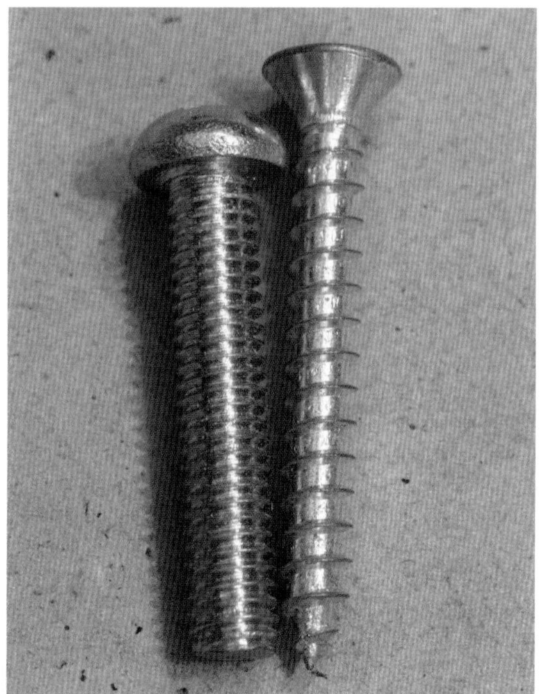

Figure 7.19. Because of the material they grip, wood screws (right) have vastly different threads than those meant for use in metal (left). The deep, thin threads allow wood screws to develop tremendous clamping and holding power.

Name	Function	Features	Price
Wood Screws	Lock parts together with or without glue	Strongest fasteners; come in brass, in nickel-plated, or galvanized, steel, and in stainless steel; variety of heads	$$
Nails	Used with adhesive	Easy to install and hide; small heads and diameters; smooth shanks; limited holding power	$
Staples	Installing plywood back panels	Good holding power; large indentation mark	$

Key: $ = inexpensive; $$ = moderately expensive

Types of wood screws

Wood screw threads vary, depending on their intended use. For softwoods, coarse threads slice deeper into the wood. Screws designed for use in hardwood may have finer threads that reduce the torque needed to install them (see **Figure 7.20**). This makes it easier to install a screw without its shaft breaking. The density of hardwoods allows the shorter threads to create a powerful grip.

Wood screws come in various lengths. With the exception of special decorative screws and those designed to secure surface-mounted hardware, wood screws are usually set into the wood deep

Figure 7.20. Because wood varies in hardness, the threads on wood screws come in coarse (left) and fine (right) configurations. In hardwoods, fine threads permit installation without breaking the shaft by reducing the amount of torque needed. In softer woods, deeper threads install easily but grab more wood to increase their grip.

Installing Wood Screws

The quickest, and in many cases the strongest, way to connect two pieces of wood is with glue and screws. Here's the basic technique for a tough utility construction that you could use to make a sturdy worktable:

Begin by fitting the pieces together, and draw their overlap so you will know where to spread the glue.

Spread glue inside the layout lines on both pieces.

Clamp the pieces together in their final orientation. One clamp may not be enough; use two or more to hold the joint steady, depending on the size of the pieces.

Drill pilot holes into the joint. Set the pilot hole drill so its point does not come out the far side.

Drive a screw into each pilot hole. Although you could remove the clamps right away, for best results, leave the joint clamped for a half hour so the glue can begin to set.

enough so that the head is flush with the surface of the wood. If the screw is to be hidden, it is sunk further below the surface to create a pocket for a wooden plug (see **Figure 7.21**). This makes it difficult to use screws in wood thinner than ½" if the heads are to be flush with the surface. To install a concealing plug, the wood must be closer to ¾" thick to leave sufficient material below the screw head to make use of its clamping power.

Wood screws are made from brass, from nickel-plated, or galvanized, steel, and from stainless steel. They come in a variety of heads to fit slotted, Phillips (cross head), and square drive screwdrivers (see **Figure 7.22**). While most wood screws have some version of a tapered head, specialty designs with a flat-bottomed head are used in pocket hole joinery and some hardware applications.

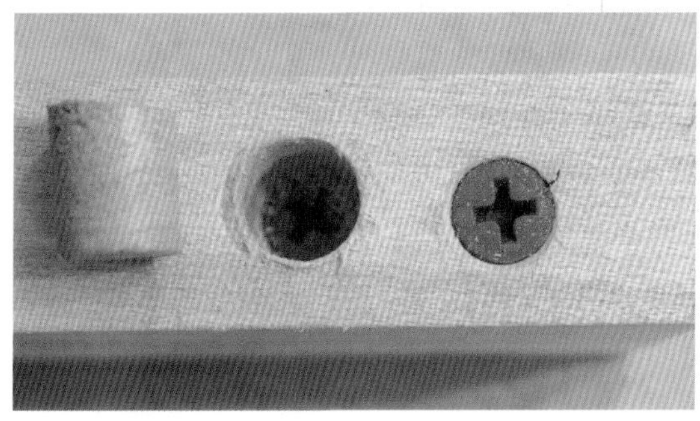

Figure 7.21. Wood screws can be installed with the head just below the surface of the wood or hidden entirely. Drilling a recess, driving the screw to its bottom, and then filling that hole with a plug cut from the same wood is the most popular method of concealing screws.

Figure 7.22. The three primary driver styles are slotted, Phillips (cross head), and square drive. Slotted screws are prone to stripping and slipping. The Phillips head remains the most common driving style, but the square drive is as good and is gaining popularity.

Nails

Finishing nails, brads, and pins are all used in woodworking. Larger nails were once used routinely in larger projects like benches, but today screws have replaced them.

Nearly all of the nails commonly used in woodworking have relatively small heads and diameters and smooth shanks (see **Figure 7.23**). This limits their holding power somewhat and is a primary reason they are often combined with an adhesive. Small nails are also useful for temporarily holding a piece while an adhesive dries. The glue ultimately provides the majority of the holding power. The smaller nail sizes can be quite difficult to drive with a regular hammer, which is one reason why woodworkers increasingly favor air-powered nail guns.

The air nailer will drive the nail slightly below the surface of the wood so you can hide the head with wood filler. If you are driving nails with a hammer, use a nail set to drive the head just under the surface.

In some situations, nails can have an advantage over screws because of their relatively small diameter and ease of installation. It is much easier to install and hide a small brad in a small trim piece, versus the head of a screw. The slender nail also is much less likely than a screw to split a small piece of decorative trim.

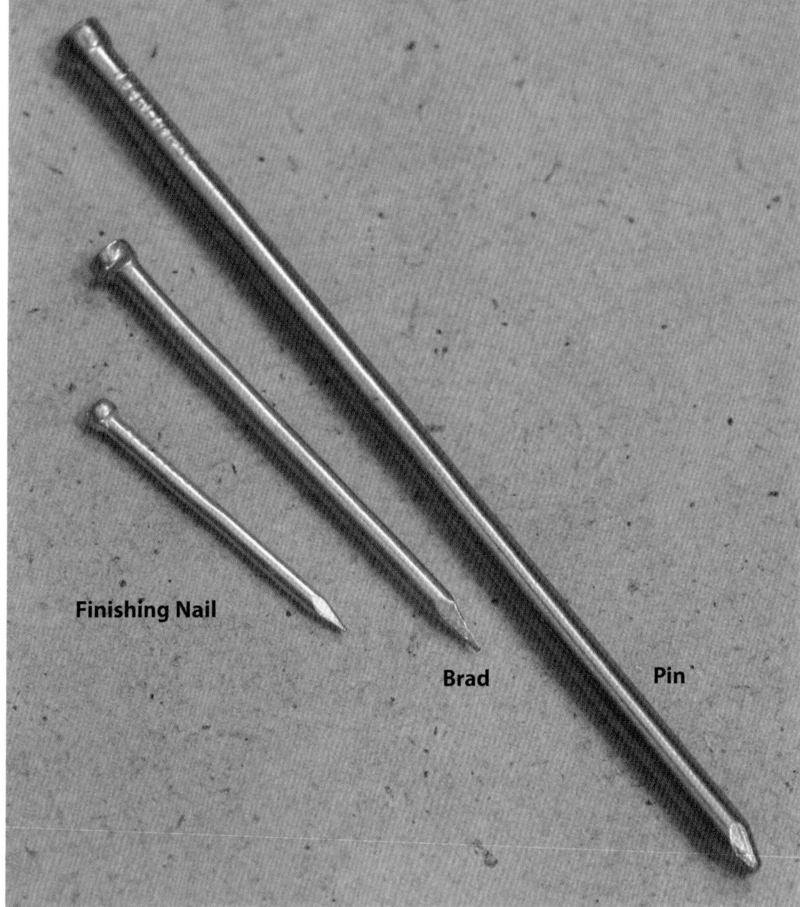

Figure 7.23. Headless finishing nails, brads, and pins are all useful in woodworking.

Installing a nail diagonally across a dado joint, where a shelf meets a cabinet side, can be much easier than placing a screw in the same position. The nail is easy to hide, especially when driven from under the shelf, and, in that application, is very strong, as shown in **Figure 7.24**.

Figure 7.24. When driven diagonally through a joint, such as this dadoed shelf, the nail provides a considerable amount of resistance to the shelf being pulled out. Combined with glue, this is a very strong joint.

Staples

Installed almost exclusively by air-powered guns, staples combine easy, accurate installation with holding power that is far superior to nails (see **Figure 7.25**). In addition to the twin legs, a staple's top strap holds thin wood more securely than the head of a brad or nail.

Because they make an indentation in the wood roughly twice the size of a nail, staples are seldom used on visible areas of a project. But the holding power of staples makes them the perfect choice for installing plywood back panels that are as thin as ¼" into a rabbet.

Common staple sizes used in woodworking range from about ½" to 1¼" long, making them useful with a wide range of material thicknesses. The power and dependability of modern air-powered staple guns make installing staples fast, easy, and very accurate.

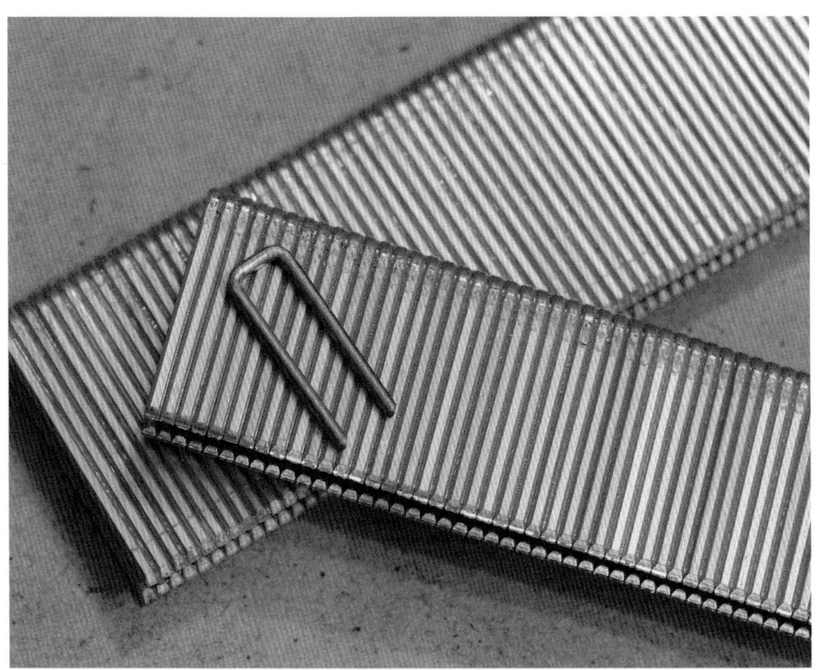

Figure 7.25. Staples, particularly the narrow crown variety shown, can be driven with an air-powered gun. The strap connecting the two legs develops a vastly more secure grip on thin plywood than a simple brad or a short finish nail.

Pilot holes

Taking the time to drill pilot holes, even when they seem unnecessary, will prevent splitting problems that always happen when they are least expected. In hardwoods, or when countersinking the head of a fastener in any type of wood, pilot holes are mandatory. Pilot holes are essential for screws in any kind of wood but are also helpful for finishing nails and brads in small pieces of trim.

Pilot holes are especially important when installing screws near the edge of a piece of wood, including into the end grain. While the shaft of most wood screws is rather small in diameter, the inconsistency of wood means it can, and will, split unexpectedly. Splits can also appear after the fastener is installed, such as when the project is moved, or after a little weight is added, such as when books are put on a shelf. Drilling pilot holes minimizes these stresses.

Another benefit of drilling pilot holes is that they help guide the screw or nail so it is installed straight or at the angle wanted. Driving screws or nails without a pilot hole allows variances in wood density, including unseen knots, to steer the fastener to an unwanted angle or worse, out through the side of the wood.

Pilot holes can be useful when driving finish nails into hardwood with a hammer. This is especially true when the nail is passing through a narrow or thin piece of wood. Drilling a pilot hole that is slightly smaller in diameter than the nail lets it develop considerable holding power without splitting the wood.

New Tools!

Pilot Bits!

You can drill pilot holes with regular drill bits, but you will need two or three different bits for every pilot hole. That's why woodworkers have pilot hole drill sets. The set usually consists of three or four different-size drill bits, each with a counterboring cutter for the screw head and a stop collar to limit depth.

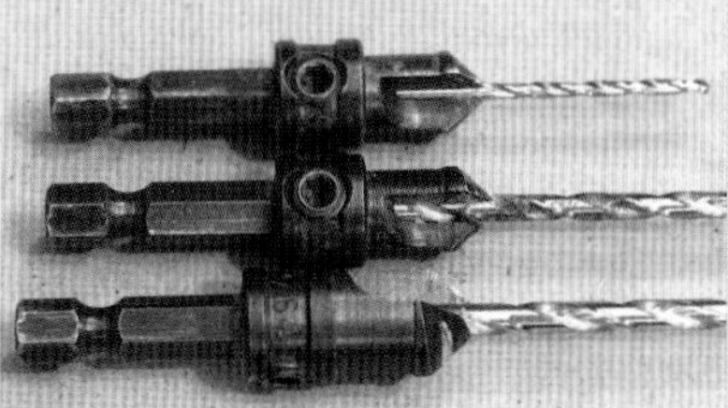

Specialized drill bits for creating pilot holes help ensure screws install at the exact angle (or lack of an angle) desired. Many have a larger bit at their base that bores the hole for a wooden plug that hides the screw.

A popular variation is the drill-driver combo. It consists of a holder that fits into the cordless drill chuck, with a double-ended device that fits into the holder: One end is for drilling and countersinking the pilot hole, and the other end is a screwdriver tip for driving the screw. That changeover is extremely quick: Just slip a collar to remove, and reinsert.

Pilot hole drill sets cost about $20, as do drill-driver combo sets.

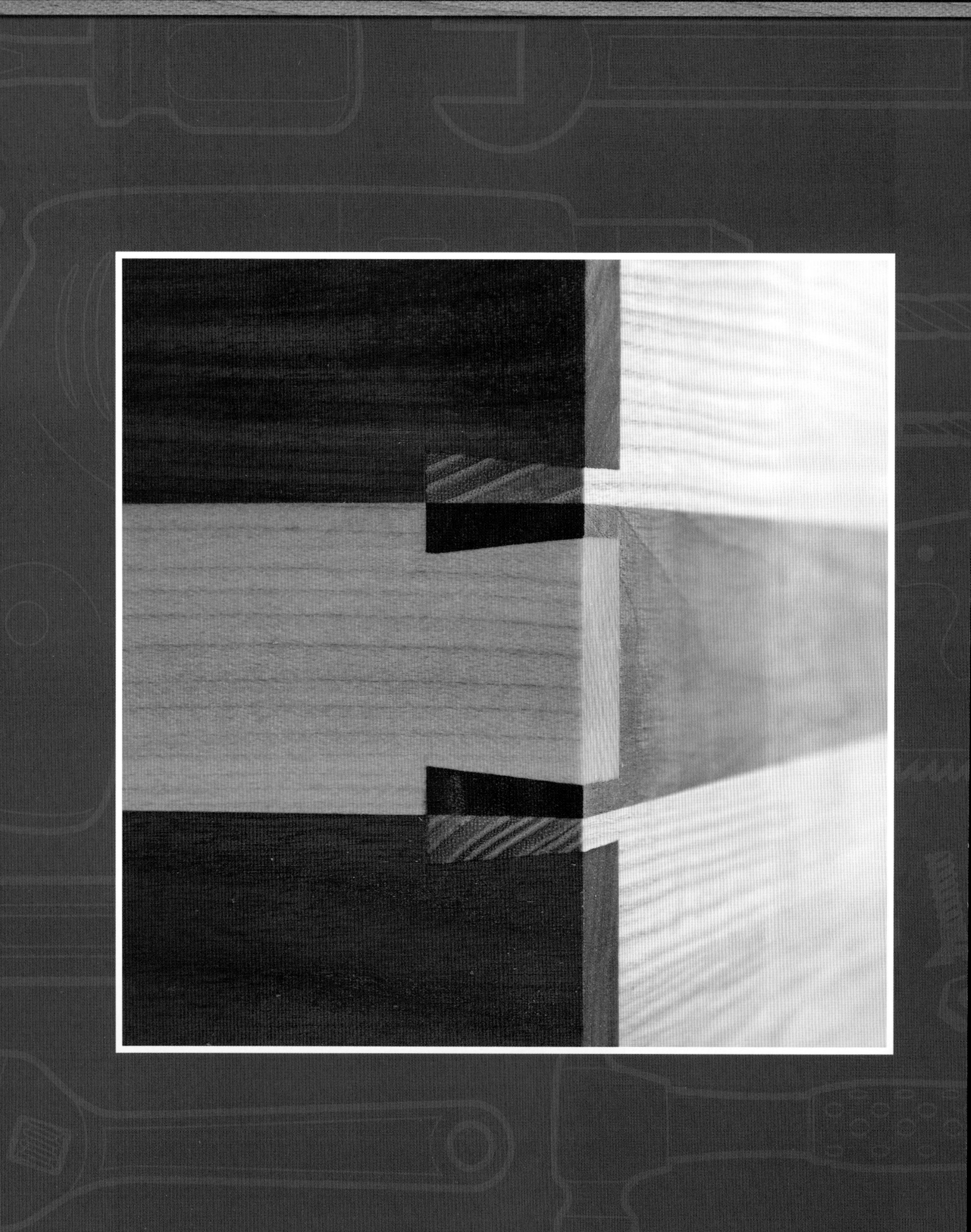

Chapter 8

Joining Wood

Woodworkers dread or crave the challenge of making joints, sometimes simultaneously, though that conflict generally emerges soon after the initial terror of dovetails subsides. Whatever your interests in woodworking, making joints will always be an important part of the projects you build.

Joints can make or break any project. Choosing the appropriate joint for the job and then executing it perfectly ensure the project will turn out square and as strong as possible. To do that, you will need to make test joints to confirm setup on joinery jigs or machines and to practice your techniques. As your skills grow, dovetails, box joints, or other visually attractive joints become options for adding your personal touch to a project.

All joints fit into four basic categories: panel, frame, box, and plywood. We'll take a look at each of these categories in more depth. Then, we'll look at a number of specific joints, from the relatively easy butt joint to the more difficult dovetail joint. I'll show you step-by-step how to make each of these joints so you can apply them to any woodworking project.

Figure 8.1. Practice making joints before you commit to your good wood, but try to use the same species or one of similar density and hardness.

Practice builds skill

Like most things, learning to walk before trying to run tends to limit the number of disasters encountered along the way. It can be tempting to jump ahead to the more complex joints like dovetails, and some overeager woodworkers have taken that path. Unfortunately, many remain in the ditches along that road, forever joint-challenged because the frustration of getting in over their heads has splintered their self-confidence.

Like woodworking itself, the craft of making joints is built on a relatively small number of basic skills. Starting with basic joints allows developing the core skills that are increasingly important as the complexity of the work increases. Following the natural progression from one joint to another helps make learning joinery a fun, rewarding process and one you may actually look forward to.

Practice is the only way to perfect joinery. Using up scrap to hone your skills is helpful and economical, but nothing beats real-world experience. Most woodworkers have at least a few cabinets on the project list for the shop. This kind of work provides low-pressure opportunities to practice joinery and put those efforts to use.

Wood for Practice

When you do use scrap to hone your joint-making skills, be aware of how the density of the various wood species affects joint fit. The problem is that interlocking joints like dovetails or even dados are much easier to fit when using pine than when using harder woods like oak (see **Figure 8.1**).

Softwoods compress far easier than hardwoods, especially when the surface is machined by a router bit or saw. A machined surface is somewhat rougher, and the fibers are displaced just a bit, enough to make them easier to compress. In woods like pine that are already soft, the compressive effect is magnified.

I inadvertently discovered this phenomenon when teaching myself to rout half-blind dovetails. After a few hours of destroying a bunch of pine, I finally had the jig and router adjusted so the joint would go together with a couple raps of my dead-blow mallet. No gaps, almost perfectly flush, I had this knocked. Then, without changing anything, I cut the same joint in oak, as shown in **Figure 8.2**, and the pieces would not go together if I crashed a Buick into them.

Thinking I had messed up the setup somehow, I cut another set in pine, and, once again, a couple raps with the dead-blow mallet seated them perfectly. I cut another set in oak, paying close attention throughout the process, and, once again, they were Buick proof.

When looking closely at the cuts to see if I had somehow shaped them differently, I noticed the pine joints had portions that were almost shiny, as shown in **Figure 8.3**. Finally, I realized that the pine was compressing and the oak was not. After adjusting the jig and router to loosen the fit in pine slightly, cutting the same joint in oak produced a snug fit that actually could be assembled.

While I frequently use cheap wood when setting up a jig or tool for cutting a new joint, I make the final test cuts using the same wood from which the project will be made (see **Figure 8.4**). My wood bill is slightly higher, but that is offset by a markedly smaller aspirin budget.

Preparing the wood

For any joint to be tight, square, and strong all at the same time, the wood must be prepared correctly (see Chapter 6, "Preparing the Wood," on page 125). If the pieces being joined are not straight, square, and consistent in thickness, the joint cannot come out correctly. This is true for the scrap you use to make test joints, too. It must be dimensioned and trimmed square to match the workpieces precisely. The simplest way to do this is to square up extra material for the project in the first place, knowing you will consume some of it testing your setups.

New woodworkers often wonder how much extra length, width, and thickness to leave for sanding at the end of the project. The answer is very little. If the wood was prepared correctly before the joinery was cut and the pieces were assembled, you won't actually be removing very much wood, maybe a few hundredths of an inch. So I like to leave only about 1⁄32" (that's 3/100") extra in width, and even less than that in thickness. When joints that interlock completely through the thickness of the wood, like through dovetails of box (finger) joints, are going to be cut in the ends of the pieces, I do like to leave a little extra length, maybe 1⁄16", because I find it easiest to sand the ends flush with the mating pieces at the end of the process. While some try to hit the length dead-on, that can be risky. If the ends of the joint are short at all, you are forced to plane or sand the entire side of the project down to meet them. It's up to you.

Another important part of stock preparation for joinery is marking the pieces clearly to identify their orientation and position within the project. It may be as simple as marking the top and outside face of each piece, but whatever markings you need to keep the parts clearly identified when cutting the joints are worth the effort. Although expert woodworkers usually mark the inside surfaces, I prefer to choose and mark the outside (presentation) sides of the wood, which I find a great help in preventing me from cutting the joint on the wrong side or the wrong way around.

Figure 8.2. When I practiced making half-blind dovetails, they fit fine in pine but not in oak. The pine is soft and compresses; the oak is hard and does not compress.

Figure 8.3. A close look at the pine shows a shiny surface, indicating that the joint fit by compressing the wood.

Figure 8.4. Here's a whole stack of practice pieces I made while learning how to cut joints in wood. I keep them as reference for the next time I want to use the joint in a project.

New Tools!

Making Joints!

As you build your repertoire of joint-making skills, you're going to have many opportunities to buy new tools, my favorite woodworking activity. Here are some you must have, plus a few shiny baubles you might enjoy drooling over.

Stacked dado set and flat-bottomed router bits

Dovetailing jig

Box joint jig

Dedicated mortising machine

Tongue-and-groove router bit set

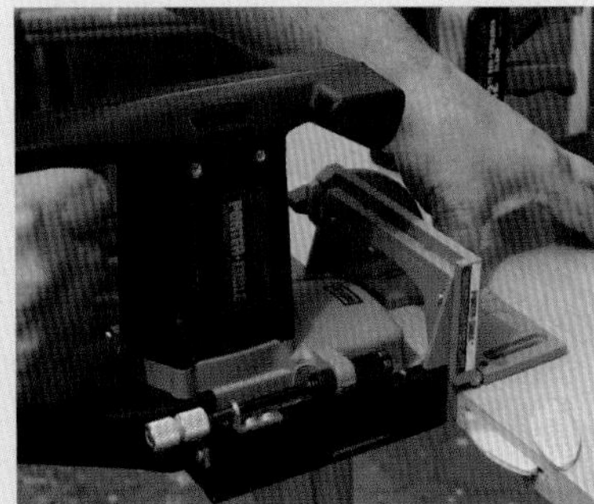
Biscuit joiner

Must have

- **Stacked dado set for the table saw.** This assembly of small saw blades, in calibrated thicknesses, allows you to saw a dado, rabbet, or groove from ¼" to about 13⁄16" wide. About $75 to well over $250.
- **Flat-bottomed router bits.** A good assortment of sizes will help you plow grooves, dados, and rabbets. $10 to $25 each.
- **Dovetailing jig with matching router bits.** Basic models cost about $75, and while they are capable of making a serviceable dovetail, there's little or no adjustability. Deluxe models are more adjustable with some able to produce variable-spaced joints. $300 to $500.

Nice to have

- **Box joint jig.** Cuts perfectly spaced square fingers that really will lace together. You can make your own jig, and you will struggle to get it working just right, or you can plunk down $200 for one of these puppies and quit struggling.
- **Benchtop mortising machine.** It resembles a small drill press but uses a square, hollow chisel with a drill bit inside it. The drill makes a round hole just ahead of the chisel that squares the hole. Make a row of them and you've got a mortise. I love mine. About $300.
- **Tongue-and-groove router bit set.** This matched pair of cutters helps make perfectly matched tongues and grooves. About $100.
- **Biscuit joiner.** It's the size of a cordless drill, but it has a small circular saw blade in a housing that controls its depth of cut. You make a matching pair of shallow cuts in two pieces of wood, and then glue in a little football-shaped plug of wood. It can join wood edge to edge, reinforce butts and miters, and make frames. About $200.
- **Mortising chisel and mallet.** The chisels are very sturdy, they're square in cross section (not bevel-edged like other chisels), and they come in precise sizes. Start with ¼" and ⅜", and get a heavy wooden mallet with which to drive them. About $30 per chisel.

Choosing joint types

New woodworkers are understandably limited in the range of joints available to them. That tends to change rather quickly because most beginners consider each new type of joint learned to be a significant indicator of progress. Achieving those joinery-related milestones makes woodworking that much more interesting, often spurring the new woodworker on to learn more, and so the process goes.

Not surprisingly, the more complicated joints are often both attractive and strong, making them even more versatile. Dovetails, for example, are extremely rugged but are just as likely to be chosen for their appearance. As your repertoire of joints grows, properties such as strength and appearance become more important than the difficulty of making them.

Choosing which joint to use may seem bewildering at first, but you can make sense of it by considering what each joint is for. There are only four basic situations, which come up over and over again in every kind and style of woodworking. I'll list them and then discuss each, though to be clear I'll have to refer to specific joints by name. In case you're not yet familiar with these basic joints, they'll be fully described later in this chapter. Here are the four basic situations:

1. **Panel (edge) joints** (long grain to long grain) make wood wider;
2. **Frame joints** (end grain to edge grain) make square frames and stands;
3. **Box joints** (end grain to face grain) make boxes and cabinets;
4. **Plywood joints.**

1. Panel (Edge) Joints: Long Grain to Long Grain

When you want to glue two boards together edge to edge to make them wide enough for a panel such as a box lid or a tabletop, you are joining long grain to long grain (see **Figure 8.5**). It's the same when you want to make a thick piece of wood by gluing two pieces together face to face, the grain in both pieces running parallel to each other. Or when you want to make a wooden angle iron by gluing the edge of one piece to the face of the other, again the grain running parallel.

You can make long-grain joints using glue alone, though woodworkers sometimes use biscuits or form interlocking tongues and grooves. Special glue line router bits that carve an interlocking profile, which helps keep the individual boards aligned during clamping, are also available. Since a properly prepared and glued long-grain joint is more likely to break in the wood than in the glue line, these reinforcements are more to help keep the surfaces aligned than to strengthen the joint.

Notice that in the long-grain-to-long-grain situation, since the wood grain is always parallel, you don't need to worry that changes in humidity will tear the construction apart. The wood might expand or contract in width and in thickness, but it will all move together, so your long-grain joints will stay together. This would not be the case if, in a cross-grain sandwich, you were to turn one piece so its grain was at a right angle to the other's. You could add all the glue and screws you wanted, but wood movement caused by changes in humidity might still break it apart.

Figure 8.5. Glued-up panel features long-grain-to-long-grain joints.

2. Frame Joints: End Grain to Edge Grain

When you make a square frame, or a T shape or an L shape, you're usually joining the end grain of one piece to the edge grain of the other. While you can make a butt joint by tacking the pieces together with glue alone, it will have little strength. You have to add hardware, such as pocket screws, or make an interlocking joint, such as a half lap (see **Figure 8.6**), a tongue-and-groove (see page 163), or a mortise and tenon (see page 166).

Figure 8.6. The half lap is an attractive frame joint.

In most of these situations, such as the corner of a square frame, the end-to-edge joint is cross-grain. Usually, the pieces are narrow enough, and the joint plus fasteners plus glue are strong enough, to avoid problems with wood movement. When wide pieces are involved, such as the headboard of a bed joining into a corner post, you have to do something to accommodate movement. The most common "fix" is to glue only the center of the wide piece and let its remaining width float in the groove. In other situations, such as a mitered picture frame, the wood grain meets at a combination of end grain to end grain and parallel. However, the amount of long grain exposed by the angled cut does not provide enough long grain for a strong joint. While the stress on a picture frame is generally low, most woodworkers will add some form of reinforcement.

3. Box Joints: End Grain to Face Grain

When you want to join wide pieces to make the front and side of a box, the end grain of one piece meets the face grain of the other piece (see **Figure 8.7**). You could get this joint to hold for a little while with glue alone, but, for a permanent construction, it needs some help. You can reinforce the joint by cutting a simple mechanical interlock, such as a rabbet, to which you would add fasteners like nails or screws or dowels. Complex joints like dovetails hold together by virtue of their mechanical interlock plus glue; they don't need any other hardware.

Figure 8.7. The rabbet makes a simple box joint.

Notice that in this situation, the grain of the wood pieces all runs around the box in the same direction. Any changes in the wood's size due to variations in humidity will affect all the pieces equally. If you were to orient the wood cross-grain so the end of one wide board met the edge of the other, changes in size due to changes in humidity soon would break any joint apart—whether or not you added glue or screws or dovetails or whatever.

4. Plywood Joints

The thing about plywood and other man-made boards is they don't have a directional grain structure like solid wood. Although plywood does move and change in response to moisture in the air, it doesn't move very much. That's because plywood is a balanced cross-grain construction of many thin layers, or plies, of wood. The layers are thin enough, and the glue is strong enough, that each layer resists any movement in the layers above it and below it.

This means that every plywood edge is a combination of long grain and end grain. While there's always some long-grain gluing surface, it lacks the overall strength of a true long-grain-to-long-grain joint (see **Figure 8.8**). Plus, if there is any stress applied to a plywood joint, the layers in one or both pieces can begin to separate and jeopardize the joint. Adding some form of reinforcement to plywood joints will help ensure they stay together for the long run.

Figure 8.8. This plywood panel can be glued into the rabbet.

This also means that when you make a plywood box, you can orient the grain of the plywood according to how it looks best. You don't have to worry about inadvertently creating a cross-grain construction. Usually you want the face grain to follow itself around the corners of a box, just like solid wood, but you're doing it for looks, not for structural reasons.

One important point about joints in plywood and other man-made boards like medium-density fiberboard (MDF): It's not a good idea to make deep dados and grooves in plywood, and you shouldn't make them at all in MDF because these materials gain much of their strength from their outside surface layers. If you rout a trench, you create a weak place that invites the board to break. These materials accept glue and hold screws pretty well, so join them that way.

Making joints

In the following pages, we will look at the primary types of joints, the ways to make them, and the tools commonly used. The joints are organized in general order of difficulty because most employ at least some of the skills used to make the ones learned before, with notes on their purpose in woodworking. Practicing each joint style until you are comfortable with that entire process makes learning the next ones easier and faster.

I've rated each joint for difficulty on a scale of 1 to 10. Nailing one board to another would be a #1 difficulty joint while cutting a curved through dovetail joint would be a #10 difficulty. While it is impossible to judge how difficult a particular joint will be for each woodworker, this scale does provide a relative indicator.

Groove, Dado, Rabbet

So what's the difference between a groove, a dado, and a rabbet? They're all trenches machined into the wood into which you can fit another piece of wood. But they're different according to grain direction, like this:

Groove

Grooves are trenches that go with the grain direction of the wood. Take a close look at a paneled door in your kitchen; you'll see that all the frame pieces have a groove running around their inside edges.

Dado

Dados are trenches machined across the grain direction of the wood.

Rabbet

Rabbets are exactly like dados except that they are machined right at the edge of the wood, so one side of the trench is missing.

Type of Joint	Function	Difficulty	Strong or Weak	Reinforcements
Butt Joint	Box corners	2	Weak	Glue and biscuits, dowels, or screws
Pocket Hole Joint	Face frames and door frames for built-in cabinets	3	Very strong	Glue and screws
Rabbet Joint	Plywood boxes; cabinet sides, tops, and back panels; solid wood boxes	4	Moderate	Glue and staples, brads, or screws
Edge Joint	Wide panels for frames, tabletops, solid wood boxes, or chests	3	Strong	Glue
Half-Lap Joint	Cabinet doors and face frames	5	Strong	Glue
Dado Joint	Shelving, partition panels	6	Strong	Glue
Tongue-and-Groove Joint	Door frames, dust panels, drawer support frames, panels	6	Moderate	Glue
Mortise and Tenon Joint	Face frames, doors, table bases, chairs, shelving	7	Very strong	Glue
Miter Joint	Picture frames, boxes	8	Weak	Glue and biscuits or nails
Box (or Finger) Joint	Cabinets, drawers, chests, jewelry boxes	8	Very strong	Glue
Dovetail Joint	Drawers, cabinets, boxes, chests	8	Very strong	Glue

Butt Joint

Box joint, plywood joint

Difficulty 2

Tools:

- Table saw or chop saw
- Combination square
- Cordless drill
- Clamps

In a butt joint, the end of one piece butts tightly against the face of the other, making the corner of a box (see **Figure 8.9**). While very simple to cut and glue, the butt joint is impossible to make strong without adding some mechanical assistance. Even with mechanical reinforcement, butt joints are weaker than most other types, particularly when subjected to twisting or diagonal forces across the corner. Butt joints are weak because they have no interlocking features themselves; they are just end grain glued directly to face grain. The end-grain side offers very little for the glue to grab onto, and even less if it is not cleanly sawn.

Figure 8.9. Butt joints commonly involve an end-grain-to-face-grain joint, creating a box corner.

Usually, butt joints are arranged so the end grain is not visible on the primary viewing side. For instance, a box assembled with butt joints would have full-length boards across the front, concealing the end grain of the side pieces behind them. Before drawing layout lines for cutting, look the wood over and decide which parts will be most visible and from where on the piece of wood they should be cut. Be sure you mark each board with which side goes in and which side will be visible.

Butt joints need some form of mechanical fastener. Biscuits, dowels, and screws are frequent choices. However, installing screws or dowels at the same time the glue joints are assembled and clamped can be hard to do without disrupting the alignment of the pieces. If you install a mechanical fastener when the pieces are out of alignment, it will be nearly impossible to correct. For this reason, I wait until after the glue has dried to install screws or dowels from the outside of the joint.

Making the Butt Joint

1 **Lay out and cut the pieces.** The key step in creating a butt joint is cutting the parts to the correct length with clean, square edges. Use a stop or gauge block to ensure that matching parts are identical in length.

2 **Verify squareness.** I always cut a test piece and check it with an accurate square to confirm the setup of my saw. This simple check takes just a minute and can prevent big problems later.

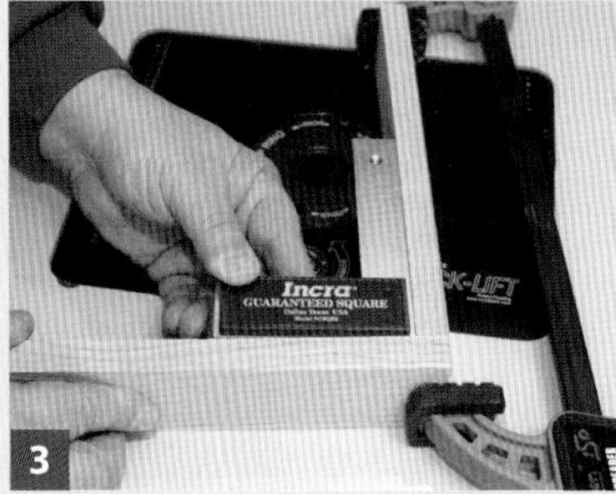

3 **Assemble.** Apply an even coat of glue to the end grain and then to the adjoining long grain against which it will rest; then, recoat the end grain if it has absorbed a lot of the glue. Be certain that the parts are clamped square to each other on a flat surface and that the joints are fully closed. Tighten the clamps, but not so much that you squeeze all the glue out of the joint. Then, leave it alone to dry.

4 **Use mechanical reinforcement.** Once the glue has set up, carefully predrill and install the screws or dowel pins. Two or three per joint (depending on its size), spaced nicely, will do the job. If using dowels, apply glue to the bottom three-fourths of the dowels and tap them in. Resist the urge to hammer the dowels in because it serves no purpose and could fracture the joint.

Pocket Hole Joint

Frame joint

Difficulty 3

Tools:
- Table saw or chop saw
- Pocket hole jig
- Cordless drill
- Clamps

Figure 8.10. Pocket hole joints are strong joints that use a combination of glue and pocket screws.

Making the Pocket Hole Joint

Lay out and drill the pocket holes. Lay out the pocket holes on the back side of the piece so that, when assembled, they are hidden from view. Be sure to mark the show side of the wood as well as the hole locations on the back side, and be sure there are no knots in the hole-drilling zone.

Size the screw according to the instructions that come with the drilling jig. The instructions will also prescribe settings for the drilling block and the stop collar on the special step drill bit for the thickness of wood being joined. Always drill and assemble a test joint to avoid such unforeseen problems as the screw breaking through.

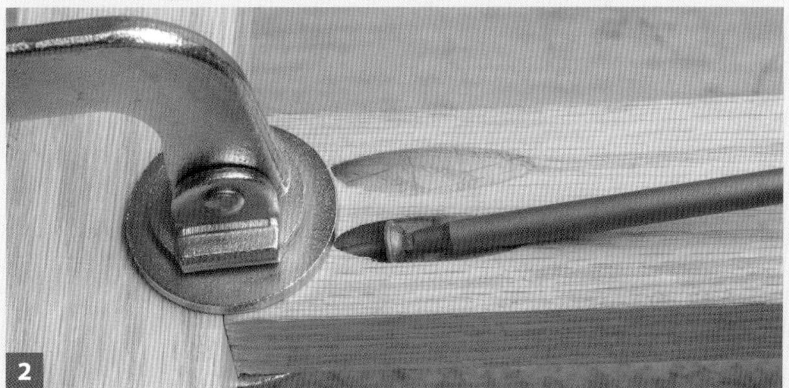

Glue and assemble. Apply glue to the end of the piece with the pocket holes in it, assemble, and clamp, making sure the pieces are flush to each other. Install the screws and check to be sure that nothing moved.

Pocket holes are drilled at a steep angle into the face of only one of the pieces; then, a long screw is driven into the pocket and runs into the adjoining piece to connect them (see **Figure 8.10**). The combination of glue and the pocket screws creates a very strong joint with tremendous shear strength. Pocket hole screws are commonly used to make face frames and door frames for built-in cabinets. In that application, they are quick to install and very strong, and eliminate the need for any additional interlock.

Pocket hole screws can also be used to reinforce edge-glued panels, such as a cabinet top. They also can be used from the underside to secure shelves that are expected to carry relatively light loads. Their disadvantage is the visibility of the holes, limiting the use of this joint to assemblies that will only be viewed from one side.

Layout and cutting of the pieces for a pocket hole joint are the same as for any other joint: You need clean, square edges with the pieces cut from the best parts of the wood, according to their visibility in the finished project.

The concept of pocket screws was developed in 1986 by Craig Sommerfeld, who went on to found the Kreg Tool Company. The process of drilling the angled holes has been dramatically simplified by purpose-designed jigs and special screws. The screws feature a self-drilling tip that will cut its own path into the second piece of wood, threads sized for the hardness of the wood, and a flat-bottomed head that maximizes the clamping power it generates.

Carefully choose the screw length according to the directions that came with the pocket hole jig. You want to be sure the screw bites deep into the second piece of wood without breaking through on the far side. Whenever possible, drill at least two pockets for each joint. Narrow pieces on some face frames may be too narrow for more than one screw.

A nice feature of pocket hole joinery is that once the screws are installed, continued clamping is not required. Usually you can continue assembling your project without waiting for glue to dry.

Rabbet Joint

Box joint, plywood joint

Difficulty 4

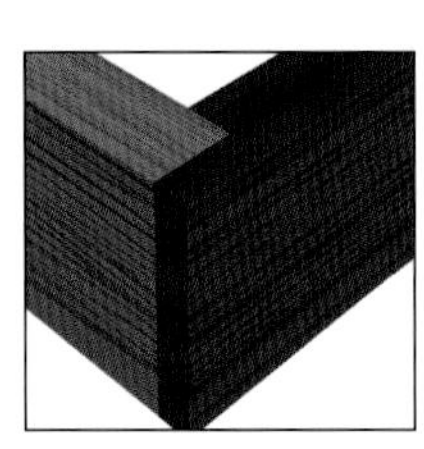

Tools:
- Stacked dado cutter (table saw) or flat-bottomed router bit (handheld router or router table) or special rabbeting cutter head (router table)
- Combination square
- Clamps

A rabbet is simply a shoulder or ledge cut along the edge of a piece of solid wood or plywood. The width and depth are sized to accept the piece that fits into it (see **Figure 8.11**). Rabbets are commonly used to join plywood box parts and to hide the end grain of crosspieces like cabinet sides, tops, and back panels. They can also be used to join solid wood box sides. Rabbet joints are often reinforced with staples, brads, or screws, the choice dependent upon which best fits the visibility of the joint. When setting a panel in the rabbet, mechanical reinforcement is often used in addition to glue. When the glue has dried, the mechanical fasteners may then be concealed by moldings, trim pieces, or plugs. Rabbet joints are generally weak without reinforcement; however, they are strong joints in plywood.

Figure 8.11. Rabbet joints use a ledge sized to accept the adjoining piece and are commonly reinforced with staples, brads, or screws.

Figure 8.12. Match the depth of the rabbet to the panel that will fit into it. You can make it up to 1/16" deeper to fully conceal the panel's edge.

To conceal end grain, cut the rabbet deep enough so the piece that fits in it is slightly recessed (see **Figure 8.12**). "Slightly" can mean a mere hair, or anything up to a full 1/16". When using a rabbet as a joint to connect two pieces of wood, make it ¼" deep, or approximately one-third of the thickness of the wood it is cut

Cutting the Rabbet

Make test cuts. Using scrap wood equal in thickness to the workpieces, make test cuts to confirm both the width and the depth of the rabbet.

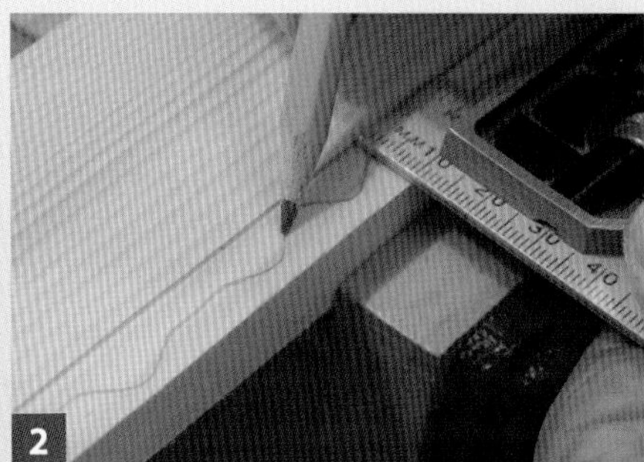

Mark the waste. Taking the time to lay out the rabbet and to mark a wavy pencil line where the material is to be removed will prevent cutting it on the wrong side of a single layout line or even on the wrong face of the wood. A careful layout process also gives you the opportunity to look for cracks or knots in the edge to be cut.

Cut the rabbets. Use a push block when rabbeting narrow stock. Be sure to keep the saw table or router table clear of debris and sawdust. Cutting a rabbet can involve removing a considerable amount of wood, so take multiple light passes rather than one full-depth cut.

into. This depth provides considerable support without compromising the strength of the piece the rabbet is cut into.

Because the plywood often used for cabinet carcasses is 23⁄32" thick (that's just under ¾"), some woodworkers dimension the rabbet to leave a specific amount of wood, often ½", rather than use an arbitrary depth. This makes it easy to cut crosspieces and braces, since with ½" of material left after cutting the rabbet, the crosspieces will be 1" less than the overall finished width of the cabinet or box.

Rabbets can be cut at the table saw with a stacked dado set (a set of matched saw blades that can be assembled to cut the width of groove or rabbet that you need). Handheld or table-mounted routers equipped with a flat-bottomed or bearing-tipped rabbeting bit are also effective.

Special rabbeting cutter heads for the router table (see **Figure 8.13**) are usually sufficiently large that router speed is a safety issue. Always follow the cutter manufacturer's recommendations for maximum safe bit speed. Some rabbeting bits are designed for use in table-mounted routers only. Whether used in a table or handheld router, making multiple light passes is safest and will produce smooth, accurate cuts with the least chance for damage to the wood.

Figure 8.13. A specialty rabbeting head for the router table uses various-size rub collars to control the depth of the cut.

Edge Joint

Panel joint

Difficulty 3

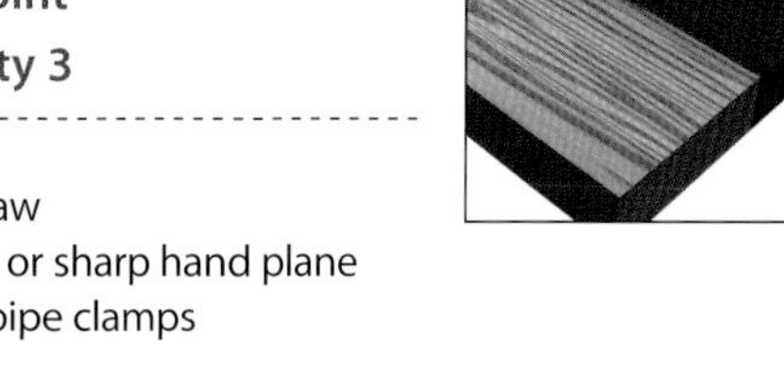

Tools:

- Table saw
- Jointer, or sharp hand plane
- Bar or pipe clamps
- Square

The long-grain edge-to-edge joint is necessary any time you want to make a wide panel out of two or more narrow boards (see **Figure 8.14**). You would do this to make a panel inside a frame, to make a tabletop, or to make a solid-wood box or chest. The joint is usually made with glue alone, and, when done right, it will be as strong as the adjacent wood. If you broke a glued-up panel, it would be more likely to break along a flaw in the wood than on the glue line itself.

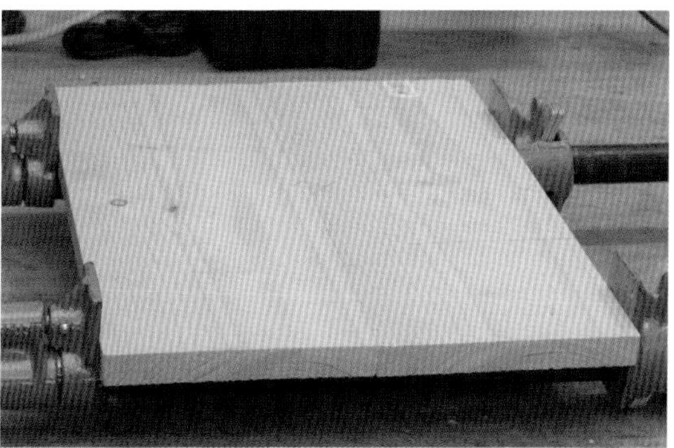

Figure 8.14. Edge joints are used to make wide panels out of narrower boards.

While this is a straightforward joint to make, it does take some care and practice to get it perfect. There are two difficulties: making sure the mating edges of the wood are straight and square and keeping the pieces in line in the clamps while the glue sets. While glue alone is usually more than strong enough for this joint, woodworkers sometimes add dowels, biscuits, or a tongue-and-groove to help align the joint and keep the surfaces flush.

Aids to Alignment

Wet glue is slippery stuff, and the big problem in gluing up a wide panel is keeping the surfaces lined up. The finished panel probably will be too wide for your thickness planer, even if you have one, and the height variations between boards can be too great to sand level. One solution is a few biscuits, if you have a biscuit joiner, or consider using a glue line router bit.

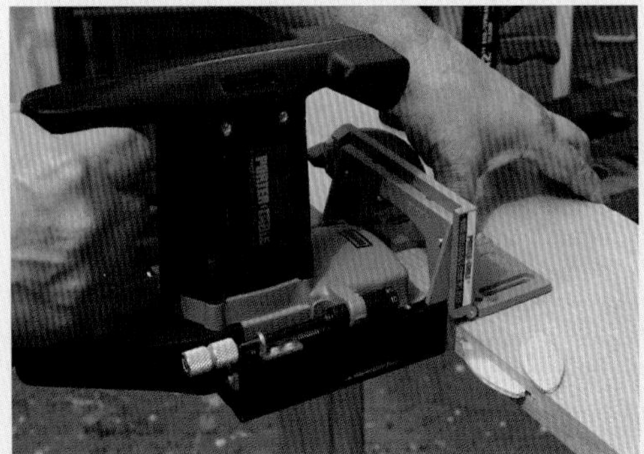

A biscuit joiner can help with alignment problems in edge joints, but biscuits do not fit tight enough to create perfect alignment on their own. Biscuits also make pretty good joints for boxes and frames.

Making the Edge-to-Edge Joint

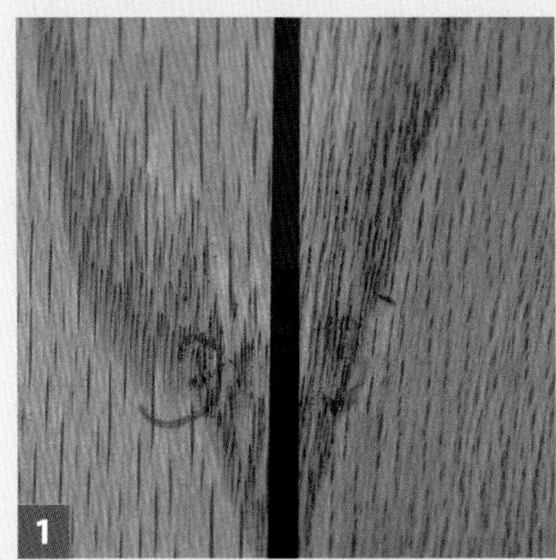

Lay out the wood. Cut the wood to length, and arrange the pieces you want to glue up next to one another. Turn them over and end for end until you get the most pleasing pattern in the figure of the wood. Then either number the joints or draw a large triangle across all the pieces. Marking the joints helps make sure the face you chose stays up in the final assembly and also prevents getting the boards out of order later on.

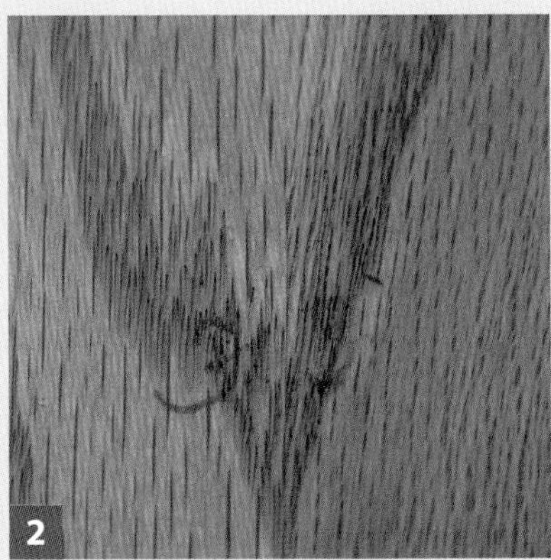

Straighten the mating edges. A sharp carbide blade in the properly aligned table saw will cut an edge that is square and clean enough to glue up. If you have a jointer, you can improve the edges by jointing them. Be sure the jointer fence is adjusted square to the table. You can also straighten the edges with a sharp hand plane. A test fit shows how straight these boards are.

Glue up the wood. How many clamps are used depends on the length of the pieces being glued. I like to have a clamp within each foot of length to keep the pressure as even as possible along the length of the joint. Also, I alternate the clamps, one on the table, the next set down over the wood from the top. This helps keep the boards aligned as well as fights the tendency of the panel to bow when clamped.

Place the clamps on the bench and set the wood on them, triangle, or marked, side up. Lightly tighten the clamps to draw the boards together. The joint should close over the full length, and the panel should remain flat. When clamping up boards without any alignment aides, you will have to align the individual boards flush to each other. Count on going back over them once or twice after clamping because they tend to slide a bit in the glue. When satisfied with the fit, loosen the clamps, paint glue onto all the mating edges, and clamp up again.

Apply just enough pressure to all of the clamps to raise little beads of glue at the joint line. Any more pressure just squeezes more glue out of the joint and will begin to force a bow in the panel.

After a few minutes, go back over the clamps and check their pressure. If sufficient glue is squeezed out, the boards actually move slightly closer to each other and can relax the clamp pressure somewhat. Make sure that the clamps are snug and that the boards have remained aligned, and then let the assembly sit overnight.

Half-Lap Joint

Frame joint

Difficulty 5

Tools:
- Stacked dado set (table saw) or flat-bottomed bit (router table)
- Combination square
- Clamps

Old but trustworthy, the half-lap joint is a very strong and useful frame joint (see **Figure 8.15**). A cleanly formed half-lap joint can be attractive because of the symmetrical way that it contrasts exposed end grain against face grain. Half-lap joints can be found on cabinet doors, face frames, and many other projects where its strength and appearance add visual appeal to the project.

Figure 8.15. The half lap is a useful frame joint that has no direct mechanical interlock and depends on glue for the majority of its strength.

The half lap is a cross-grain joint with locating shoulders but no direct mechanical interlock between the pieces of wood. It depends on the glue for its strength, though some woodworkers do like to reinforce it with screws or dowels.

Half-lap joints are often made on the table saw with a stacked dado set. By using an accurately adjusted miter guide and a gauge block on the fence, this setup is easy and safe. Half laps can be made on a router table using a flat-bottomed bit, a miter guide, and a stop block; the method is the same as with the table saw. They can also be made on the table saw by first sawing the shoulder, then cutting the cheek with a tenoning jig that holds the wood up on end, or on the band saw after cutting the shoulder with the table saw.

Making the Half Lap

Set up and cut the wood. Set up a gauge block (see Using a Gauge Block on page 131) so the maximum cut width is slightly more ($1/32$" is plenty) than the width of the piece that will fit in it. When assembled, having the end-grain portions protruding slightly makes it easier to sand the joint smooth. Cut the shoulder first; then, slide the workpiece along the miter gauge, and make multiple passes to remove the rest of the waste wood. If chipping is a problem, put a backer board between the miter guide and the workpiece, and slow down.

Cut the half laps. Raise the blade or bit so it removes slightly less than half of the material thickness, and begin making test cuts in two pieces. Fit the pieces together, note the difference where they meet, and then raise the cutter half that amount. Recut those pieces, match them up again, and continue until the surfaces are flush when assembled. Taking small bites on each pass, cut the half laps in all of the workpieces.

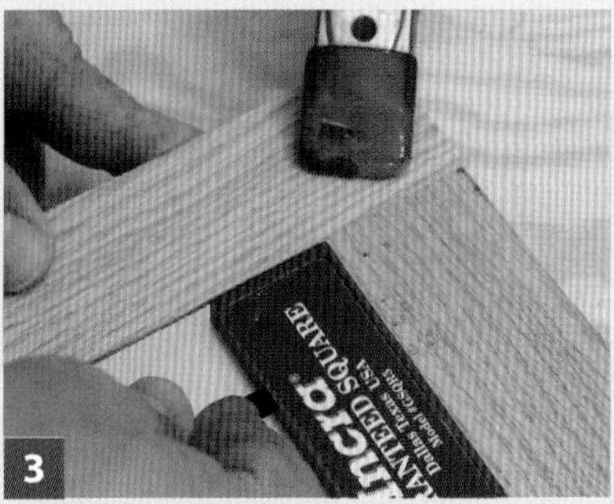

Assemble. There may be small ridges in the half-lap surfaces, depending on the cutter used. In most cases, lightly sanding these ridges to flatten them slightly is all that is needed, but be careful you do not destroy the fit. Apply glue to all the mating faces of both pieces (including the shoulders), assemble, and secure with one or two clamps. Using a square, make sure that the joint is aligned correctly, and set it aside to dry. Then, sand the edges smooth and, if you like, round the edges or add a decorative edge profile.

Reinforce the joint. The tremendous surface area of a half lap means glue alone makes properly fitted half laps strong. However, some woodworkers like to add two short screws on the back side to lock the joint while the glue dries. A pair of brass screws set in flush with the surface can add a nice, old-style touch to some projects. Another way to dress up a half lap is to install a pair of dowels through the joint, arranged diagonally.

The trick to making good-looking half laps is starting with pieces of wood that are identical in thickness. Cutting both pieces from one board is usually close enough, though having a jointer and a planer in the shop to accurately size all of the project wood is a big plus. The wood must be straight and flat.

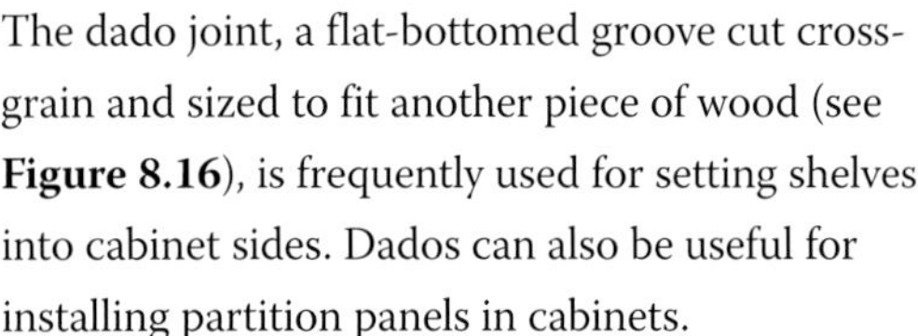

Dado Joint

Box joint, plywood joint

Difficulty 6

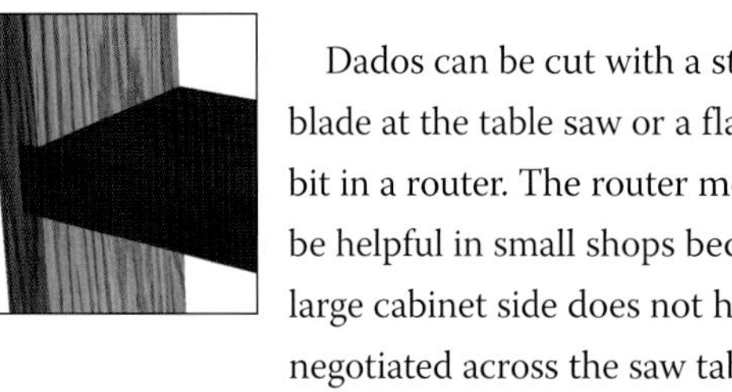

Tools:
- Stacked dado cutter (table saw)
- Flat-bottomed router bit (router/router table)
- Combination square

The dado joint, a flat-bottomed groove cut cross-grain and sized to fit another piece of wood (see **Figure 8.16**), is frequently used for setting shelves into cabinet sides. Dados can also be useful for installing partition panels in cabinets.

Like a rabbet, the depth of dados is usually held to approximately one-third the thickness of the wood into which it is cut, or a bit less. Going deeper gains little in vertical loading strength but will begin to compromise the strength of the piece into which it is cut. While a properly fitting dado assembled with a complete coat of glue will restore most of that strength when dry, few woodworkers depend on it. Most woodworkers cut the dado only as deep as needed, leaving as much of the original thickness as possible to retain as much of the strength as possible.

In width, the dado should match the wood that will fit into it, with a hair of clearance for the glue. If the board just drops into the dado, it's too loose. If you have to drive the wood into the dado with a mallet, it's too tight. It is the combination of the wood fitting the groove with just enough space for the glue that makes a good dado joint strong.

Dados can be cut with a stacked dado blade at the table saw or a flat-bottomed bit in a router. The router method can be helpful in small shops because a large cabinet side does not have to be negotiated across the saw table or router table. Clamping the workpiece to a bench or support and using a router to cut the dado require far less shop space. There are also commercial and shop-made jigs that make cutting accurate dados relatively easy; the key is a perfectly square fence to guide the router across the workpiece.

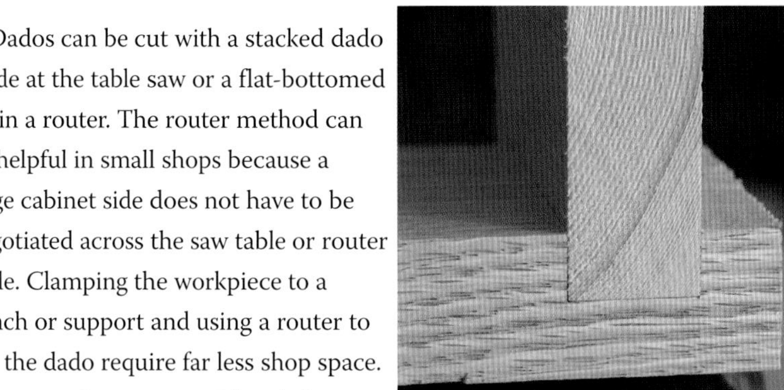

Figure 8.16. The dado joint consists of a flat-bottomed groove sized to fit another piece of wood.

The quality of the cutter has a lot to do with how clean the edges of the dado are and how flat its bottom is. There is nothing more disheartening than to cut a perfectly sized and located dado, only to have the edges chip out.

Cutting a dado the correct width to match modern plywood thicknesses can be frustrating. Stacked dado sets usually come with shims that are placed between the plates to fine-tune the width. You can also buy a dial head dado set that allows making tiny width adjustments without having to remove the blades from the saw. Router bits with diameters matching common plywood thicknesses are available from many bit manufacturers. You can cut a dado of any width using a narrower cutter and taking two or more passes, but the likelihood of error increases with each additional pass.

Cutting the Dado Joint

1 Draw layout lines. If you draw a single layout line, sooner or later you will cut the dado on the wrong side of it. I use two lines that define the width of the dado, along with a wavy line through the middle to mark the wood that will be removed. This also helps you match both sides of a project to be sure the dados line up before cutting them.

2 Test cut the wood. The only way to be sure the dados are correctly sized is to make test cuts. Also, check the thickness of all of the wood that will be inserted into the dados because small differences in thickness will become a big problem. You can sand off a small difference, but planing all the wood to uniform thickness before starting will make your dado life much more enjoyable.

3 Cut the dado. Quality dados can be cut with a stacked dado blade at the table saw or a flat-bottomed bit in a router. On the table saw or router table, use a properly aligned miter gauge to guide the wood. With a handheld router, use a quality square to be sure the fence is actually 90 degrees to the edge of the workpiece.

Tongue-and-Groove Joint

Frame joint

Difficulty 6

Tools:

- Standard table saw blade
- Stacked dado blade (table saw)
- Flat-bottomed router bits or dedicated tongue-and-groove bit sets (router table)

Another age-old form of end-to-edge joinery, tongue-and-groove joints are used frequently for making door frames, dust panels, drawer support frames, panels, and more (see **Figure 8.17**). The advantage is that the groove that forms half of the joint is also available for inserting a plywood panel when making door frame and dust panel projects.

Figure 8.17. Tongue-and-groove joints are popular for a variety of projects, such as door frames and panels, and their mating parts can aid in alignment.

Centering the Cutter

Adjust the fence of the table saw or router table so the cutter is as centered as possible. Start the machine, make one pass over the cutter, and then shut it off. Turn the stock end for end, and slide it up to the bit. If the cutter does not slip into the groove, note the amount of error, and adjust the fence in whichever direction is needed by half of the total error noted. Using another piece of scrap, repeat the process until the groove just slides over the bit when the workpiece is reversed, proving the groove is centered.

Making the Tongue-and-Groove

1

Set up and cut the groove (alternate method). On the table saw or router table, set the cutter height to ½". Adjust the fence to center the cutter by eye on a piece of scrap the same thickness as the workpieces. On the table saw, you can center the cut by making one pass over the cutter, turning the test piece end for end, and making a second pass. This technique will expand the groove slightly, but, since the tongue will be fitted to the groove, that is not a big deal.

On the router table, it is important to center the bit so that a second cut is not needed; otherwise, you could be in a dangerous climb-cutting situation. Reversing the board to make the second cut could have the wood contacting the bit on the back side, which could cause the bit to grab the wood and throw it off the table. When satisfied with the setup, cut the groove in all of the workpieces.

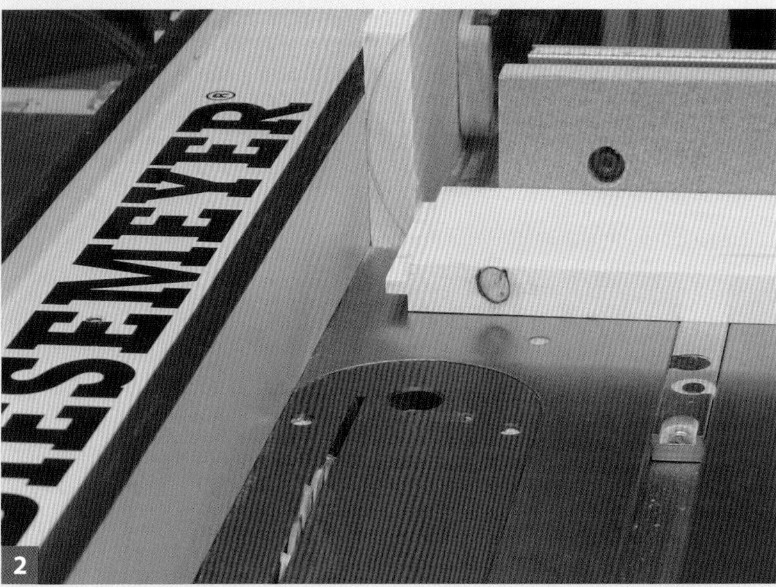

2

Set up and cut the tongue. Cutting the tongue employs the same techniques used to make a rabbet joint (see page 158), only the cuts are usually shallower and made on both sides of the workpiece. When using a stacked dado cutter, increase its width to about ¾" so a portion of it can be buried in a sacrificial fence. Secure a sacrificial fence to the saw's rip fence, and then adjust so ½" of the dado stack is exposed. At the router table, install a flat-bottomed bit with a diameter in excess of ½", and adjust the fence so ½" of the bit is exposed.

Raise the bit slightly above the table, and make a pass on both sides of the wood. Check the resulting tongue against the groove, and make small corrections to the bit height if needed. Repeat the test cut until the tongue fits the groove with a little bit of friction. When satisfied with the setup, cut the tongue in all of the workpieces.

More Than Enough Wood

When making tongue-and-groove joints for a project, cut more than enough wood to avoid having to recreate the setup. Centering the groove and corresponding tongue in the stock can result in dimensions that vary slightly from the size of the cutter used. Trying to recreate that exact setup later is at best an inexact science. Cutting a little extra stock the first time is easier and less aggravating. Save pieces of scrap a few inches long from each of the finish cuts. These can be used for setup blocks later if you do need to cut additional stock to match what's already in the project.

The edge-to-edge version of the tongue-and-groove joint is also popular for making variations of bead-board paneling. The tongue-and-groove keeps the pieces together and in line, including without glue when used to make a free-floating panel or back in a cabinet.

For frame joints, the depth of the groove and the length of the tongue can be altered as needed, but ½" is a common dimension when working with materials in the ¾"- to ⅞"-thick range. Increasing the depth of the groove (and the length of the tongue) serves little purpose, but shortening them can weaken the joint. If you cut the tongue just a hair short, it will fit tight, and there will be a little space for glue at the bottom of the groove.

Tongue-and-groove joints often are made on the table saw with a stacked dado set, using only the two outer blades to produce a ¼"-wide cut. Make the groove with the wood up on edge and the fence set to center the cut in the thickness of the workpiece. To make the tongue, use a gauge block on the rip fence (see Using a Gauge Block on page 131) with the wood flat on the saw table, guided by the miter fence.

On either the table saw or the router table, I prefer to sneak up on the cutter height for the tongue. Use an already grooved piece as a gauge by laying it flat next to the cutter and adjusting so the top of the cutter is slightly below the bottom edge of the groove. Remember that since you cut from both faces, twice the amount of change will be taken off the workpiece. Make test cuts in scrap of the same thickness until you get it right. Too loose will produce a sloppy joint while overly tight risks splitting open the groove when assembled. I consider the fit to be ideal when I can work the tongue into the groove by hand.

Matched tongue-and-groove router bit sets are available for use in router tables. These bit sets are slightly less versatile than the table saw in terms of the range of stock thickness they can handle, though most are designed to be compatible with material around the ¾"- to ⅞"-thick range (see Tongue-and-Groove Router Bit Set on the next page).

Tongue-and-groove joints can also be made on a router table using a ¼" straight bit to cut the groove and a flat-bottomed or rabbeting bit to cut the tongue.

Tongue-and-Groove Router Bit Set

These two-bit sets combine cutters and guide collars so that one bit cuts the groove and the other forms the tongue. Setup has to be perfect because the workpieces must each be cut in one pass. Flipping them over for a second pass will alter the width of the tongue-and-groove, ruining the fit. The good news is that this setup is relatively easy to do with a little practice and that most routers mounted in tables have enough power to make the cuts in a single pass. Also, some bit manufacturers offer setup blocks that make this alignment easier yet.

This two-bit set has one cutter for the groove and a matching cutter for the tongue. It is very efficient but must be precisely set up.

Step 1. Start with the grooving bit because it is easier to center on the wood. The grooved parts can then be used to help adjust the tongue cutter. Install the grooving bit, and adjust the fence so its face is even with the operator's side of the guide bearing. Using a piece of scrap the same thickness as the workpieces, eyeball the groove cutter as close to center as you can.

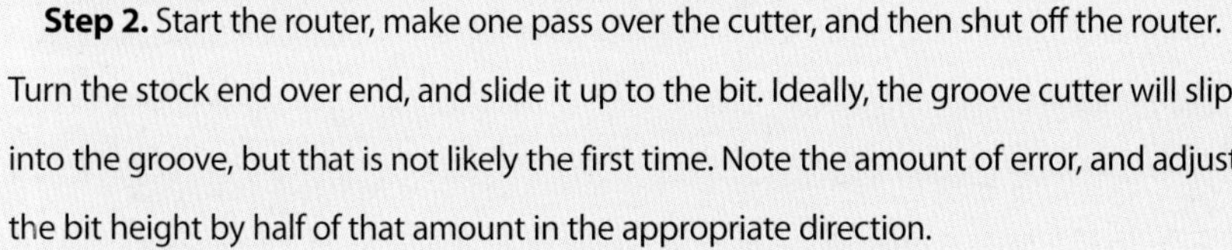

Step 2. Start the router, make one pass over the cutter, and then shut off the router. Turn the stock end over end, and slide it up to the bit. Ideally, the groove cutter will slip into the groove, but that is not likely the first time. Note the amount of error, and adjust the bit height by half of that amount in the appropriate direction.

Step 3. Repeat this cut on a fresh piece of scrap, and check your progress until the groove slides over the cutter when flipped over. Save the last piece of scrap to use as a gauge later when setting up the tongue-cutting bit.

Step 4. When satisfied with the setup, cut the grooves in all of the appropriate workpieces.

To set the groove cutter, make a test cut, then flip the wood end over end and see if it lines up. Adjust the setup until it does.

Step 5. Install the tongue-cutting bit, and set the fence so it is even with the operator side of the bearing. Slide the grooved test piece against the tongue-cutting bit, and adjust the height until the edges of the tongue cutters align with the edges of the groove.

Step 6. Cut a tongue in a piece of scrap, and shut off the router. Flip the stock end over end, and align it with the bit. If the tongue does not slide between the cutters, note the amount of error, and adjust the bit height by half of that dimension.

Step 7. Repeat the cut, and check the steps on fresh pieces of scrap until you are satisfied with the setup; then, run the tongues on all of the workpieces.

Step 8a. When the joint is assembled, the tongue should fit the groove snugly with the surfaces of the two pieces flush to each other. You might have to sand these joints to make them absolutely flush, but the discrepancy should be very small if your setup was right.

Step 8b. If the tongue does not fit the groove properly, check the literature that came with the bit set for instructions on altering the width of the tongue cut. Better bits have provisions for changing shims between the cutters and the bearing to change the thickness of the tongue the bit cuts.

To set the tongue cutter, line it up with the groove test piece.

Mortise and Tenon Joint

Frame joint

Difficulty 7

Tools:

- Stacked dado cutter (table saw)
- Flat-bottomed bits (router table)
- Drill press
- Mortising machine, or router table, or mortising chisel and mallet

Long a favorite of woodworkers, a well-made mortise and tenon joint is neat and very strong (see **Figure 8.18**). The mortise is a rectangular hole in a piece of wood, and the tenon is the matching piece that fits into the mortise. The tenon is made smaller than its parent piece of wood in order to create two, three, or most often four shoulders. The shoulders contribute a great deal to the strength of the joint, in particular to its resistance to racking stress.

Figure 8.18. The mortise and tenon joint is a strong joint that is useful as a structural element for a wide variety of projects.

Its strength makes the mortise and tenon useful as a structural element in a wide range of projects, including face frames, doors, table bases, and chairs. Variations such as the through mortise and tenon can add visual appeal to a project. It is the basic joint used for centuries in timber-framed houses. Though normally a frame joint, the mortise and tenon can also be used to make virtually anything with a frame and even to join shelves to uprights in a bookcase.

Normally you make the mortise first, and then make the tenon to fit. That's because it is much easier to adjust the tenon. The general dimensions of the tenon and its shoulders depend on the overall size of the piece into which they are cut and on the purpose of the joint. Having a larger shoulder at the top and bottom can be important when the joint is located near the end of a structural member, such as a leg, because it leaves more wood beyond the mortise to help resist breaking through under a load.

The length of the tenon can also be a point of discussion. I try to cut tenons at least 1" long if there is sufficient material for the mortise. However, I seldom go beyond 2" long (see **Figure 8.19**), even when there is room for deeper mortises. There is little in the way of strength to be gained by making the tenon much longer than 2". If the load is severe enough to break a 2"-long tenon, the rest of the assembly is in danger of failing anyway.

Figure 8.19. I seldom make tenons longer than 2", as shown here, since making them much longer does little for the strength of the joint.

The fit of a mortise and tenon joint should be snug but not so tight that it must be hammered together. My ideal tenon fit is when it can be almost fully seated by hand and then pulled closed with slight clamp pressure. If the fit is too tight, you risk splitting the mortise open or scraping most of the glue from the joint during assembly.

While all four sides of the tenon should fit the mortise closely, the end of the tenon cannot touch the bottom of the cavity. Leaving $\frac{1}{16}$" to $\frac{1}{8}$" of free space between the end of the tenon and the bottom of the mortise guarantees that the shoulders will fit tightly against the surface and allows room for glue that becomes trapped when the joint is assembled.

There are several variations of the mortise and tenon joint, many of which enhance cosmetics more than strength. A traditional favorite is installing pegs through the mortise and tenon, a technique that was used many years ago to lock the joint together. The strength of modern glues makes this unnecessary. However, adding the pegs is an easy way to enhance the look of this joint on some projects. I suggest learning to make good mortise and tenon joints first before you experiment with ways of dressing them up.

Mortising Methods

For most woodworkers, cutting the mortise is the most difficult part of the process. Locating the mortise properly is largely a matter of good layout technique. Cutting the mortise square with even sides is what gives people fits, especially when using a router or a mallet and chisel to make them.

Using a mallet and chisel to cut mortises is skill intensive and consequently is the most difficult method, at least initially. Learning to make a relatively slender, straight-sided hole more than an inch deep is no small task. There are many who enjoy this type of work and are able to achieve a high degree of accuracy with hand tools. I have tried it and appear to lack the interest, patience, and skill to even begin to enjoy the task. You may be different.

Though handheld and table-mounted routers are capable of cutting mortises, this can be difficult and somewhat dangerous. Routing a mortise with a handheld plunge router means using a fence attached to the router base. To avoid having to balance the router along a relatively narrow surface, you also need to arrange blocks around the workpiece in a vise so there's plenty of support for the router base.

On a router table, the workpiece has to be plunged down over the bit to begin the cut and then lifted off at the end. Starting and stopping these cuts without messing up the ends can be more than a little difficult. You can improve the odds by rigging up some blocks to limit where the workpiece can go. For me, having all of this happening with the bit hidden from view does not generate the warm, fuzzy feeling I am looking for.

Cutting a mortise with a chisel and a mallet is skill intensive.

If you do decide to go with routed mortises, note that the router bit leaves round corners instead of square ones. You have the choice of chiseling the corners of the mortise square or of rounding the edges of the tenons to match, which is easy to do with a rasp and coarse sandpaper. Another choice is to make matching mortises in both pieces, then connect them by gluing a loose tenon into both. You can run miles of round-cornered loose tenon stock on your router table easily enough, but remember that this technique requires cutting two perfectly placed mortises.

Having said all that, I prefer to use the dedicated mortising machine. It is easy to set up and use. The hollow chisel arrangement can cut an overlapping row of square holes, and you can see the bit as it works. Being able to cut many mortises with one setup does wonders for consistency of size. That makes forming tenons much easier since you do not want to custom fit each joint individually.

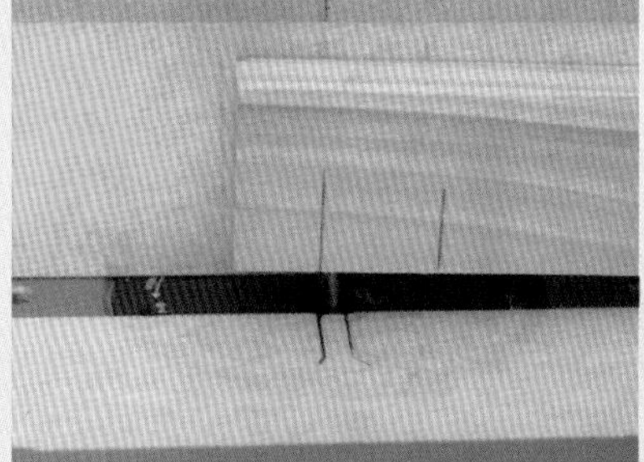

Cutting mortises on the router table requires you to start and stop the cut accurately. The bottom lines show the edges of the router bit. The upper lines are the start/stop indicators that, when aligned with the bit markings, size the mortise cut on a router table.

Clean Up Now

When mortise and tenon joints are assembled, some glue probably will squeeze from the joint. While I believe in letting squeezed-out glue dry when joining flat panels, the corners around a mortise and tenon joint make it impossible to scrape away dried glue without damaging the wood. I keep a damp rag handy when assembling mortise and tenon joints so I can wipe away any excess glue as soon as I see it.

Making the Mortise and Tenon

1

Cut the mortises. Be sure to lay out all four sides of all the mortises so there is no doubt regarding where they are to be cut. Set up the mortiser depth stop so the depth is 1⁄16" to 1⁄8" deeper than the tenon is long, and use its hold-downs. Stops can be set up on the router table if you are using that. Brush off or vacuum up the chips after each workpiece since any strays can hold the next piece of stock at a small angle and interfere with accuracy.

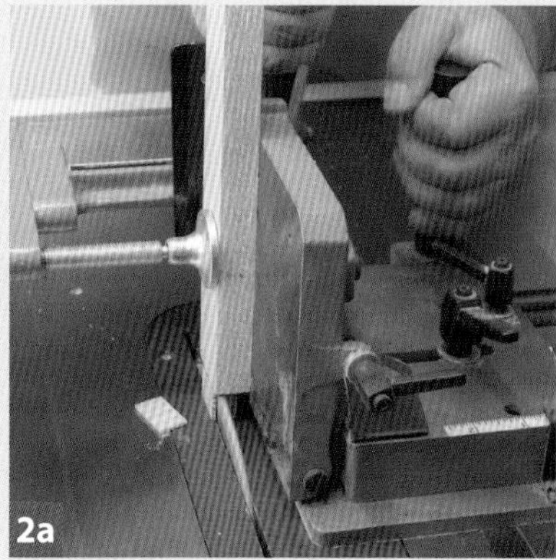

2a

Form tenons on the table saw. On the table saw, you can form tenons using a stacked dado set. You can do it with the workpiece flat on the table, guided by the miter gauge, or you can clamp the workpiece up on end in a tenoning jig. Either way, the idea is to take equal cuts on both faces of the tenon test piece. Slowly increase the depth of cut until the tenon fits the mortise. Cut the wide faces of all the workpiece tenons; then, cut their narrow faces, adjusting the height of the cutter if necessary to produce the right tenon fit.

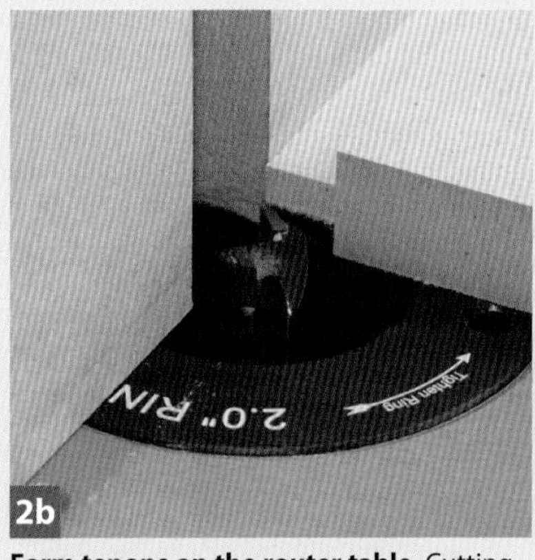

2b

Form tenons on the router table. Cutting tenons is essentially the same on the router table as on the table saw (see Step 2a). However, using the router table adds a step because it is advisable to saw a scoring cut around the tenon shoulder to minimize chipping. Another way to eliminate chipping is to score a deep shoulder line with a combination square and a sharp knife before you start routing. Cut the wide faces on all of the tenons, and then cut their narrow faces. With the workpiece held against a miter guide, use the fence or stop block to make sure all four tenon shoulders are exactly the same distance from the end of the tenon.

3

Assemble. Apply a thin coat of glue to the sides and ends of the mortise and all surfaces of the tenon. I put a thin coat of glue on the tenon shoulder, more as a sealer than to try to increase the strength of the joint, since the shoulder area is pure end grain. Then clamp the joint with just enough pressure to seat the shoulders against the mortised piece. Make sure the assembly is square, and allow it to dry.

Have It Your Way

There are many ways of making mortise and tenon joints, all of which have large numbers of proponents. You can make the mortise by chopping with a chisel and a mallet, by drilling, by routing, or by using a dedicated mortising machine. You can make the tenon by using a handsaw, band saw, table saw, or router. You can combine these methods in any way that suits you. Most important is that you make mortise and tenon joints the way that is most comfortable and enjoyable to you. It is your shop, and you get to decide how things will be done in it. In my shop, I use the dedicated mortising machine and for tenons, the table saw. I enjoy doing it that way and get the best results.

Miter Joint

Box, frame, and plywood joint

Difficulty 8

Tools:
- Table saw or miter saw
- Specialized router bits
- Miter clamp or rubber bands and an adjustable-length strap clamp
- Hand-operated screw
- Angle finder or 45-degree square

A miter is simply a cut at 45 degrees so that matching miters on two pieces of wood will mate to form a square corner (see **Figure 8.20**). Miters are often used for picture frames, where they can be glued and nailed together. They're also attractive as box joints, since the end grain can be completely hidden, which is the application I'm discussing here. Projects with more than four sides are also assembled with miter joints, though the angle of the miter depends on the number of sides in the construction.

Figure 8.20. A miter joint is formed by two boards cut at 45 degrees to create a square corner. These joints are often used for frames and boxes.

While they may look simple, trying to cut gap-free miter joints is how many new (and veteran) woodworkers learn to fill gaps. Cutting miter angles close is relatively easy; getting them perfect, meaning no gaps at any corner, is a real challenge. Increase the number of sides and the gap problem does not get any better. I'd like to tell you there is a simple way to cut perfect miters, but that just is not how it is. Going through the process of setting up with an accurate gauge and then fine-tuning that setup by making test cuts is the only way to make good-fitting miters.

Clamping miters together can be a real challenge. The idea is to put pressure on all of the joints without forcing them out of alignment; most common clamp styles are useless. Some woodworkers use large rubber bands but more common is an adjustable-length strap clamp.

Though attractive, miter joints run across the grain at the end of a board. That produces a semi-end-grain-to-end-grain gluing situation that limits the strength of the joint. In many situations, the strength of the joint is not a big issue since small boxes and frames see little stress in use. Where strength is an issue, the joint needs some kind of mechanical interlock, such as biscuits.

In some situations, the wood is oriented so the joint runs parallel to the grain, for example when you want to make a tall, hollow box to use as a column or table leg with the grain running vertically. That is a long-grain-to-long-grain situation, and the glue will hold the joint very well.

The good news is that miter joints get easier with experience. I think this is more from knowing what not to do than how to make them easily. The best teacher I know is practice and getting to know your equipment.

Tip!

Nailed Miters

Picture framers usually use miter joints. They glue them and clamp them with special-purpose clamps; then, they guarantee each joint with one or two long finishing nails. They stand the frame up on edge, drill pilot holes, and drive the nails straight down through one side of the miter and into the other.

Cutting Miter Joints

1

Get the angle right. High-quality saws simplify cutting accurate miters, but some trial and error remains likely to perfect the joint. Use a good angle finder or a 45-degree square to check the actual angle of the blade on miter saws and to check the angle of the miter guide on table saws. Confirming the accuracy of that setup with test cuts is mandatory.

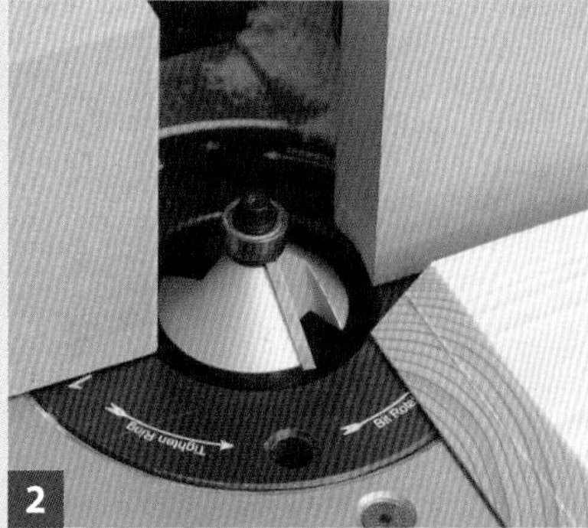

2

Use special router bits. Router bits are available with cutters angled for making specific miter angles, but they are not foolproof either. If the router is not exactly square to the table, gaps will show up in the finished joint. Setting the fence correctly to cut a full angle without reducing the overall dimension of the workpiece can become a spontaneous test of character. Here again, some router bit manufacturers have setup blocks available that make the initial setup much easier. Test cuts to perfect the setup are still required but will generally be fewer in number.

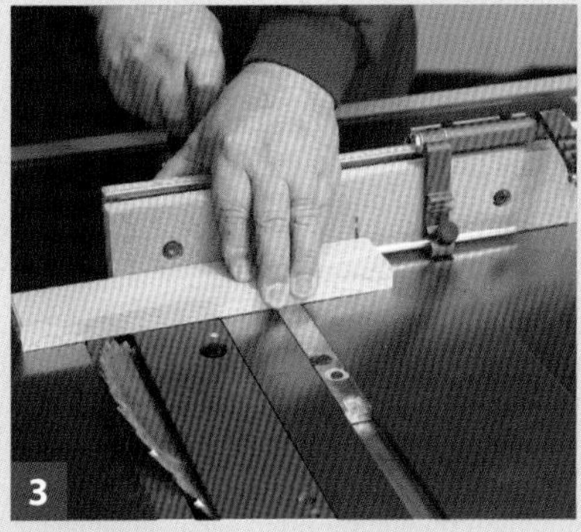

3

Dry fit and cut the pieces. After determining the miter angle and confirming it with a test cut measured with an accurate gauge, it is a good idea to cut all of the necessary pieces from scrap and dry fit them together. If the pieces can be assembled to form the shape wanted without any gaps, you are ready. If not, make tiny adjustments to the saw to perfect the angle. The setup shown also has a flip stop to ensure that all of the pieces are identical in length. Take your time to get the stop block positioned correctly, and then cut all of the pieces.

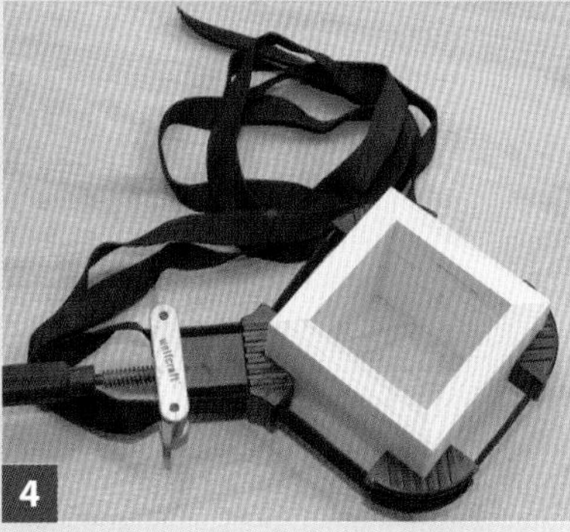

4

Assemble. The webbed strap surrounds the assembled pieces and a hand-operated screw applies uniform pressure. Check the assembly to be sure it is still aligned before tightening the belt just enough to force the joints closed. Then, leave the shop and don't go back in until the glue has had plenty of time to dry.

Tip!

A Fence that Grips

When sawing miters using the miter guide, adding a wooden face to the fence and covering that with 100-grit sandpaper can increase the accuracy. When the blade cuts a steep miter, the force of that cut tries to slide the wood along the fence. If it moves even slightly, the joint is ruined. The sandpaper adds a tremendous amount of grip, making it much easier to hold the piece motionless during the cut, and if you clamp the workpiece to the guide instead of hand holding it, your problems are over.

The force of sawing tends to slide the wood along the miter gauge, so add traction by gluing sandpaper to the fence. A clamp also helps a lot.

With some saw blades, you might find it best to cut the miter 1/16" longer than needed and then take a trim cut to reduce it to the final length. Taking that little trim cut substantially reduces the stress on the blade, and it tends to clean the end of the piece more accurately.

Box (Finger) Joint

Box joint

Difficulty 8

Tools:
- Stacked dado set (table saw)
- Flat-bottomed bit (router table)
- Box joint jig
- Combination square

A box joint, also called a finger joint, has square fingers and spaces on the ends of both pieces of wood, offset so they lace together like your own fingers (see **Figure 8.21**). It can be made on the table saw or the router table, using a simple jig that you can buy or make. When the joint fits neatly and is glued together, it is enormously strong. A well-made box joint is not just strong; the exposed end grain can be very attractive when stained and finished, which is another reason why box joints are used to make cabinets, drawers, chests, and jewelry boxes.

Figure 8.21. A box joint is a very strong joint with fingers that lace together.

Woodworkers have made their own box joint jigs for decades. Using a correctly made jig, this joint is very easy. However, if the jig is improperly spaced at all, box joints are nearly impossible to close because even tiny spacing errors compound as the number of fingers increases. The problem lies in the width of the cutter and the spacing between it and the locator pin. The cutter width, space, and pin all must be identical or the fingers will not be sized or spaced correctly.

The cutter can be virtually any width as long as the space and the pin match it exactly. Most often, box joints are made using ¼", ⅜", or ½" widths, mostly because those cutter sizes are already in the shop and the width of the fingers produced look proportionately right on the majority of projects. All of the box joint jigs I have made use a ⅜" cutter because I like the look and the finger size seems to fit most projects.

To make the jig, follow the instructions in Making the Box Joint Jig on page 172. Before using the jig, prepare all of the workpieces, making sure they are cut square and that opposing sides are exactly the same length. Mark their top edges and their position in the finished box so they can be kept in the correct order while cutting the joints.

There is another option that will make your box joint life much easier. I use a commercially made box joint jig, as shown in **Figure 8.22**. Machined from metal, the spacing is perfect, which translates to perfect box joints without any cussing and scrap. After using it, I conceded defeat and threw away my shop-made box joint jigs. The box joint jig made for the photos in this book actually worked pretty well, but I tossed it also. I have learned not to argue with perfection.

Before putting the box joint jig away, cut a set of fingers in a piece of scrap 12" to 18" long. This strip can be used as a gauge to see how the joints will fit on different widths of stock when designing a box using box joints.

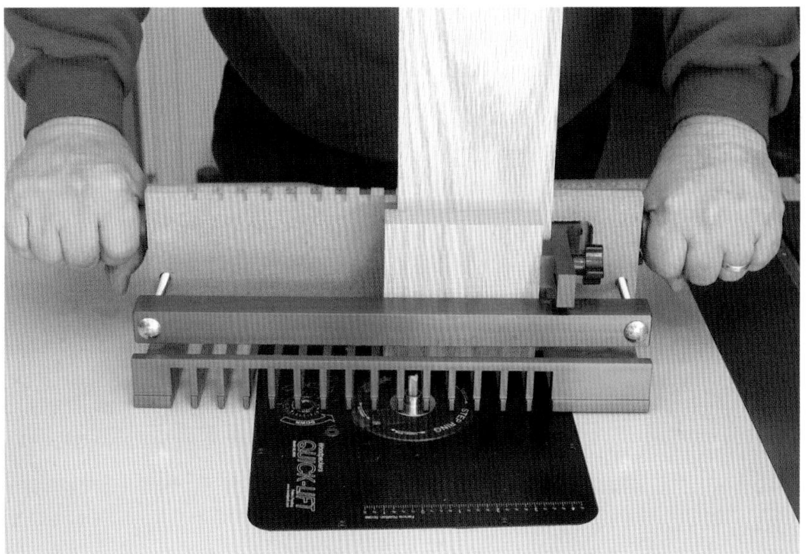

Figure 8.22. This very nice box joint jig is more accurate than my shop-made ones, so it's what I use now.

Making the Box Joint Jig

Box joint jigs usually use the miter guide, fitted with an auxiliary fence made from a piece of plywood or MDF (medium-density fiberboard). Nearly all factory-supplied miter guides have two holes in the fence meant for attaching a wooden face. The wood is sized as you think necessary to support the workpieces to be joined. I have found that box joint jigs between 18" and 24" long and 6" to 8" tall work best for the project range I normally build.

The easiest way I have found to get the spacing correct between the cutter and the pin is to use a spacer block that is precisely twice as wide as the cutter. The procedure described here uses a ¾"-wide spacer block to produce a jig that matches a stacked dado cutter set at ⅜" width in a table saw or a ⅜"-diameter bit on a router table. If your router table does not have an adjustable fence, use a board clamped to the table to take its place. For the initial cut to make the jig, set the cutter height to ⅜". When using the jig, set the cutter height to slightly exceed the thickness of the workpiece.

Clamp the box joint jig fence to the miter guide, making sure it extends beyond the cutter about 4". Place the spacer block against the end of the jig, move the table saw (or router) fence against the spacer, and lock it down. Remove the spacer (leave the fence where it is), start the machine, and then make a single pass over the cutter, creating a slot in the auxiliary fence. Shut off the machine.

Move the miter guide back to the starting position, remove the clamp, and slide the jig fence over so it contacts the rip fence. With the spacer block removed, this indexes the jig fence over exactly ¾". Clamp the jig fence to the miter guide again, making sure it remains in contact with the fence. Install screws through the holes in the miter guide to permanently secure the jig fence in place. You're done with the rip fence now; move it out of the way. Increase the cutter height to ½", start the machine, and make another single pass over the cutter to make a second slot. Higher cutter settings may be used later and will enlarge this opening as needed without affecting the jig, but I like to start low and close to help reduce backside chipping.

Now make a piece of hardwood ⅜" square and about 10" long. This will yield the locator pin and spacer that are used while making the first cuts on two faces of a box. It is important that this piece be exactly ⅜" square because it is what indexes the workpiece to create the proper spacing.

Cut a 5"-long piece of the locator pin stock, and fit it into the slot in the jig fence next to the blade path. The locator pin should extend out from the jig face with its rear edge flush with the back of the jig fence. Glue the locator pin in place, making sure it is square to the face of the jig fence, and allow it to dry. After the glue has dried, I predrill and countersink a screw through the locator pin and into the jig fence for extra security.

The box joint jig consists of an auxiliary fence fastened to the miter guide with a cutter-wide slot in it and a wooden pin that exactly fits the slot.

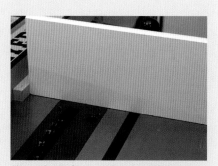

Clamp the jig fence to the miter guide, and fit the spacer between it and the rip fence. Remove the spacer, and cut a slot in the jig fence.

Slide the jig fence over so it contacts the rip fence, and screw it to the miter guide. Move the rip fence out of the way and then saw a second slot.

Glue the locator pin into the first jig slot, and square it to the face of the jig fence.

Making Box Joints

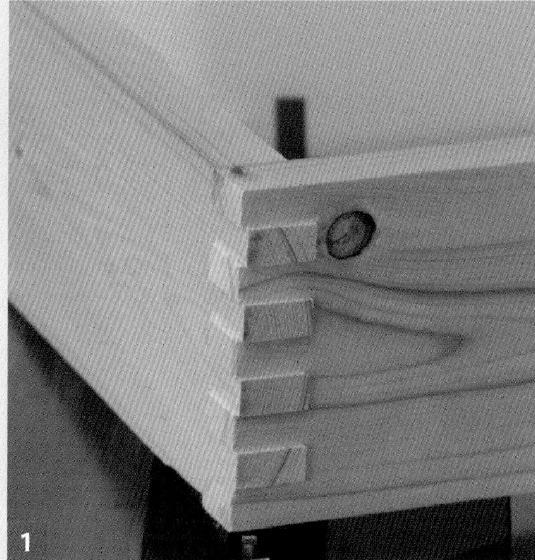

Set up the cutter. Lay one of the workpieces next to the cutter, and adjust the cutter to about 1⁄16" higher than the wood. This ensures the joint will be cut a little deeper than necessary. When assembled, the ends of the fingers will protrude slightly from the sides and easily can be sanded flush. If the cutter is too low, the fingers will end below the surface of the sides, and you will have to plane or sand the sides down to match.

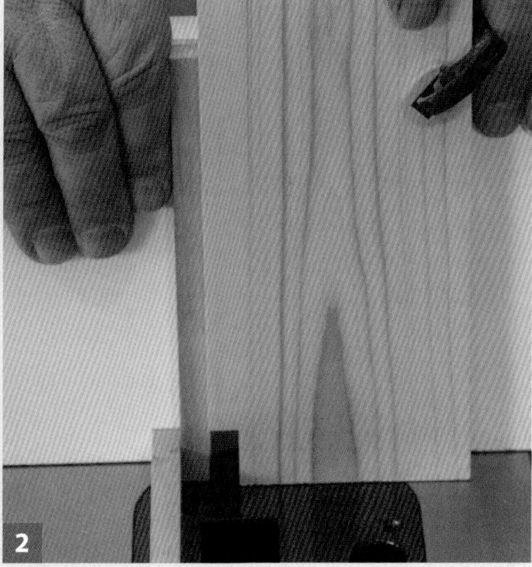

Make the first cut. Because you usually want a full pin at the top of the front piece for appearance, make the first cuts in the two sides. Use the remaining piece of 3⁄8"-thick locator pin stock as a spacer. Stand both sides on end against the jig fence, top markings toward the locator pin. Insert the spacer pin between the sides and the locator pin; then, clamp them to the jig fence, and remove the spacer pin. Using the spacer pin indexes the side pieces over so a space is cut for the top finger of the front panels. Make the first cut.

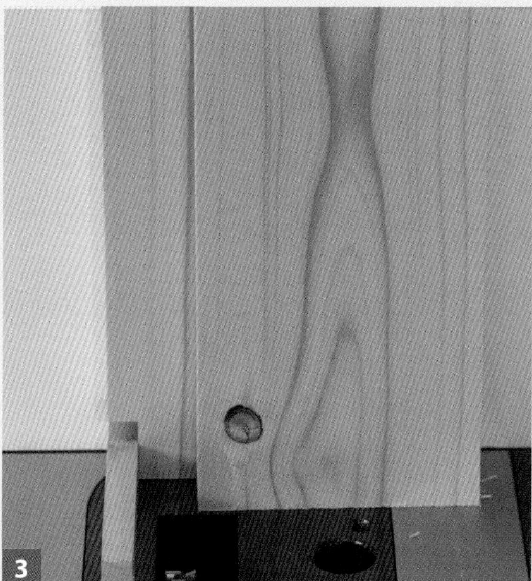

Complete the remaining cuts. Slide the pair of sides to the right so the notch you just cut fits over the locator pin, and then clamp them to the jig fence again. Make the second cut. Continue making cuts, setting the last cut made over the locator pin, until the entire width has been cut, including a full or partial notch at the bottom edge. Then, flip the workpieces end over end so the uncut end is at the table surface and the top markings remain on the locator pin side. Make the cuts in that edge the same way, including using the spacing pin for the first cut on the side pieces only.

Cut the mating pieces. The front/back panels are cut exactly the same way except that the spacer pin is not used for the first cut. This creates a full pin at the top edge of the panel that corresponds with the notch at the top of the sides. If the box joint jig was made right and the stock was prepared accurately, you should now have a set of joints that will tap together with no gaps and produce a flat, square box. Of course, that seldom happens the first time in the real world. As with any new technique, practicing the box joint is the only way to master this very useful joint.

Fitting the Fingers

Because the spacing of the fingers cannot be altered, I have found it easiest to cut the stock 1⁄2" to 3⁄4" wider than needed, cut the box joints, and then rip the stock down until a full or half pin remains at the bottom edge. Most projects are easily altered to accommodate this small change in height.

Cut the Panels and Sides in Pairs

You can cut each piece individually, in pairs (front and back together or sides together), or all four at once, adding the front/back panels to the stack after the first cut is made in the side pieces. I have had the best results cutting the pieces two at a time because it is easier to accurately clamp and handle two rather than four pieces, and easier to keep track of what I am doing.

Dovetail Joint

Box joint

Difficulty 8

Tools:
- Table saw or chop saw
- Dovetail jig
- Router with dovetail bits and guide collar
- Chisels and mallet
- Square

Figure 8.23. In addition to being beautiful, the dovetail joint is also one of the strongest wood joints.

Figure 8.24. Through dovetails go right through both pieces of wood and are visible on both sides of the corner.

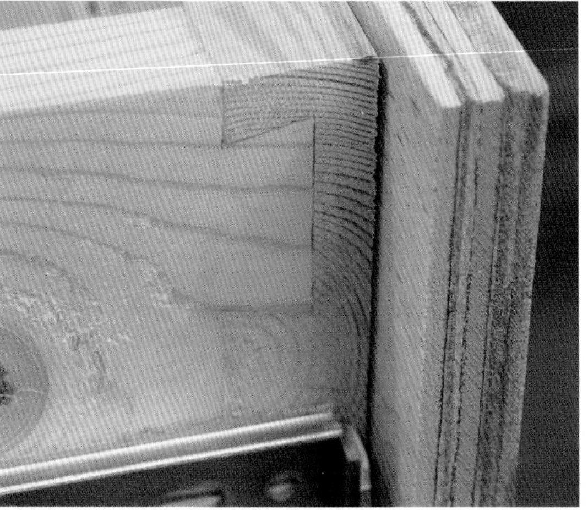

Figure 8.25. Half-blind dovetails go through one piece but stop short of the surface of the other. This drawer has an added front, so the dovetails could have gone through without showing.

Long regarded as one of the most beautiful joints, the glued dovetail is also one of the strongest joints that can be made in wood (see **Figure 8.23**). While dovetails are frequently used to make drawers, cabinets, and box-based items such as jewelry cases, woodworkers continue to find ways of applying dovetails to add their own touch of craftsmanship to a wide range of the projects they build.

Through dovetails go right through both pieces of wood and are visible on both sides of the corner (see **Figure 8.24**); they're common on chests and boxes. Half-blind dovetails show on one side but stop short of the surface of the other piece (see **Figure 8.25**); they're common in drawers. Full-blind dovetails stop short of both surfaces and are completely invisible once the joint is closed. Some folks might enjoy the very private satisfaction of knowing they are in there, but not me!

Dovetails can be intimidating for new woodworkers because of all of the angles that just look hard to make. While dovetails are more difficult to cut than most other types of joints, how you do it, the equipment used, the amount of experience, and your level of interest all contribute to how easy, or difficult, this task is to master.

A point in the dovetail's favor is that there are but three primary methods for making them: using a router and dovetail jig, using hand tools, or paying someone else to do them, in that order of popularity. Some books have instructions for making them on the band saw, scroll saw, or table saw, but I have never been able to achieve good results using those procedures.

Few choose paying someone to cut their dovetails since that presents no challenge, offers no bragging rights, and could set a dangerous fiscal precedent.

Dovetail Jigs

Though virtually any router can handle dovetailing, the quality of the jig can have a huge impact on the accuracy and variety of the joints produced, as well as on how difficult it is to use. Dovetail jigs cost from $75 to well over $400, but, after that, all you need is a router and a few bits. Lower-priced jigs usually lack variable spacing, capacity, and good instructions. The most common complaint I hear about the bargain-priced dovetail jigs is the terrible instructions that come with many of them. The folks most likely to understand these instructions are those already familiar with using a dovetail jig.

A high-quality jig, like this Leigh D4, can accommodate virtually any size workpiece and dovetail spacing.

Most higher-priced jigs are made to higher tolerances from better materials, have more features and capacity, and are more consistent. Plus, they tend to have good instructions that someone new to making dovetails can comprehend.

The Leigh D4 dovetail jig is commonly regarded as the standard by which all others are measured. While it is exceptionally well made from quality materials and is capable of variable spacing of through and half-blind dovetails, one of its big selling points is the incredibly detailed instruction manual that comes with it. In addition to the best text and illustrations in the business, the Leigh manual has a troubleshooting section that covers most of the problem areas of cutting dovetails and provides logical, understandable solutions for them.

Dovetail jigs rely on a perfect match of guide bushing and bit.

Dovetail jigs require that a specific diameter guide bushing and bit (diameter and angle) combination be installed in the router. If these pieces are not included with the jig, the instructions should spell out exactly what is needed. A common complaint from new dovetail jig users is that the joints will not fit despite following the instructions precisely. Frequently the cause is that the bushing and/or bit being used is not exactly what is required for the jig. In terms of bit, bushing, and dovetail jig compatibility, close is not close enough. Just because you already have a dovetail bit does not mean it will work with the jig you bought.

Through dovetails are easier to make on most jigs than half-blinds primarily because tiny changes in bit height have dramatic effects on how the half-blind joint fits. I have learned the hard way that bit height changes in excess of 1⁄64" at one time are too much. If the fit is close, you can easily overcorrect, so go slow and small. Once the correct bit height is determined, cutting half-blind dovetails is fast, accurate, and surprisingly easy.

The process of fitting half-blind dovetails has frustrated some woodworkers sufficiently that after getting the bit height set correctly, they refuse to remove or adjust that bit until it or the router breaks. One exasperated woodworker told me that if a fire were to start in his shop, his half-blind dovetailing router would be the only thing he would risk his life to save. That's extreme, but dedicating a router to half-blind dovetails can be a good idea if cutting them is a frequent task and your shop budget can handle this understandable extravagance.

Farming out dovetails could negatively impact the time-honored tradition of needing (justifying) more new tools!

Some folks like to debate over whether to make dovetails with a router and jig or with hand tools, but either method is legal, so you can choose whichever you like, or choose both.

Hand cutting dovetails (see **Figure 8.26**) involves a substantial learning curve, but, if this technique is intriguing to you, learning will be part of the enjoyment. While using hand tools to make joints is not high on my personal whoopee list, I admire those with the drive, patience, and skill to master the techniques. However, don't imagine that hand cutting is the cheap way out since a good set of chisels can cost $100, not to mention sharpening supplies, plus specialty layout and measuring tools. The cost of the tool kit will end up close to the cost of a good dovetail jig, though to be fair you will find lots more uses for sharp chisels.

While very popular, using a router to cut dovetails is not without its own learning curve. However, once you become familiar with the process and learn how a particular jig works, cutting accurate dovetails is relatively fast and easy (see **Figure 8.27**). Like any joint, the wood that dovetails are cut in must be prepared properly. If the ends are not square, the power of the dovetail joint makes it impossible to tweak the joint to straighten the assembly.

Because dovetail jig instructions are so specific, providing general step-by-step directions here would be confusing. However, I can offer some general strategies and tips that might help you along in the learning process. Considering the outcome of my hand-cut dovetail attempts, you will want to find another source of information if that is how you choose to make this joint.

Figure 8.26. Hand cutting dovetails with a dovetail saw and chisels takes practice and skill, but some do enjoy the challenge.

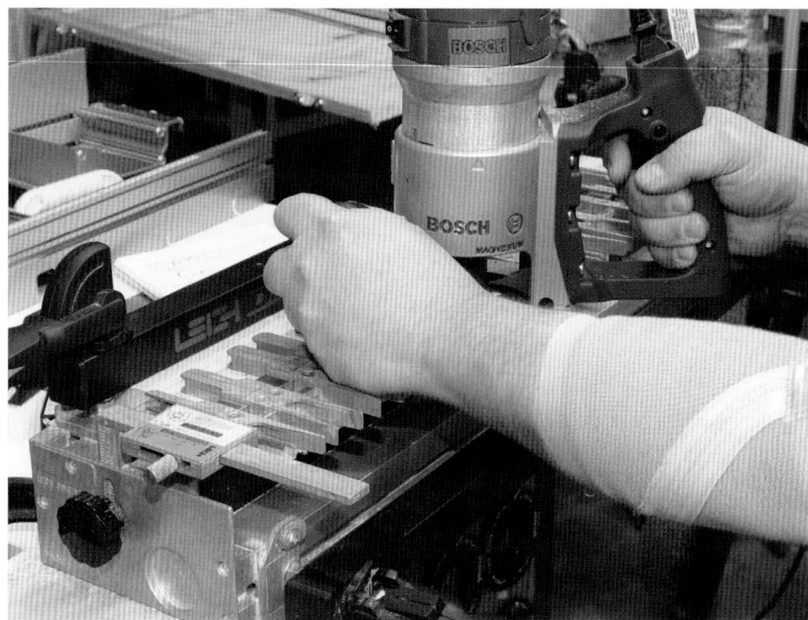

Figure 8.27. A good jig makes short work of cutting dovetails, though it will take time to set up and learn to use.

Making Dovetails

1

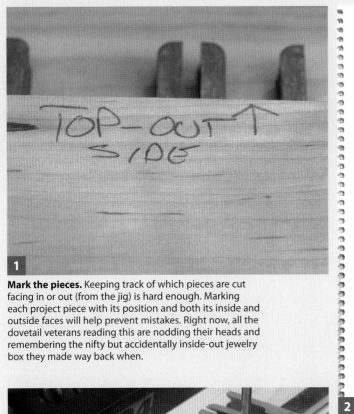

Mark the pieces. Keeping track of which pieces are cut facing in or out (from the jig) is hard enough. Marking each project piece with its position and both its inside and outside faces will help prevent mistakes. Right now, all the dovetail veterans reading this are nodding their heads and remembering the nifty but accidentally inside-out jewelry box they made way back when.

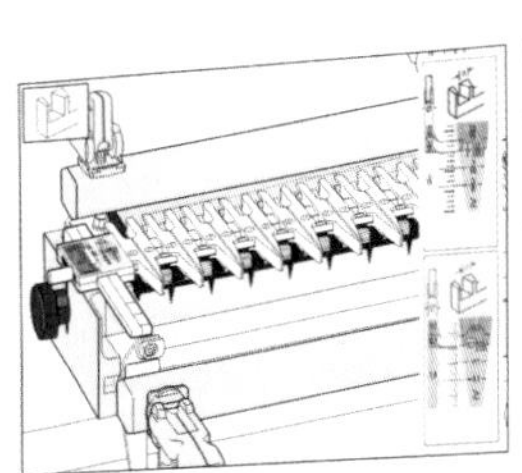

8-7

Place the finger assembly on the support brackets in the TD PINS mode, flat on the spacer board, and with the scale set on the ½"[12,7mm] setting for now. Don't worry about the scale's specific meaning now. Each scale's use will be fully explained in the appropriate section.

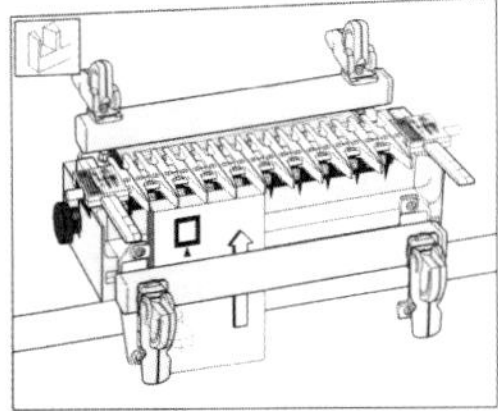

8-8

Although you will cut the tails first, adjust the guidefinger layout in the TD PINS mode. The adjustment screws are on top in this mode, and it is easier to visualize the finished joint pattern. **Clamp one of the pin boards** in the left side of the front clamp, against the side stop, with the top edge flush under and touching the guidefingers, and the outside face away from the jig body.

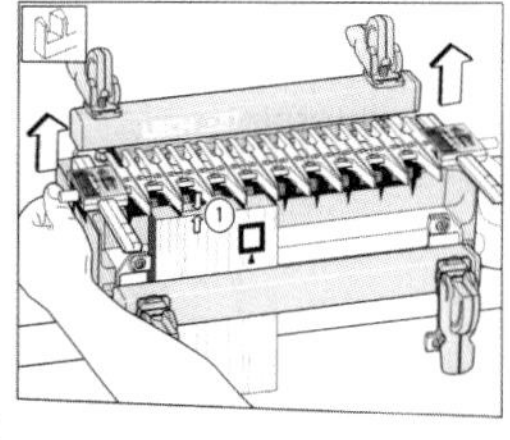

8-9

Loosen the support bracket knobs and raise the finger assembly about 1/16"[2mm] ① above the boards and retighten the knobs. This will allow easy and accurate guidefinger adjustment.

2

Follow the sequence. Dovetail jig instructions follow a specific sequence regarding which pieces are cut first and may have other steps in the procedure that come in a specific order. Sticking with the procedure described in the instructions is not an option—it's the law. Altering that order is a prescription for disaster.

3

Use scrap to practice joints. Whenever I get a new jig, some of the scrap (or cheap) wood in the shop is sacrificed in order for me to become familiar with using it. Reading instructions and having experience with similar jigs is fine, but nothing beats actually using a new jig according to the instructions. Then, with a little practical experience, cutting joints in project wood is less frightening.

Chapter 9

Finishing

Woodworkers often have a love/hate relationship with finishing. They love how it looks when completed (if it comes out as expected), but hate the process of applying it. Some, myself included, have the good fortune to be married to someone who enjoys finishing. This bit of good fortune is all that prevents many from having a house full of unfinished or hastily painted projects.

The range of finishing options is immense, as are the tastes of woodworkers. We will look at the basics of getting a project ready for the application of a finish and the more common types of finishing materials. Many finishes contain volatile materials that can present health and fire hazards if handled improperly. Before opening a finish container, take the time to read and understand the instructions, and then adhere to them.

Personal protection

Reading and following the manufacturer's instructions for using, applying, and storing finishes is not only important to the results, but also crucial to the safety of you and anyone who enters the work area. Adequate ventilation is a basic requirement for using finishes safely, and a face mask designed for solvent protection may also be necessary with some finishes. Wear rubber or synthetic gloves (see **Figure 9.1**) to prevent the possibility of chemical components causing irritation to, or being absorbed through, the skin. Gloves also eliminate the embarrassment of going to work for the next week or two with wood-colored hands.

Figure 9.1. Wearing rubber (or vinyl) gloves not only prevents staining or finishing your hands, but also prevents absorbing volatile chemicals through your skin.

Finishing Checklist

Finishing is not a complicated process. You'll have the best results if you learn and follow a logical finishing sequence. Mine goes like this:

- Begin to sand the wood, starting with 100-, 120-, or 150-grit paper, depending on how rough it is.
- Raise the grain with distilled water, and sand.
- Repair and fill defects, and sand the patch.
- Work the grit sequence, ending at 220 or even 320 grit.
- Fill the grain of open-pore hardwoods, such as oak.
- Apply a pre-stain conditioner for softwoods, such as pine.
- Stain, if staining is necessary or desired.
- Sand again at 220 or 320 grit.
- Apply the topcoat: paint, varnish, oil, lacquer.
- Sand between coats, following label directions.
- Wait for the finish to dry thoroughly.
- Wax or buff to the final polish, if appropriate for the finish used.

Finishing Product	Uses	Features
Sandpaper	Smoothes a rough surface to remove scratches, dents, defects	Available in a wide variety of grits; can be used by hand or with machines
Grain Filler	Fills open pores	Easy to apply; does not fill cracks and gaps
Gap Filler	Fills cracks and gaps	Hides cracks and gaps; works best with small defects
Stain	Alters or enhances wood color	Available in many colors and formulas
Paint	Covers the surface of the wood with color	Many colors and textures available
Varnish	Protects wood from dirt and damage	Fast drying; available for indoor or outdoor use
Oil	Enhances depth and contrast of figure	Variety of kinds available; drying time fast or slow; hardens surface
Food-Safe Finish	Protects furniture, toys, and utensils	Strict adherence to manufacturer's guidelines

Sanding

One of the hard lessons to learn in woodworking is that applying a finish will not conceal a rough surface. In fact, it usually highlights scratches, dents, and defects that you either did not see or hoped would magically disappear during finishing. Particularly annoying is the near certainty that a scratch or gouge will become a prominent feature. Sanding is the answer.

Choosing the initial sandpaper grit is important to both the quality of the final surface and how long it takes to develop it. The abrasive should be rough enough to remove surface imperfections quickly, but fine enough that it does not create unnecessary scratching. Unfortunately, there are no hard-and-fast rules to guide this selection. Experience with the various species of woods, experimentation, and restraint will be your best allies.

In most cases, 120-grit abrasive is suitable for the initial sanding. Occasionally, rougher grits may be needed, but those instances become less frequent as your experience with preparing and working with wood grows and the scale of your built-in defects decreases.

As soon as the larger defects begin to sand away, change to a finer grit. This helps limit the amount of material removed and the chances of sanding in waves or depressions that can be nearly impossible to see before finishing. Learning when to change grits is another judgment call that becomes easier to make after doing it a few times. It's usually best to change to the next finer grit without skipping grits (see **Figure 9.2**). If, for whatever reason, you have to go back to a coarser-grit abrasive, you'll have to work through the sequence again.

Figure 9.2. Working your way through a range of grits when sanding speeds the process and results in a better finish. Most woodworkers sand down to 220 grit, but some go much finer to achieve the look they want.

Sandpaper: The Nitty Gritty

Sandpaper comes in grits from coarse to super fine. The higher the number, the finer the grit, and, therefore, the more abrasive particles it has. Use a coarser paper to remove imperfections or level a surface. Select a finer grit to prepare wood surfaces for staining and to sand in between coats of finish. For best results, change from each grit to the next finer one since this is the best way to remove the scratches created by the sandpaper.

Grit	Use
40-60 (Coarse)	To do heavy sanding, stripping, surface roughing
80-120 (Medium)	To smooth surfaces, remove light scratches
150-180 (Fine)	For final sanding before finishing wood
220-240 (Very Fine)	For sanding between finish coats
280-320 (Extra Fine)	To remove dust and bubbles between coats of finish
360-600 (Super Fine)	To remove surface blemishes, alter luster

The grit size can usually be found on the back of the sandpaper, as well as the type of grit and if the paper is intended for use with softwoods (open coat) or hardwoods (closed coat). The terms "open coat" and "closed coat" refer to how much space there is between the grit particles, and therefore to how quickly the paper will become loaded with sanding dust. Some papers indicate the particle spacing with a letter from A to D, with A being the most widely spaced, following the grit number on the back.

Aluminum oxide, which makes tan-colored sandpaper, and garnet, which is orange, are the most common abrasive materials used for woodworking. Aluminum oxide lasts longer than most other sandpapers, but garnet of the same grit number will produce a smoother surface. This is so because aluminum oxide is extremely hard and durable, while garnet (a natural mineral) breaks down as you sand, continually exposing sharp new grains. Black sandpaper is made with silicon carbide and usually can be used dry or with water. It is for sanding between coats of finish.

Types of Abrasive

Material	Use	Features
Garnet	Hand sanding	Maintains sharpness longer
Aluminum Oxide	Machine sanding	Available in a wide variety of grits
Silicon Carbide	Wet and dry sanding; rubbing out finishes; sanding between coats	Available in a wide variety of grits
Aluminum Zirconia	Removing lots of material	Maintains sharpness longer
Steel Wool	Fine sanding; creating matte finish from glossy finish; sanding raised grain	Be sure to vacuum up dust

The final choice in sanding is how fine of a grit to use last. Many woodworkers find that 180 grit or 220 grit gives them the smoothness they want and still leaves enough tooth for the finish to grab. Others continue to 320, 400, and finer grits. I find that 220 to 320 grit provides the surface I look for, but you may want to experiment with finer grits to see if they provide a more appealing look to your projects.

Dust Control

Though many sanders have some form of on-board dust control, they can still produce significant amounts of airborne particles that are bad for the project and worse for your lungs. When possible, connect sanders to a shop vac or dust collector, and if you have one, run an ambient air cleaner designed for woodshop use.

Despite other dust control efforts, wearing an effective dust mask is a good idea and should be a standard part of your finishing attire (see **Figure 9.3**). Disposable dust masks are cheap.

Aside from breathing the dust, the big problem is the havoc that airborne dust can wreak with the finish itself. There are few things more maddening than brushing the last coat of varnish out thin and smooth, then returning to the workshop to find that fine particles of sanding dust have settled in it. That's why it's so important to suck up as much sanding dust as possible in the first place and then wait a few hours for what dust is in the air to settle out. Then, use a tack cloth (see Tack Rags on the next page) to remove remaining dust before applying a finish as well as between coats.

Figure 9.3. Even with a vacuum attachment and an ambient air cleaner, wearing a dust mask during sanding is a good habit to get into. The best dust collection systems are not 100% effective, but your lungs are exceptionally effective at retaining whatever particles you inhale.

New Tools!

Sanders for Finishing!

The choice of which finishing sander to buy is harder than ever because of the many useful machines on the market. Belt sanders and disk sanders are useful for smoothing major woodworking errors and removing old finishes like polyurethane and paint. Beyond that, they are not used in the finishing process. Here are a few sanders that will be useful:

Random Orbit Sander—These little machines remove material quickly without the heavy scratching that plagues belt and other straight-line machines. Look for variable speed control, very helpful in many sanding situations and between coats, and a hook-and-loop pad attachment, which allows you to change grits without throwing the old sanding pad away. About $60.

The random orbit sander can remove lots of material quickly or polish the wood to a very smooth finish, depending on the grit of the disk installed on the pad.

Palm Sander—These little vibrating units are very popular, especially for the last stages of sanding with fine-grit paper. Cheap, effective, and easy to use, palm sanders can produce exceptionally fine surfaces that are hard to match with any other machine. Their limitation lies in the relatively slow rate at which they remove material, so they are frequently used for final surface sanding and sanding finishes in between coats. They use quarter-sheets torn from regular sandpaper. About $40.

While palm sanders do not remove material as quickly as the random orbit models, they can produce remarkably smooth surfaces and can be easier to fit into tight corners.

Detail Sander—Detail sanders have a triangular pad so they can get into the tightest of corners. Many have changeable heads with other shapes for more specialized sanding tasks. Some have an orbital action and some vibrate. About $30 to $125, depending on features and attachments.

Rubber Block—While you are shopping for finish sanding equipment, don't neglect the plain old rubber hand-sanding block. It is cheap, it is easy to change the sandpaper, and it has many uses during the final construction and finishing processes. It is also a frequent choice for sanding between coats on smaller projects. Under $10.

Sanding Technique

Any sander is capable of carving grooves and gouges into the wood if the operator applies uneven pressure or rocks it onto an edge to increase its effectiveness (see **Figure 9.4**). Aggressiveness with a sander can be tempting when you encounter a tough defect, but it usually creates more problems than it cures. Keeping the sander flat on the surface and relying on the grit of the paper to increase or decrease the rate of material removal will save time, effort, and projects.

Keeping the sander flat on the surface is especially important when working at or near a corner. A clean, crisp edge makes the corner of a project look clean and square. Tilting the sander or running off the edge can round portions of an otherwise square corner, making it look wavy or crooked.

In most cases, the weight of the sander, combined with the motion of the abrasive, will be the most effective and produce the best finish. Once you learn to trust the capabilities of the sander and to avoid leaning on it, you may also be surprised by the extended life of the sandpaper. If you can resist applying excessive pressure to the sander and just let the grit do the work, the resulting surface will be far more pleasing.

While random orbit and palm sanders can be used across grain far more easily than belt sanders, moving them generally with the grain, particularly in the final stages of sanding, produces the best results. In addition to producing the smoothest finish, following the grain helps keep you oriented to avoid missing some areas and resanding others.

Early in the sanding process, moving a sander across the grain may be necessary to flatten small high spots or ridges, particularly along the joint lines of glued-up panels. However, as soon as those defects are removed, return to following the grain to refine the surface.

Figure 9.4. If you rock a sander up on an edge to help remove a scratch, you will almost certainly carve a depression that did not have to be there. Keep the pad of the sander flat on the surface, and let the sander and abrasive do their work.

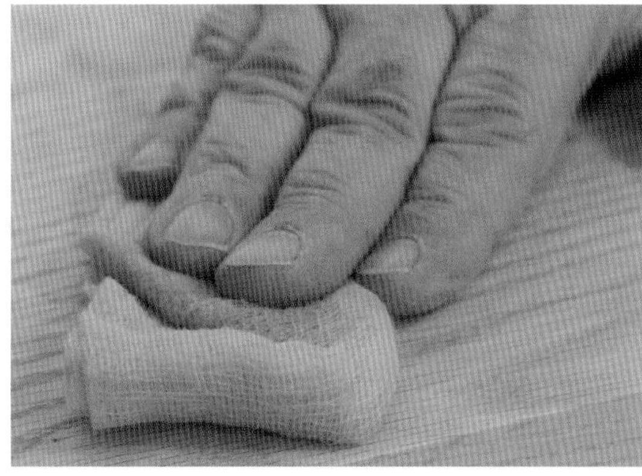

Figure 9.5. After sanding, whether before finishing or between coats, using a tack rag is the only way to remove the fine dust that is left behind.

Tack Rags

One of the mysterious properties of wood is its ability to retain dust. Wiping down wood with a rag or blowing it off with an air gun are good starts, but to be sure the dust is gone, nothing beats a good tack rag and a little effort.

Tack rags are cheap. Stripping and refinishing a project because of dust contamination in the finish is not. Use tack rags in between sandpaper grit changes to pick up both dust and any stray abrasive grains. Then, tack off very thoroughly after you've finished sanding and before you apply any finish (see **Figure 9.5**). Replace the tack rag at the first sign of contamination. It is cheap insurance.

Raising the Grain

A frequent source of frustration occurs when you apply the first coat of stain or finish and the grain in the wood pops up. Sanding the grain back down at this point can result in irregular coloring and a rougher surface than anticipated. The cure is to raise the grain intentionally during the sanding process. I find it works best to raise the grain as soon as the surface begins to feel smooth (see **Figure 9.6**).

To raise the grain, dampen a clean rag with distilled water, and wipe down the surface of the wood. The idea is to thoroughly dampen the surface of the wood but not to soak it. The added moisture will expand the wood fibers. Allow the surface to dry, and then continue sanding through the grits. Once grain has been raised and sanded off, it tends to have little or no further reaction when finish is applied.

Using distilled water for this grain-raising process is a safeguard against contaminating the wood with minerals that may be found in tap water. If the levels of those contaminants are high enough, they can color the wood or finish, usually in noticeable splotches.

Figure 9.6. Dampening the wood early in the sanding process and then allowing it to dry raises the grain so it can be sanded flat. If you wait, the first coat of stain or finish may raise the grain, but then sanding it away without damaging the surrounding finish can be a difficult task.

Figure 9.7. The piece of pine on the left had a pre-stain conditioner applied, and then both pieces were stained in the same way, per the instructions on the can. The untreated piece on the right looks splotchy.

Softwoods and hardwoods

As the density of the wood decreases, the rate at which it absorbs finishing materials increases. Often, density changes significantly within one piece of wood. This varying rate of absorption can make a finish look splotchy, a technical term in woodworking describing a noticeable difference in coloring or tone. While this can occur with hardwoods, it is far more prevalent in softer varieties, particularly in the pine family.

Applying a sanding sealer helps control color variations in most woods, but using a pre-stain conditioner on the softwoods like pine is even better. A pre-stain conditioner is essentially a colorless stain that is absorbed into the wood, creating a uniform surface for the stain or finish that follows (see **Figure 9.7**).

The instructions printed on finishing material containers often specify the need for pre-stain conditioners on specific wood varieties, but experience and experimentation on scraps (of the same wood) are what make so-so finishers look like experts.

Regardless of how many times you have used a finish on a specific species of wood, testing it on piece of scrap from that project is always a good idea to prevent surprises. Working with a natural material like wood means you never know for sure how it will respond to finish until you test it.

End grain

Like softwood, end grain absorbs more finish than the rest of the piece. This happens with any type of wood, finish, and application method. Fight it if you want, but the truth is that end grain is going to be darker than long grain, and the sooner you become okay with it, the more relaxed your finishing life will be.

The absorption properties of end grain can enhance the appearance of some joints. Rather than fight end grain, use the difference in color as an accent (see **Figure 9.8**). Through dovetails are prime examples of this. The contrast between the end grain and long grain in a nicely fit set of through dovetails calls attention to them and gives the project a more professional look.

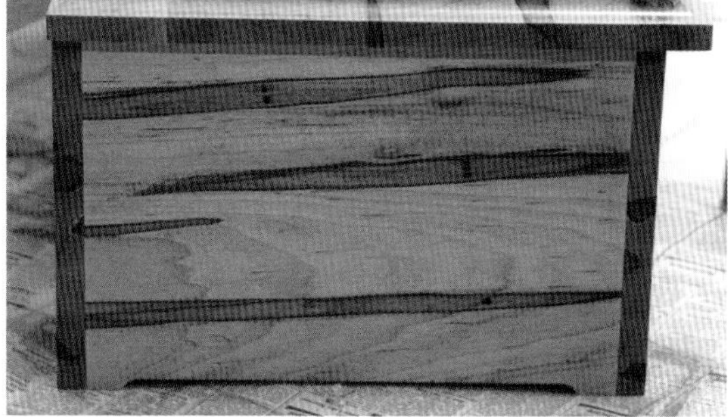

Figure 9.8. End grain always turns darker than long-grain portions of the wood because it absorbs the stain and finish materials faster and deeper. The joints in many projects take advantage of this contrast in color to enhance the look.

Grain filler

Surface prep: Sand and tack off
Application: Rag
Features: Colored to match wood
Uses: Fill pores in wood

Grain fillers are for filling the open pores of woods like oak (see **Figure 9.9**). These fillers can be thinned to make them easier to apply to broad surfaces. Thinning also helps get the material down into the pores of the wood. You can apply them with a drywall knife or with a rag. Either way, you push the filler into the wood and then wipe off the excess. Grain fillers are not much good for cracks and gaps, however.

Figure 9.9. A grain filler is for leveling and filling the pores of open-grain woods like oak.

Buffing

One way to achieve a highly refined finish is to use buffing wheels loaded with special compounds that smooth the surface of the wood and remove tiny scratches. These compounds are applied to fabric wheels that are spun by a grinder motor or are mounted in a woodworking lathe. The combination of the fabric wheels and buffing compounds can smooth a surface to a state that would be very difficult to match with traditional sanding techniques and tools. This technique is best for small projects, woodturnings, and woodcarvings that can be easily managed by hand against the buffing wheels.

Once the project surface has been prepped with the smoothing compounds by one fabric wheel, another fabric wheel is loaded with some form of wax, usually carnauba, which is buffed into the surface. If the surface was prepared well, buffing it with wax can really bring it to life. The shine produced by buffing is very difficult to match. If you desire, the shine can be toned down to a soft sheen by using other types of wax and buffing techniques.

Buffing does not take the place of thorough sanding. Before the fabric wheels can do their job, you have to do yours by sanding through the full range of papers, down to at least 220 grit. If your goal is a glass-smooth shine, count on sanding down to at least 320 grit. It is more work, but the results can be spectacular.

Buffing small projects produces a remarkably smooth, glossy finish that is hard to beat with any other process. It is also surprisingly quick to do.

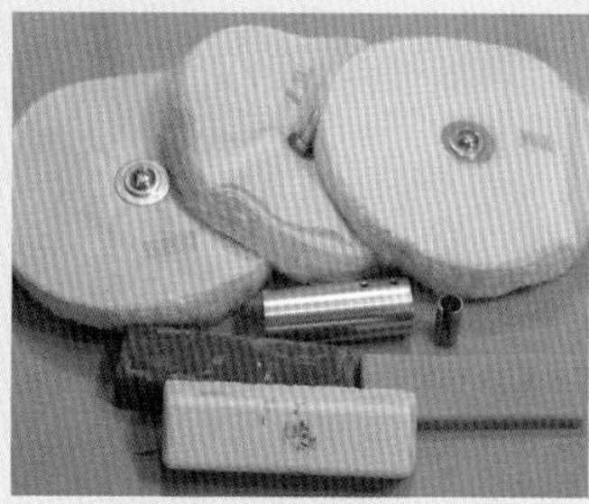

This buffing kit from Beall Tools includes three fabric wheels and buffing compounds to go with each. This three-step process can produce consistent, glass-smooth surfaces on wood projects small enough to be safely held to the wheels.

Gap filler

Surface prep: Sand
Application: Putty knife
Features: Colored to match wood
Uses: Fill cracks and gaps

While many products are designed to fill cracks and gaps, most woodworkers consider them a last resort. Trying to match filler to the surrounding wood is difficult when applying a transparent stain or finish. Frequently, what may have looked to be a close match before finishing becomes a dramatic color difference afterward.

The problem is that many fillers absorb stain and finish at a different rate than end grain or long grain. The result can be a third shade or color that calls attention to the filler.

There is a good side to the problems of using fillers since they inspire woodworkers to create gap-free joints that do not require any filling. You may never seem to escape this problem entirely, but as your joinery skills improve, the need to fill cracks and gaps will be substantially reduced.

An old but effective trick is to use the sanding dust from the piece being worked on as the filler (see **Figure 9.10**). This does not work much better than commercial fillers, but it is fast and cheap and doesn't do any harm. This technique is most effective at filling gaps 1⁄16" wide or less. After rubbing a little fast-setting glue into the gap, work sanding dust from that piece of wood into the glue, building the combination a little higher than the surrounding wood. While some wait for the glue to dry, I hand sand the repair immediately, keeping the abrasive flat on the surface and using minimal pressure. This levels the filler and adds a little fresh sanding dust to the mixture, helping to blend it with the surrounding wood (see **Figure 9.11**).

For wide gaps and spaces in joints, the best filler may be a sliver of wood with its grain oriented the same way as the adjacent parts, whittled to a precise fit and glued in place. This can be a nearly invisible repair.

Whatever type of filler is used, it's best to do these repairs early in the sanding process. Sanding the filled area through all of the remaining grits minimizes the visual impact of the repair and ensures removing excess filler or glue that could affect the appearance of finish in that area.

Figure 9.11. After sanding and staining, the patch made from the glue and sanding dust is clearly visible. It would have been better to cut a tight joint in the first place. As your experience in woodworking grows, this kind of repair is needed less frequently.

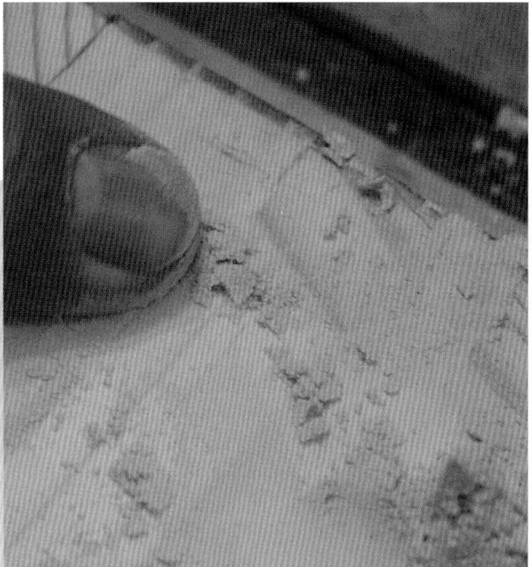

Figure 9.10. After rubbing glue into small gaps around these dovetail ends, I'm rubbing sanding dust from that same piece of wood into the glue.

Save That Dust

Empty your sander's dust container before starting a new project. Then, when sanding is complete, empty the catch container into a sealable plastic bag, and mark it with the species of wood. These bags of dust can be handy when you encounter a gap on another project using the same wood.

Stain

Surface prep: Sand and tack off
Application: Brush on or wipe on
Features: Many colors available
Uses: Change wood's natural color

Stains are used to alter or enhance the color of wood. Staining always occurs after the last of the sanding. The decision on whether or not to use a stain, and how much to change the color of the wood, is purely a matter of taste. The woodworker or the person for whom the project is being built may want a specific color that can be attained during the finishing process.

Stain can be used to highlight the wood figure and to blend light and dark areas to achieve a consistent color over a project. It is especially useful with woods like cherry and walnut, where the sapwood is much lighter and contrasts sharply with the darker heartwood. A stain can make the wood uniform in color, though it will also make it somewhat darker everywhere.

Applying stain to achieve the desired coloring can be more complicated than you might expect. It's mandatory to save scrap pieces of the wood being stained for testing before applying the color to the project itself. To really see how the stain will look on the project, the scrap must be prepared exactly as the project has been, including sanding and the application of any pre-stain conditioners.

Stains are available in a wide variety of formulations—pigments, dyes, water-based, oil-based, and even gel (see **Figure 9.12**). Pigment stains are like paint, with color particles suspended in a water-based or oil-based medium; they are somewhat opaque. Dyes are pure color, without any solid particles; they are transparent. Dyes penetrate the wood fibers more than pigment stains do and will allow more of the wood figure to show through. This deep penetration by dyes also means that if you make a mistake, or just do not like the result, sanding out the dye is going to be a real problem. Gel stains are thickened so they stay on the surface of the wood. Depending on how quickly the gel dries, you can control the color by varying how soon you wipe off the excess. Apply the stain with a foam brush, and then wipe it off with a cotton rag.

Figure 9.12. There are many types of stains, from water-based to oil-based and even gel-type formulations. All come in a wide range of colors, which, with experience, allows matching a new project closely to an existing one.

Stain/Finish Combination

A relatively new innovation is a combination of stain and finish that is premixed at the factory. While this idea does speed the finishing process, it has limitations. Combining stain and topcoat does nothing to preclude the need for surface preparation, including pre-stain conditioners on absorbent woods. The number of coats applied controls their depth of color. If the desired color is achieved before the desired surface finish, additional coats of clear finish can be applied over the combination product. The clear finish should be from the same product line, and it must be the same type of finish for the best results. Use water-based clear over water-based finishes and oil-based clear over oil-based finishes to be sure of compatibility.

Stain Is Not Mandatory

Some people believe that it's always necessary to stain the wood. It is not. Wood will be totally happy with no stain at all on it, and if you like the color of the natural wood, you need not stain it. Oil finishes, like tung oil and oil-based varnishes, will make the wood both darker and more yellow than its unfinished color. Water-based varnishes will also make the wood seem darker, but most of them do not add any yellow color. If you want to see how a finish is going to affect the wood, test it on a piece of scrap.

Types of finishes

Everything from common paint to exotic oils can be used to enhance the appearance of a project or make it more resistant to specific environmental threats. With few exceptions, finishes are applied according to the manufacturer's recommendations, though woodworkers may increase the number of coats to best highlight or protect the wood.

Paint

Surface prep: Sand and tack off
Application: Brush on or spray on
Features: Infinite colors and degrees of shine
Uses: Protect and color wood

While it may seem odd to cover quality wood with paint, on some projects, woodworkers do consider paint to be a good choice. Sometimes a painted project fits a specific décor better or is easier to match to an existing set. Paint is also the base for faux finishes. Whatever the reasoning, paint remains a viable option.

Not all woods take paint equally well. The resins in woods like pine may bleed through paint, creating dark patches; these woods should be primed with a shellac-based sealer. Open-pored woods like oak will still be open pored after you paint them, an effect you may or may not like; they should be filled before painting. Poplar is the traditional wood for painted finishes because it accepts paint exceptionally well. It is often used for high-quality interior moldings that will be painted.

Like other finishes, the range of paints available makes it possible to apply the one that best fits the intended use of the project. Interior, exterior, gloss, semi-gloss, and flat or matte paints can all be precisely matched to an existing or desired color, allowing the woodworker a new level of creativity. You can also use artists' colorful acrylic paints on wood, though for additional protection you might want to apply a clear varnish afterward.

Figure 9.13. Polyurethane varnishes are popular because they are durable and relatively easy to apply.

Polyurethane Varnish

Surface prep: Sand
Application: Brush on or wipe on
Features: Fast-drying, easy application, very durable
Uses: Indoor and outdoor projects

Currently the 400-pound gorilla in the finishing world, polyurethane-based varnishes have become extremely popular because of their durability and relative ease of application. This has become especially true since the introduction of fast-drying, water-based polyurethane that is as tough as or tougher than the solvent-based versions (see **Figure 9.13**).

Applying polyurethane is much like any other finish and requires no special equipment or surface preparation. There is even a gel-type polyurethane that is designed to be wiped on rather than brushed. Formulations for indoor and outdoor use are available, including a super-tough spar polyurethane that rivals the venerable spar varnish used for decades in the marine industry.

Applying Water-Based Polyurethane

Water-based polyurethane has a milky appearance when applied. That has shaken more than a few first-time users. That cloudy appearance goes away, and it dries crystal clear (I don't know how, so don't ask); but, until you see it happen a few times, it can be disconcerting.

Oil

Surface prep: Sand and tack off
Application: Brush on or wipe on
Features: Penetrates and hardens wood; enhances wood with deep, rich finish
Uses: Indoor only, great for exotic and figured woods

Longtime favorites like Danish oil and tung oil remain popular for finishing exotic and figured woods. The deep, rich look they add to the wood enhances the features that make it beautiful and interesting to view; they will cause light-colored woods to darken and yellow somewhat. I especially like the look Danish oil gives to mahogany and walnut, particularly to through dovetails in these woods (see **Figure 9.14**). The depth and contrast makes a well-formed set of through dovetails stand out without overpowering the look of the project.

After normal surface preparation, oils are brushed or wiped on, allowed to set a certain amount of time (specified on the container), and then wiped off. Usually a few applications are necessary to achieve the desired results.

Oils penetrate the wood surface and harden in the wood with little or no surface build. You cannot make a true gloss finish using oil, though you can buff it to a very pleasant shine and you can wax it with paste wax. Some oil finishes, like boiled linseed oil, are traditional for furniture, but they may take a very long time to dry completely.

Figure 9.14. Oil finishes, such as this Danish oil, are very popular for woods like walnut, mahogany, and other figured species. When dry, topcoats like polyurethane can be applied, or the surface can be waxed and buffed to a very high sheen.

Figure 9.15. Food-safe finishes are necessary when the piece will hold food or will be used by a child who is apt to chew on it. If the container does not specify it as food safe, do not assume it is.

Food-Safe Finishes

Surface prep: Sand and tack off
Application: Brush on or wipe on
Features: Nontoxic
Uses: Projects that will be used with food

Finishes specified as "food safe" are nontoxic and are frequently used on objects such as bowls, utensils, and cutting boards. The Food and Drug Administration (FDA) has specific criteria that finishing materials must meet to be considered food safe. Manufacturers will specify "food safe" on product labels or literature for products that conform to these standards (see **Figure 9.15**). I strongly suggest you rely on the manufacturers' expertise rather than on assurances from Internet "experts" when choosing this type of finish. While it is true that many finishes are safe for food once they have thoroughly dried, some finishes may contain lead, an ingredient in some oils that helps them dry. Lead is quickly being eliminated from finishes, but this is nothing to play with. Stick with what is listed on the label.

Mineral oil is a favorite finish for butcher blocks and cutting boards because it is nontoxic and, unlike vegetable or other cooking oils, does not go rancid.

Rub the mineral oil into the wood. Most likely you will need to apply several coats. Allow it to soak in, and then wipe off the excess. To maintain the surface, occasionally reapply mineral oil. The frequency of recoating depends on usage. If the surface starts looking worn, a new coat of mineral oil generally fixes it up. If the object is washed, reapply the mineral oil.

Food-safe finishes are frequently used on furniture and toys meant to be used by children. Be very sure of a material's food-safe qualifications when finishing children's objects. Also be sure pieces are fully dry before being presented for use. Many woodworkers let a project intended for a child (or that will be available to them) sit for 30 days to be sure the finish has completed chemical drying and has released the gases associated with drying. Here again, erring on the side of safety is a smart move.

Other Choices

While these are a few of the more popular finishing options, the range of choices available to woodworkers is immense. Most find a few techniques and materials that produce the look they want and that they are best at applying. Exploring the various finishing techniques on different species of wood is part of the learning process that can be as much fun as it is educational.

Shellac

Surface prep: Sand and tack off
Application: Brush on or wipe on in many thin coats
Features: Easily renewed
Uses: Antique furniture and period reproductions

Shellac is a very old finish that dissolves in alcohol. It is a common finish on fine antique furniture. Shellac's big virtue is that it hardens by the evaporation of the alcohol, and it can be softened or dissolved at any time. This makes it possible to repair and renew. Shellac can be brushed on, or wiped on with a tight cloth pad. It's best when applied in many very thin coats.

Lacquer

Surface prep: Sand and seal
Application: Brush on or spray on
Features: Hard, shiny film; repairable
Uses: Very durable for indoor furniture

Lacquer is a modern finish that usually is sprayed on, but a number of brands of brushing lacquer are also available. It builds quickly to a hard, shiny film that also is repairable.

Wax

Surface prep: Sand and tack off
Application: Rag or brush
Features: Lightest possible finish, some have added dye
Uses: Furniture

Though usually used to impart a final polish to other finishes, wax can be used by itself on raw wood. It makes the lightest possible finish, which might be just what you want. Many waxes are formulated specifically for furniture, and they all work about the same way. Some even have a dye added so they will impart some color to the wood.

No-frills finish application

The labels on finishing material containers describe methods for applying that product that are known to work. Following these instructions is a good way to ensure achieving an attractive finish. After you gain experience with a finish, you may develop different ways to enhance its appearance.

Foam brushes are often recommended by the finish manufacturers (see **Figure 9.16**). In addition to their low price, foam brushes are easy to handle and eliminate having to clean tough finishes from reusable bristle brushes. Foam brushes drip less easily, and they don't leave any loose bristles behind either.

The key to using any brush (foam included) is to lay the finish onto the wood with flowing strokes, with the direction of the grain (see **Figure 9.17**). Trying to scrub a finish into the wood with any kind of brush is going to create bubbles and irregular film thicknesses that can distort the coloring and coverage when the finish dries. Work quickly, but being aggressive with any brush also shortens its useful life.

Maintain a Wet Edge

When you are brushing finish onto a woodworking project, always keep a wet edge and overlap the brush strokes from the wet area into the dry. If you let the working edge dry, you'll have streaks and a thickened line of finish there.

Figure 9.16. Foam brushes are easy to use, are cheap, and eliminate trying to clean a more expensive bristle brush.

Figure 9.17. Keeping a wet edge by overlapping the strokes of the brush helps get a consistent layer of stain or finish onto the project.

Applying several thin coats of finish is always better than trying to flood one or two thick coats onto the surface. It is much easier to develop an even thickness of finish over the entire project when it is applied a little at a time. The multiple coats also help eliminate light and dark spots caused by applying more finish in some areas of the project. Naturally, the most noticeable of those spots will be in the middle of the most visible part of the project.

It's important to follow recommended dry time between coats, but this can be difficult to judge. The dry times listed on the container are for average conditions, including temperature (air and the wood) and humidity. If the shop is cool or humid, more time will be needed for the finish to set up properly before sanding and applying the next coat. If the shop is hot, the finish may begin to dry while you are still brushing it on. This temperature sensitivity can apply to how much time is allowed before wiping away excess stain, as well.

Sanding Between Coats

Sanding between coats of finish reduces high spots in the last coat without disturbing the layer of finish in the grain or pores. Sanding between each subsequent coat reduces the difference between the high and low spots, bringing you closer to the elusive glass-smooth surface.

Sanding between coats also ensures a secure bond between the layers of finish. Scuffing the surface breaks the shine or gloss and gives the next coat something to lock onto. A lightly sanded surface is said to have more tooth—tiny irregularities into which the next coat affixes itself. Some finishes, like lacquer, bond without sanding because each new coat dissolves a bit of the one before. Other finishes, like urethane varnishes, have to be sanded because they cure chemically, and, once that process begins, they cannot be dissolved.

Sanding between coats is best done by hand with a sanding block, as shown in **Figure 9.18**, but, on a large piece, you can do it carefully with a random orbit sander or a palm sander. Finish instructions often specify the ideal abrasive for this task. Follow the instructions. Using more aggressive grits will not make this task quicker but could easily ruin the job by breaking through previous coats and creating bare spots.

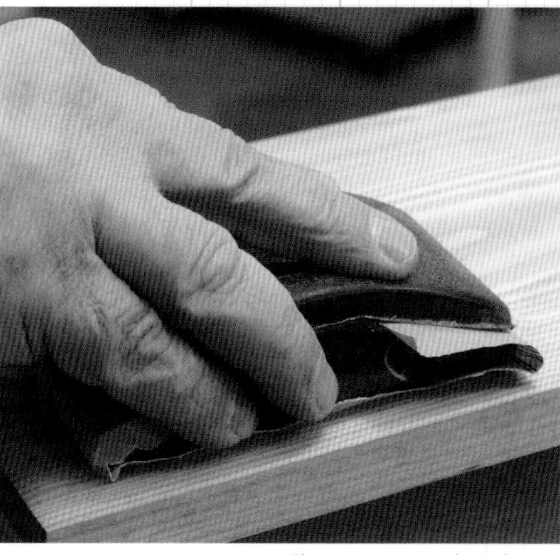

Figure 9.18. Hand sanding between coats knocks down any high spots and creates "tooth" that helps the next coat bond securely to the surface.

Another potential trouble spot is sharp corners where sanding effects are concentrated on a very small area, making it easy to break through the previous coat. When it is necessary to sand near or on a corner, doing it by hand reduces the chances of creating a major problem. Using a sanding block held flat on the surface also helps prevent concentrating the sanding at an edge.

Remember that tack rag I talked about earlier and its importance? It is equally important to use a clean tack rag to remove sanding debris between coats. The dust created when sanding between coats can be exceptionally fine, almost talcum-like, which makes it difficult to remove with anything but a good tack rag. If you don't get it off, it will create bumps and nibs in your finish.

Drying versus drying before use

While many finishes, food safe or not, dry to the touch relatively quickly, they usually require a longer time to fully cure. Some of the materials within a finish need more time to evaporate completely, and some of the finish material that remains behind needs a long time to fully cure. Using an object before the specified cure time has elapsed could damage the finish itself or expose people handling it to a small, but unnecessary, danger.

Here again, temperature and humidity levels can extend both of those times considerably. When in doubt, wait another day or two before handling the project, and another week or two before subjecting it to hard use.

Chapter 10

Skill-Building Projects

The projects in this chapter start with a basic lidded box, then move up to a tote box, a bedside bookcase, shop wall cabinets, base cabinets (with and without drawers), and finally a coffee table. Some of these projects may appear easy, but building them square with tight-fitting joints may not be so simple.

These projects are arranged in a specific order, beginning with those using the most basic techniques, and then moving to ones that are more difficult. They are designed to help you refine the skills—choosing wood and tools, preparing the material, making joints, assembling, and finishing—that you can use to build virtually anything you like. Then, you'll hone some more specific skills like installing hinges, cutting miters, making tongue-and-groove joints, and experimenting with pocket hole joints.

Please resist the urge to jump ahead just because a later project would fill part of your gift list. I chose these projects not only for their general usefulness, but also for how they help develop the basic set of woodworking skills. Each project can be easily modified, allowing the new woodworker to apply that base set of skills to a huge range of new projects. When encountering a skill that you find a little tough to master, building a different version of the project can make learning more interesting and more rewarding.

Boxes and frames

Many woodworking projects are based on one or more box shapes. Cabinets, bookcases, and jewelry boxes are all based on the basic box form, as are drawers and other compartments inside them. The practice gained from making small boxes, particularly cutting identical-length square-ended pieces, will be invaluable when building larger projects. The size of the project may differ, but the procedures for building it straight and square do not. Once you master the basics of building a simple square box with tight joints, altering the dimensions to create a large range of projects of your own design is much easier.

Another project element that you will discover in these projects is how to build square frames for face frames, cabinet doors, and cabinet sides. Plywood box projects, like shop cabinets, often rely on a strong square-cornered frame glued to the front opening for rigidity. The frame not only finishes the raw plywood edges, but also squares and stiffens the plywood construction, and it creates a sturdy attachment for hanging doors and mounting drawers.

Project materials

While any type of wood can be used to build these projects, the most economical approach is to use simple pine or poplar for the first versions. Then, as your comfort level with a technique increases, moving on to more expensive, more attractive woods will induce less anxiety.

All of the primary material I used in these projects is ¾"-thick solid pine and regular plywood because they are readily available and, in many cases, that is the easiest thickness to work with. The smaller projects could be made from thinner wood, for example ½" thick, but until a thickness planer finds its way into your shop, standard-thickness wood will work fine. The larger projects, like a bookcase or shop cabinets, need the strength of ¾" material.

In some cases, approximate dimensions are provided for parts, particularly back, floor, and door panels. Small variances in cutting, preparing, and assembling other portions of a project can impact the actual size of parts that fit within a space. New woodworkers are sometimes dismayed by this uncertainty, but it's just how it is in woodworking. Whether you are a new woodworker or a veteran, you'll usually find it best to wait until the surrounding parts can be dry fit before you measure for the final size of the panel or part that goes within or between them.

There's variation in any project, so it's always best to dry fit the parts together before measuring for the actual size of parts like floating panels that will fit inside and in between. Waiting to measure for these parts during a dry fit of the assembly will save time, frustration, and money.

Back Panels

I've intentionally omitted plywood back panels from the bookcase and shop wall cabinet projects. Because they are used against a wall, the back panel is not needed. Also, because these are teaching and learning projects, even though many woodworkers rely on a back panel to hold a project square, I think it's best for you to learn how to assemble the primary structure of your projects square without the assistance of a back panel. This is an important skill that is best developed from the start. Assembling a project square starts when you prepare the first piece of wood, and paying close attention to that process makes building projects easier, the parts fit better, and the finished piece more professional. It's easy to add a back panel during construction, and many woodworkers naturally take advantage of the strength and squareness that a back panel provides—but that is in addition to making the project square and strong on its own, before adding the back. So if you want to add a back, you can, so long as you aren't relying on it to keep your project together. You'll see how it's done when building the base cabinet projects later in this chapter.

Preparation

Even though I have given you shop drawings and materials lists, you'll find that your project will go much better if you take some time at the start to think it through for yourself. Read the steps, look at the illustrations, and make your own parts lists and size calculations. You may see a detail you would like to handle differently or a feature you would like to add. The sooner you make these decisions, the better—and the more of them you make, the sooner you'll build confidence in the workshop.

You may also want to refer to Chapter 6, "Preparing the Wood," on page 125, to review some of the concepts we covered. Remember that straight, square, and properly prepared wood will allow you to concentrate on making the projects, not fighting problems in the wood.

Hinged box

This little box has an overhanging hinged lid with a routed edge. The corner joints are simple glued rabbets. You may be surprised by how many basic skills you'll use to make it, skills that will serve you well.

Making this little box with hinged lid, our first box project, will require a number of basic woodworking skills, starting with preparing the wood so that each piece is square in every direction and that the opposing pieces are identical in length. This is fundamental to all woodworking, even with a project as small as this.

The four corners will be joined with a glued rabbet joint, strong enough for this little box. Rabbets have the additional advantage of allowing you to saw the groove for the box bottom from one end of the wood to the other, without the groove showing after assembly. Note that the groove for the bottom is set a full ½" up from the edge of the box pieces. This extra room allows you to rout recesses along the bottom edges that form a little foot at each corner.

The basic box form is perfect for learning new joinery skills. You have the option of trying any other joint you like, including box joints and through dovetails; just remember to add the appropriate amount of extra length needed for that joint. If you will be using a jig, the instructions that came with it will specify this dimension.

Bottom and Lid

The box bottom is a piece of ¼" plywood that you'll trap in the groove when you assemble the box. I like to leave the plywood loose in the groove, which would be essential if it was a piece of solid wood, in order to accommodate any wood movement. Since it is plywood, wood movement is very slight, and you could glue it in if you wanted (see To Glue or Not to Glue on page 201).

The hinged lid is a flat panel that I made by edge joining two narrower pieces of wood and then trimming to final size. Mine has a routed profile for visual interest; you may prefer to leave yours square or to rout a chamfer or a round-over.

Little boxes like this project make great test subjects as your joinery skills grow. Small changes in construction techniques, materials, and edge treatments allow you to make a never-ending range of boxes. Adding box joints or dovetails can dress up the look (and strength) of a box considerably. Most important is that you take your time, becoming proficient at the basic joinery skills before moving on to more complicated types.

Core Skills

- Selecting project wood
- Cutting the wood square and to length
- Cutting a rabbet or other suitable box joint
- Making an edge joint to glue up the top
- Making the right-size dado for a plywood bottom
- Assembling the box so its corners are square
- Routing the box sides with stopped cuts to form feet
- Installing hinges
- Finishing the box

Tools

- Table saw or chop saw
- Dado set on table saw, or flat-bottomed router bits
- Cove router bit for decorative edges
- Router table
- Cordless drill and bit for pilot holes
- ½"-diameter straight bit
- Combination square
- Screwdriver
- Random orbit sander
- Clamps

9½"
11"
Top
1 needed

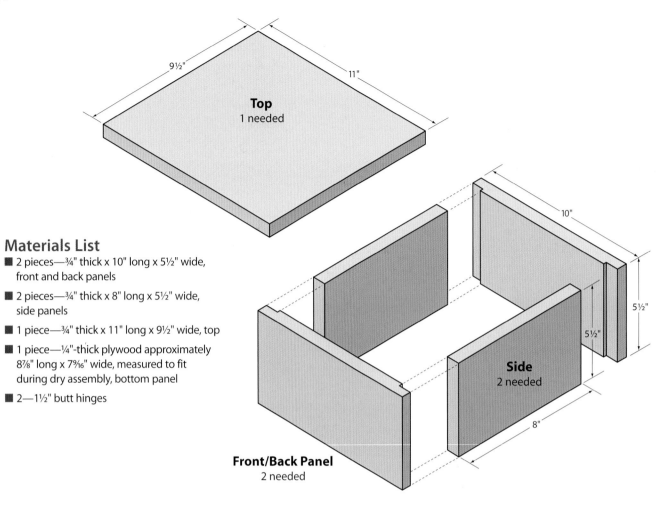

10"
5½"
5½"
Side
2 needed
8"

Front/Back Panel
2 needed

Materials List

- 2 pieces—¾" thick x 10" long x 5½" wide, front and back panels
- 2 pieces—¾" thick x 8" long x 5½" wide, side panels
- 1 piece—¾" thick x 11" long x 9½" wide, top
- 1 piece—¼"-thick plywood approximately 8⅞" long x 7^9^⁄~16~" wide, measured to fit during dry assembly, bottom panel
- 2—1½" butt hinges

Consider Proportions

In advance of making the box, you might consider its design and proportions. I've deliberately used 1 x 6 wood, which measures 5½" wide, for the box sides because I don't want to introduce additional sawing and measuring in this first project, and I've chosen the length of the pieces to go with that width.

You might like to build this box to some particular proportion for a specific purpose, maybe to store a set of tools or accessories. Measure what you want to store inside the box, and then modify the given dimensions in width, length, or height; the procedures to build and assemble it remain the same. If you expect really heavy loads, consider adding finishing nails or screws (drill pilot holes in either case) to reinforce the rabbet joints.

Remember to keep the wood grain running in the same direction in all of the front and side pieces. Don't forget to account for the length you need for a corner joint and the depth you need for the bottom. You'll find that it is a juggling act between the sizes you want and the wood and tools you have, but that's design: The best designs don't come out of thin air; they always arise from real problems with built-in limitations. So have some fun with it!

This storage box was made the same way as the lidded box in the step-by-step project. Once you understand the procedures, it's easy to make a box the size and proportions you want.

1 Using the table saw or chop saw, carefully cut the front, back, and side panels to size. I used a work stop on my miter guide to ensure cutting identically sized pairs of pieces. A gauge block clamped to the rip fence will also work (see Step 2). When using a gauge block, cutting the shorter pieces can be difficult if the wood is not long enough to allow for gripping it and keeping it stationary while not forcing you to hold it close to the blade.

2 Remember that when using a gauge block clamped to the fence, the workpiece is measured from the block to the side of the blade facing the fence (see Using a Gauge Block on page 131). Be certain the workpiece is not in contact with the gauge block when it reaches the saw blade.

3 Stand the front, back, and side panels on edge on a flat surface. Decide which side of each panel will face out and which edge of each panel will be on top when assembled. I identify the top and inside surfaces of each piece with markings that indicate its position and orientation in the project.

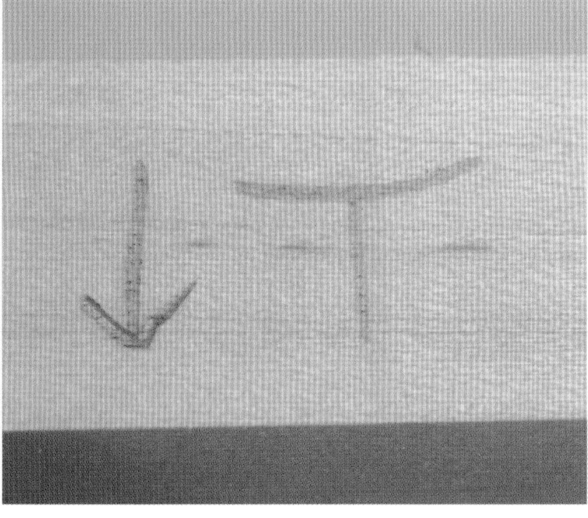

4 This dry fit also shows how the piece would look if you built it using butt joints: not very impressive or strong. Adding glued rabbets to the ends of the front and back panels not only increases the strength of the joint, but also adds a bit of interest.

Developing a Marking System

However you mark your pieces, make sure that it is easy for you to remember—the important thing is to develop the best way for you and to use it consistently. Keeping project pieces in the right order through joinery and assembly requires clear, understandable, consistent markings. It's all too easy to cut the joints on the wrong side or have the panel chosen for the right side wind up on the left.

A common trick of woodworkers is to cut the pieces for a box from one piece of wood. If you cut the back, the right side, the front, and then the left side, the grain runs around the box consistently. This can be especially attractive with highly figured woods. Even more subtle grain structures can be enhanced with this method.

5 Set up your router, router table, or table saw to cut a ¼" deep by ¾" wide rabbet along the inside ends of the front and back panels. Actually, you want a rabbet that is 1/32" to 1/16" wider than the wood that fits in it. This small overhang makes it easier to sand the corners flat, smooth, and true (see Sand the Inside First on the next page).

Take Two Passes

Depending on what you are using to cut the rabbet, it may be best to cut it in two passes. You can either set the cutter to half the height or half of the final width, whichever is easiest for you. The point is to reduce the amount of material removed in a single pass to limit the chances of chipping. Use the scrap to adjust the fence so that the rabbet will be cut to its final size, remembering to include the extra 1/32" to 1/16" of width if needed for overhang; then, make the second pass.

6 The plywood box bottom fits in a groove cut around the bottom edge of the front, back, and side panels. Use a normal ⅛"-thick blade in the table saw and a push block to protect your hands. Using one of the rabbeted pieces as a gauge, set the blade slightly below the rabbet so the groove won't show in the finished box. Set the fence ½" from the side of the blade to make room for the routed feet. Make one pass along the bottom inside edge of the front, back, and side panels. Adjust the fence slightly farther from the blade for a second pass on all of the pieces, and continue until the plywood just slips into the groove. **Note:** Using a test piece before making the cuts in the project wood is a good way to confirm the setups.

Extra, Short, or Dead-on?

I like to make the end grain of joints extend a little bit past the mating piece, and then sand it down flush.

When you make rabbet joints and many other kinds of joint, you have to decide whether you want to hit the width dead-on, make it 1/32" to 1/16" extra wide, or make it short by the same amount. Which is best depends on how you like to work.

For my style of work, I always make the rabbet a little bit extra deep. This means the end of the rabbeted piece—the box front and back in this project—will overhang the side pieces that fit into it by that small amount. I can sand the overhangs flush with the end of the box using my random orbit sander, and there is not much to sand.

Somebody who likes to use hand planes probably would do it the other way around, making the rabbet a little short. That way the sides of the box would stick out beyond the end of the rabbet, and he or she could plane the sides down flush with the joint. That's a lot of wood to remove by sanding, but it's no problem for a sharp bench plane.

Somebody else who enjoys the challenge of perfect accuracy might try to shoot the joint dead-on the first try. That way there would be nothing to sand flush; it would already be flush.

Like I say, which is best depends on how you like to work.

7 Carefully measure the depth of the groove for the bottom, double that dimension, and subtract 1/16" to determine how much overlap the bottom panel needs. Dry clamp the box together, bottom edge up, on a flat surface. Measure the bottom opening, and add the overlap to the length and width. Cut the bottom panel to this size, slip it into the groove, and reclamp. The bottom panel should not hold the joints open, and it should move in its grooves slightly. Trim the panel to get this fit right.

8 Lay out the parts of the box in their proper orientation to be sure they are assembled correctly. Apply glue to both rabbets of the front panel and the ends of the sides that will fit into those rabbets. Set the side panels into the rabbets, and slip the bottom panel into the grooves—with or without glue on the bottom panel or in its grooves, depending on your preference (see To Glue or Not to Glue, below). Apply glue to the remaining rabbets and side panel ends. Install the last panel over the edge of the bottom panel, and fit the sides into the rabbets. Stand the assembly flat on the bench, and clamp as needed to hold the rabbets closed uniformly. Use a damp rag to wipe up any excess glue that has emerged along the joint lines inside the box.

Sand the Inside First

Sanding the inside surfaces is easy before they are assembled. This may seem like a minor and logical point, but, if I didn't bring it up now, many of you would be trying to figure out how to sand the inside surfaces after assembly—just as I and a bunch of woodworkers have done.

So what you teach yourself to do is sand the inside surfaces to 150 to 220 grit before assembly. If there are joints involved, like the rabbets for this little box, be careful you don't sand so zealously that you round their edges. And be sure to wipe the dust and abrasive grits off the newly sanded surfaces with a tack rag while they're easy to get at.

During this sanding, the position-identifying marks you made earlier will go away. I put a piece of masking tape on the inside surfaces after they are sanded and tack ragged off and write the marking on that. You have to maintain the identifying marks on the pieces until they are actually assembled.

To Glue or Not to Glue

Remember from Chapter 5, "Selecting Wood," that solid wood changes size along with changes in the humidity (see Wood and Water on page 120)? That's why you would not glue a solid wood panel tightly into the groove inside a box or frame. If you did, normal wood movement—easily 1/4" per foot of width, dry winter to wet summer in many parts of the United States—would force the construction apart.

This little box has a plywood bottom trapped in a groove. Plywood moves a little bit but nothing like solid wood. If you want the plywood to contribute to the strength of the box, go ahead and glue it in, but don't use too much glue because you'll have a very tough time cleaning the excess that squeezes out from down inside the corner. Me, I like it that the box bottom is snug fit in the grooves and that it doesn't have to be glued in. So even though it's plywood, I don't glue it.

9 If all went well, your box is now square, but the front and back panels extend slightly beyond the sides. Carefully sand those edges smooth with your random orbit sander, keeping the sander flat on the surface to avoid rounding the corners. Give the entire outside surface a light sanding to be sure there are no high spots, dried glue, or other irregularities.

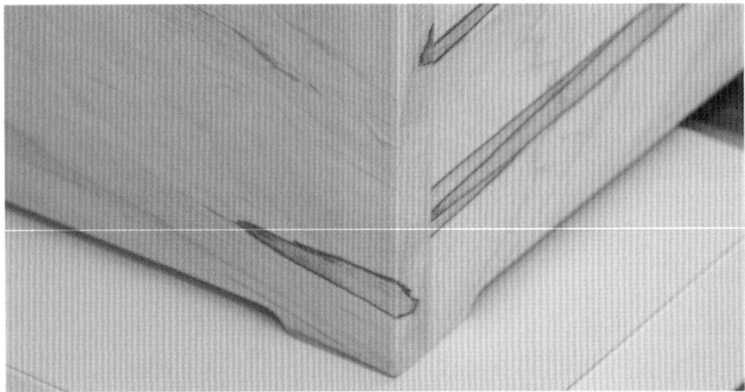

10 To make a box that does not rock on a flat surface, rout reliefs around the edges to form feet at the corners. While you could sand the bottom of the box perfectly flat, most surfaces won't be, meaning the box will rock anyway. The relief lets the feet of the box straddle small irregularities.

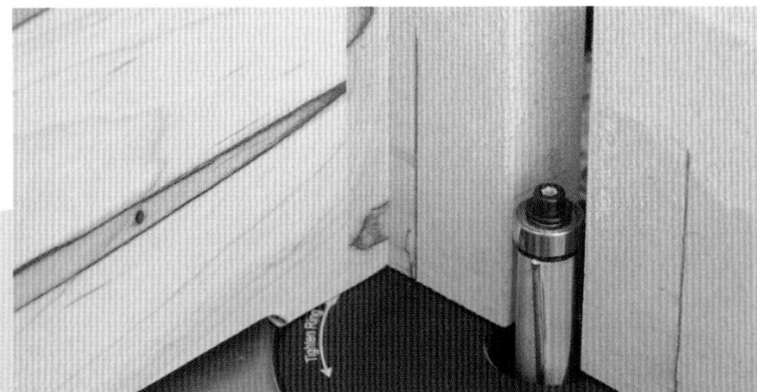

11 Install a ½"-diameter straight bit in the router table, set the fence halves close to it on each side, and then adjust the fence so that ¼" of the bit is exposed. Draw vertical lines on the fence 1" from both sides of the bit to indicate where the ends of the box will start and stop. To reduce the chance of chipping, make a plunge cut at the right end of each long cut, as described in Stop Cuts on the next page. Then, rout the long relief cuts in all four sides of the box.

How Square Is That?

Measure the diagonals with a tape. When they're exactly the same, the box corners are precisely square.

After you assemble the box but before the glue dries, you want to be sure that everything is square. Set the box on a flat surface—I like to use the top of the table saw, covered with a piece of flat MDF—and measure the corner-to-corner diagonals from outside to outside. They should be exactly the same. If they're not, put a clamp with a couple of protective corner blocks across the longer diagonal and just barely tighten it. Measure again. It won't take much clamp pressure to pull the diagonals so they're exactly the same, which means the corners are all perfectly square. Finally, check that this correction hasn't moved one of the joints and that the box is still sitting flat on the table. If it did, adjust the joints and push the box down flat again, adding a clamp if necessary, and remeasure the diagonals.

Tip!

Cutting Reliefs

When cutting reliefs, adjust the bit to a height that exposes the cutters to the full thickness of the box sides with the box lying on its side. If the bit has a bearing on its end, make sure that is above the wood because you want the fence to be in control of the cut depth.

Stop Cuts

The router cuts that form the feet on this little box are stopped cuts, meaning they must begin and end short of the box corners. If you simply plunged the box over the bit at the starting point and routed to the end point, there is a good chance the wood would split or chip near the end of that cut. You can avoid this calamity by making the far end of the cut first, then routing up to it. Here's how:

Set up the router table with a straight, ½" bit, and bring the fence halves close to the bit. Draw vertical lines alongside the bit, but set away by the amount of wood you want to leave uncut. These are your starting and stopping reference lines.

Now use the reference lines to make a plunge cut—a little divot, really—at the right-hand end of the cut. Do it by laying the box on its side and holding the left corner of the box side against the fence; eyeball it so the right end of the box side lines up with the rightmost line you drew on the fence, and push the right end straight toward the fence and into the cutter. Pause, then carefully pull the box straight away from the fence. You should have made a little scallop in the right-hand end of the box side where that foot is going to begin. Slide the box ¼" to the right, and make another plunge cut to widen the first one, again plunging straight in and then pulling the box straight back off of the bit.

Now, hold the right corner against the fence, and align the left corner with the vertical line you drew to the left of the bit. Slowly push the left corner against the fence. With the box held tight against the fence, slide it from right to left down the fence, making a consistent cut until you reach the previously cut area toward the right end. Do not slide the box beyond that because if it contacts the previously cut edge, the foot probably will chip out. Repeat this process on the remaining three sides.

You may notice a small ridge where the long cut meets the plunge cuts at the right end. Sanding this ridge away by hand is safer than trying to rout it flat.

Use the right-hand reference line to make the stop cut at the right end of the cut.

Start the long cut at the left end, aligning the box corner with the reference line on the fence.

Complete the long cut at the right-hand stop cut.

12 Set the box on a flat surface (a table saw's machined top is good) to see if it rocks on the newly formed feet. If it does, lay a piece of 100-grit or 120-grit sandpaper flat on the table surface, put the tall foot on the paper and rub the box back and forth a few times. Repeat until the box sits flat.

13 Choose wood with attractive grain for the box top, and glue it up edge to edge to make a panel a little larger than you'll need in length and width. When the glue dries, scrape off any excess glue, and saw the top to its final size. Pick which side will face up and which edge will be at the rear of the box; then, turn the top over, and place a small piece of tape along the rear edge on the inside surface to avoid confusion when routing a decorative edge and installing hinges.

Rout That Edge

Routing a decorative profile in the side and front edges of the top is not necessary, but it is very effective at enhancing the visual appeal of the project.

14 Because butt hinges will be used, you can't rout the whole back edge. Install the edge profiling bit in a router table (I used a plain cove bit), and adjust the fence so it is even with the bit's guide bearing. Lower the bit so it takes a light initial cut. You will raise the bit about 1/16" per pass until you achieve the desired look. Taking small cuts is the best way to get a smooth, chip-free cut. Rout the ends of the lid, rout the long front side, and then make the partial cuts (if any) on the back edge (see Partial Cuts, below).

Partial Cuts

The partial cuts on the rear edge give the box top a more interesting look and are relatively easy to do. Draw vertical start and stop lines on the fence 1½" to each side of the bit's cutting edges. The left end of the top can be cut by simply sliding it into the bit from right to left and stopping as the left corner reaches the vertical line.

To start the right side partial cut, you have to plunge the box top into the bit. Hold the left side against the fence, and slowly pivot the wood into the bit, aligning the right corner with the vertical line drawn to the right of the bit. Once the top is against the fence, move it from right to left to complete that cut. These partial cuts should be made after routing the end grain.

Repeat all of the cuts, raising the bit about 1/16" between passes until you get the profile you want.

The lines drawn on the router table fence indicate the end points of the decorative cove being routed into the hinge edge of the box top.

15 To locate the hinges, lay the top upside down on the workbench with its rear edge facing you. Place the upside-down box on the top, center it left to right with its rear edge flush with the rear edge of the top, and clamp the assembly to the bench. Space a pair of plain flat hinges just inward of the routed cuts, and center the hinge knuckle over the seam between the top and the box. Mark the hole centers and drill pilot holes for the screws. Seat the screws, remove the clamps, and check the operation of the top.

Installing Hinges Properly

For a box top to swing open and closed freely on its hinges, the hinges must be square to the rest of the box. Work with the top and the box clamped in position upside down on a workbench and center the hinge over the seam between the box and its top. Then, mark the holes, drill pilot holes, and seat the screws.

16 Remove the hinges, finish sand all remaining surfaces to at least 220 grit, and wipe down the entire box and top with a tack rag to remove any remaining dust. Apply a finish, allow it to dry completely, and then reinstall the hinges to complete the project. The boxes in the photo below were treated with three coats of Watco Danish oil (natural). After drying for several days, the exterior surfaces were buffed and waxed with carnauba wax.

Tote box

Here are a few of the tote box variations I have built. Adapting this project for garden tools, household repair supplies, cleaning supplies, or virtually any other need is easy, and the building techniques do not change.

You can buy a plastic tool tote for a couple of bucks, and you can make one for about the same investment in wood. Which would you rather have? Once you understand the basic construction techniques, these wooden totes can be easily modified to fit a range of needs for home handyman tools, household repair supplies, gardening tools, and cleaning tools. The joints are glued rabbets. If considerable weight is to be carried, add screws or nails—drill pilot holes first—to the rabbet joints for security.

This second box project is a toolbox. Your investment in the materials is relatively low, making it a great project to deepen your understanding of wood as a natural material. Along with a review of basic box-making skills—cutting wood square and to length, making and reinforcing rabbet joints, applying varnish—this tool tote makes you think about wood movement, cross-grain construction, and what you can get away with in the climate where you live.

The ends of this tote box are shaped differently from the box project, but the same techniques are used to build it. The range of tote boxes you can design is limitless. After applying the last coat of finish, my wife, Beth, put her finishing supplies in this one and kept it.

Core Skills

- Selecting project wood
- Cutting the wood square and to length, with opposite sides being exactly the same length
- Cutting a rabbet or some other suitable box joint
- Sawing a taper
- Making the right-size dado for a plywood bottom and fitting the bottom into it
- Locating and drilling holes
- Assembling the box so its corners are square
- Finishing the box

Tools

- Table saw or jigsaw
- Cordless drill, ¾" bit, pilot hole bit
- Dado head on table saw, or router with ¼" flat-bottomed bit
- Combination square and tape measure
- Hammer and nail set
- Clamps

Materials List

- 2 pieces—¾" thick x 18½" long x 7¼" wide, sides
- 2 pieces—¾" thick x 7¼" wide x 11" tall, ends
- 1 piece—¼"-thick plywood approximately 17⅝" long x 7¼" wide (measured to fit during construction), bottom
- 1 piece—1"-diameter hardwood dowel x 20" long
- Glue
- 12—2" finishing nails
- 2—1"-long brads

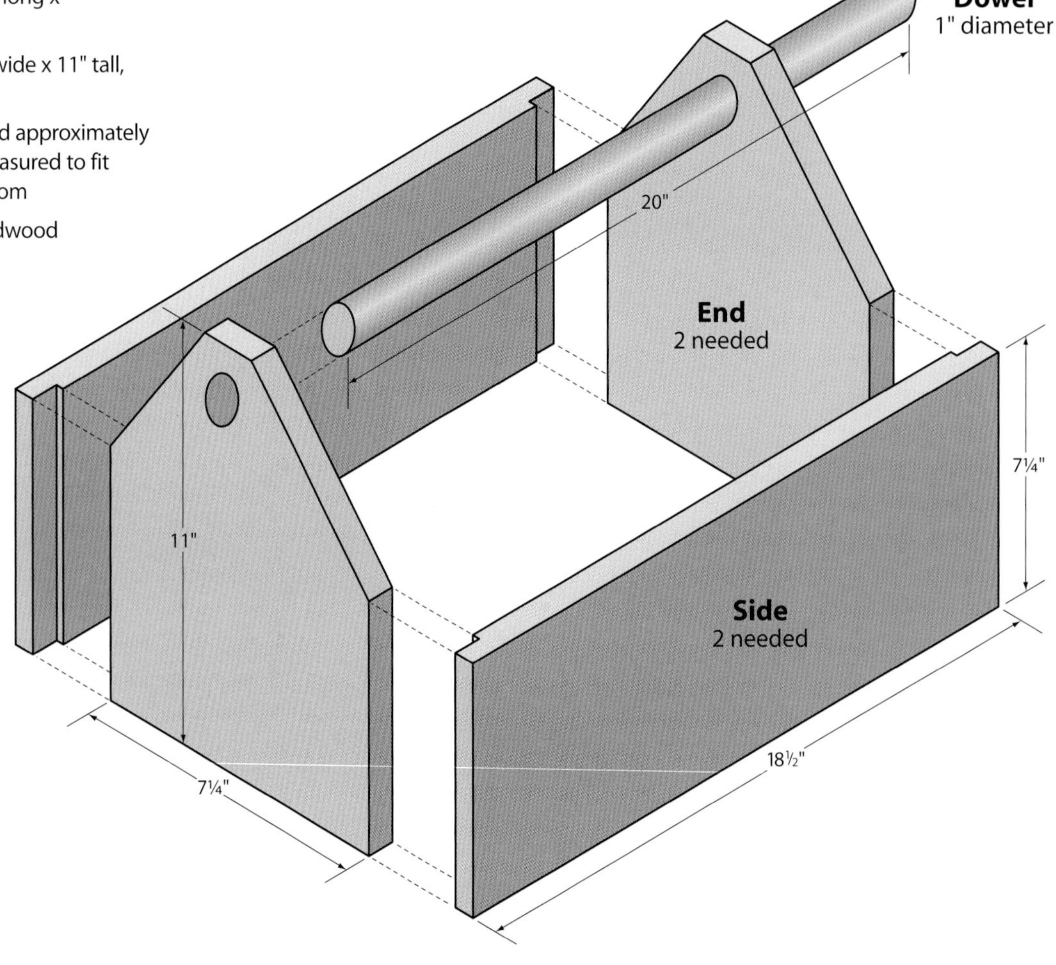

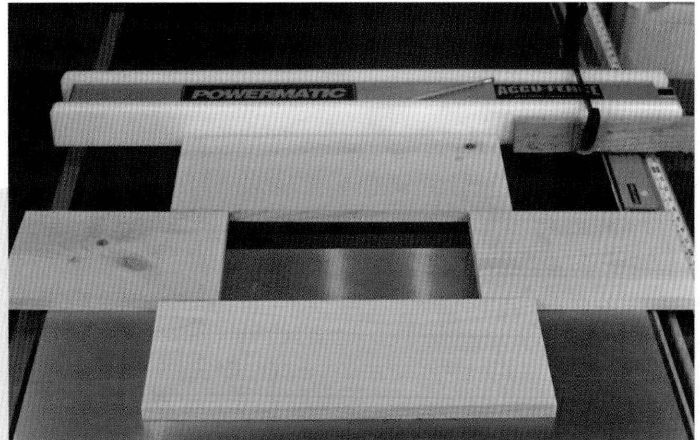

1 Cut the side and end pieces, making sure the opposing faces are identical in length, as when building the Hinged Box on page 196. Note that the grain on the ends of this tote runs vertically, which you may prefer not to do.

2 Cut ¼"-deep rabbets in the ends of the sides, making their width slightly more than ¾" to allow for sanding the joint smooth (see Extra, Short, or Dead-on? on page 200).

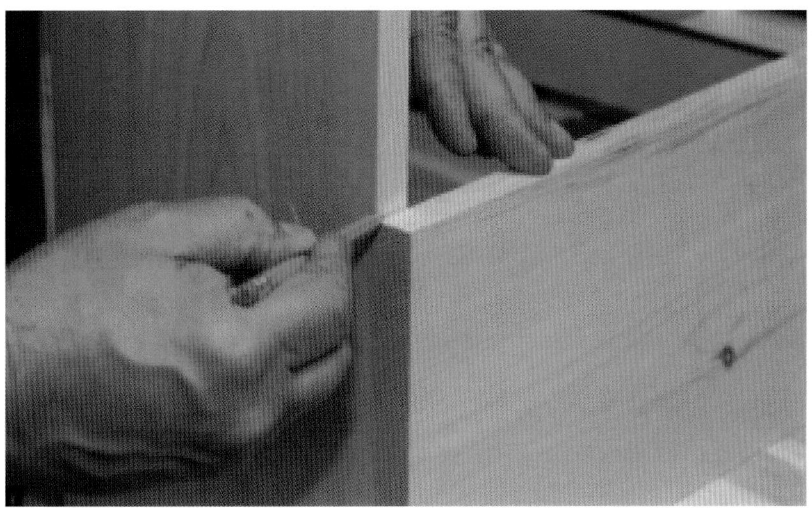

3 Dry fit the sides and end panel blanks, and temporarily clamp them together. Draw a line on the edges of the end panels where they meet the top of the sides. Mark the top of the end panels, and then remove the clamps.

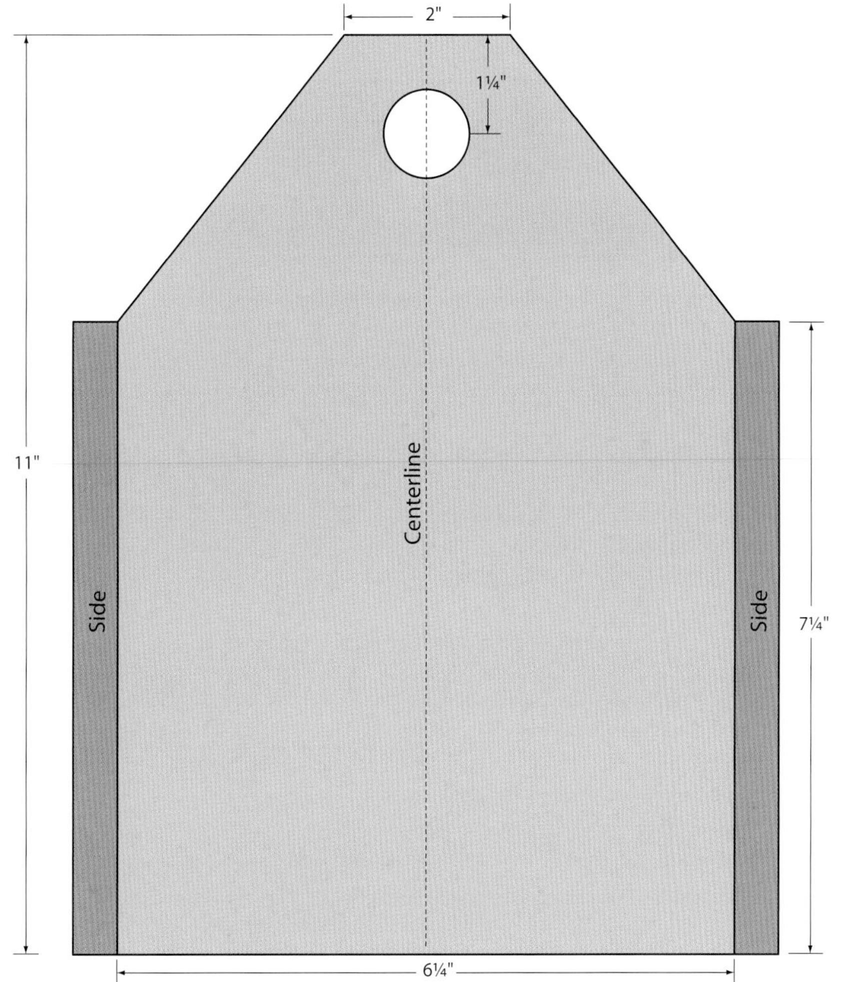

4 Mark the center of the top edge of the ends, extend a line down the face 1¼", and mark the center of the handle hole. Draw marks on the top edge of the ends, 1" to both sides of the center mark. Connect these marks with the lines marking the top of the sides. These are the cut lines for tapering the end panels.

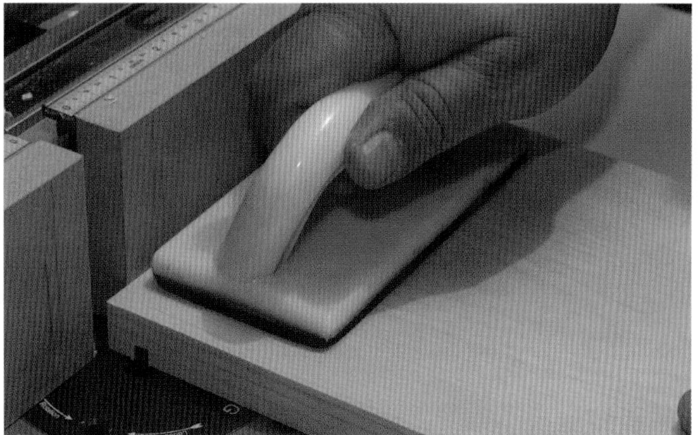

5 Rout a ¼"-deep groove beginning ½" above the bottom edge of the sides and ends, sizing it to the plywood used for the bottom. Because the groove is the same depth as the rabbets, you can cut it the full length of the pieces without it showing in the finished rabbet joints.

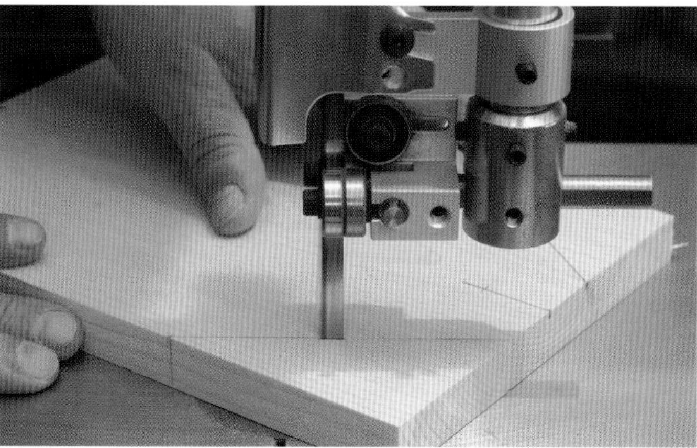

6 Cut the tapers in both ends on the table saw, and drill a 1"-diameter hole at the marks. Sand the edges of the tapers, being careful not to sand below the marks where the sides meet the ends.

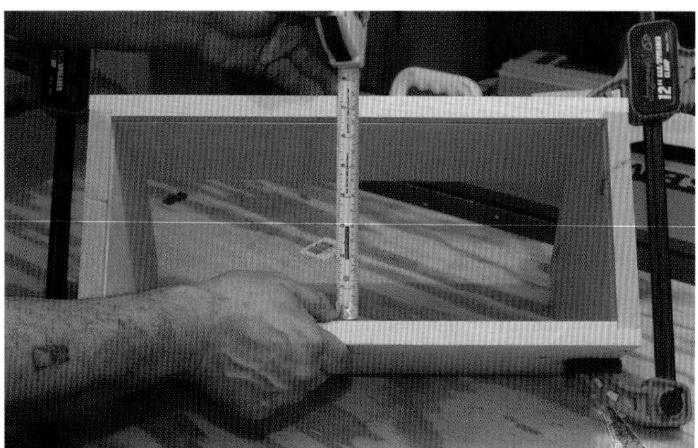

7 Dry fit the sides and ends; clamp and measure the bottom opening. Determine the bottom size by doubling the actual depth of the groove, subtracting 1⁄16", and adding the result to the length and width of the bottom opening.

Clamp in the bottom to be sure that it has a slight amount of movement and that the joints close fully. If necessary, trim the bottom panel so it has approximately 1⁄16" clearance side to side and end to end. When satisfied that all parts fit properly, remove the clamps, and finish sand all interior surfaces to 120 or 220 grit. Check to be sure that the handle dowel fits through the holes, and sand the dowel if that fit is tight.

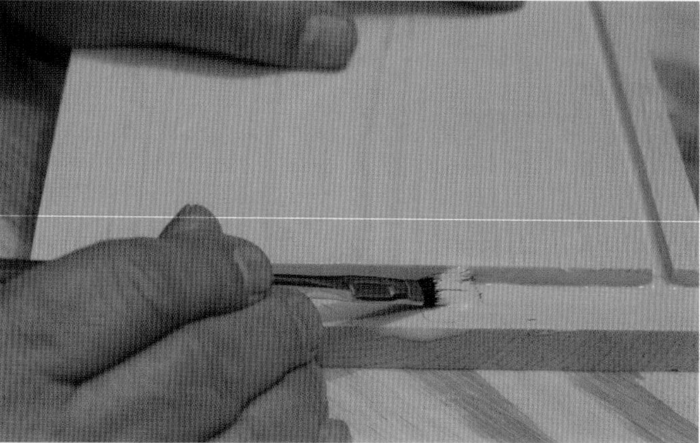

8 Apply glue to the rabbets and the corresponding portions of the ends, and assemble the pieces, inserting the bottom (see To Glue or Not to Glue on page 201) before installing an end, and then clamp. Measure the diagonals—they should be the same—to be sure that the assembly is square before allowing the glue to dry completely. If the diagonals are not the same, the box is out of square (see How Square Is That? on page 202).

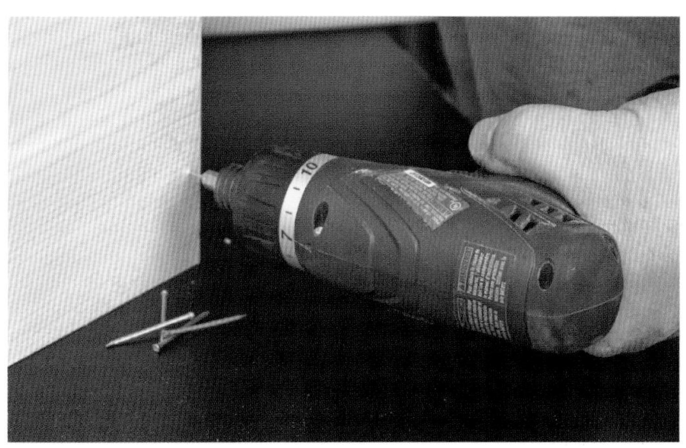

9 Find a dozen 2" finishing nails, and find a drill bit that is smaller than they are. Mark and drill three straight holes through each rabbet joint into the ends of the side pieces. Drive the nails flush, set them just below the surface, and fill the holes with wood putty.

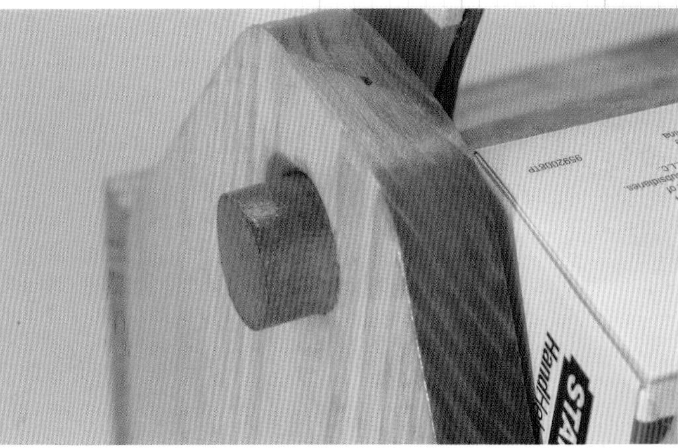

10 Insert the handle dowel through the holes in the ends, and extend it ¾" at each end; then, mark and cut the dowel to length. Apply a few dabs of glue to the handle just to the right of the ends, and then slide the handle into its centered position, giving a twist to spread the glue inside the hole. Using a damp rag, wipe away any excess glue. Allow the glue to dry. As a safety, drill a pilot hole and drive one 1"-long brad through the top of each end and into the dowel to lock it in place.

11 Finish sanding the outside surfaces, and apply the finish. The tote box in the photos was stained with Olympic Early American water-based stain and then given two coats of Olympic (clear) water-based polyurethane.

Bedside bookcase

A bookcase is nothing more than a box with the bottom in the wrong place and a crosspiece or two or three. It has dado joints, but the cutting, fitting, and assembly remain the same as with the box projects. Making the bookcase taller or wider has little impact on building it—the goal remains to build it square with tight joints.

A bookcase is simply a box with more crosspieces and the bottom moved up a little. Dados secure the shelves to the sides to make use of the vertical strength of that joint. The heavy loads that can be expected with a bookcase demand strong joints.

This bedside bookcase was built from red oak, but it could be made from pine or poplar to keep the cost down while refining this set of skills. Later, better materials can be used, especially when building larger versions that require the strength of hardwoods.

The shelves in this bedside bookcase are almost 12" apart. If you measure your stuff, you will find that CDs are 5" tall, DVD movies and paperback books are under 9" tall, and hardcover books are up to 12" or 13" tall and 9" wide. So if you want to make the case a few inches taller try 1 x 10 lumber (which measures 9¼" wide) for the sides, with 1 x 12 for the top. It would also look good using 5/4 lumber, which measures about 1 1/16" thick, with wider dados to match.

With this third box project in this chapter, you will learn to install shelves and a top, make a stopped dado, and assemble a multi-piece project squarely. This project also demonstrates the importance of cutting equal-length pieces.

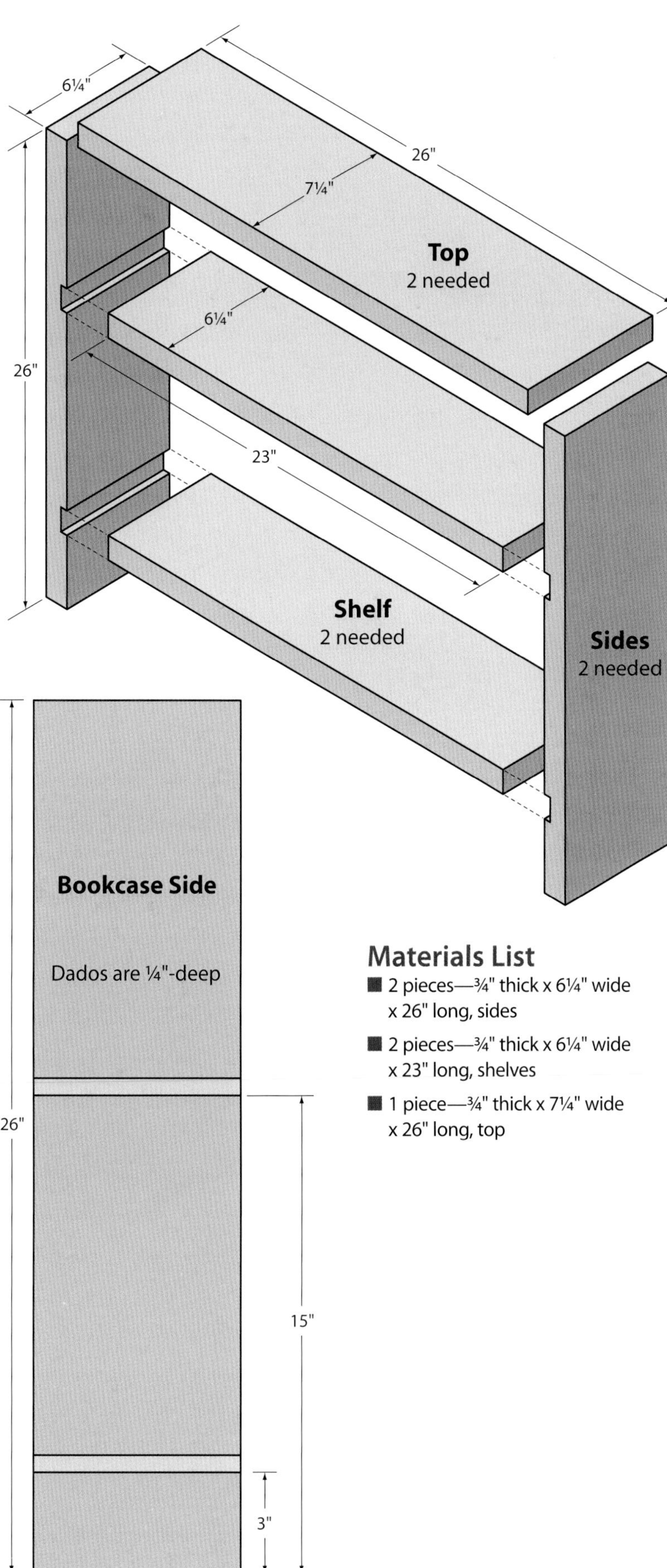

Materials List

- 2 pieces—¾" thick x 6¼" wide x 26" long, sides
- 2 pieces—¾" thick x 6¼" wide x 23" long, shelves
- 1 piece—¾" thick x 7¼" wide x 26" long, top

Core Skills

- Ripping wood to width
- Crosscutting to length and squareness
- Cutting through and stopped dados
- Assembling a medium-size project and keeping it square
- Staining and varnishing

Tools

- Table saw
- Router
- Router guide and ¾" cutter for dadoing
- Combination square and tape measure
- ½" chisel
- 30" pipe clamps or bar clamps
- Drill

1 If you are building the bookcase to the size specified here, you probably will have to rip the boards for the sides and shelves to their finished width. In pine, to end up with 6¼" wide, you would begin with 1 x 8 material, which measures 7¼" wide. It is helpful to crosscut the pieces to length first so the pieces are manageable. If you have a jointer available, true up one edge of each piece, and mark the opposing edge so the final rip can be taken off that edge. This both sizes each board's width and makes the edges parallel to each other at the same time. Remember that the sides and shelves are 6¼" wide while the top is 7¼" wide.

2 Lay out the dado locations on the sides. Cut a dado in a test piece the same thickness as the sides, and check its depth (¼" deep) and how well the shelf material fits in it. When satisfied with the test dado, cut the dados in both side pieces. If you find the pieces awkward to maneuver on the table saw, try dadoing with a handheld router instead (see Router Dado Guide on page 216).

Tip!

Matching Measurements

Note that all of the dado locations were measured from the bottom of the sides. Choosing a single point of reference from which to take measurements, when possible, makes it easier to be consistent, especially when multiple pieces are involved. This is a good habit to get into whether following a set of plans or designing your own projects. Consistency is always important.

Another aid to consistency is laying out pairs of parts together. Lightly clamp the two pieces together with their reference ends flush, make the measurement on one piece, and use the combination square to draw the mark across both pieces.

3 Dry fit the shelves and sides, temporarily clamping the assembly together. Check the joints to be sure they all fit correctly and that the case is square. The most common problem is irregular dado bottoms: Any high spots will hold the joints apart. Pare off the high spots with a sharp chisel. When satisfied with the fit, disassemble and sand the inside surfaces of the sides and both surfaces of the shelves. Put a piece of tape on the shelves to indicate the good side.

Fixing Irregular Dados

Irregular dado bottoms can keep your shelves from fitting correctly and squarely. Those high spots will hold the joints apart, ruining the final appearance of your project. To fix this problem, simply pare off the high spots with a chisel.

5 Stand the shelf assembly upside down on its top with the front edge of both facing you. Center the shelf assembly left to right, with the rear edges of the shelf sides flush with the rear edge of the top. Lay out the stopped dados on the underside of the top by carefully tracing around each side piece.

When to Rout?

If you plan edge treatments such as a round-over or a bevel, as is on the bookcase in the photos, routing those features before assembly will be easy, especially if they are to be applied to any of the inside edges. Be careful to stop edge treatments before the dados to avoid creating gaps there. Avoiding the dados is just one reason I only routed the bevel on the outside edge. Adding the profile only on the outside edge gives the whole piece a different look.

4 Apply glue to the dados in the sides and the ends of the shelves. Insert the shelves into their dados, making sure their front edges are flush with the edges of the sides, and then put clamps at the front and back of each dado. Apply just enough pressure to seat the shelves in the sides. With the assembly lying on a flat surface (on the back set of clamps), check to be sure the shelves are 90 degrees to the sides. If a correction is needed, loosen the clamps slightly, rap the bottom of the side that needs to move up until the assembly is square, and then tighten the clamps. Check the assembly for square after tightening the clamps, and, when satisfied, allow the glue to dry thoroughly.

Assembly Time

Before you glue up the bookcase, do a dry test-run. Get out all the clamps you expect to need and your measuring tools, and put the whole piece together without glue. Then fetch everything you forgot to have handy.

This might be a good time to use one of the glues with an extended setup time. Getting this assembly square before the glue dries is crucial and may take longer than expected, especially the first few times you do it. Also, no nails or screws were used when assembling the bookcase in the photos. A pair of screws through the sides and into each end of the shelves would add considerable strength, though with a small piece like this, they are not necessary.

6 Use the dado guide to rout a ¼"-deep dado for each side, being sure to stop about ½" from the front edge of the layout tracing. This operation can be done on a router table or with a handheld router, using the shop-made dado guide on page 216. Because the dados are relatively close to the end of the top, one of them will have to be routed using a plunge motion to begin the cut.

Router Dado Guide

While this dado guide has been around as long as electric routers, it remains a favorite of woodworkers. Though it is simple to make, this guide makes cutting accurate dados across long boards, including stopped dados, easier and safer than trying to control a large piece of wood on the table saw or router table.

The dado guide can be made however long you like, though 30" covers the needs of most woodworkers. If a job requires a longer version, making one is fast. In addition, this guide works with one router (base diameter) and bit combination. If you commonly cut more than one dado width, dado guides will have to be made for each of them.

This simple jig makes cutting dados, and stopped dados, in a long board easier and safer than trying to control a long piece of wood on the table saw or router table.

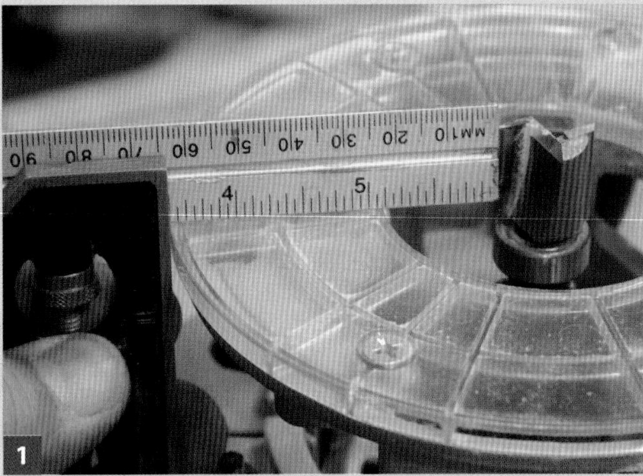

Install the bit and adjust its height so you can measure the distance from the outer edge of the router's base to the edge of the cutter. Add ⅛" to get the initial width of the guide's base; you'll trim it later. Cut a 30"-long piece of ¾"-thick stock about 2" wide. This piece acts as the fence, plus provides a place for the clamps that secure the guide to the workpiece. Cut a piece of ¼"-thick plywood 30" long and at least ½" wider than the fence and initial base width combined.

Glue the fence along the edge of the plywood. Clamp the guide to a bench so the raw edge of the plywood hangs free. Make sure at least 1" of the jig is hanging off the back so that the router does not cut into the bench. Adjust the bit depth so it will cut the plywood, start the router, and make a pass (left to right) along the full length of the guide, keeping the base firmly against the fence. This pass trims the plywood to its final size, making that edge an accurate indicator of where the router is going to cut the dado.

Align the plywood edge of the dado guide so it splits the layout line, and clamp in place. Check that the jig is aligned to the correct side of the layout line, that it's square to the edge of the wood, and that the clamps won't interfere with the router. In this case, moving the router from the left to the right keeps the cutting action of the bit pulling the router toward the fence on the jig.

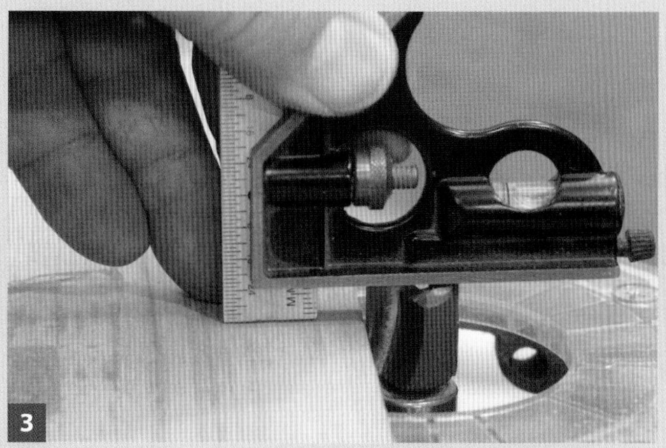

3

With the guide between you and the dado, remember that the opposite side of the bit is doing the cutting so the router has to travel from right to left. This makes cutting dados near the ends of a board accurate and safe. When setting the cutter depth, lay the dado guide on the base, and measure the bit height from it. Forgetting to add the thickness of the plywood jig base to the depth of cut is a common mistake.

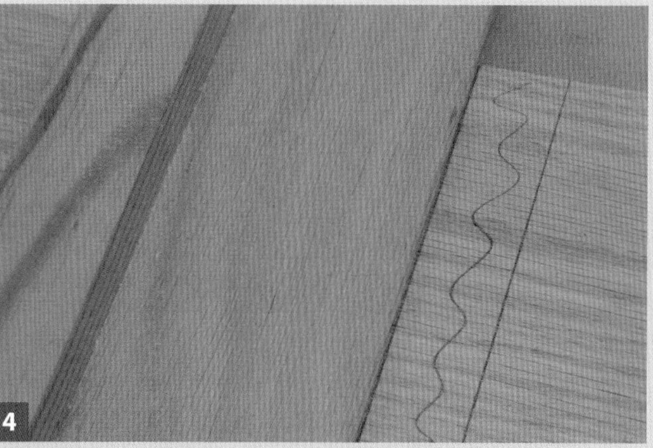

4

Always draw out the dado to be cut. Marking both sides of the dado, drawing a wavy line between them that marks the waste, and then double-checking to be sure it is placed correctly will prevent frustrating, costly errors.

Using a Dado Guide with the Router

Using the dado guide is simple, as long as you remember which way the bit is turning and cutting. The router must always be moved so that the cutting action of the bit pulls the router against the fence, not away from it.

Allow for the Plywood Jig Base

Remember to add the thickness of the plywood jig base to the depth of your cut when you are cutting dados. Forgetting to add the thickness of the plywood jig base to the depth of a cut is a common mistake.

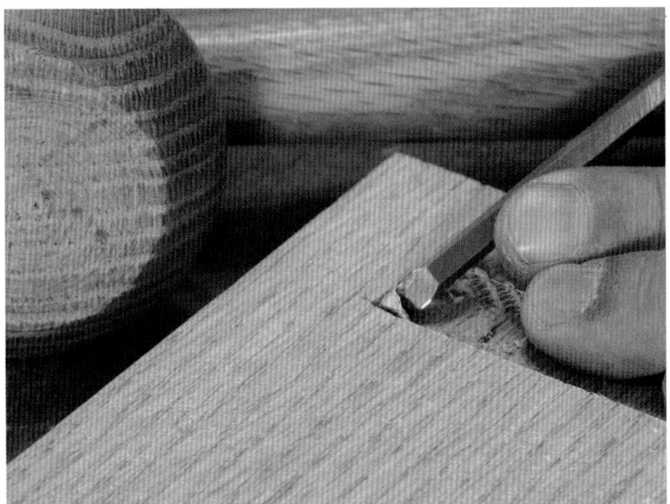

7a After routing the dados, you have a choice of squaring their front ends with a chisel, or of cutting the front edge of the sides back just enough to slip over and conceal the rounded end of the dado left by the router bit. Make sure that when completed, the dado is long enough for the case side to fit in it, with the back edges flush with the back edge of the top.

7b I like to notch the piece that goes into the stopped dado so it covers the rounded end. Temporarily seat the sides into the dados. Draw a line on the sides along both edges of the dados, running the lines back about ¾". Remove the side assembly, and carefully hand saw a notch into the front edges, cutting back about ⅝". Remember that the layout lines for this cut are at the surface, so the cut has to just leave the line, not split it.

Using a Plunge Base

Most router kits come with a plunge base, and this is the perfect job for it. Practice making dados in some scrap to get the feel of the plunge action before making the actual cuts on your project piece.

Stubbornly Not Square

Sometimes an out-of-square condition can be stubborn. In those situations, I use a long pipe clamp (or two hooked together on large projects) across the longest diagonal to squeeze the assembly so it is square. Make sure that squeezing diagonally doesn't lift one corner of the worktable, and if it does, clamp it down flat. After measuring and confirming that the assembly has been pulled square, put an additional half-turn on the long clamp to overcorrect slightly. When the glue dries and you remove the clamps, the assembly will spring back slightly and be perfectly square. Or very close to it.

Rounding Sharp Edges

Finish has a hard time clinging to sharp corners, but rounding them slightly with a sanding block cures that and softens those edges to the touch, as well.

8 With the notch cut, the side assembly should fit into the dados in the top and slide forward so the notch covers the rounded portion of the dado at the front with the sides' rear edges flush with the back edge of the top. When satisfied with this fit, remove the side assembly and clean any debris out of the dados. Apply glue to the dados and the top edge of the sides, put the side assembly into the dados, and clamp to apply pressure to the joints. Check to be sure that the assembly is square before allowing the glue to dry completely.

9 Finish sand the entire project. Use a sanding block with 150-grit paper to break any sharp corners along the edges. Use a tack rag to remove any remaining sanding dust, and apply the finish of your choice. The bookcase in the photos was given two coats of Olympic Vermont Maple oil-based stain, followed by three coats of Olympic oil-based clear satin polyurethane.

Hand Sawing Notches

You want to conceal the end of the dado with a small notch cut in the case sides, but the bookcase sides-and-shelf assembly is too awkward to pilot over the table saw. You'll have to use a handsaw.

Saw the dado-concealing notch in the case side with a small handsaw.

If you don't already have a small back saw, tenon saw, or dovetail saw, this is a good opportunity for you to go tool shopping. You want a saw between 12" and 15" in length, with a folded metal back, a comfortable handle, and a tooth-per-inch count around 12 to 16.

Clamping the bookcase to the bench will keep it from moving while you are cutting. Stabilizing the assembly lets you concentrate on making a precise cut. Hold the saw at about 45 degrees to the wood, brace the side of the blade with the thumb of your other hand, and make a few short strokes, letting the saw's own weight provide the downward pressure. Once it begins to bite, level the handle as you cut down the layout line. This might be a good time to pause and practice making a similar cut in scrap wood.

Here's the piece of wood that was removed.

Bookcase Options

While the bookcase in this project is nicely sized for a small room or at the bedside, larger versions are often desirable. When making a taller bookcase, the sides must be widened to between 10" and 12" for stability, and the shelf spacing increased as needed to accept the book sizes you expect to store. An easy way to check your dimensions is to cruise a local furniture store with a tape measure. Find a bookcase that is approximately as tall as you want to build, and take a quick measurement of the sides to see how wide they are and of the shelf spacing. You don't have to copy those dimensions exactly, but they will give you an idea from which to base your design.

Adding a 2"-wide strip of hardwood under the full width (at the rear) of the top or one of the upper shelves, secured with glue and screws, provides a secure bracket through which one or two screws can be driven into the wall studs behind the bookcase. This would prevent it from tipping over should someone pull on the front for some reason. Depending on whether the room has a baseboard, you might need to make a cutout at the bottom of the sides to clear it so the bookcase can stand flat against the wall.

Remember that shelf lengths over 30" long will sag when loaded with books, even when made from solid hardwood. When you need a wide bookcase, build two narrower ones and connect them side by side, or add vertical center braces between the shelves at the center. And when you want a tall case, especially if you will have to move it up and down stairs, consider stacking two shorter ones instead; just be sure they are secured to each other and to the wall.

In the living room, you may want to have backs on your bookcases. Use ¼" plywood, rout a rabbet in the case sides to receive it, and trim the shelves by ¼" to allow for it. It's probably simplest to just let the back butt against the underside of the top piece. Attach the back to the case sides and shelves with glue and staples or small nails.

Shop wall cabinet

Wall cabinets are essentially bookcases with doors. A cabinet is easy to build if you follow the techniques learned in the previous projects. If your shop is like mine, more storage space is always welcome—I built two of the project cabinets while I was at it.

Cabinets for the workshop are great ways to develop basic cabinet-making skills without the cost of the high-grade woods used for in-the-house versions that you are likely to build in the future.

For this fourth box project, the shop wall cabinet, I went to the local home center and selected wood from their stacks. Despite choosing the best boards I could find, there remained some warp and twist defects that would have to be dealt with during construction. Since most new woodworkers do not have a jointer or a planer, those machines were not used to prepare the wood for these projects.

The wall cabinet has rabbet joints with dados for the shelves, reinforced by screws. It also has an edge band plus frame and panel doors. Because I did not install a back panel, the side pieces are identical in terms of the dados and rabbets. If you decide to add a back panel, the rabbet you'll cut along the back edge of the sides creates a left and a right piece. Make sure you mark the sides with their place in the cabinet to avoid making two rights or two lefts. I promise this is very easy to do.

Edge Band and Doors

In this project, you'll learn how to face your cabinet with an edge band that does some of the job of a full face frame. If all you really want is a set of wall-hung shelves, you can leave the class after Step 6 and the French cleat demonstration. Just sand, apply the finish of your choice, and install. However, if cabinets are what you really want, you will have to continue on and add an edge band, doors, and hardware.

Take a look at your kitchen cabinets to see what a face frame looks like. It's narrow pieces of wood, joined at the corners and fastened to the front edge of the cabinets. The face frame stiffens the box and creates a foundation for hanging doors. Since your cabinet is made from solid wood with glue and screws reinforcing the corners, you can apply a solid-wood edge band instead of a fully joined face frame. That's why you can assemble it right on the front of the wall cabinet.

Making tongue-and-groove doors is relatively easy and can be done on a table saw using a standard ⅛"-wide blade. Beginning with accurately cut, square pieces is crucial to building a square, flat door that will stay that way regardless of the door style or type of joinery used.

Wall Cabinet Options

The design and procedures used to build this wall cabinet can be easily modified, but consider the weight of the possible contents and how that could affect materials, joints, and mounting choices. The bottom cubby, left uncovered by the doors, can be changed to hang pipe clamps by cutting slots slightly wider than the diameter of the pipe or width of the bar. When hanging clamps, adding corner braces to help prevent sagging under the weight is a good idea. Or, the bottom crosspiece could be left off and a bar installed from side to side to be used for hanging C-clamps and spring clamps.

This same design can be lengthened to make a floor-standing cabinet with a base made from 1" x 4" wood. I built one like this and found that the narrow width and narrow doors allowed it to be installed in a corner of my shop that kept it out of the way while adding much-needed storage space.

I added a back panel to this tall version and ran screws through that to secure the cabinet to the wall. I also built three boxes (using the same procedures as for the box project) to fit on the lower shelves. One is for fasteners, one for electrical stuff, and one for plumbing supplies.

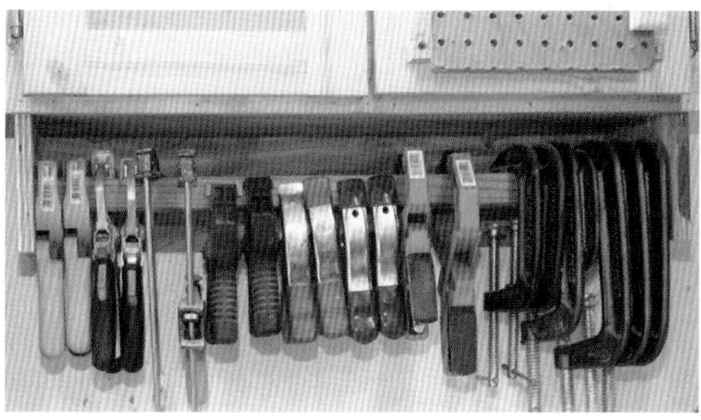

On this cabinet, I left the bottom crosspiece off but added a 1½" by 1½" bar on which I hang all my hand clamps and C-clamps.

This tall floor cabinet is really a very tall wall cabinet with a quick base made from 1" by 4" stock. The doors are much longer and narrower but are built exactly like the ones in this project.

Core Skills

- Selecting wood
- Sawing to length and width
- Making dados and rabbets for joints
- Making tongue-and-groove frame joints for paneled doors
- Applying an edge band
- Gluing and clamping
- Drilling pilot holes and driving screws
- Mitering

Tools

- Table saw
- Dado cutter (table saw) or router with ¾" flat-bottomed bit
- Combination square and measuring tape
- Cordless drill/screwdriver with pilot hole bit
- 30" bar or pipe clamps
- 6" corner squares with small clamps
- Stud finder
- Wood rasp
- ½"-diameter flat-bottomed bit
- Collar for router

Materials List

Cabinet

- 2 pieces—¾" thick x 35" long x 7" wide, sides
- 5 pieces—¾" thick x 24" long x 7" wide, top, bottom, and shelves
- 1⅝" constructions screws

Edge band and doors

- 2 pieces—¾" thick x 1½" wide x 26½" long, top and bottom
- 2 pieces—¾" thick x 1½" wide x 30½" long, sides
- 1 piece—¾" thick x 1½" wide x 27½" long, center bar

Note: Edge band part dimensions are approximate. Measure on your assembled cabinet to be sure of the actual lengths needed. Also, if a rail and stile bit set is to be used for the door joints, consult the instructions that came with the bit set to see if the door rail length must be altered to accommodate the built-in overlap created by the profile.

Doors

- 4 pieces—¾" thick x 2¼" wide x 28½" long, stiles
- 4 pieces—¾" thick x 2¾" wide x 8½" long, rails
- 2 pieces—¼" thick x 8⅜" wide x 23⅞" long (approximate), panels

Note: Measure the actual dimensions of the plywood panel during a dry fit after machining the rails and stiles. Details on taking this measurement are in the door section of the instructions that follow.

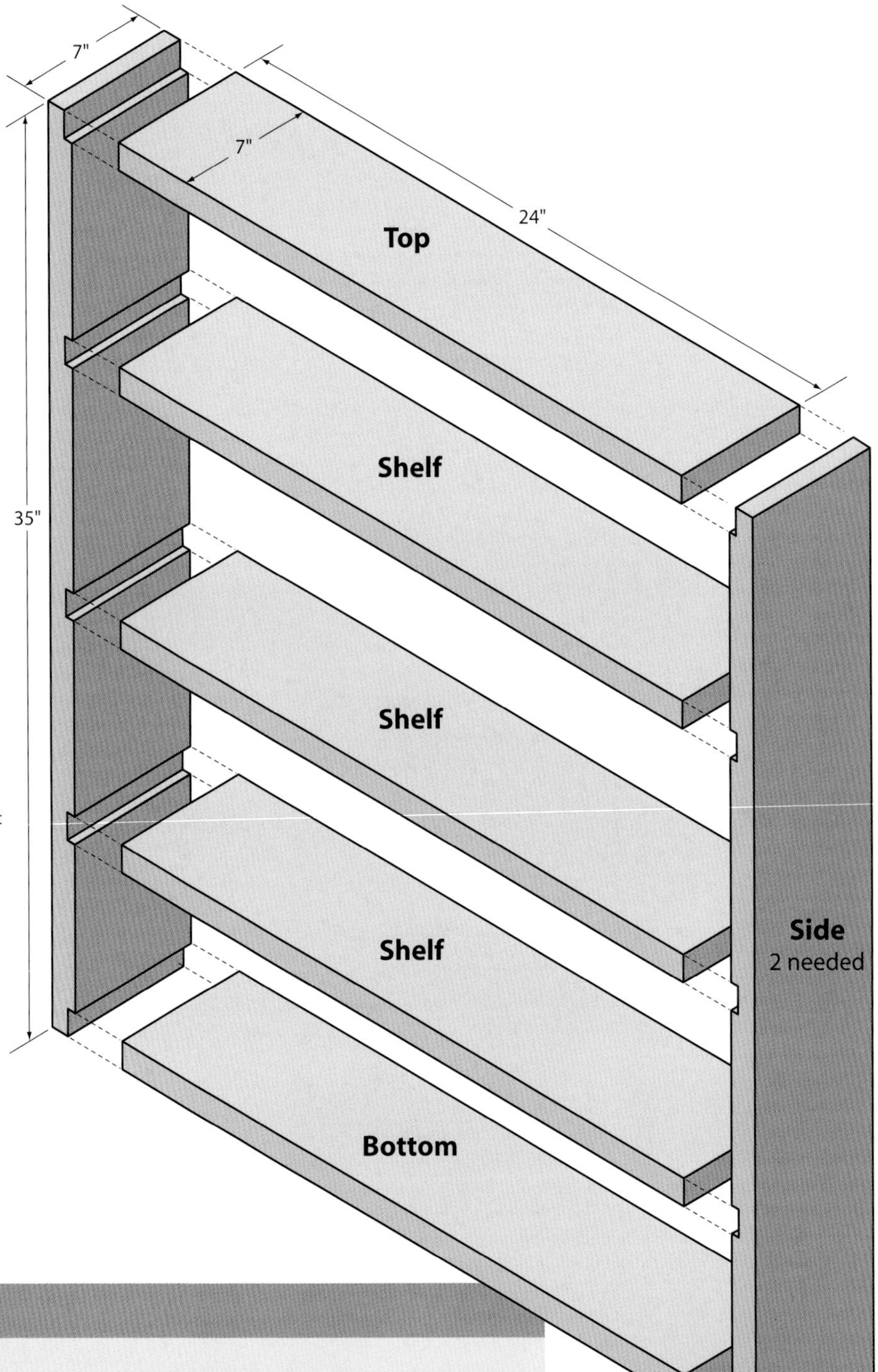

Tip!

Selecting Wood

Before cutting the pieces for the shop wall cabinet, I inspected the lumber and laid out the cuts to make use of the straightest sections. Often relatively straight pieces can be cut from a warped board, substantially reducing the problems these defects cause during machining and assembly. For the shop wall cabinet, I paid particular attention when picking out the sections to be used for the sides.

Using the straightest wood available for these pieces made assembly go easier. It's also important, when selecting pieces that will have joints cut in their ends, not to crosscut next to a knot. The knot itself and the wood surrounding it can be very hard and difficult to cut clean joints in. Also, knots have a nasty habit of breaking loose while being cut and becoming potentially painful missiles.

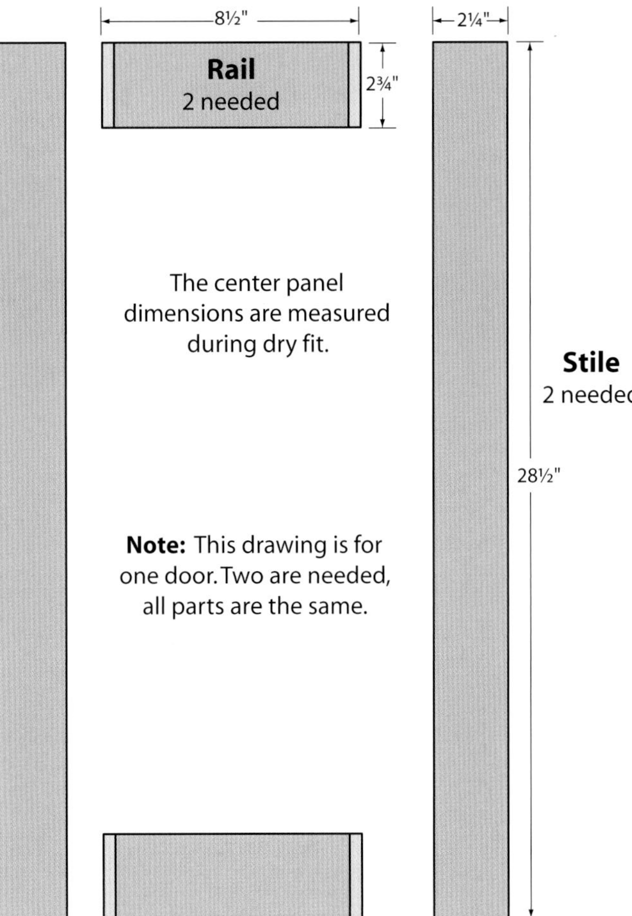

Be Consistent

To create identical sides, make matching cuts from each setup in both side pieces. That way, if a dado setup is off by 1⁄16", the mistake cancels because you will have cut both sides with the same error. Nobody will notice a shelf that is 1⁄16" higher than intended, but everybody will see the problem if one end of that same shelf is lower or higher than the other.

This method makes dados that match, but using wood as it comes from the home center can mean some variance in thickness, as you will learn when you dry fit the shelves. Usually the error is rather small, and oversize pieces can be sanded to fit or planed. Trying to force the oversize piece into a dado can split the side and all but ensures an out-of-square project.

New Tools!

Making Cabinets!

- **Aluminum corner squares.** I like to use 6" aluminum corner squares as an aid to assembling and clamping cabinets like these. When they are clamped to a corner, they will hold it square and leave my hands free for gluing or drilling pilot holes or whatever. About $20 to $50 a pair.
- **Pilot hole bit set.** Driving screws without predrilling a pilot hole is risky on a good day and foolish on most others. The pilot hole ensures that the screw doesn't wander and also that the wood doesn't split, both of which are likely to happen on the same cabinet. You can buy sets of bits to match common screw sizes. You can also find a double-ended drill/quick-release chuck set that has a pilot hole bit on one end and a screwdriver on the other. About $25.
- **Stud finder.** These handy gadgets use some mysterious electrical property to locate studs inside a wall. I don't know exactly how they work (please don't write and tell me), but I do know they make finding studs easy when attaching heavy stuff to a sheet rock-covered wall. You can't live without one. About $30.
- **Wood rasp.** A simple wood rasp is an excellent tool for removing small amounts of wood to perfect a joint and for many other uses. I have a four-way rasp, spent about $10 to get it, and use it frequently. You can get better versions, but plan to shell out $15 or $20 for them.

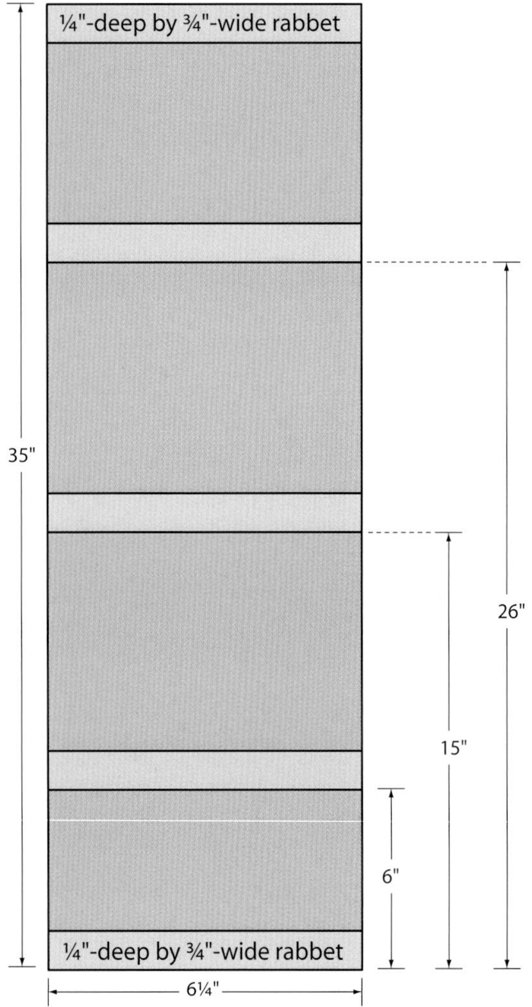

1 With the cabinet sides on a bench, choose the inside and outside faces and bottoms of each, and mark them to avoid confusion when laying out and cutting the joints. Lay out the rabbets at the top and bottom of each side. Lay out the dados on each side piece, remembering that all of the dados are measured from the bottom edge of the side to the bottom of the dados. Draw the width of the dados, and add a wavy line where the wood will be removed to help prevent mistakes. Make sure the dados and rabbets align with each other on both pieces.

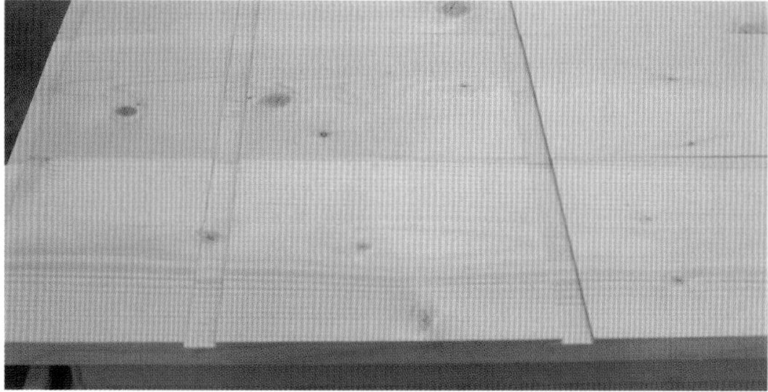

2 However you choose to cut the rabbets and dados, whether on the table saw, router table, or with a handheld router guided by a jig, confirm the depth and width of the cuts on a piece of scrap before tackling the workpieces. This may seem like a simple thing, but it is important and easily can be forgotten.

3 Dry fit the shelves and sides, temporarily clamping the assembly to check that it goes together square. Clamp-on squares help get it right. If the shelves were cut to the same length, there should not be a problem. However, if you do find a problem, it is much easier to correct it now than after glue has been applied and the setup clock is ticking.

Squareness and Pilot Holes

I use 6" aluminum corner squares clamped to the side and shelf to make assembly easier and more accurate, as shown in Step 3. The squares hold the pieces in position while my hands are free to drill pilot holes and install screws. Taking the time to drill a pilot hole prevents splitting in the shelves, but more importantly ensures that the screw does not wander in the end grain. This helps the screw to pull the shelf down square. When screws are run in without the benefit of a pilot hole, they can deflect enough to pull the shelf out of alignment, making it even more difficult to end up with a square project.

4 When satisfied with the test fit, take apart the assembly and sand all internal surfaces to 220 grit. Wipe away the dust with a tack rag, being sure that there is no dust or debris stuck in the dados. Apply glue to the dados and the ends of the shelves only. On a flat surface, assemble the sides and shelves, and clamp with light pressure. Make sure that the shelves and sides are flush at the front edge of the cabinet and that everything is square. Because this wood was not perfectly straight, I had to sand a couple of the shelves during the dry fit so they would fit into their dados properly. Drill two pilot holes through the sides and into the ends of each shelf. You can eyeball these holes, but I like to measure and make a layout mark that ensures placing the screws in the center of the shelf thickness.

5 Install a 1⅝" screw in each end of the shelves. Set the assembly aside while the glue dries.

6 Dry fit the top and bottom pieces into their rabbets. I found one end of the bottom that was warped slightly and required persuasion to fully close the joint. I fixed that with a speed clamp. Apply glue to the rabbets and to the ends of the top and bottom, assemble, and clamp. Check the joints and apply additional clamps as necessary to seat the top and bottom panels. Drill pilot holes and install two 1⅝"-long screws through the sides and into each end of the top and bottom. Check the assembly to be sure it remains square before setting it aside for the glue to dry.

7 This edge band consists of strips of wood 1½" wide that are mitered at the corners and glued to the front of the cabinet. To install the edge band, start at the top of the opening and do each side in turn. While the goal is for each miter to fit with no gaps, that is not always easy. Hold each piece in position, and note what part of the miter is making contact. Use a rasp or sanding block to remove a little material from that spot, check it again, and continue until the piece does fit.

French Cleats

A French cleat, used to hang a wall cabinet or to attach a floor cabinet to a wall to prevent the cabinet from tipping over, is a pair of wooden strips, each with one edge beveled at 45 degrees. One strip is mounted to a wall with heavy screws or lag bolts driven into the studs. The other strip is built into a cabinet near its top. The wall-mounted strip has its bevel pointed up and slanting away from the wall. The cleat in the cabinet has its bevel pointed down and its point flush with the back edge of the cabinet. Use quality wood for the cleats, and mount both strips solidly; ¾"-thick plywood is commonly used, but equally thick hardwood works also.

1

I use two ¼"-diameter lag bolts 3½" long to mount the cleat to the wall. Remember that the lags must reach through the ¾" thickness of the cleat itself, plus ½" or ⅝" of drywall, in many cases, before engaging the wood of the stud. Drill a pilot hole for lags to avoid cracking the stud.

When installing the wall-side strip, use a long level to draw a faint line on the wall marking the height of the cleat's bottom edge. Run a strip of masking tape along the bottom of this line, locate the studs, and mark their edges and then their center on the masking tape. Hold the wall-side cleat alongside the tape, and transfer the center of the stud locations onto the cleat so you can drill through holes for the fasteners.

2

Glue and screw the mating cleat to the cabinet sides and under the rear edge of the top or an upper shelf to be sure it cannot pull out. Reinforce the mounting of the top or shelf with screws through the sides if they were not installed when building the cabinet. Clamp the cleat in place while you drill pilot holes and drive the screws. A little overkill is a good thing when hanging a cabinet that always seems to hold more weight than anticipated.

Lags with Washers

I always use ¼ "-diameter lags with a flat washer under their heads to secure French cleats to studs. The addition of the washer engages a little more wood, something that can't be a bad idea considering the weights and forces that may be placed on these devices, and ensures that you don't twist the head of the lag down into the cleat, weakening its hold.

3

To hang the cabinet, lift it so the bevel of its cleat slips over the bevel of the wall-mounted side, and then lower the cabinet so they interlock. If you ever want to reposition the cabinet or move it to a different shop, lift the cabinet off the cleat, remove the lag screws, and you are good to go.

To install a French cleat on a cabinet that has a back, just set the back into the cabinet by the thickness of the cleat. You can glue the cleat to the plywood if you want, but it still must be reinforced with screws through the sides and top.

8 Cut a 45-degree angle on one end of a piece of edge band material, and hold it on the cabinet with the short side of the angle aligned on the inside corner and its inside edge flush with the inside edge of the cabinet. Mark the stock at the opposite inside corner of the cabinet. To prevent errors, make the mark from the inside corner of the cabinet, and run it out to the edges of the edge band piece at roughly a 45-degree angle. Cut the piece about ⅛" longer than needed, check it on the cabinet, and shave the miter until the inside corners align. Glue the piece in place, and secure it with a few brads.

9 Fitting the bottom piece of the edge band is done a little differently because you can't simply hold it in position and mark it. With a 45-degree miter cut in one end, turn the material upside down, align the point with the point on a side piece, and then mark the point on the opposite side piece, again extending the layout mark to indicate the direction of the cut. As before, cut the piece ⅛" longer than needed, and trim it to fit.

Miter Challenge

Gap-free miters at all four corners are the goal. However, making them takes practice. I like to build the edge band right on the cabinet front so that I can miter and fit each piece as I go. The alternative method is to make the edge band on the bench as a unit with joined corners, whereupon it becomes a true face frame, and then glue the assembled frame to the front of the cabinet. But for that to work out right, you need a lot of confidence in your ability to make a mitered frame to precise dimensions, which only comes with practice. Try both methods to see which you like best.

Miter Madness

When marking edge band pieces for miters, I found that adding a slanted line indicating the direction of the miter angle eliminates frustrating mistakes when cutting it, which otherwise are all too easy to make. If the cabinet is to be painted, gaps can be filled with drywall joint compound. After painting, you never have to admit there were gaps in the corners. With some practice, you won't need the filler or the lie and can use a clear finish to show off your mitering skills.

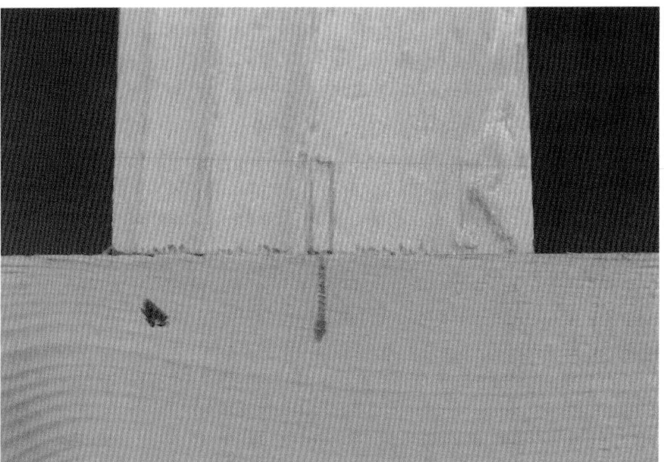

10 Locate and mark the center of the top and bottom edge band pieces, and cut the vertical center stile to fit. Ideally, this center stile will slip into place with just a tap or two. That friction, combined with a good coat of glue at each end and a dab of glue where the center rail crosses each of the shelves, will hold it securely. I added a single brad, driven through the center rail and into each shelf. Reinforcing those joints adds substantial support to the center of the shelf.

11 To make the doors, cut all the rails and stiles, choose which side goes out and which edge goes toward the inside, and mark the pieces accordingly. Each of the rails and stiles gets a full-length groove centered on its thickness that both forms the joint and accepts the center panel. Set the ⅛"-thick table saw blade to a height of ½". Use a piece of scrap the same thickness as the workpieces to make the setup. Center the cut by eye, run the test piece, and then turn it end for end and run it again. This automatically centers the groove. Add a featherboard to hold the stock against the fence.

12 Try fitting the plywood to be used for the center panel into the groove. If it is tight or won't fit, adjust the fence away from the blade slightly, recut the test piece, and check its fit over the center panel plywood. The plywood should slip into the groove easily but not sloppily. If not, move the fence slightly further from the blade, and recut the test piece until a good fit is achieved. Then, run all of the rails and stiles.

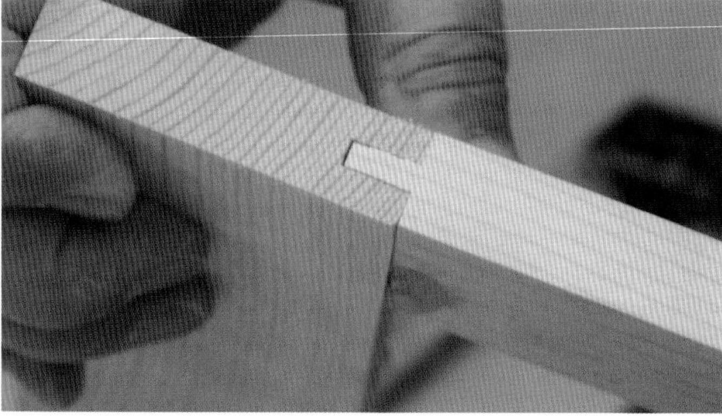

13 A tongue (tenon) must be cut in both ends of all four rails to fit into the grooves. These cuts can be done with a router bit or stacked dado set, but we'll use the same blade in the table saw. First, use one of the grooved pieces laid flat on the table next to the blade to set the blade height slightly below the bottom edge of the groove. Second, use a gauge block to set the rip fence for a tongue that's just under ½" long. Making the tongue slightly shorter (1/32" is enough) than the depth of the groove allows the tongue to fit into the groove fully and leaves room for excess glue at the bottom. Lock the fence and move the gauge block toward the operator's end before clamping it securely to the fence. Now nibble away at both sides of the test tongue.

14 Try fitting the test tongue into the groove. The ideal fit allows the tenon to slip into the groove fully by hand but does not have any slop. Most likely the tongue will be too thick, so adjust the blade upward slightly and recut it. Small adjustments make big changes, so go slowly. Then, cut the tongues on both ends of all four of the rails.

Rails Run Across, Stiles Stand Up

In a face frame or a cabinet door, the horizontal pieces are called "rails" and the vertical ones are called "stiles." Usually the stiles run the full height of the door or panel, with the rails trapped between them.

15 Assemble the set of rails and stiles, and clamp with just enough pressure to close the joints. Insert the blade of a combination square into the bottom of the groove, slide the body against the edge, and lock it. Set the combination square against the inside edge of the rails and stiles, and draw marks to indicate the bottom of the grooves on each side and the top and bottom. Make the marks directly across from each other. Measure between those marks and subtract ⅛" to determine the height and width of the plywood center panel. Cut one panel and dry assemble a door to be sure the joints close. When satisfied with the panel fit, cut the other one, and sand them both.

16 To assemble the doors, apply glue to the tongues and in the last 2" of the grooves in the stiles. Assemble the rails and stiles, slipping the center panel (not glued, see To Glue or Not To Glue on page 201) into the groove. Place in clamps, making sure the ends of the rails and stiles are flush before applying just enough pressure to close the joints fully. Make sure the doors are flat and square in the clamps before allowing the glue to dry completely. Then unclamp and sand all of the surfaces.

17 Many hinges can be surface mounted, but cutting a shallow mortise to sink the hinge leaf flush with the wood makes the door fit tighter. I use a simple template to guide a router equipped with a ½"-diameter flat-bottomed bit and a collar. The template is a piece of ¾"-thick wood with a cutout that is ⅛" larger than the hinge leaf side to side and is ⅛" wider. I set the hinges 4" in from the top and bottom of the doors. To make sure the doors are installed squarely, clamp a straight piece of wood along the bottom edge of the cabinet as a temporary alignment support.

Rasp to Fit

Because you are not using wood processed through a thickness planer, the actual thickness may vary from piece to piece. That means the thickness of the tongue can also vary slightly. If the tongue on some pieces is too thick, rather than trying to recut them on the table saw, I use a rasp to fit them to the groove. Another method is to wrap a piece of sandpaper around a square block and use that. Yet another method is to shave them with a shoulder plane. Very little material will have to be removed, making any of these methods a good choice.

CA Glue Hardens Pine

When using softwoods like pine for an edge band, face frame, or cabinet door frame, I install the doors and hinges, then remove them. Put a drop of thin CA (cyanoacrylate) glue in each of the hinge screw holes, and let it dry before reassembly. The CA glue penetrates the wood around the threads, making it stronger and better able to hold the small screws securely.

Base cabinet

These useful shop cabinets have legs at the front and wheels at the back, making them easy to move around. They can be made any height.

The semi-mobile design of this base cabinet has become a favorite of mine because there is never enough storage or workspace in my shop. Being able to roll these cabinets and the work surface on top of them to wherever they are needed is even better. The idea of two wheels and two legs came from the frustration of trying to use locking casters that often had a mind of their own. Once again, simplicity emerged as a functional and cost-effective alternative.

These cabinets are made of plywood, with glued rabbet joints. While good-fitting dados and rabbets along with glue make strong joints, augmenting them with screws is a good idea. This is especially true of these shop cabinets that will be moved frequently and could be subjected to heavy loads from time to time. When you cut dados for shelves, however, don't make them too deep, or you will weaken the plywood. Dados ¼" deep in ¾"-thick (okay, 23⁄32"-thick, really) plywood is more than sufficient.

Doors and Drawers

In this fifth box project, you'll learn to construct drawers. Drawers are useful and also optional, and the materials lists and instructions cover both choices. If you want the drawer, it's built using the same techniques as the box in the first project.

The door is the same as those on the wall cabinet. The individual parts are bigger, but the grooves and tongues are cut exactly the same way. The center panel for this door is much larger but is sized exactly like the wall cabinet versions.

However you detail them, there are quite a few parts in this cabinet. The big thing to learn here is how to manage all those parts. Marking them clearly, including which side faces out and their position in the cabinet, will keep track of them. Laying the sides next to each other and comparing the layouts for dados and rabbets will help cutting or assembling them without error.

More Choices

The interior of the base cabinet, was purposely left open to provide storage space for larger items I never seem to have a place for. Adding shelves is as easy as installing cleats or adjustable shelf standards on which the shelves rest or adding dados in the sides for permanent shelves.

This base cabinet design is easily modified to serve a wide range of needs. It can be a tool base, an assembly table, or an outfeed table for your table saw. In addition to what the top surface is used for, the cabinet provides flexible storage space, something no shop seems to have enough of.

I built two of the base cabinets so they can be put back-to-back to make a temporary work surface when needed.

Can you tell I had a new set of raised panel cutters and templates in the shop when this miter saw cabinet was built? Shop cabinets are great for practicing with new tools.

Core Skills

- Laying out and sawing plywood cabinet parts
- Cutting dados and rabbets in plywood
- Marking and making left and right sides
- Assembling a plywood cabinet
- Building an edge band
- Making a drawer box and installing it
- Making and installing cabinet doors

Tools

- Table saw
- Dado cutter or router with flat-bottomed bit sized to match the wood being used
- Combination square and tape measure
- Hammer and nail set
- Handsaw or jigsaw
- Clamps
- Drill
- Utility knife

Note: If a rail and stile bit set is to be used for the door joints, consult its instructions to see if the door rail length must be altered.

Base Cabinet

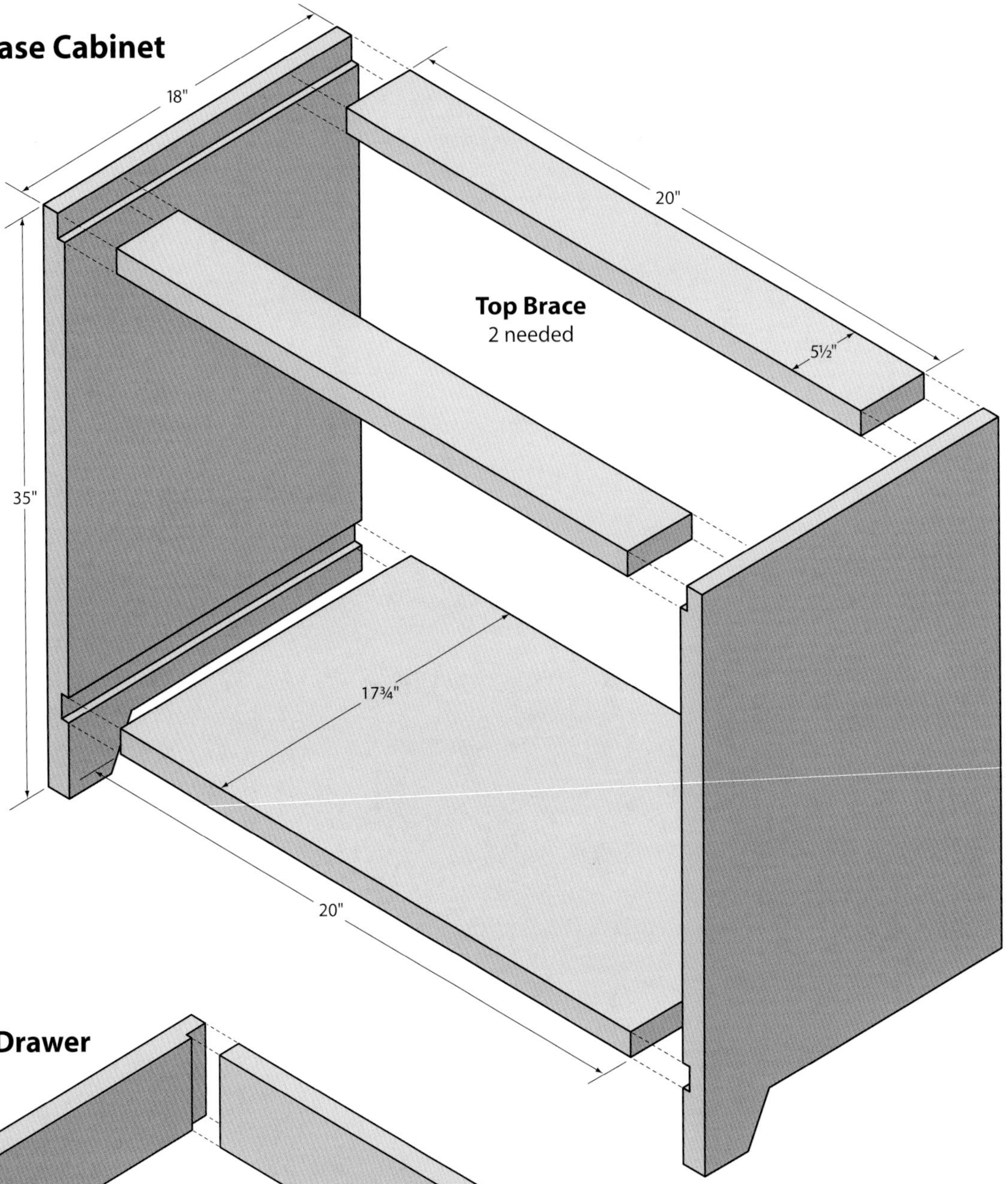

18"

20"

Top Brace
2 needed

5½"

35"

17¾"

20"

Base Cabinet Drawer

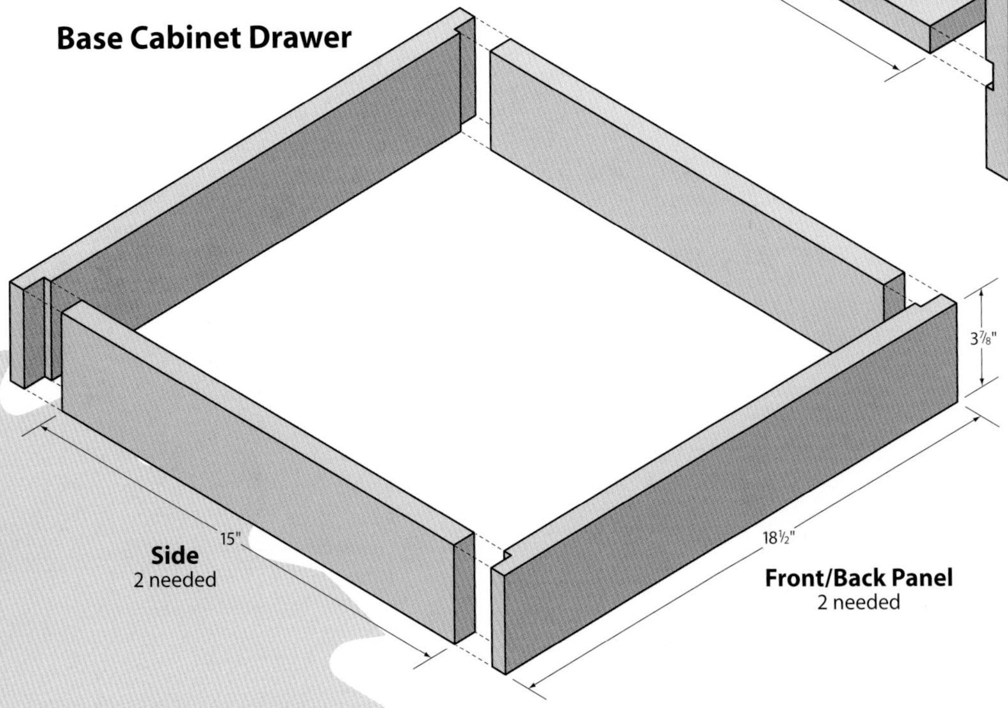

3⅞"

15"

Side
2 needed

18½"

Front/Back Panel
2 needed

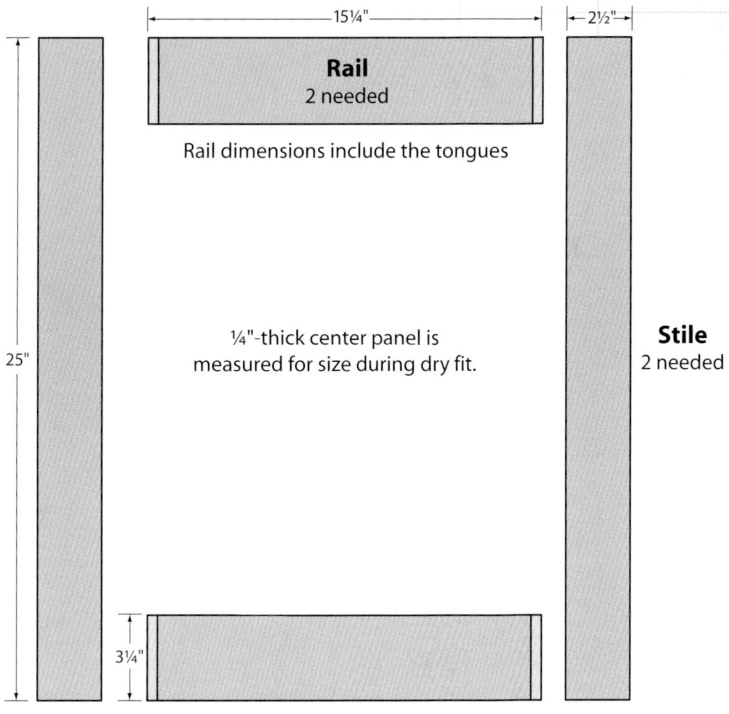

Base Cabinet Door (with Drawer)

Note: When no drawer is used, the stiles are 30½" long. The rails remain unchanged.

Materials List

Cabinet

- 2 pieces—¾" thick (plywood) x 18" wide x 35" long, sides
- 1 piece—¾" thick (plywood) x 17¾" wide x 20" long, bottom
- 2 pieces—¾" thick (plywood) x 5½" wide x 20" long, top braces
- 1 piece—¾" thick (plywood) x 23¾" wide x 21" long, top
- Top banding—¾" thick x 1" wide, cut to fit along front and sides of top (no banding on the rear edge)
- 1 piece—¼" thick x 20" wide x 32⅜" long, back (measure for size after cabinet is built)

Drawer

- 2 pieces—¾" thick x 15" long x 3⅞" wide, drawer sides
- 2 pieces—¾" thick x 18½" long x 3⅞" wide, drawer front/back (measure to fit, as described in instructions)
- 1 piece—¼" thick x 18⅜" wide x 13⅞" long, drawer bottom (measure for size during dry fit)
- 4 pieces—¾" x ¾" x 17" long, drawer runners

Note: If box joints or through dovetails are to be used on the drawer, measure the width of the drawer cavity and subtract ⅛" to determine the size for the front and back panels. If half-blind dovetails are being used, consult the instructions that came with the dovetailing jig for information on sizing the drawer parts.

Edge band with drawer (sizes are approximate, cut to fit)

- 3 pieces—¾" thick x 21" long x 1½" wide, rails (horizontal pieces)
- 2 pieces—¾" thick x 24" long x 1½" wide, stiles (vertical pieces)
- 2 pieces—¾" x ¾" x 4" long, stiles at the sides of drawer opening

Edge band no drawer (sizes are approximate, cut to fit)

- 2 pieces—¾" thick x 21" long x 1½" wide, rails
- 2 pieces—¾" thick x 29½" long, stiles

Door with drawer

- 2 pieces—¾" thick x 15¼" long x 3¼" wide, rails
- 2 pieces—¾" thick x 25" long x 2½" wide, stiles
- 1 piece—¼" thick x 15⅛" wide x 19⅞" long, center panel (measure for size during dry fit)

Door no drawer

- 2 pieces—¾" thick x 15¼" long x 3¼" wide, rails
- 2 pieces—¾" thick x 30½" long x 2½" wide, stiles
- 1 piece—¼" thick x 14⅞" wide x 24⅞" long, center panel (measure for size during dry fit)

1 The lower edge of the dado for the bottom panel must be located equal to the overall height of the wheels, plus ½" above the raw bottom edge of the cabinet side. In my case, a 2"-diameter caster is 2½" tall including its bracket, which mounts directly to the underside of the bottom panel. That means the dado for the bottom panel was cut with its lower edge 3" up from the bottom of the raw panel. Saw or rout the lower dado, the ¾"-wide rabbet along the top, and the 3⁄16"-deep x ¼"-wide rabbet along the back edge of the sides. Remember that there are left and right sides. Marking them early in the process will help prevent problems later.

2 To define the front leg and the end of the cut that runs to the rear of the cabinet sides, you have to do a little layout. Measure back 1½" from the front edge of the side, and draw a line upward, angled at 30 degrees and a few inches long. The angle needs only to be close since it is primarily aesthetic, not structural. Now, draw a line parallel to the bottom edge, located ½" below the dado that will accept the bottom panel. Connect this line to the angled line that defines the slanted side of the leg.

3 You can saw the foot with any kind of saw, but, if it is the table saw, you have to stop the cut for completion with a jigsaw or handsaw. Remember that while the right side can be cut with its outside face up, the left side must be cut with the outside face down (and the layout must be drawn on the inside surface).

Base Cabinet Dados & Rabbets

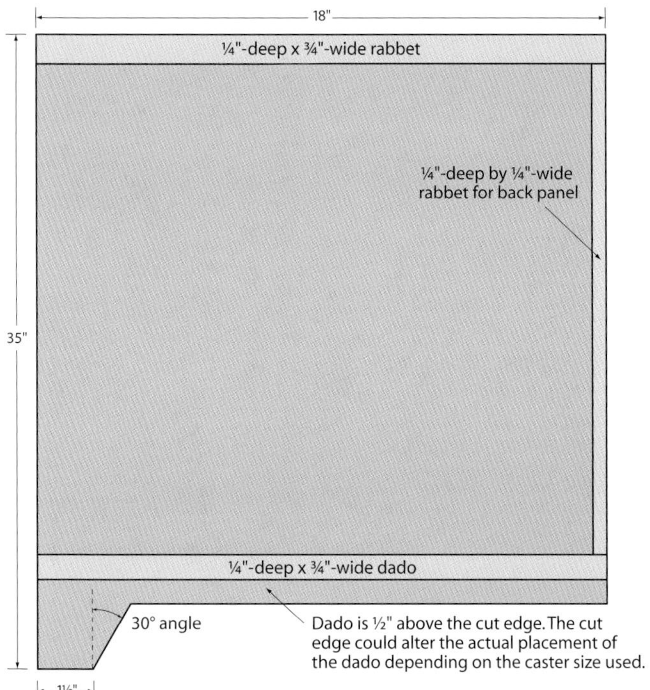

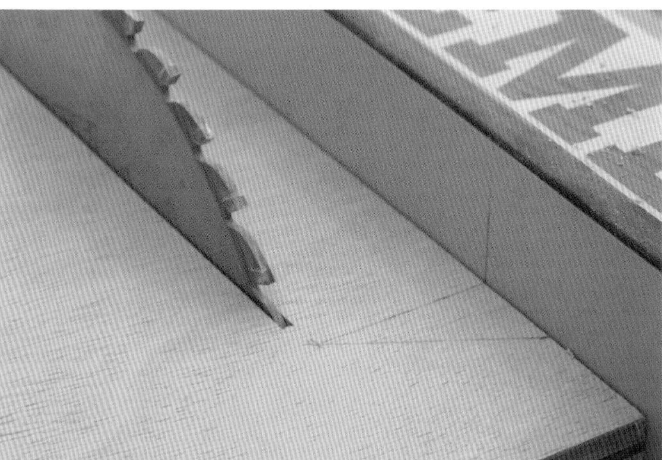

4 Set the blade-to-fence distance to place the cut ½" below the dado. I raised the blade as high as it goes without the blade washer rubbing on the underside of the throat insert and then, using a square, drew a vertical line on the fence even with where the blade starts cutting. Using a square, draw a line from where the horizontal line meets the angled line defining the foot, out to the edge of the wood at the fence to mark a stopping point. When you reach the line, shut off the saw and wait for the blade to stop completely before sliding the workpiece away from the blade. Finish the cut with a jigsaw or handsaw, and then sand the edge smooth.

5 Drill small pilot holes in the dado from the inside to locate four or five screws that will be installed from the outside during assembly. Apply glue to the dados in both sides, and install the bottom, making sure it is flush with the front edge of the sides. Check the sides and bottom for square; then, install 1⅝"-long screws through the sides, countersinking their heads just below the surface.

6 Apply glue to the top rabbet where the top braces go and install them, making the front one flush with the front edge of the side, and the rear brace flush with the bottom of the back rabbet. Install two 1⅝"-long screws in each end of both top braces. Check the assembly for square before setting it aside to dry.

7 After the glue dries, turn the cabinet upside down and attach the wheels. Install the wheel brackets approximately ⅜" from the back and side. Use heavy screws or through bolts with locking nuts.

8 If you are including a drawer, use glue and brads to install the drawer runners now. One runner fits against the underside of the top braces, flush with the front edge of the sides. The second runner goes 4" below the first. Cutting a pair of 4"-long spacers from scrap can be used to get the lower runner parallel to the top one. Use glue and brads to secure the drawer runners.

9 The drawer complicates the edge band. To simplify this process, you will not miter the ends of the edge band. Since this cabinet will probably be painted, mitered corners are not visually important. All edge band parts are installed with glue and brads.

10a No drawer. Install the top rail of the edge band with its top edge flush with the upper edge of the top braces. Install the bottom rail; then, cut and fit the stiles between the upper and lower rails. The stiles fit flush with the outside edge of the sides.

10b Drawer. Frame the opening. Install the top rail of the edge band with its bottom edge covering the upper drawer runners. Install two pieces of ¾" x ¾" stock on the sides of the drawer opening, butting against the upper edge band rail and ending 1⁄16" below the upper surface of the bottom drawer runners. This spaces the next edge band rail down so the drawer does not drag on it. Install that rail, too. Install the bottom rail covering the bottom panel. Cut and fit the stiles to fit between the upper and lower rails. The stiles fit flush with the outside edge of the sides.

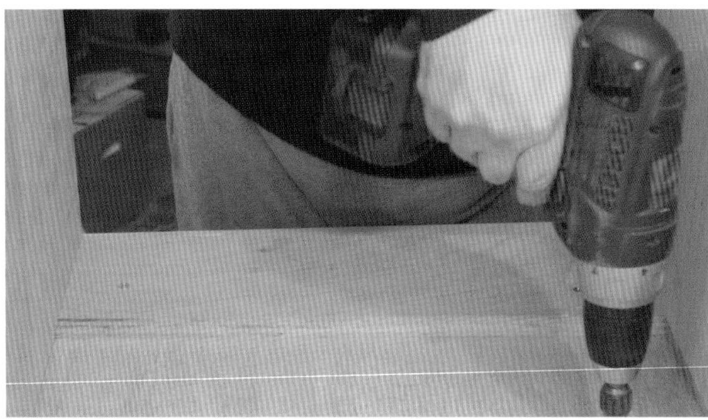

11 Before installing the top, make sure there are no glue beads or other irregularities that would interfere. Spread glue on the top braces before laying the top panel onto them, centered left to right, back edge flush with the back of the cabinet. Clamp it, and install large-diameter (#10 or #12) screws from underneath, through the top braces and into the top panel. Be sure the screws are not so long that they could break through the surface of the top.

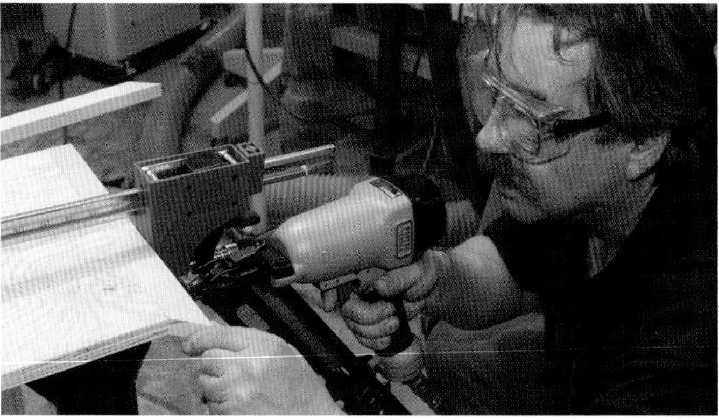

12 Install the ¾" thick x 1" wide edge banding around the sides and front of the top panel, mitering the front corners and stopping at the rear edge. Use glue and long finish nails or countersunk screws to reinforce the banding. **Note:** If you are not installing the drawer, go on to Step 16.

13 To make the drawer, cut the rabbets and then the ¼"-deep groove around the bottom of the sides, front, and back. The groove should be ¼" above the bottom edge of the drawer parts. While cutting the grooves, fit them to the plywood floor material. Dry fit the sides, back, and front panels, measure the bottom opening, and add ⅜" to the length and width to size the bottom panel. Dry fit to be sure the drawer closes; then, glue the rabbets and assemble the drawer, slipping the floor into its groove. Clamp the assembly, and make sure it is square before setting it aside to dry.

Drawer Box

The drawer is built using the same techniques used to build the box in the first project. The difference is that the rabbets are cut in the sides rather than the front and back as you did on the box. Putting the rabbets on the sides and reinforcing the joint with finishing nails or screws adds a tremendous amount of shear strength to resist the forces of pulling it open.

Sizing the Drawer

The key to making a drawer that fits the cavity correctly is cutting ¼"-deep rabbets and sizing the front and back panels correctly. To determine their length, set the sides on the drawer runners against the sides of the cavity, and measure the distance between them. Add ⅜". This accounts for the ¼"-deep rabbets plus ⅛" total side clearance.

14 After the glue dries, sand all four sides and the top and bottom edges to be sure they are smooth. Rounding the rear corners slightly will smooth the operation, as will applying paste wax to the drawer runners and the bottom edge of the drawer itself.

15 After installing the hinges and pull knobs on the door and drawer, install them on the cabinet and check their operation. If the drawer is hard to operate, a small amount of sanding or planing on the top or bottom edge usually remedies that. To limit the drawer, push it in until its front face is flush with the edge band. Glue a small block of wood to the runner so it just touches the back of the drawer.

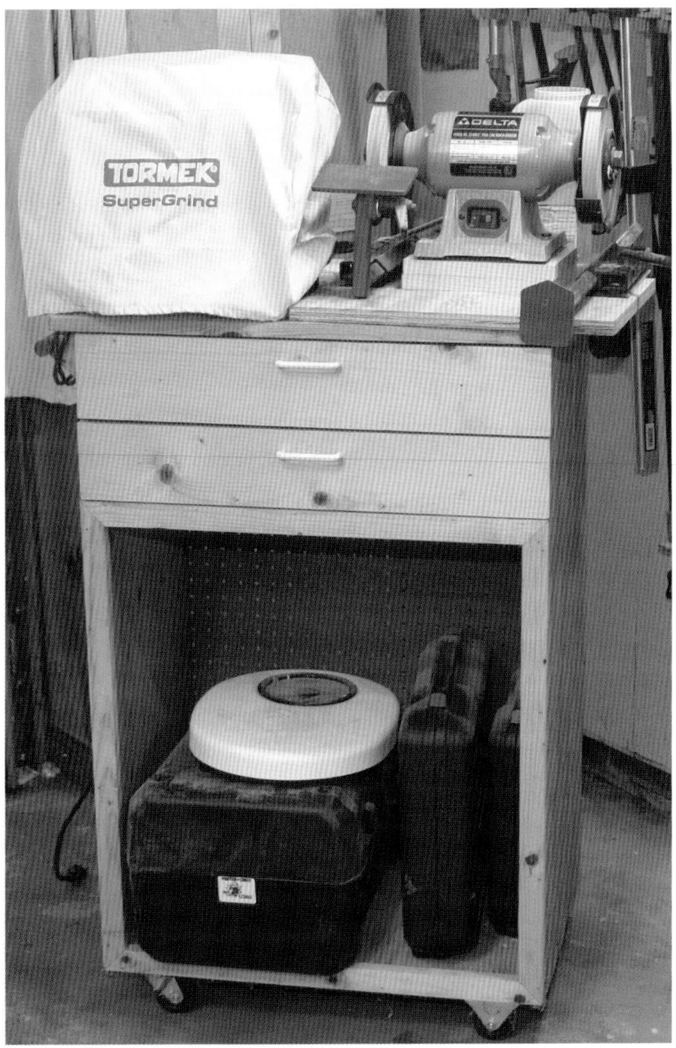

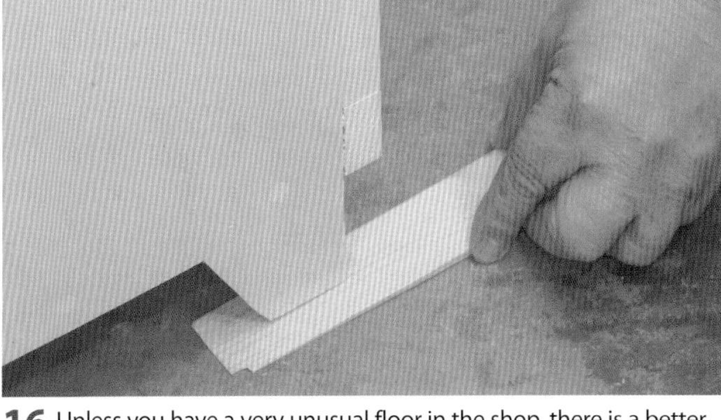

16 Unless you have a very unusual floor in the shop, there is a better than even chance that the base cabinet will rock on its legs and wheels. Depending on how uneven the floor is at various points, the wobbling can get worse or better. Place a shim under the leg that's off the floor the most. I use common wooden shims, available at any home center. Fit the shim under the leg until the rocking stops, mark the shim, apply glue, and reinstall it. After the glue dries, trim away the excess shim with a sharp utility knife—score it, then snap it.

17 Remove the hardware and finish sand to 220 grit the cabinet, door, and drawer. Some makers would varnish the whole drawer inside and out; others would just varnish the front outside. Apply the finish of choice, allow to dry thoroughly, and reinstall the hardware. Check the drawer and door for correct operation, and the project is done.

Coffee table

While easy to build, this coffee table uses the core set of skills required to build a wide range of table styles and sizes.

As our sixth and final project, we'll construct a coffee table. This project is simple but uses the same skill set needed for a large range of table projects. While the scale of the parts will change, the core skills of gluing up the panel for the top and constructing a table-leg-and-frame assembly remain essentially the same.

In the course of this project, you'll learn pocket hole screw technology, a relatively new but popular method of creating simple and strong joints. If you feel comfortable, or adventurous, you'll find that table projects are great for practicing mortise and tenon joints, the traditional method for connecting the legs and apron pieces.

I used a router table and a few common bits to enhance the appearance of the table. A handheld router equipped with a fence could be used for some of these operations, but a router table is safer and easier. As the diameter of the bits used exceeds 1", a router table becomes mandatory for both safety and the quality of the profile produced.

I made the coffee table shown in the photos from red oak, but virtually any species from pine to the most exotic hardwoods could be used. I prefer hardwoods because of their strength, stability, and appearance, but making your first tables from pine can be a good confidence builder.

Building the tabletop will require you to glue up a wide panel of wood from a number of narrower pieces. I started with four boards, all more than 30" long and varying in width. I arranged them to get the best-looking figure pattern. Whenever gluing up a panel, I add 1" to each side of the finished size to allow trimming to final dimensions. The amount of this trim allowance decreases as your skills build, but it never goes away entirely. You will always need a little extra wood to work with.

If you have a jointer and a thickness planer (or access to them), squaring the boards, planing them to identical thickness, and making sure that the edges are straight and square will make the glue-up easy and accurate. This preparation, along with good clamping practices, will produce a flat panel that requires little sanding.

The Versatile Table

This coffee table can be modified in length, width, height, or overall scale. The procedures remain the same; only the parts dimensions change. Adding stretchers between the legs, for strength on larger tables or to support a shelf, is as easy as cutting another set of reduced-width aprons and installing them exactly like the original versions around the top of the frame. The only change would be using one screw at each end of the narrow stretchers.

Tables are one of woodworking's core projects. Once you master the basics of building a solid table, there are no limits on the variations you can build.

Core Skills

- Selecting project wood
- Matching wood figure for a panel glue-up
- Cutting the parts square and to precise length
- Gluing up a large panel
- Using a router to enhance appearance
- Making pocket hole leg-to-apron joints
- Assembling a table frame flat and square
- Mounting a tabletop using metal clips
- Finishing the table

Tools

- Table saw
- Chop saw
- Dado set on table saw, or router table with flat-bottomed router bits
- Pocket hole jig and screws
- Router bits for decorative edges
- Cordless drill and bit for pilot holes
- Combination square and tape measure
- Random orbit sander
- Clamps

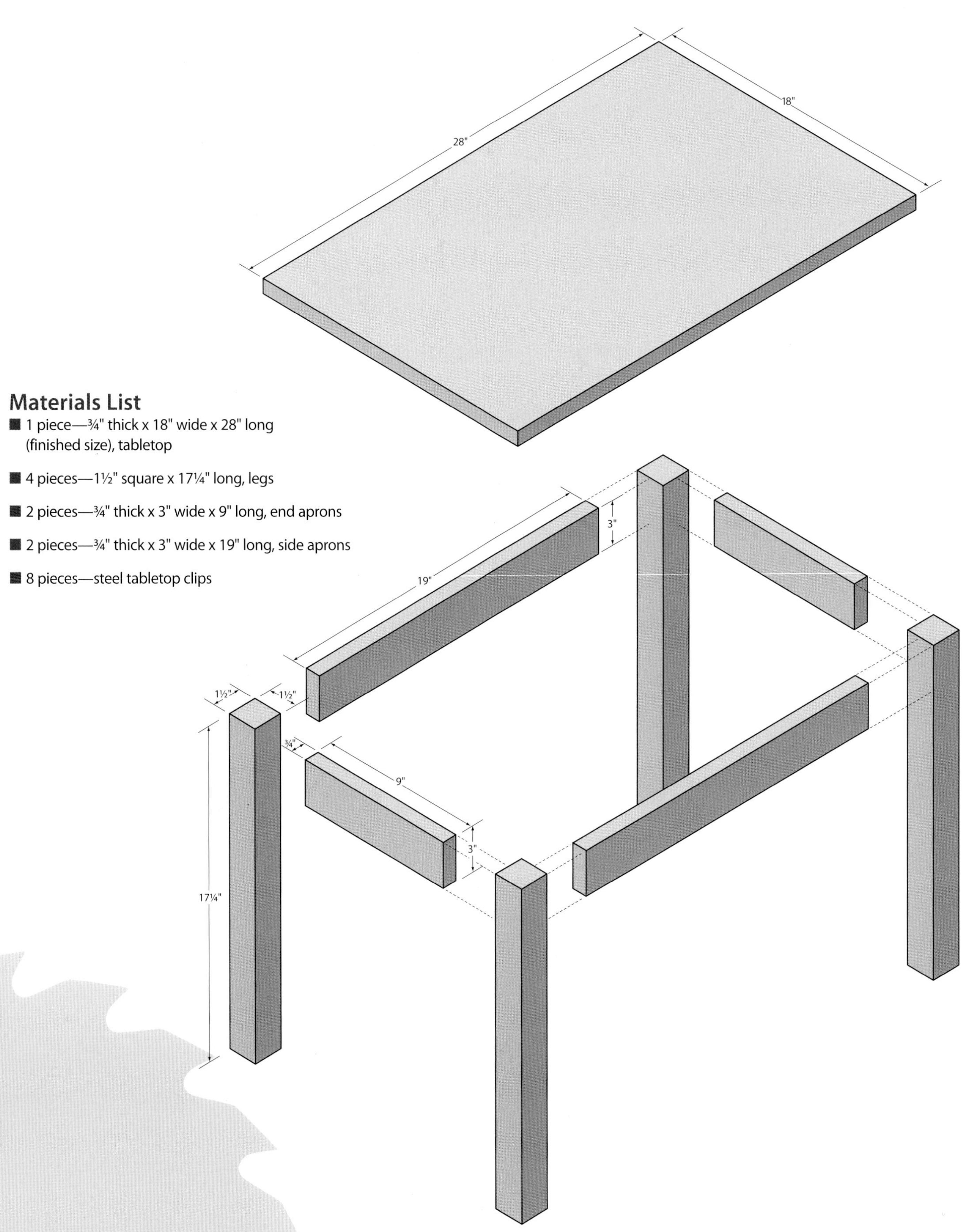

Materials List

- 1 piece—¾" thick x 18" wide x 28" long (finished size), tabletop
- 4 pieces—1½" square x 17¼" long, legs
- 2 pieces—¾" thick x 3" wide x 9" long, end aprons
- 2 pieces—¾" thick x 3" wide x 19" long, side aprons
- 8 pieces—steel tabletop clips

1 When making a tabletop, always choose the best-looking wood figure in each board, and then arrange them for the best board-to-board match. Don't worry about which way the growth rings go.

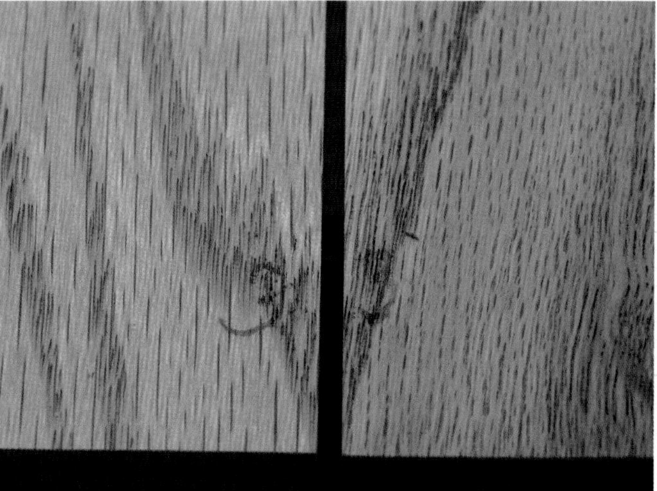

2 Once I had arranged the four boards, I numbered each joint so I could restore its position after the machining processes. It helps to reapply any numbers that machining removes. I also marked a 30" cut-off line on each board, eliminating unattractive figure and defects near the ends.

Gluing Up the Top

My tabletop is held together entirely by glue, a thin and uniform coating on all mating edges. I didn't use any joint reinforcement techniques or hardware. With straight and square edges on all the boards, glue alone is more than sufficient to keep the panel together.

Once you have applied light clamping pressure, check all of the joint lines to be sure they are flush, and use a dead-blow mallet to tap them into alignment. Make sure the joint lines are flush; then, snug the clamps down just enough to raise little beads of glue from the joints. Apply additional clamps as needed to maintain uniform pressure on the panel. I like to have a clamp every foot or so and alternate them top and bottom.

Let the panel assembly sit in the clamps for a few minutes, and then go back and check the alignment of the individual boards. If excess glue was trapped in a joint, a board may float out of alignment. If you don't tap it back into place before the glue sets up, there will be lots of sanding in your future. When you're satisfied with the alignment, snug the clamps down, and then leave it alone! You might be able to handle the panel in a few hours but leaving it to dry overnight is much safer.

With the boards prepared, lay out the clamps on a flat surface, and open them wider than the full set of boards. Apply glue, assemble the boards according to your marks, and apply light clamp pressure.

You might find it difficult to keep the edges aligned while clamping, and most joint enhancement techniques are meant to solve alignment problems, not to add any strength. My favorite panel joint enhancement is the profile cut by a glue-line router bit. Biscuits are also popular because they are easy to install. Dowels can be effective but are quite difficult to install with the necessary precision.

3 When the glue has dried, remove the top from the clamps, and scrape away glue beads. Sand both sides smooth with the random orbit sander, paying particular attention to the joint lines. Start at 80 grit or 120 grit, but switch to finer disks as soon as the top surface flattens, ending at 220 grit or 320 grit.

4 Trim the top to its final dimensions. I jointed one long edge, put that against the table saw fence, and ripped the panel to its final 18" width, making those edges parallel at the same time.

5 I used a shop-made panel-cutting sled to saw the top to final length (28"). You could also use a handheld circular saw with a straight board as a clamped-on fence.

6 To rout the edges of the tabletop, I used two profiles: a ⅜" round-over bit to ease the bottom edge, and a ½" cove bit to shape the upper edge. I did not have a final depth of cut in mind but rather made several light cuts until the cove looked right.

Routing the Edges

The edges of the coffee tabletop can be left square, but routing a profile adds a more finished look and enhances the overall appearance. The choice of which bit profiles to use is wide open, but the more common ones are round-overs, ogees, and bevels. Take a look at the catalog or website of the bit manufacturers to see a selection of profiles.

When profiling the edges of a panel like the coffee tabletop, first rout the end grain on both ends, and then rout the sides. When routing across the end grain, the wood is likely to chip as the bit exits the wood. A backer block may help but can be awkward because of the panel size—and that makes it dangerous. Routing the long-grain sides after the end grain removes any chipped wood.

Make several light passes to produce the best finish and to avoid excessive chipping and tearout. Get in the habit of routing the end grain first and then the long-grain sides. Regardless of how light the cuts are, sticking with this sequence—along with a clean, sharp bit and moderate feed rate—will produce the best results.

To remove chipping that often occurs as the bit exits the wood, rout the end-grain edge first and then the long-grain sides.

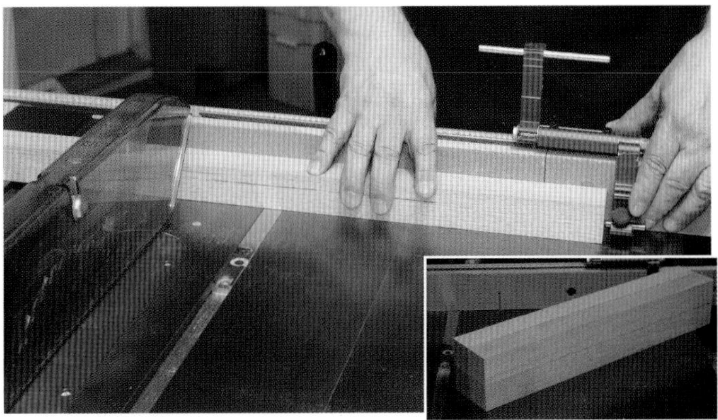

7 Cutting identical-length legs and matching pairs of aprons is crucial for making a table that doesn't rock. Use a stop block on a properly aligned table saw miter guide or on the miter (chop) saw.

8 I used part of a ¼" round-over bit profile to ease all four long edges of the legs. Balance the cut by making one pass on all four long edges; then, turn the leg end over end, and make a second pass.

9 Round the bottom of each leg to prevent chipping when the table is dragged across the floor. The round-over bit has a bearing that limits the depth of cut, but you should also use a safety pin (also called a starter pin) to help ease the wood into the bit.

10 These formed steel clips will secure the tabletop to the frame, so you need to cut a groove for them along the top inside edge of the apron pieces. The groove is ⅛" wide by ¼" deep, so you can cut it on the table saw using a standard blade. Cut the groove along the inside top edge of all four apron parts.

Use the Router Table

Using two profiles can be difficult with a handheld router because the first cut can remove the very part of the edge that the next bit's guide bearing needs to follow. In a router table with a fence, using multiple profiles is easy and safe because you set the fence flush with the front of the bearing. The fence controls the depth of cut. As long as a little bit of straight edge remains, even a narrow or rounded one, it's easy and accurate to guide the workpiece past the bit.

Locating the Groove

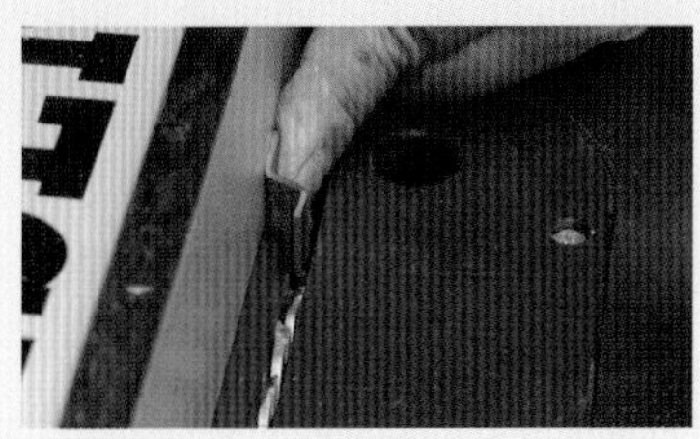

When you use steel tabletop clips, you want the apron groove that holds them to be in exactly the right place. With the table saw unplugged, adjust the blade height to ¼". Hold one of the clips against the fence, and adjust the fence-to-blade distance so the top edge of the clip is even with the edge of the blade nearest to the fence. This places the groove so the installed clips will have a small amount of preload, helping them hold the top securely in place without creating too much pressure.

11 I used a plain V-shaped bit in the router table to cut a shallow groove ½" above the outside bottom edge of the apron pieces to add a subtle shadow line and give the entire piece a more finished appearance.

12 I roughly centered the pocket holes between the tabletop clip groove and the bottom edge of the apron. Don't place the holes too close to the edge of the apron. After drilling two pocket holes in both ends of all four aprons, give the legs and frame parts a final sanding.

13 To add another visual point of interest, I used a flat hardboard spacer to set the aprons ¼" in from the outside face of the legs. This setback (or reveal) also butts the ends of the aprons squarely against the flat portion of the leg.

Pocket Hole Screws

I like pocket hole technology because it produces strong, attractive joints quickly and easily. Plus, the cost of the various jig versions is reasonable enough to fit even fledgling shop budgets. Pocket hole screws will never entirely replace traditional joints such as the mortise and tenon. However, they are useful in general woodworking and are a good alternative while you develop joinery skills.

The pocket hole jig block has two or three drill guide bushings that direct a specially shaped drill bit so it bores a pocket and pilot hole aimed at the center of the wood thickness. The jigs are adjustable to accommodate several thicknesses. The square-drive pocket hole screws are self-tapping, so only one side of the joint has to be drilled. Pocket hole screws have a flat-bottomed head. When seated, these screws generate a substantial amount of clamping force, and when combined with glue, the joint is surprisingly strong.

The most frequent error seems to be drilling the pocket holes on the wrong side of the workpiece. For our purposes, remember that the tabletop clip groove is on the same side of the apron as the pocket holes. Most pocket hole jigs have two or three drilling guides spaced for making two holes in a range of stock widths.

Pocket hole screws are self-tapping and have a flat head that pulls the joint together with surprising strength. Install them with glue.

14 Assemble the ends of the frame (short aprons) first for easier access. Apply glue to both ends of the apron, and then lay out the parts on a flat surface with the apron piece resting on the ¼" spacer, clip-groove side facing up. Align the top of the legs with the top edge of the apron, and clamp.

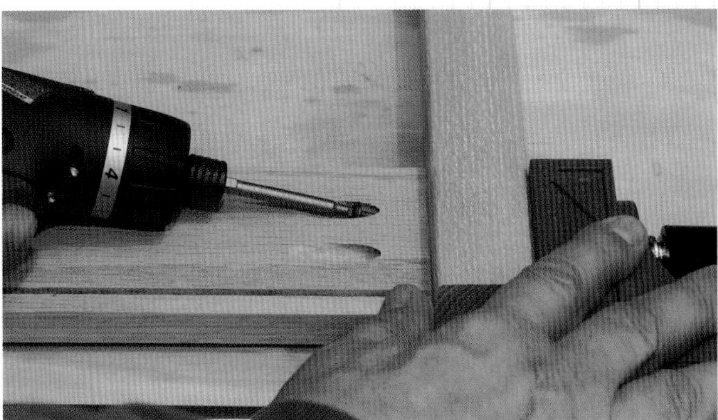

15 Drive pocket hole screws into each hole, seating them firmly. There is nothing to be gained by overtightening these screws. They will form a very strong joint.

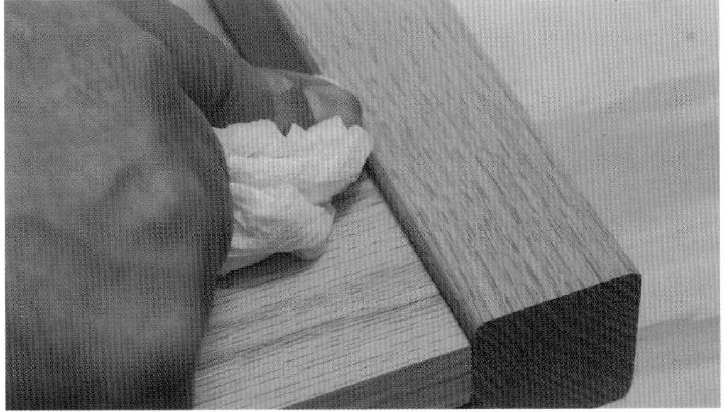

16 After installing all four screws, remove the assembly from the clamps, and use a damp rag to wipe up any squeezed-out glue. Repeat the assembly process for the other frame end.

17 Repeat the process to join the long side aprons to the end assemblies. If the apron ends were cut square and if the legs are square, the assembly should also be square, but check it anyway.

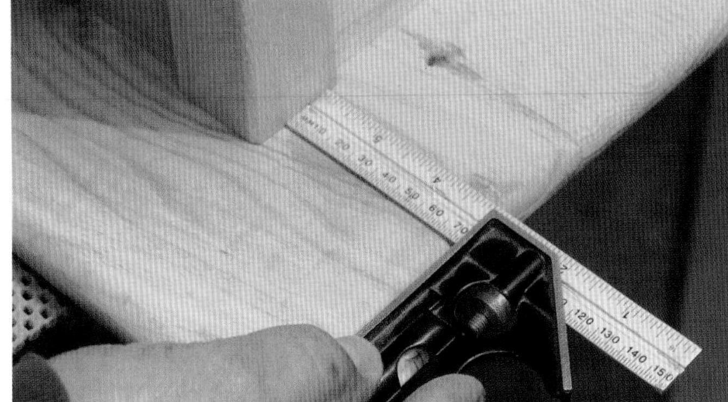

18 Lay the top and frame upside down on a padded surface. Use a combination square to help you center the frame 3" from the edges of the top. Draw around the inside edges of all four legs, and make an orientation mark so you can return the top to the same position.

Square Enough?

It is difficult to correct an out-of-square condition on assemblies like this table base. The best option is to place a clamp across the longest diagonal and apply enough pressure to pull the assembly into squareness.

Unless the frame was excessively crooked, with a difference of more than ½" when measuring the diagonals, I would leave it alone. The top of the frame will be hidden from view, so an out-of-square condition will be invisible to everyone but you. Remembering this kind of problem encourages new woodworkers to perfect their stock preparation techniques for future projects.

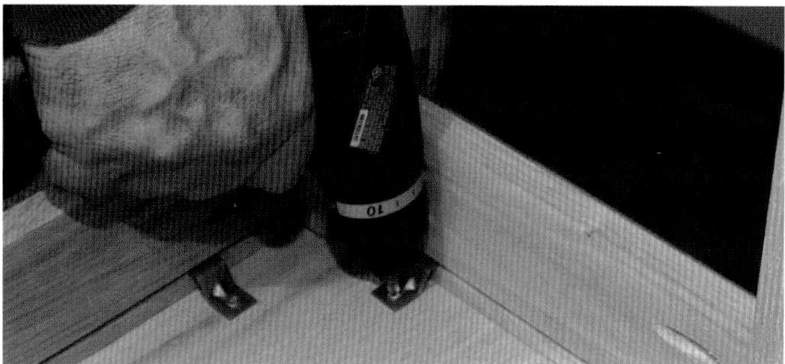

19 Slip a steel tabletop clip into the groove a couple inches from each leg, two per side. Drill shallow pilot holes and install a ½"-long #6 wood screw to secure each clip. If the clips do not snug up in the apron grooves, clamp them in a vise and bend them a little by tapping with a hammer.

20 The final construction step is to make sure the table does not rock when placed on a truly flat surface—whenever the size allows, I use the cast-iron surface of my table saw. For larger tables, use a heavy sheet of MDF.

21 When sanding is complete, use a new tack rag to wipe the dust from all surfaces. This crucial step does not take long but if skipped can ruin the finish. I used red oak oil-based stain, followed by three coats of clear satin polyurethane varnish.

Tip!

Take It Apart

When satisfied with the assembly and stability, remove the frame from the top for finishing. There is no sense in working around the frame when it comes apart so easily. Also, with the frame and top separated, it's easy to apply a full coat of finish to all of the surfaces. This goes a long way toward slowing down moisture exchange with the atmosphere.

Leveling the Table

It's frustrating that there are few truly flat surfaces in the average home, or in the workshop for that matter. Floors covered with tile, wood, or other hard surface materials may look perfectly flat, but they seldom are. This becomes painfully evident when an otherwise wobble-free table is set on them.

If your table wobbles on the table saw surface, there are two ways to correct it. The best, and most labor intensive, is to identify the long leg or legs and shorten it or them just enough to eliminate the wobble. The other way is to add a set of adjustable feet, which may also serve as glides or floor protectors.

The good news is that unless you have made serious errors during cutting or assembly, shortening one leg usually corrects the problem without throwing the table out of level to any noticeable degree.

With the table on the cast-iron surface, slip a sheet of 100-grit sandpaper (grit up) under the long leg. While holding a little downward pressure on that leg, pull the sandpaper across the bottom of the leg. Each pull removes a small amount of material, sneaking up on the exact length needed. I remove the sandpaper to check my progress after every three or four pulls to avoid making the long leg the short one. When the wobble is almost gone, switch to 150- or 220-grit paper to complete the repair. A few strokes with the finer paper also readies the end of the leg for finishing.

In the case of a major wobble, the only answer may be sawing a slice from one or more legs, followed by this sanding technique to finish the repair. In that situation, I would find an attractive set of leveling feet instead.

Place a sheet of sandpaper under the long leg, apply a little downward pressure to the leg, and pull the sandpaper to remove a little wood.

Glossary

Air Dried Lumber. Lumber dried through exposure to the air, without artificial heating. The lumber is usually stacked (separated by narrow pieces of wood called stickers), covered, and then left to season one year for every 1" of thickness.

Aliphatic Resin. The most commonly used glue in woodworking. Usually called yellow glue, this adhesive is water-soluble in its liquid state, does not produce harmful vapors, and is non-toxic. Some newer versions are moisture-resistant and have longer open times.

Alternate Top Bevel (ATB). A common tooth pattern on many circular saw blades. Generally, one tooth is beveled to the right, one is beveled to the left, and another is ground straight. While ATB designs may vary in number and order of teeth, their purpose is the same: The angled teeth slice the wood fibers along the edges, and the flat tooth cleans the cut.

Annual Growth Ring. A layer of wood produced by a single year's growth of a tree. In most species, each layer forms a distinct dark-colored ring within the tree, resulting in the darker lines found in wood.

Anti-Kickback Pawls. A pair of spring-loaded, toothed arms, one installed on each side of the splitter, that grip the wood, preventing it from moving back toward the operator during a cut. Usually found on a table saw or radial arm saw.

Apron. The horizontal framework that supports a tabletop.

Arbor. The revolving spindle to which a table saw blade is attached.

Back Saw. A handheld saw with a thin blade reinforced by a folded metal spine along its top edge.

Bench Dog. A metal or wooden peg that fits into round or square holes in a workbench top, forming end stops that hold a workpiece in place.

Bevel. An edge at any angle other than 90 degrees. Bevels are often used as a form of decoration on wood and are also found on the cutting edge of tools such as chisels.

Biscuit. A football-shaped piece of pressed hardwood (usually beech) that is used to align and reinforce joints. The biscuit is set into crescent-shaped slots cut into the edges of two pieces of wood with a biscuit joiner.

Blade Parallelism. The key table saw alignment, in which the face of the blade is made parallel to the miter slot in the table surface. Blade parallelism is crucial to the performance of the blade and the saw as well as to safety.

Blade Stabilizers. A pair of large, flat washer-like pieces, one installed against each side of a circular blade (primarily on the table saw), that limit flexing of the blade during cuts.

Board Foot. A common unit of measurement used when buying lumber. One board foot equals the volume of a piece of wood 1" thick by 12" wide by 12" long, or 144 cubic inches.

Bookmatch. A pair of identical resawn boards, usually sliced thin, that are cut from the same piece of wood and laid side by side, like the pages of a book, to produce a mirror-like grain image.

Bow. A warp over the length of a board.

Box Joint. A joint consisting of a series of interlocking square cuts (sometimes called fingers) often used to make the corners of boxes. When properly cut and glued, box joints are exceptionally strong and can be very attractive. Also called a finger joint.

Brad. A thin finishing nail with a small head. Brads are used to secure small pieces or to hold a piece in position while glue dries.

Brad Point Bit. A specialized drill bit designed for cutting clean holes in all types of wood. The most prominent feature is a spear-like point that helps keep the drill on a layout mark. Some brad point bits also have extended cutters at the outer edges that slice the grain for a cleaner edge. These bits are available in most common drill sizes.

Butt Joint. A joint in which one board sets squarely against another (usually end to wide face), with no interlocking features in either. Though very simple to make, butt joints are also very weak and must be reinforced with mechanical fasteners such as screws, biscuits, or dowels.

CA (Cyanoacrylate) Glue. An adhesive that forms a hard bond almost instantly. CA glues are most commonly used to tack small pieces in place while more permanent glues dry. Super Glue is a brand of CA glue.

Cfm. Cubic feet per minute. A measurement of the amount of air that flows through an air cleaner or dust collector, that is generated by a compressor, or that is required to operate an air tool.

Chamfer. An angled edge, frequently used as a form of decoration on wood. A chamfer is similar to a bevel but usually not as wide.

Chuck. A device that secures a bit or cutter in drills and lathes.

Clear. A piece of wood with no knots or defects.

Closed Coat. Sandpaper with grit completely covering its surface, primarily used for sanding harder woods. See also "Open Coat."

CNC (Computer Numerically Controlled). A high-precision machine control system used by manufacturers to produce parts that are identical to tolerances within thousandths of an inch.

Collet. A chuck-like device on a router that locks the router bit in place.

Combination Square. A square with 90-degree and 45-degree surfaces on the body and a sliding blade, often with multiple resolution scales printed on it.

Compound Cut. A cut made with two angles, one to the face and one to the edge of a board; for example, a cut made across the flat face of a board at a 45-degree angle with the saw tilted to also cut a 20-degree bevel in the thickness.

Contact Cement. An adhesive primarily used for bonding laminates and other sheet coverings to wood substrates.

Cope and Stick Joint. A technique for building a frame (such as on a cabinet door) using router bits that cut matching profiles in the sides of the stiles and ends of the rails.

Coplanar. The alignment of two surfaces. Coplanar is often used to describe the alignment of the infeed and outfeed tables of a jointer or the upper and lower blade wheels of a band saw.

Countersink. To drive a screw into a hole so that its head is below the surface. Also, a tool that cuts the stepped hole for a screw's threads and its head.

Crosscut. To saw a board across its width, perpendicular to the grain.

Cup. A common defect across the width of a board, in which the edges are raised above the center of the board, creating an arch.

Dado. A flat-bottomed groove cut across the grain of wood.

Dado Joint. A joint made by cutting a flat-bottomed groove (dado) in one piece of wood and then fitting another piece of wood into the dado. Dado joints are most commonly used to install shelves into the vertical sides of a cabinet.

Dovetail Joint. A joint consisting of a series of interlocking pins and sockets. Named for its resemblance to a dove's tail feathers, this joint is considered one of the strongest and best-looking in wood. See also "Half-Blind Dovetail Joint" and "Through Dovetail Joint."

Dowel. A round, wooden pin used to reinforce simple joints.

Edge Guide. A clamped-on board or other straight piece used as a guide for a handheld saw or router. Also, a guide attached to a router for making a cut using the edge of a piece of wood as a guide.

End Grain. The grain structure at the ends of a board. Also called short grain, this grain structure is made up of the ends of the wood fibers, which can be difficult to glue or cut. When end grain is part of a joint (end grain to end grain, or end grain to long grain), the ends of the wood fibers afford glue very little to grip. Also, cutting across the end grain tends to fray the ends of the fibers. See also "Grain" and "Long Grain."

Epoxy. A two-part adhesive that is very strong, water-resistant, and has varying open times. Epoxies are especially good for gluing metal to wood.

Face. The wide surface, or "top," of a board as opposed to the narrow, thickness edges.

Fastener. Any of various nails, screws, or staples used to attach one piece of wood to another.

Featherboard. A board with lightweight, flexible fingers cut into one end that is used to apply pressure against a workpiece to maintain its contact with a fence, reducing the risk of kickback.

Feed Direction. The direction in which wood is fed into a cutter. To maintain control, wood must be fed against the rotation of a cutter. If the wood is introduced to a cutter in the same direction that the cutter is rotating, the cutter will simply grab the wood and throw it out of the machine.

Feeler Gauges. A set of thin metal strips of varying thicknesses used for checking small dimensions when setting up tools or jigs.

Fence. A rail that guides wood or a cutting tool.

Finger Joint. See "Box Joint."

Finish. A material applied to wood to protect it or enhance its appearance, such as oil, stain, or paint.

Finishing Nail. A nail with a very small head designed to be driven below the surface of the wood and then concealed with putty or another filler.

Flake Board. See "Oriented Strand Board (OSB)."

Flat Sawn. Boards made by slicing a log through and through. Flat-sawn lumber has whorls and long Vs on the surface and broad arcs on the ends. Also called plain sawn.

Footprint. The total physical size of a machine, not just the area taken up by the leg set or base. Footprint is calculated by measuring straight down to the floor at the machine's largest dimensions, including fence rails, permanent table extensions, or any other parts that project out from the primary mass. See also "Useprint."

Forstner Bit. A specialized drill bit designed for boring very clean, flat-bottomed holes in wood. Forstner bits have a centering point with one or two horizontal shaving cutters and a surrounding circular cutter that cleans the edges of the hole. Commonly available in sizes from ¼" to more than 2", some Forstner bits have a smooth outer edge, while others, particularly the larger sizes, have saw-like teeth cut into the edge.

French Cleat. A pair of wooden strips, each with a 45-degree beveled edge, used to hang cabinets. One strip is mounted to the wall, and the other to the cabinet.

Gauge Block. A piece of wood clamped to a fence that positions workpieces for accurate cutting and helps prevent kickback.

Glue Line Router Bit. A specialized router bit that cuts an interlocking profile in the edges of two boards being joined. Typically, one board is cut face up, and the one being joined to it is cut face down. This profile both increases the available gluing surface and helps keep the joint aligned.

Grain. The direction of the fibers in wood. Wood is essentially a bundle of small tube-like fibers that run vertically through a tree. This bundle of fibers is what gives wood its strength but also what complicates cutting and shaping. Trying to plane, shave, or rout wood against, rather than with, the grain is likely to cause chipping or splitting.

Gullet. The curved area at the base of a saw blade tooth. Gullets help carry chips and dust out of the kerf and also introduce air to the cut to help control the temperatures of the blade and the wood.

Half-Blind Dovetail Joint. A type of dovetail joint in which the sockets cut into the edge of the wood do not go all the way through the wood, hiding the joint when viewed from the front. See also "Dovetail Joint" and "Through Dovetail Joint."

Half-Lap Joint. A simple but very strong joint made by removing half of the thickness on opposing sides of two pieces of wood so that, when joined, the surfaces are flush with each other. Typically used at 90-degree corners, half-lap joints are occasionally used in end-to-end and angled joints.

Hardwood. Wood cut from deciduous trees (with broad leaves), such as oak.

Hook Angle. In circular saw blades, the angle of the teeth in relation to the center of the arbor hole. This angle varies between 5 degrees and 25 degrees, with the larger, more aggressive angles found on ripping blades and other designs made for relatively fast cutting. As the number of teeth increases, the hook angle is generally reduced to help promote ultra-clean cuts.

Hot-Melt Polyurethane Glue. An adhesive that has the strength and waterproof qualities of liquid polyurethane but a much shorter open time. Hot-melt poly glues are primarily used for tacking parts in place while more permanent adhesives dry or mechanical fasteners are installed.

Infeed. The side of a machine from which wood is introduced or fed. Also, a table or surface on which wood rests as it is fed into a machine.

Jig. A fixture used to hold wood in correct position for accurate cutting or machining.

Kerf. The width of material removed by a saw blade. Standard table saw blades remove about ⅛" of wood, while thin-kerf models cut about 3/32" of wood away.

Kickback. A dangerous event in which a piece of wood is thrown out of a table saw or router table and back at the operator.

Kickout. A hazardous situation in which a piece of wood is grabbed by the router bit and ejected at a high rate of speed. Kickout most often occurs when the wood is fed into the router bit in the same direction that the bit is rotating, rather than against the rotation.

Kiln Dried Lumber. Lumber that is dried to a specific moisture content, usually 10% or less, in a chamber having controlled air flow, temperature, and relative humidity.

Knockdown. A table or rack that can be disassembled when not in use.

Laminate. Plastic or other man-made material that is attached to a flat piece of wood to achieve a custom look and/or to protect the wood's surface.

Lift Plate. A table-mounted plate to which a router is attached. Lift plates have a mechanism that raises or lowers the router to change the height of the cutting bit.

Long Grain. The grain structure along the face and long edges of a board. Gluing long grain to long grain is always preferred because adhesives can grip around the fibers, creating a very strong joint. See also "End Grain" and "Grain."

Measuring Diagonals. A method of checking square or rectangular box-type projects for squareness. The dimension measured from the top right corner to the lower left corner should be identical to that measured from the top left corner to the lower right corner.

Medium-Density Fiberboard (MDF). A manufactured sheet material made by combining wood sawdust and adhesives under pressure. Sold in many of the same sizes as plywood, MDF can be purchased plain but is frequently used as the base for laminate-covered materials.

Medium-Density Overlay (MDO). Plywood with a paper (usually Kraft paper) covering on one or both flat faces. The paper covering provides a flat surface that takes paint very well. Available in common plywood sheet sizes, MDO can be difficult to find in some areas. Asking a local sign painter is often the best way to track down a supplier.

Miter Box. A box with slots cut at precise angles to guide a handheld saw when cutting miters and other joinery.

Miter Gauge. An adjustable fence mounted on a bar that rides in the miter slots on table saws, band saws, and other woodworking machines to guide material across the blade or cutter in a straight line. A miter gauge usually has an adjustment feature to lock the fence at a known angle for making miter cuts. Also called a miter guide.

Miter Guide. See "Miter Gauge."

Miter Joint. A joint formed by cutting complementary angles on two pieces of wood that are then joined to produce a specific angle. Most common is cutting 45-degree angles on two pieces to form a 90-degree joint. Miter joints vary in strength, depending on the orientation of the wood.

Morse Taper. A standardized taper used to mount various tool components, such as drill chucks and drive centers, on lathes.

Mortise. A square or rectangular hole that makes up half of a mortise and tenon joint. The other half, the tenon, is cut to fit the mortise snugly.

Mortise and Tenon Joint. A joint made by cutting a square or rectangular hole (mortise) in one board and a projection (tenon) in the mating board. The tenon is then inserted into the mortise, forming a hidden but extremely strong joint.

Nominal. The size of lumber before it is planed. The actual dimensions of a board will be less than its nominal size due to shrinkage and milling; for example, a board that is nominally 2" X 4" actually measures 1½" X 3½".

Ogee. A traditional S-shaped profile cut by a router or shaper bit.

Open Coat. Sandpaper with grit covering less than 70% of its surface, primarily used for sanding softer woods. See also "Closed Coat."

Open Time. The period from the time an adhesive is applied until the time it begins to harden, or set up. While fast setup is often desirable in speed building, a longer open time is preferred with complicated assemblies, such as when having to align several pieces at once. Also called set time or working time.

Oriented Strand Board (OSB). A manufactured sheet material made by combining chips or flakes of wood, the fibers roughly aligned in opposing layers, with adhesives. OSB is frequently used as sheathing in home building and has limited usefulness in woodworking for back panels or projects with low appearance demands. Also called flake board.

Outfeed. The side of a machine from which wood exits. Also, a table or surface on which wood rests as it exits a machine.

Pilot Hole. A hole pre-drilled in wood so that a screw can be driven easily into the wood without splitting it. The diameter of the hole is slightly smaller than that of the screw so that the screw's threads are still able to grip the wood.

Pin Nail. A small nail, usually driven by an air-powered gun, used to tack pieces of wood in place while an adhesive dries.

Plain Sawn. See "Flat Sawn."

Planer Tooth. See "Raker Tooth."

Pocket Hole Joint. A joint made by drilling a hole at a steep angle (pocket hole) into the face of a piece of wood and then driving a long screw through the pocket and into an adjoining piece of wood. Commonly used to make face frames and doorframes for cabinets, pocket hole joints are very strong.

Polyurethane Glue. An adhesive that is waterproof, strong, and has a long open time. Poly glues are ideal for outdoor projects.

Push Block. A flat, rubber-bottomed pad with an elevated handle; used to push stock safely across the table of a machine.

Push Handle. A long, flat piece of wood or composite with an elevated handle and a "heel" near the rear that hooks over stock; used to push stock safely across the table of a machine.

Push Stick. A straight piece of wood or plastic with a formed handle on one end and a notch on the other end that hooks over stock; used to push stock safely across the table of a machine.

Quarter Sawn. Boards cut from a log in a pattern that aligns their wide faces across the annual growth rings. Quarter-sawn lumber has long, straight lines on the surface and short arcs on the ends. It is considered the best cut and is the most expensive.

Rabbet. A ledge or shoulder cut along the edge of a piece of wood.

Rabbet Joint. A joint made by cutting a ledge (rabbet) in one piece of wood to a width and depth sized to accept another piece. Commonly used to conceal the end grain of crosspieces such as cabinet back panels, rabbet joints are often reinforced with mechanical fasteners.

Rail. The horizontal part of a door frame, face frame, or similar structure. On doors, rails always run between the vertical stiles that extend fully from the top to the bottom of the door. The rails are usually 10% to 30% wider than the stiles to enhance the visual appeal of the door.

Raker Tooth. A tooth in circular and band saw blades that clears chips or sawdust from the kerf. Also called a planer tooth.

Reading the Grain. Determining the direction and angle at which the grain in wood runs. Whenever possible, cutting or machining should go with the grain; working against the grain can cause the edges of the grain to lift, resulting in a rough surface or even a failure of the wood.

Relief Angle. The downward bevel on the back of cutting teeth that prevents them from dragging on the bottom of the cut as they swing through an arc.

Resaw. To cut a board from edge to edge through its width in order to produce two thinner boards. Also, a band saw specially equipped for resawing.

Rift Sawn. Boards sawn somewhere between flat sawn and quarter sawn. Rift-sawn lumber tends to have straight lines on the surface, possibly with some whorls and Vs, and has diagonal lines on the ends.

Rip. To saw a board along its length, parallel to the grain of the wood, making the board narrower.

Rough Sawn. Boards cut to approximate size but not planed smooth. Usually, rough-sawn wood is thick enough that it can be planed and jointed to common finished dimensions.

Runout. The wobble in a rotating piece, such as a table saw blade, table saw arbor, or router shaft.

Set Time. See "Open Time."

Shank. The metal shaft of a router bit that is inserted into the collet of the router.

Shear. A joint or fastener is said to be in shear when forces being applied try to push through it rather than applying twisting or torquing forces. For example, the end of a shelf captured in a dado is in shear when the weight of the books pushes down on it. Typically, a joint or fastener can withstand considerably more shear force than leveraged force such as twisting or torquing.

Short Grain. See "End Grain."

Snipe. A shallow depression inadvertently made at one or both ends of a board, usually with a thickness planer but occasionally with a jointer. Snipe occurs when the board is not adequately supported by a table or other surface as it enters or exits the machine.

Softwood. Wood cut from coniferous trees (with needle-like leaves), such as pine.

Spline. A thin piece of wood cut to fit into grooves in another piece to help align the two. The grain in the spline must run across the joint, not parallel to it.

Splitter. A simple device, usually made of flat steel, that prevents the saw kerf from closing on the back of the blade as tension within a piece of wood is released during a cut. Splitters are an integral part of most blade guard/anti-kickback assemblies on table saws.

Square. A tool used to ensure that one edge of a layout or assembly is 90 degrees to another edge. Squares are also available for measuring 45-degree and other angles and for checking the alignment of machines.

Stacked Dado Head. A specialized tool consisting of a series of blades and chippers that can be arranged to produce various-width dados and grooves.

Stile. The vertical part of a door frame, face frame, or similar structure. Stiles always run the full height of a door, with the horizontal rails captured between them. The stiles are usually 10% to 30% narrower than the rails.

Tack Rag. A cloth (usually cheesecloth) that contains a sticky resin. Tack rags are used to wipe fine dust from wood before finishing it.

Tearout. The tendency of a cutter to chip or split a workpiece, typically at the end of the cut.

Tenon. A projection at the end of a wooden part, cut to fit snugly into a mortise to make a tenon and mortise joint.

Through Dovetail Joint. A type of dovetail joint formed by cutting the angled pieces completely through both pieces of wood being joined. Through dovetails are often used in box-type projects because of their strength and visual appeal. See also "Dovetail Joint" and "Half-Blind Dovetail Joint."

Tongue-and-Groove Joint. A weaker form of a mortise and tenon joint, in which a spline (tongue) on one board fits into a groove cut into a mating board.

Useprint. The amount of space required to actually cut or machine wood on a machine, not the physical size of the machine itself. If useprint is not considered, the useable capacity of the machine may be reduced by obstructions.

Warp. A curve or arch in a board.

Working Time. See "Open Time."

Zero-Clearance Insert. A composite, metal, plastic, or wood insert covering an access hole surrounding a blade or cutter. The opening in the insert is cut to fit the blade or cutter very closely to provide maximum support for the wood and to prevent small pieces from becoming wedged between the cutter and the insert itself.

Index

More Great Books from Fox Chapel Publishing

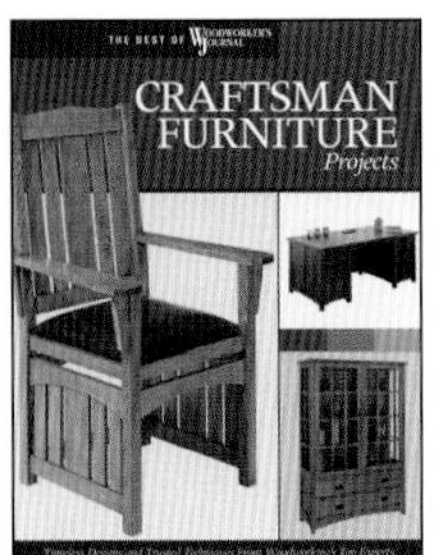

Craftsman Furniture Projects
By Editors of Woodworker's Journal
17 Craftsman-style projects from the experts at *Woodworker's Journal.*
$17.95
ISBN 978-1-56523-324-9

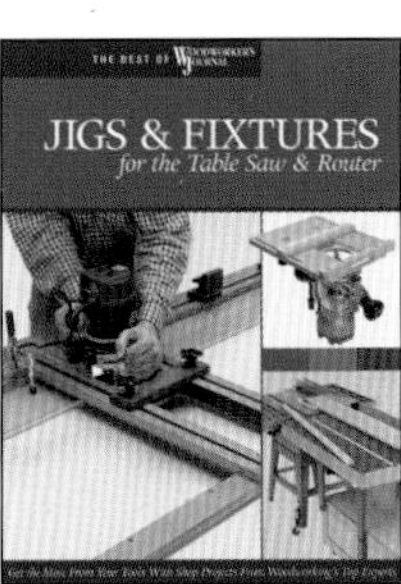

Jigs & Fixtures for the Table Saw & Router
By Editors of Woodworker's Journal
Learn the tricks of the trade with over 25 jig and fixture projects from the experts at *Woodworker's Journal.*
$17.95
ISBN 978-1-56523-325-6

Boxes, Clocks, Lamps & Small Projects
By Editors of Woodworker's Journal
Features over 20 small, well-designed projects from the experts at *Woodworker's Journal.*
$17.95
ISBN 978-1-56523-328-7

Woodworker's Pocket Reference
By Charlie Self
Everything a woodworker needs to know in an easy-to-read, quick-to-find format.
$14.95
ISBN 978-1-56523-239-6

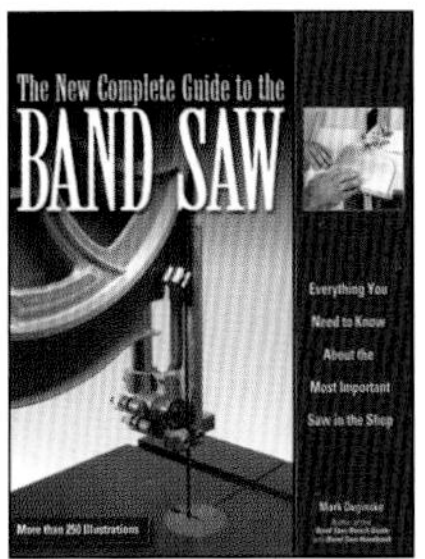

The New Complete Guide to the Band Saw
By Mark Duginske
Learn to master the workshop's most important saw. Contains over 500 photographs and illustrations.
$19.95
ISBN 978-1-56523-318-8

Foolproof Wood Finishing
By Teri Masaschi
Take the mystery out of finishing with easy-to-follow exercises designed by one of the nation's premier finishing instructors.
$19.95
ISBN 978-1-56523-303-4

Look For These Books at Your Local Bookstore or Woodworking Retailer

Or call 800-457-9112 • Visit www.FoxChapelPublishing.com

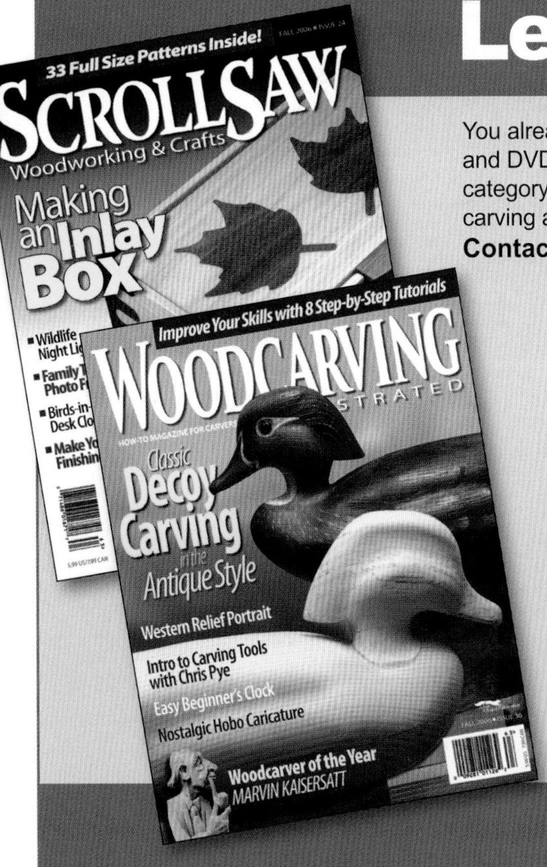

Learn from the Experts

You already know that Fox Chapel Publishing is a leading source for woodworking books, videos, and DVDs, but did you know that we also publish two leading magazines in the woodworking category? *Woodcarving Illustrated* and *Scroll Saw Woodworking & Crafts* are the magazines that carving and scroll saw enthusiasts turn to for premium information by today's leading artisans. **Contact us today for your free trial issue!**

WOODCARVING ILLUSTRATED

- Written BY carvers FOR carvers
- Improve your skills with premium carving patterns and step-by-step instruction for all skill levels
- Learn from today's top artists with helpful hints and new techniques for every style of carving
- New product and tool reviews
- Stay in touch with the carving community with biographies, show coverage, a calendar of events, and galleries of completed work

SCROLLSAW Woodworking & Crafts

- Written by today's leading scroll saw artists
- Dozens of attractive, shop-tested patterns and project ideas for scrollers of all skill levels
- Great full-color photos of step-by-step projects and completed work presented in a clear, easy-to-follow format
- Keep up with what's new in the scrolling community with tool reviews, artist profiles, and event coverage

To Get Your Free Trial Issue or Subscribe:
Call 800-457-9112 or Visit www.FoxChapelPublishing.com